# PRODUCTION, POWER AND WORLD ORDER

THE POLITICAL ECONOMY OF
INTERNATIONAL CHANGE
John Gerard Ruggie, General Editor

# PRODUCTION, POWER, AND WORLD ORDER

## Social Forces in the Making of History

### ROBERT W. COX

Volume 1 in the four-volume series
**Power and Production**

New York • Columbia University Press • 1987

Columbia University Press
New York        Guildford, Surrey
Copyright © 1987 Columbia University Press
All rights reserved

Printed in the United States of America


Library of Congress Cataloging-in-Publication Data

Cox, Robert W., 1926–
    Production, power, and world order.

(Power and production; v. 1) (The political economy
of international change)
    Bibliography: p.
    Includes index.
    1. Industrial relations—History.   2. Power
(Social sciences)—History.   3. Capitalism—History.
4. International economic relations.   I. Title.
II. Series: Cox, Robert W., 1926–. Power and
production; v. 1.   III. Series: Political economy of
international change.
HD6971.C78   1987        337        86-26387
ISBN 0-231-05808-X

This book is Smyth-sewn
Book design by J. S. Roberts

To Jessie, Susan, and Janet

THE POLITICAL ECONOMY
OF INTERNATIONAL CHANGE
John Gerard Ruggie, General Editor

# TABLE OF CONTENTS

# PREFACE

The purpose of this book is to consider the power relations in societies and in world politics from the angle of the power relations in production. Its central premise is that work is a fundamental activity that affects a range of other important human relationships and the organization of society as a whole. This premise is taken as a guide to inquiry—an injunction to explore the connections between work and politics as a basis for formulating some appropriate concepts and theoretical propositions. In this way, the book suggests an approach to the study not only of work but also of forms of state and of world order.

This is one of a series of four volumes that have been written as a collaborative effort. Jeffrey Harrod is the author of two of the four and I am the author of the other two. This book, which is first in order of the series, deals with the conceptual framework used in all four of the volumes. It includes historical and factual illustrations intended to bring the key concepts and theoretical propositions to life without attempting to give them an exhaustive demonstration.[1] It considers the three levels of production, the state, and world political economy in their interrelationships.[2] The book may therefore be read as an overview or introduction to the study comprising the four volumes, highlighting implications of the study for a political economy of the state and world order.

The study begins by classifying the totality of world production into patterns of production relations called modes of social relations of production. It then examines the dynamics of these modes, their interrelationships, and how they are affected by the nature and activity of states and of international forces. The three volumes that follow this one go much more thoroughly into the different patterns of production relations. Specific modes of social relations of production are treated as Liebnizian monads, as self-contained structures each with its own developmental potential and its own distinct perspective on the world. This is consistent with the study's approach to the issue of power in societies and in world order. It begins with the arena of production and looks out from it. Of course, such a standpoint is incomplete. It can be completed by considering forms of state in the same way and then by conceiving structures of world order that include both patterns of production relations and forms of state. This study points in that direction.[3]

Each of the remaining volumes deals with a group of monad-modes. The second volume, written by Jeffrey Harrod is entitled *Power, Production, and the Unprotected Worker*. It deals with the subordinate patterns of production relations in societies in which the dynamic of development is capitalist—including countries both more and less advanced along the capitalist road. Workers in these subordinate patterns are relatively more exploited and insecure than those in the dominant patterns. The third volume, also by Jeffrey Harrod, tentatively titled *The Established Worker: Corporatist Social Relations*. It deals with the dominant patterns and with workers who enjoy relatively more advantageous and more stable conditions, hence, the designation "established." The fourth volume, and the second to be written by me, will deal with production relations in noncapitalist development, illustrated by the experience of the Soviet Union, China, and other countries of what has been called "actually existing socialism."

The grouping by monad-modes, several of which coexist and interrelate within any society, may at first appear unusual since most studies take countries or national societies as their framework. It is consistent with the method of this study that the specific forms of production relations should be the starting point. The monad-modes are, however, presented in the different volumes so as to show their linkages in different types of national society and also their place in the world complex of production. They show societies from different perspectives—volume two from below, volume three from above. In volume four, noncapitalist societies, like capitalist societies in the previous volumes, are also viewed from the perspective of the different patterns of production relations they contain. Each of the four volumes stands on its own and can be read independently, but each in some measure implies all the others.

Jeffrey Harrod and I have worked closely together over a number of years in developing the concept of social relations of production and in its application to the variety of modes discussed in the study. There are also a number of points that each of us has developed on his own without benefit of mutual consultation, though long awareness of our respective thought processes makes these individual developments broadly consistent with the common core of ideas. By assuming separate responsibility for different volumes, we have sought to maintain the conceptual unity of the study as a whole while allowing ourselves freedom to elaborate parts of it each in his own manner.

In putting this book into final form for publication, I am conscious of my debt, both intellectual and moral, to Jeffrey Harrod. He is the person with whom I have most consistently discussed the ideas presented here over a period of some fifteen years. Inevitably, I have absorbed many of his thoughts and insights and integrated them into my own—often, perhaps, without being fully aware of what was happening. That is in the nature of a fruitful intellectual collaboration. Moreover, we have stood together in some of the most important issues and conflicts that have affected our lives during the same period. Comradeship and loyalty have reinforced intellectual affinity. Thus, though I bear the full and final responsibility for what is written below, it must in a very real sense be considered as one of the fruits of a joint endeavor.

Others too have helped by their advice and criticisms, especially in the final stages of preparation of this book. I am indebted particularly to Tchavdar Beyazov, Salvatore Biasco, Fred L. Block, Robert O. Keohane, James H. Mittelman, and Georges Spyropoulos, who all gave a critical reading to an early draft of the manuscript. Their cogent and at times painfully incisive comments forced me to rethink the way my argument was presented and, in effect, to rewrite the book in its present form.

They may be no happier with it now than they were then, but the experience has been salutory for me. John Gerard Ruggie has excelled in his editor's task of reinforcing valid criticism of others, adding his own, and cajoling a sometimes reluctant author to exhaust the full potentialities of a book. Jessie Rankin Cox not only assisted in the research for this project over more years than either of us care to remember and helped to translate my prose into more comprehensible English; she also at some crucial moments made me see the virtue in some of my critics' comments. Kate Wittenberg and Leslie Bialler worked over the manuscript with an editor's sympathetic understanding of an author's autonomy and made it more accessible to the reader.

I owe a special debt to the late Bernard Gronert. He it was who first encouraged me to submit the book project to Columbia University Press and who later suggested to Jeffrey Harrod and me that the project was too big for a single volume. Without his sponsorship and understanding it is difficult to see how we could have successfully developed and completed the job.

Several people who have had nothing directly to do with this book bear nevertheless a share of responsibility for having helped an erstwhile international civil servant along an unorthodox route into academic life and thereby brought about the conditions in which such a book could be written. I would like to mention in particular David A. Morse, who as director-general of the ILO, understood that freedom is being able at the crucial moment to act in accordance with an inner necessity; Jacques Freymond and Kenneth Thompson, who opened the way to my first full-time teaching experience at the Graduate Institute of International Studies, Geneva; William Fox, Leland Goodrich, and Herbert Deane, who were my sponsors at Columbia University; John Holmes, upon whose initiative I returned to Canada after some thirty years abroad; and, finally, Harold K. Jacobson, who has been friend, intellectual stimulus, and model of scholarly conduct these many years. I wish to record here the sense of obligation I bear to each of them.

York University,
Toronto,
February 1987

# THEME

Production creates the material basis for all forms of social existence, and the ways in which human efforts are combined in productive processes affect all other aspects of social life, including the polity. Production generates the capacity to exercise power, but power determines the manner in which production takes place. This study approaches the understanding of current historical change from the standpoint of a reciprocal relationship between power and production.

The first stage in this enterprise is to translate the general category of production into concepts that express concrete historical forms of the ways in which production has been organized—into modes of social relations of production. This is the subject matter of part 1. The next stage is to examine historically specific forms of power in state and world-order structures—how they have shaped production relations and been conditioned by forms of production relations. This is the subject matter of part 2.

These historically derived concepts are presented in both synchronic and diachronic form—synchronically, from the standpoint of their coherence as wholes; diachronically, from the standpoint of the internal contradictions that have led or can lead to transformations. They focus, in the case of production relations, on the differentiations among producers that can be the basis of class formation, and, in the case of states, on the mutations of class configurations that foreshadow the transformation of state structures.

In part 3, the tools of analysis developed in the first two parts are applied to the tendencies and options of the present—

to the conditions not chosen by themselves under which people will make the history of the future. Tendencies in the structural transformation of states that affect production relations are considered in relation to the weakening of a hegemonic world order. Tendencies in production relations that set the conditions under which political power is exercised are considered within the framework of the changing structure of accumulation.

These tendencies are not unidirectional. They contain their own contradictions. The world economic crisis that began in the 1970s is examined to see what transformations in structures of production, states, and world order they portend. The world economic crisis appears as a threshold—a phase of transition between the definable structures of the recent past and the as yet unclear structures of the emerging future. Those future structures will be made by the human material of history, shaped as it is by its own past. It is fitting, then, to end with a look at this human material in its collective aspect—at class formation and the prospects of politicization of class toward the formation of new state structures.

To assert the centrality of production, indeed, leads directly to the matter of social classes. Production organization creates the distinctions of power between employer and worker, lord and peasant, that form the basis for class differences, but other factors enter into the formation or nonformation of real historical classes. Salient among these in recent history have been political parties and other agencies of collective action that can evoke and channel class consciousness.

Now to make class analysis a principal feature of the study of historical change may seem old fashioned. Most-favored theories in the social science of advanced capitalist societies eliminated class some time ago; politics, it was thought, was about individual "actors" and associations of individuals, their perceptions and interactions in decision-making processes conditioned by "political cultures." Some non-Marxists conceded that class might have explained conflict and change in the early industrial past but had become irrelevant in more recent times.[1] Some Marxists have even joined in the conspiracy to remove class from the panoply of contemporary historical explanation. Rudolph Bahro, a radical critic from within Eastern European socialism, considers that class has been transcended ever since productive forces have been able to produce abundance and that the real social issues now turn upon arousing consciousness directed toward psychic emancipation.[2] André Gorz, a socialist critic from within Western European capitalism, perceives the industrial work force as now totally conditioned by and bound up with the capitalist organization of society and completely incapable of leading a movement to transform that society. The eradication of capitalism, he argues, can come only from areas of society that stand outside social classes and prefigure their dissolution.[3]

Events also seem to challenge the continuing relevancy of class. The conventional wisdom was that mass unemployment had become politically intolerable in advanced capitalist countries since the depression of the 1930s. Yet Western capitalist countries experienced very high unemployment in the early 1980s and workers remained quiescent, cowed. Why was there no reaction proportionate to the magnitude of the injury? Does this not refute by implication the notion that class struggle is the driving force of history? In the Third World, the most notorious of recent revolutions has raised the banner of Islam, not class. Only in Eastern Europe, where class is supposedly withering away (even if the state is not) has a class-based opposition arisen in the Polish Solidarnošc—though similar movements have not become apparent in other Communist Party-led countries.

These various grounds for discarding class analysis, whether arising from theory or practice, each points to some defect or inadequacy in past use of class analysis. They may be interpreted as calling for a rethinking of class through a development of the classical tradition of political economy. That tradition inquired into class formation and dissolution and class conflict; class relations provided the link between economy and politics, between production and power. In that respect, so the present work argues, the classical tradition remains valid. But past definitions of class that had some basis in mid-nineteenth-century European societies cannot just be taken over and applied mechanically and uncritically to a late twentieth-century world that manifests a great diversity of social class situations. In order that class analysis again become a valid and useful tool for understanding society in such a way as to be able to change it, a fresh approach to the dynamics of class formation is necessary. This means starting at the beginning with production so as to consider how the diversity of ways in which production is carried on and the variety of social relationships generated in production processes condition the social forces that can become bases of power in state and world order. It also means following the reverse course to consider how power institutionalized in world order and in the state shapes and controls the development of production relations.

To understand how and why changes take place in both the forms of political power and the organization of production, it is necessary to find a concrete and specific way of grasping the variety of actual forms of production and polity. Persistent patterns of production relations and forms of state derived from historical experience can be expressed as ideal types. Ideal types "stop" the movement of history, conceptually fixing a particular social practice (such as a way of organizing production or a form of state) so that it can be compared with and contrasted to other social practices.[4] To conceptually arrest movement in this way also facilitates examination of the points of stress and conflict that exist within any social practice represented by a type. Thus there is no incompatibility between the use of ideal types and a dialectical view of history. Ideal types are a part of the tool kit of historical explanation.

Ideal types are a way of representing historical structures. The term *structure* has been used in such a variety of ways that it is useful to be clear at the outset how it is used in this book. Some authors have used "structure" to mean innate ideas or patterns of relationship that exist independently of people; they think of people merely as bearers of structures.[5] No such meaning is intended here. There is, of course, a sense in which structures are prior to *individuals* in that children are born into societies replete with established and accepted social practices. However, these practices, whether taking the forms of languages, legal systems, production organization, or political institutions, are the creation of collective human activity. Historical structures, as the term is used in this book, mean persistent social practices, made by collective human activity and transformed through collective human activity.[6]

The system of power that emerges from these linked historical structures begins with the way the world's work is done through a series of connected structures of production relations, each of which is a power relationship, some more dominant and oppressive, others more equitably balanced. Production not only takes place through a power relationship, but also creates resources that can be transformed into other forms of power—financial, administrative, ideological, military, and police power.

Production has, however, only a certain logical precedence in the sense of providing the material basis for any form of state. It has no historical precedence; indeed, the principal structures of production have been, if not actually created by the state, at least encouraged and sustained by the state. Competitive capitalism required a liberal state in order to break through the shackles of mercantilism. Central planning was the creation of the bolshevik state and state corporatism of the fascist state. In historical time, production has been more shaped by the state than shaping of it. Why different forms of state have devised and imposed specific patterns of production relations and how they have done so requires explanation.

Each particular society comprises several connected types of production relations. For example, centralized collective bargaining is flanked by nonunion open-labor-market relations, self-employment, and household production; central planning is flanked by cooperatives, the self-employed, and, again, household production; the industrial enclaves of Third World countries are flanked by peasant agricultural production, subsistence agriculture, and a variety of "informal" production relationships in the urban sector. The state that consecrates one of these types of production relations as the dominant form, the most legitimate, the hegemonic form, also structures the relationships among the different coexisting forms. How the state does this has to be explained because it in turn explains the structuring of power within the society.

The hierarchy established among types of production relations (which, as just noted, is one of the tasks undertaken by the state) constitutes a structure of accumulation. The extraction of surplus flows from the subordinate and weaker levels of production to the dominant and stronger. Peasants, cheap labor, and housewives provide inputs to big industry and feed industry's workers. Central planners extract from communal agriculture. There are two main modes of development in contemporary history: capitalist and redistributive. Their common feature is accumulation and expanded reproduction. They have replaced earlier modes that lacked the dynamic of expansion. How capitalist and redistributive modes accumulate differs. They have structured differently the process of extracting surplus through different linked patterns of production relations.[7] To explain the mechanisms of accumulation in each mode and the crises to which each is subject delineates the physiology of power in these two kinds of society.

The structure of production in a particular society gives the basis for its class structure. The organization of production creates, however, only the potential for class. Whether or not classes in fact emerge depends on factors affecting consciousness—in particular the form taken by political party organization and its level of development. Class and party are the channels of encounter between production and the state. They explain where the balance of influence lies, whether it comes primarily from the social forces generated in the production process or from the state.[8]

The nature of the state is also defined by the class structure on which the state rests. This is not to say that dominant classes instrumentally use the state to their advantage. Rather, state actions are constrained by knowledge on the part of the state's agents of what the class structure makes possible and what it precludes. This has nothing to do with specific manipulation of state policies or the actions of particular "actors" but with general understandings about the tasks and limits of the state. The structure defining these tasks and limits, which becomes part and parcel of the state itself, is what Antonio Gramsci called the historic bloc.[9] To lay bare the nature of the particular historic bloc is to demystify the state and open the possibility of constructing an alternative historic bloc and thus an alternative state.[10]

Complexes of production relations, classes, and historic blocs do not exist in isolated national compartments. They are linked to a world order that bears directly on them, as well as influencing them through their national states. There have been important qualitative and structural differences between successive world orders in the modern era. It is a misleading oversimplification to regard all interstate systems as essentially the same insofar as they all lack a supreme world authority. The qualitative differences between world orders touch the nature and incidence of wars, the manner of resolving disputes, and the creation and distribution of wealth and poverty. These differences between one structure of world order and its successor are shaped by the forms of state and of production, and stabilized structures of world order in turn provide a framework conducive to certain forms of state and of production.

A principal distinction between structures of world order lies in whether or not the order is hegemonic. The Pax Britannica of the mid-nineteenth century and the Pax Americana of the mid-twentieth century were both hegemonic world orders. The intervening period, which saw two world wars and a great depression was not. I am using the term *hegemony* here as meaning more than the dominance of a single world power. It means dominance of a particular kind where the dominant state creates an order based ideologically on a broad measure of consent, functioning according to general principles that in fact ensure the continuing supremacy of the leading state or states and leading social classes but at the same time offer some measure or prospect of satisfaction to the less powerful.[11] In such an order, production in particular countries becomes connected through the mechanisms of a world economy and linked into world systems of production. The social classes of the dominant country find allies in classes within other countries. The historic blocs underpinning particular states become connected through the mutual interests and ideological perspectives of social classes in different countries, and global classes begin to form. An incipient world society grows up around the interstate system, and states themselves become internationalized in that their mechanisms and policies become adjusted to the rhythms of the world order. In nonhegemonic phases of world order these tendencies are reversed. Social classes and the organization of production revolve more exclusively around the state. States advance and protect the interests of particular national social classes and production organizations, using all the political, economic, and military means at their disposal as necessary.

The system of power outlined here is an open system. At any one time, concentrations of forces tend to maintain the system's structure. Disturbances in any one part can be counteracted by mobilizing strength from other parts of the system. Yet change is possible and does happen. Change can occur at all levels—in production relations, in class relations, in the emergence of new historic blocs and of alternative forms of state, and in the structure of world order. Most likely, where change does occur, it will be through mutually sustaining relationships at all of these levels. The main purpose of this enquiry is not to depict an inexorably self-reinforcing system of power, but to pinpoint the places within the system where conditions are most propitious for change—to undertake the preliminaries necessary for a strategy of social and political transformation.

It is, of course, important not to underestimate the forces for system maintenance while looking particularly for the opportunities contending forces have to break through. Forces for change can be disposed of easily when isolated in particular countries and particular classes. Accordingly, the critic's attention will be directed toward the possibilities of building alliances of opposition forces, not indiscriminately, but having mutual coherence within the global system.

With this in mind, the book focuses on certain strategic links in the system of power outlined above, namely:

- the effects of prevailing patterns of production relations in differentiating categories of producers (more and less powerful) as bases for class formation;
- the effects of different forms of state on the structuring of production relations and on the relative rates of growth of different patterns of production relations and on the balance of power between classes;
- tendencies at the world-order level affecting both the organization of production and forms of state, notably

the international division of labor and the internationalizing of the state within a hegemonic world order;
class formation and dissolution and the potential it creates for transforming production relations, forming new
historic blocs, and generating alternative forms of state
and world order.

# Part 1

# The Social Relations of Production

The social relations of production arise in three analytically distinct ways.

In the first place, the social context of production determines *what* kinds of things are produced and *how* they are produced. The "what" expresses the priorities of a society, which in turn reflects the social power relations of that society; the "how" expresses the prevailing manner in which established social power organizes production—i.e., the form of dominant-subordinate relationships among producers. Some people have more say in determining the priorities than others, whether they exercise that influence through the market or through a central plan. Some people control the production process and others are controlled and perform the tasks, whether in virtue of property ownership or high bureaucratic status. The structure of social power is thus the first aspect.

The second aspect is internal to the production process, namely, the complementarity of roles required in most production. Even the most primitive kinds of production, such as subsistence farming, involve a division of labor and a relationship of authority within the producing unit, i.e., the family, and in the case of more sophisticated forms of production, the network of relations is much wider and more complex. The complementarity of roles is bound together by a structure of authority that governs the production process. Complementarity is a better term than cooperation, because cooperation carries the connotation of harmony whereas the groups bound together in the production process manifest conflict at least as frequently as harmony in their relations.

The third aspect is the distribution of the rewards of production. In part, this is determined by custom, or in other words by the structure of social power, i.e., by the first aspect mentioned above, which dictates that some roles are more rewarded than others. In part, the distribution is determined by the power struggle within the production process, i.e., by the second aspect, through which some groups may be able to increase their rewards relative to others. Looked at over time, both factors are reducible to the power struggle, since the structure of social power can be thought of as the cumulative consequences, taken as a starting point, of previous struggles among social groups.

The three aspects analytically distinguished here—accumulated social power that determines the nature of production, the structure of authority as molded by the internal dynamics of the production process, and the distributive consequences—are dialectically related in a single historical whole: the social relations of production. Within this whole, contradictions arise among the three aspects. A sense of deprivation in rewards by one group of producers, for instance, leads this group to struggle effectively for greater control of the production process, and this results over time in a change in the structure of social power.

The terms *production relations, social relations of production,* and *power relations of production* are different ways of expressing the same relationship—different ways each of which contains a different emphasis. Production relations is the broadest term, including the relationship between the people involved and the world of nature, i.e., technology, as well as the relations between the various groups of people and the legal and institutional forms to which these relations give rise and which structure them. The term *social relations of production* focuses attention more specifically on the pattern or configuration of social groups engaged in the process, and the term *power relations of production* focuses on the dominant-subordinate nature of this pattern of social relations. The three terms all refer essentially to the same basic relationship and are used in this study not exactly interchangeably but to highlight the aspects of the relationship relevant to a particular context.[1]

To think through the concept of production relations, it is useful to begin with the general notion of work in the most universal, comprehensive, and substantive manner. Work can be defined as action toward the transformation of nature for the purpose of satisfying human needs and desires. The direct satisfaction of human needs and desires is not work, e.g., eating, conviviality, sexual activity, and sleep. Work is what is done to make these direct satisfactions possible—producing the food, building the physical structures within which actions to satisfy human needs take place, creating the symbols that evoke such activity, and building the social institutions and moral codes that channel and regulate this activity. It is important to underline here that work produces both the physical conditions and the social and moral conditions for satisfying human needs. Nature is transformed in two senses: first, physical transformations like the growing of food, i.e., the ordering of nature to meet human requirements, and the making of tools and utensils; second, the making of symbols and social institutions that make possible the cooperation among people required to do the first. The nature that is transformed through work is both physical and human nature. Nature, in this sense, is an artifact. Work takes place in an artificial world—a world made by people—and the artificiality of this world is maintained and expanded by work.

Work is sometimes an individual activity, though it is more frequently a collective activity. Even when work is an individual activity—as in the work of a single craftsman who produces a complete product—it takes place in a social context. Production relations are those social relations that govern the way work is done. Following this line of definition, production relations govern every kind of work. Production relations exist in subsistence agriculture and in domestic housework, as well as in the large modern factory. Production relations govern the itinerant peddler in India, the shoeshine boy in Mexico City, the pimps and prostitutes of Taipei, the advertising executives of Madison Avenue, the stockbrokers of Wall Street, the bank employees of Zurich, and the police, soldiers, and civil servants of all countries. In respect to their work—which is how we have identified people in relation to what they are—all these different kinds of people act within discernible patterns of production relations. What they produce may be valued positively or negatively according to different social perspectives, but that does not alter the fact that they produce whatever it is within determinate relations. These relations include dominance and subordination, and accordingly those who are dominant and those who are subordinate are to be considered as equally part of the production process—as producers in the sense of being participants in this process. Thus the employer, as well as the employee, the general, as well as the foot soldier, are encompassed by production relations. Those who produce for direct consumption, e.g., housewives, do so within production relations as surely as those who produce goods for sale on the market—e.g., wage workers. The concept of production relations covers the whole universe of work.

To study production relations in concrete terms, it is necessary to break the general concept down into a set of specific types or patterns. Such a typology, distinguishing patterns of production relations, will make it possible to estimate which forms are growing and which declining, which types are most frequently to be found alongside which other types, and so forth. Such types will have to be defined empirically, that is, translating the general concept into a particular form by condensing or summarizing observed patterns in such a way that one such concrete form is clearly distinguishable from another. The kinds of models that depict distinct types of production relations are in this study called modes of social relation of production.

These modes are defined as types, structural models that cannot be expected to account for every bit of evidence, but that should be able to comprehend the most recurrent and most decisive events. The adequacy of the typology is to be judged by the following criteria: (1) Is the set of modes large enough to reflect the diversity of production patterns on a world scale at the present time, without bias toward particular patterns, such as those most familiar to the author? (2) Is the set small enough to be manageable as a research tool and to give the advantages of parsimony? (3) Are the modes sufficiently clear and distinct to permit their use in classifying and comparing real situations?

A mode of social relations of production is not isolated; it exists in relationship to other contiguous modes and in a society regulated by a state. It may have more far-reaching links in the world economy. In principle, all of these factors in the broader context are in some measure necessary to explain any particular mode of social relations of production. However, at the outset it is convenient to treat the mode as a monad (see Preface), as something that can be understood in its own terms as a structure that has its own origins, history, and development. Adopting this perspective on the mode, the effects within the mode of these external factors can be seen. At the next stage, in part 2, the perspectives of the state and world order will be adopted, showing the determining role of the state in the origin and development of production modes. Before that demonstration, it is useful to have a clear idea of what these modes are and how they have evolved.

Before proceeding to discuss the existing modes of social relations of production, however, something should be said about the general characteristics of such modes. What kind of historical structure are we looking for? What are the dimensions or common characteristics of a mode of social relations of production?

# CHAPTER ONE

# THE DIMENSIONS OF PRODUCTION RELATIONS

The threefold nature of production relations noted above—the power relations governing production, the technical and human organization of the production process, and the distributive consequences—suggests some of the factors that might distinguish different modes of social relations of production. The objective delineation of each mode, taking account of these factors, is matched by an intersubjective content—the common understandings shared by the people embraced by the mode in respect to the relationships and purposes in which they are involved.[1] Specific institutions embody and stabilize this match between objective and subjective aspects of the mode. The fit of objective, subjective, and institutional aspects defines the mode. The actual or potential disjunctions among these three aspects pinpoint sources of transformation.

## POWER RELATIONS

The social and political power context of production determines the *what* and the *how* of production. In each mode there is a dominant and subordinate group of people. The dominant group controls production; the subordinate works under its control. To explain this basic cleavage, it is necessary to refer to factors whose origins lie outside of the immediate production process in the ambient society.

The dominant and subordinate groups in a production process are drawn from the social milieu, which includes social classes. Production takes place in a preexisting context of social power. The dominant group is usually drawn predominantly from one class and the subordinate from other classes. This statement leads, of course, to a kind of circular reasoning, because the production process itself generates class distinctions and class privileges and disadvantages. The point is that when one first begins to study a mode of social relations of production, it is discovered in an existing society with a class structure. The classes in that society are historical realities produced by collective experiences. They originated in production in previous history but transcended the specific activity of production to become human aggregates, collective ways of feeling and of acting. The social power of dominant classes may be thought of as originally grounded in the control of production—the material basis of all societies—and as being the accumulation of production power from the past. Resources derived from production have been translated over time into positions of social influence and prestige. These dominant social groups draw upon resources of wealth, status, and prestige that are not immediately derived from the production process. The subordinate groups, for their part, consist of members of classes formed or in formation, or they are declassed persons, e.g., former peasants turned wage laborers. A working class in process of formation has a greater power potential with which to confront the dominant group than an atomized assemblage of declassed peasants has. On the other hand, a working class that comprises only an elite of skilled workers, separated in their unions and working conditions from other working people who have less employment security and from other subaltern groups like self-employed farmers, may be more inclined to seek a *modus vivendi* with the dominant groups. The class context of the society, accordingly, affects the power positions within production relations.

Political power is the power to control the machinery of the state or to influence government policy. Political power may be derived directly from power over production combined with social power, as, for instance, when the capitalist classes gained influence in the states of western Europe during the 1830–1848 period. On the other hand, seizure of political power may be the means whereby a new group takes control of production away from an established class, as in the Bolshevik Revolution. The struggle of political parties, especially where there are strong parties based in the working classes, can alter the power context of production. Nationalization of industries introduces the notion of accountability of management to public authority. Labor movements may gain access to economic policymaking with influence over the development of production. The state cannot be considered as merely the direct instrument of a dominant class. The state is an arena of class struggle, but it also comes, especially during periods of relative stability in class struggle, to embody certain general principles bearing on the regulation of production that act as a constraint on class interests narrowly conceived.

The personnel of dominant and subordinate groups in the production process are drawn from existing social classes. In the past, dominant groups have derived their power from military control of land, from ideological or religious sanction, from property ownership, or from state bureaucratic rank and office. Subordinate groups have been composed of chattel slaves, serfs bound to a particular stretch of land, coerced labor of different kinds such as the encomienda decreed by the Spanish monarchy for the benefit of the overlords in its American possessions, "free" unprotected wage labor, and workers protected by law and collective bargaining. These differences in status derive from prevailing social and political power.

## THE ORGANIZATION OF PRODUCTION: LABOR ALLOCATION AND TECHNOLOGY

The internal dynamics of the production process are conditioned, in addition, by the way in which labor is allocated, and the struggle for control over the production process is conditioned by technology.

The means of allocating labor have included direct coercion (do this, or risk severe punishment!); custom (peasants are expected to spend part of their time tilling the lord's fields, but they also have certain rights to graze their animals on the commons); administrative disposition (a state agency allocates workers to jobs); and market transaction (the hiring of an individual worker by an employer).

There are still plenty of cases of direct coercion, although legal systems in principle outlaw it. Customary obligation is less than formerly prominent in peasant agriculture but may still be considered to be the basis of household production, which represents a very substantial part of total use-plus-exchange value produced. Administrative disposition is associated with redistributive economies organized by central planning. In the Soviet Union, this has in effect given place to labor market allocation, and in China under the Four Modernizations (since about 1979) growing emphasis has been given to ways of introducing more "flexibility" in employment, although without embracing the still-repugnant concept of a labor market.

Although the principle of a free and open labor market has formed part of the ideology of capitalist societies and was once enforced by law when "combinations in restraint of trade" in the form of trade unions were proscribed, all modern societies have reacted against this extreme. As Karl Polanyi has argued, labor is a "fictitious commodity" and to treat labor as a commodity goes against the deepest tendencies of all societies except that which, in the early nineteenth century, was subordinated to the self-regulating market.[2] To the extent that workers have gained collective strength and the state has responded to this strength, the labor market has become modified, institutionalized, and regulated. Consequently, only the weakest elements of the labor force now find themselves in a "pure" labor market. The stronger are sheltered by collective bargaining, labor legislation and administration, and the personnel management practices of large corporations.

Technology has the effect of structuring relations in the work process between those who command and those who execute orders. The transition from a workshop in which a variety of skilled craftsmen work together cooperatively, to an assembly line in which fragmented tasks are coordinated in a continuous process, to an automated factory, is a transition between three different structures of control over work.

In a simple, popular view, technology has a natural history from neolithic through postindustrial times following its own internal logic of discovery and application. Society, in this view, adapts to technological progress. It is more realistic to see technology as being shaped by social forces at least as much as it shapes these forces.[3] Technology is the means of solving the practical problems of societies, but what problems are to be solved and which kinds of solutions are acceptable are determined by those who hold social power.

To control the production process is often a determining motive in the direction given to technological development. The beginning of factory production of textiles, bringing workers together under one big roof instead of delivering materials to them in their separate cottages, was motivated by the employer's desire to enforce discipline, to better regulate production, and to avoid loss and pilfering of materials. Social control, not the invention of new and bigger machinery, began the movement to factories. Machinery appropriate to the scale of production followed.[4] Similarly, the "scientific management" of Taylorism responded to a specific desire of employers to gain control over the pacing of work, i.e., once again a motive of social control.[5]

## DISTRIBUTION OF THE PRODUCT

How is the product divided? Two lines of division are important. There is the division of the product between those who command and those who execute, between dominant and subordinate groups, and, of that which is retained by the dominant group, the division between what is consumed or hoarded and what is invested. The latter distinction marks the difference between the simple reproduction of the old regime and the expanded reproduction of modes of development that accumulate—the expansive capitalist and redistributive modes.

The same methods apply to determining the shares of dominant and subordinate groups as apply to the allocation of labor: brute force, custom, administrative disposition, and market transaction. These methods seldom if ever apply in a pure form.

Brute force shades into custom. In the fifteenth and sixteenth centuries, Turkish suzerainty was rather milder in its exactions from Balkan peasants than nearby European feudalism was, but by the seventeenth century, as the tide turned against the Ottoman empire, it had become much more harsh.[6] Force remade custom.

Custom influences the notions of relative returns to different kinds of work under both administrative disposition and market transaction systems. Sophisticated methods may be designed for evaluating job contents, but people are still much influenced by customary differentials. These customs are, however, influenced by different cultural contexts. Some entertainers in present-day America and Europe command extremely high incomes. The market rewards them as "stars." In China, opera singers' incomes are very modest indeed; they are middle-school graduates, situated in an income hierarchy according to their educational attainment.

## INTERSUBJECTIVE IDEAS: ETHICS AND RATIONALITIES OF PRODUCTION

Participants in a mode of social relations of production share a mental picture of the mode in ideas of what is normal, expected behavior and in how people arrange their lives with regard to work and income. Peasants think of their lives differently than wage workers do. Casual wage laborers think of their lives differently from skilled, unionized workers. Middle- and upper level bureaucrats in big public or private corporations have yet another set of lifetime expectations bound up with their work. These sets of collective images constitute the intersubjective meanings of the different modes.

Of more limited focus but closely related to these different intersubjective meanings are characteristic attitudes toward work or the ethics of production relations.

In discussing this it is useful to recall some of the distinctions that have been made in social theory. One such distinction is that between a community in which social bonds and obligations are regarded as natural and arising out of relationships that transcend production, e.g., family, kinship, and traditional hierarchies, and the more artificially constructed association in which obligations are created by contract and limited to specific purposes.[7] The sense of obligation obviously differs between these two patterns. Obligation has a more nearly absolute quality in the first and a more conditional or relative quality in the second.

Another distinction is that between behavior directed by external sanctions and behavior governed by internally accepted norms of conduct. This has a particular application to work, distinguishing patterns of labor control in which it is assumed that work will be performed only under threat of punishment or deprivation from patterns in which it is assumed that workers are largely self-motivated and require less external control.

Self-motivation, in turn, can be divided into an instrumental type in which work is performed in order to gain some other reward (income) and an absolute type in which work is its own reward or the manifestation of one's character, which incidentally may bring material rewards but is not pursued solely for that purpose. Such an absolute work ethic is what Max Weber perceived in the asceticism of the Protestant sects.[8]

Several tendencies in production ethics that take account of the above-mentioned distinctions can be suggested for distinguishing within this dimension of production relations.

One such tendency is found in the custom-regulated division of labor extending from isolated subsistence-farming communities to the modern nuclear family. Work is thought of, not as the consequence of compulsion, but as an activity flowing naturally from social bonds transcending work.[9]

Another tendency simply assumes that coercion is necessary in order to compel people to work or more specifically to compel them to work for someone else's benefit. Forms of direct personal and legal coercion have been practiced on a wide scale in the past, e.g., in slavery and the encomienda system, and are known to exist at present in some peasant production. In the contemporary world, the impersonal coercion of the market is also a commonly recognized form.

Clientelism gives rise to a different ethic, one in which there is an expected exchange of protection and loyalty between master and subordinate. The relationship is instrumental and thus conditional (by contrast to the social obligation inherent in the natural community mentioned above), but it extends beyond work to many other aspects of life. Dominance and subordination in the production process becomes but one manifestation of a status differentiation that pervades a broader social relationship. In the past, clientelism has generally been of a personal kind, of lord to peasant, master to servant. In the contemporary world, increasingly prevalent is the bureaucratized relationship within large institutions and corporations. Enterprise corporatism thus purports to offer a kind of community shielded from the atomization of the marketplace, and one not without material rewards for those who enter into it.

Another form of production ethic is mediated by contract. Here the relationship is partial and the exchange is negotiated either individually or collectively in specific detail. Implicit in the contractual form is a conflict of interests, a conflict that becomes suspended and regulated at least for a time by the terms of the contract. Contract is associated with an instrumental valuation of work.

A further form of ethic can be characterized as inspirational. It is associated with historical epochs in which a new work ethic is being generated with goals transcending immediate material satisfaction. The inspirational ethic derives from a claim over the individual by the new community to be created. It arouses a sense of obligation to work largely unrelated to immediate material compensation—the material rewards being understood as deferred to some future time and accruing to the collectivity rather than to the individuals whose efforts are expended. A reasonable hypothesis is that the inspirational ethic is inherently unstable—that the commitment it evokes cannot be maintained over long periods of time—and tends to become transformed into either a contractual or an institutionalized, clientelistic ethic.[10]

Ethics of production characterize the quality and intensity of producers' participation in the production process. The whole body of intersubjective meanings associated with a mode of social relations of production also incorporates a bias favoring the dominant group over the subordinate group, despite an appearance of reciprocity. Lord and peasant are supposed to be bound together by reciprocal obligations, yet the onus of these obligations falls more heavily on the peasant. Revolt by the peasant challenges not just the political and social order but also the divine order. It is heresy, as well as rebellion. Worker and employer are represented as social partners in a productive enterprise: workers contract to work and capitalists are expected to manage efficiently and to invest in expansion. Yet there is a bias in the intersubjective expectations. When workers collectively withhold their labor because employers do not offer high enough wages to satisfy them, it is called a labor strike and may be seen as a disturbance to social order. On the other hand, when capitalists do not invest because they do not see the likelihood of earning a sufficient profit, it is not called an investment strike, and it is not considered to be a disturbance of social order. Governments intervene to limit and regulate labor strikes; they are more likely to take steps to raise profitability in order to encourage investment.

The other aspect of the subjective side of a mode of social relations of production comprises the common orientations to action of particular groups. Specific social groups tend to evolve a collective mentality, that is, a typical way of perceiving and interpreting the world that provides orientations to action for members of the group. The term *rationalities* is used here to designate such coherently worked out patterns of thought, which correspond to practices in a specific social context.[11] The plural form indicates that human reason is a practical tool that has in the course of history provided guidelines for action to advance the interests of a variety of different social groups in a variety of material circumstances. Rationalities are the interpretative structures of thought and mental rules for making decisions that are characteristic of specific social groups. Thus, the typical mental processes followed by administrators and bureaucrats for reaching decisions of practical consequence differ from those of business entrepreneurs and again from those of elective officeholders. Similarly, the trade union leaders of "business unions" think and calculate differently than revolutionary syndicalists do. Members of these different groups tend to look for different kinds of facts, to process them according to different decision rules, and to devise different strategies of action based on the same facts. Each approach is, however, (or can be) coherent and rational in its own terms.

Remaining strictly within its own terms, a specific type of

rationality may perceive certain actions that derive from other rationalities as being dysfunctional or irrational or nonlogical, i.e., as resulting from a misperception or miscalculation on the part of the other. What appears as irrational to one rationality can, however, be quite rational to another. The breaking of machinery appears as irrational to the larger industrial capitalist but was rational to the Luddite worker and to some small capitalists. The aim of the social analyst, as distinct from that of the practitioner, may be defined as an ability to appraise the relativity of different forms of rationality and to show the connection of each with its social context.

## INSTITUTIONS

To the configurations of objective and subjective factors constitutive of each mode there corresponds a typical institutional complex. Indeed, it is by the institutions that the mode may often most easily be recognized. Nevertheless, we cannot regard the institutions as determining the mode. There may, in some cases, be a hiatus between the formal institutions and the real structure of relationships. The objective and subjective factors just discussed in their reciprocal interaction are to be regarded as the determinants of the real or essential structure of relations. The mode is identified by its real structure. The formal institutions have, however, an important function in legitimating the real relationships.

In distinguishing institutional aspects, various factors have to be considered. One is the degree of bureaucratization of decision making. Bureaucratization can be either external (i.e., imposed on production relations by the political authority) or internal (i.e., arising within the producing unit itself).[12] In the most organizationally complex modes there is a combination of internal and external bureaucratization. Another important dimension of the institutional structure is the extent of autonomous participation encouraged or tolerated, of which a particularly sensitive indicator is the existence and tolerance of opposition.

Direct domination is a relationship of personal subordination. Direct, personal dependent status is not modified or mediated by any formal organization. One can hardly speak of institutionalization since institutions imply rules and procedures, and this is an arbitrary relationship.

Corporatist institutionalization bureaucratizes production relations and eliminates, coopts, or controls opposition. The fundamental notion of corporatism is that common interest should override separate interests of the participants in the production process. Corporatist institutions have been created at the national level, at industry levels, and at the level of individual enterprises. They all involve formal representation of workers and management. In advanced capitalist countries, national wage or incomes policy boards are a form of corporatist representation; they are intended to reach a consensus or social contract between government, employers, and unions on wage policy. In Mussolini's Italy and Vargas' Brazil the state imposed a form of corporative organization on industrial employers and workers. Corporatism is institutionalized within some big enterprises through welfare and personnel policies designed to attract the loyalties of workers to the enterprise and through union representation directed to the enterprise level—practices pioneered in but by no means confined to Japan. The form of trade union representation characteristic of redistributive, centrally planned economies is also corporative insofar as it is designed to promote harmony between workers and management at the workplace and between both and the central plan's goals. The theory underlying corporative institutions in capitalist and redistributive development is, of course, different: in the one case, corporatism is intended to overcome class struggle; in the other, class struggle is supposed to have been superseded by nonantagonistic or purely technical contradictions.

Delegated bargaining accepts conflict, and therefore opposition, and institutionalizes it through organizational relationships (e.g., collective bargaining) that are often very highly bureaucratized. Delegation of representation through bureaucratic organization can be very remote from the rank and file and indirectly appointed. In North America, decentralized negotiations concerning workers in particular plants are sometimes conducted on the union side by bargaining agents who are union bureaucrats appointed by the central officers of the union and who may be strangers to the factory or the town in which it is located. In Scandinavia, centralized negotiations are conducted with such sophistication by union and management technicians that the resulting collective agreements are sometimes scarcely intelligible to rank-and-file workers.

Self-management is a form of institutionalization that rejects both external and internal bureaucratization. Individual self-employment of its very nature is a nonbureaucratic form of self-management. Syndicalism, an old tradition within the labor movement, has in current times attracted renewed interest (most commonly under the label of "workers' control") as a reaction against bureaucratization and a demand for more direct participation of workers in determining their own conditions. Its current manifestations vary from the shop stewards' revolt against the conventional leadership of the Trades Union Congress (TUC) in Britain, to the demands for a self-management form of socialism by the *Confédération française democratique du travail* (CFDT) in France, and also to some of the demands of *Solidarnošc* in Poland.

A hiatus may develop between formal institutions and the real structure of relations. For example, where formal institutions suggest delegated bargaining, the real relationship could take on the character of corporatism if institutionalization of union-management negotiation became stabilized and routine, if external bureaucratization increased with the inclusion of union and management personnel in government-appointed economic councils and other advisory boards, and if the conflictual element in the relationship became subordinated to a doctrine of common or public interest. Conversely, in late Franco Spain the formal structures of corporatism had begun to operate in such a manner as to provide official cover for unofficial negotiations carried on by illegal workers' internal factory commissions, in fact a form of delegated bargaining. In Yugoslav experience, institutions that are self-managing in form tend in substance to cloak the reality of enterprise corporatism. The important thing is not to accept institutional structures at their face value but to inquire into the objective-subjective nature of social relations underlying formal institutions.

## RECIPROCAL RELATIONSHIP
## OF FACTORS

Figure 1 summarizes the reciprocal relationship of the objective, subjective, and institutional factors in a mode of social relations of production. Several examples may help to illustrate how these relationships work dynamically to transform a mode.

One illustration can be provided in the transformation of peasant production under European feudalism. The objective power of the dominant class was derived from its control of land. In theory, the rights in land of the lord were conditional; in practice, because of the fragmentation of political authority, they became virtually absolute, as they indeed later became in civil law. Access by the peasant to land was conditional upon service to the lord, though in practice it became a customary right.

Subjectively, arrangements consecrated by custom were

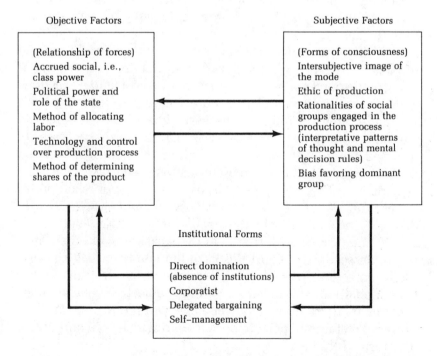

Figure 1.  DIMENSIONS OF A MODE OF SOCIAL RELATIONS OF PRODUCTION

overcast by religion. Institutionally, the mode was regulated by customary law, which in principle was to be interpreted in conformity with divine law but in practice was administered by the lord.

A shift in the relationship of forces came from several sources. Demographic decline in the fourteenth century (e.g., the Black Death) reduced the productivity of land and thus the income of the lord. Internecine warfare (e.g., the Hundred Years War) weakened the nobility as a class as they struggled with each other to control land. The growth of towns in western Europe offered an avenue of escape for peasants from feudal exactions. Correspondingly, the subjective sanctions were also weakened particularly in the west. Religious movements inclining into heresy challenged the authority of the social order—the poverty doctrines of the spiritual Franciscans, the Dolcinians of northern Italy, and later the Anabaptists in Germany and Bohemia. The existence of the towns and of free citizens within them provided an alternative image of social order, displacing the feudal order from the absolute to the relative.[13]

Different results ensued in eastern and western Europe. In the west, a weakening of the power of the nobility and a strengthening of the power of peasants led to an easing of feudal exactions and a growth of freehold land tenure, i.e., in practice to a growth of small-holder farming. In the east, where towns offered no alternative life for absconding peasants, the lords successfully imposed a more onerous serfdom. In Germany, midway between these extremes, the Protestant Reformation tried to stem the peasant tide by consecrating the lords as the scourge of rebellion (in the peasant war of 1525), but though the peasants were militarily defeated, the subjective legitimacy of the mode was shattered.[14]

Analogies can be drawn to the weakening of other land-based classes in the Third World of the late twentieth century. Their place in the state has been lessened from the rise of other commercial-industrial classes, and the subjective beliefs underpinning their traditional power have worn thin, leaving this power to rest upon open violence toward which civil authorities may turn a blind eye.

Another illustration, this one focusing on the factor of technology and control over the production process, is provided by Taylorism. In the early manufactories, skilled workers controlled the pace of work; their unions also exercised a degree of control over the supply of skilled labor. Employers counterattacked with a redesigning of production processes, fragmenting work so that it could be done by unskilled hands, recombining the fragments through industrial engineering controlled by management. This shift in power in favor of employers had consequences in the subjective and institutional sides. Craft unionism gave place to industrial unionism, and pride in craft skill was displaced by consciousness of social goals more geared to security of income than to the nature of work (social insurance, full employment)—goals that could be attained through political action.

A further illustration is drawn from the redistributive mode of development. Here industrial workers have been given the status of the most prestigious class. Their ranking on the subjective side of the register is very high. But this does not correspond to real power in objective terms. Management of the central plan and of the major industrial enterprises is in the hands of officials who, in their vast majority, are not of the working class, and workers, in practice, have a subaltern position. This hiatus between subjective status and objective power was articulated by Edward Gierek during the Polish worker revolt against the ruling bureaucracy in December 1970: "You work well, and we will govern well!"[15] Crisis in this redistributive mode of social relations of production has typically come over the determination of shares in the product. One source of crisis, latent and building up over time, is resentment by labor of waste and corruption by the bureaucracy in the administration of the social surplus produced by labor. Another, more usually the trigger of revolt, has been a decision to raise consumer prices, in other words to reduce the workers' share in the product.[16] In the one case of prolonged crisis—the creation, official recognition, and subsequent outlawing of Solidarnošc in Poland—there was a temporary movement in the institutional sphere from corporative to delegated bargaining and self-management forms.

Twelve modes of social relations of production are identified here as differentiating production relations in the late twentieth century world. These twelve modes are:

- subsistence
- peasant-lord
- primitive labor market
- household
- self-employment
- enterprise labor market
- bipartism
- enterprise corporatism
- tripartism
- state corporatism
- communal
- central planning

This number excludes modes like slavery, which have virtually ceased to exist on a significant scale.[17] It also excludes forms that may possibly be more extensive in future, e.g., self-managed, autonomous worker collectives. There is nothing sacrosanct about the number twelve. This denomination of modes has been arrived at through a long process of (1) positing an initial set of modes by inference from personal knowledge and experience,[18] (2) confronting these definitions with the criticism of people who have experience of studying production relations in different parts of the world, (3) considering deviant and marginal cases in regard to whether they suggest new categories or changes in the definitions, and (4) revising the set of mode definitions, and so forth, continuing the process. As a result, the twelve modes defined here seem to cover all significant patterns of production relations in the late twentieth-century world of work. But the task is never complete. As experience accumulates and the questions suggested by it are sharpened, further revision will doubtless be necessary. That is in the nature of the concrete universals with which scholars try to understand society: there is a continuing dialogue between experience and the development of concepts. The setting down of a concept is but a moment—though a critical moment—in the process of understanding.

It has been pointed out above that configurations of production relations vary according to modes of reproduction and development. This can be taken as a guideline for the order of presentation of the twelve modes. We can begin with those of the greatest antiquity, which find their origins in societies of simple reproduction and then proceed with the modes of social relations that came into existence through capitalist development and, finally, with those generated by redistributive development.

This ordering encounters, however, some problems. The modes do not appear one at a time successively, in one or more series. Each of the modes considered here coexists with other modes and changes through time. Modes once dominant, such as the peasant-lord production of the precapitalist era or the enterprise labor market of early capitalism, become subordinate in later configurations. They adapt to their changed position in the total configuration of which they are a part. Furthermore, some modes have bifurcated into residual and novel elements. The residual retain the characteristics of an old configuration while the novel are more integrated with a new configuration. The enterprise labor market has a residual element in small non-unionized businesses; it has a novel form in the widespread use of semiskilled immigrant labor by large enterprises, for instance, in the European auto industry. Furthermore, there are some instances where what resembles a well-known mode in the context of a social formation that is very different from the formation in which that mode originated leads us to speak of an analogue rather than an actual instance of the mode. For example, the inner-city poor of the larger U.S. cities manifest many similarities to the marginal populations of Third World cities or the "reserve army of labor" that Marx and Engels observed in mid-nineteenth-century England. However, the political and institutional context of the United States is sufficiently different in its impact on these groups that they are more properly to be regarded as an analogue to the Third World embodiment of the mode that we call primitive labor market. Another such instance is the survival and especially revival of individual and small-scale enterprise in the context of redistributive central planning. The fact that these social relations of production are in effect regulated by the plan and coordinated within it makes them analogous rather than identical to the enterprise labor market and self-employment modes of capitalist development.

Thus in presenting each of the twelve modes discussed below as a monad (the term used in the preface), it is necessary not only to depict it at its origin but also to follow it through as a historical development, to note the variations of the mode and to be able to explain them. The sketches that follow can do no more than suggest something of this complexity.[19] It is a necessary step toward making use of these concepts of modes of social relations of production in the explanation of change at the levels of social formation, state and world order.

# CHAPTER TWO

# SIMPLE REPRODUCTION

Taking the historical processes of reproduction and development as the framework for presenting variations in production relations, the starting point is simple reproduction. Simple reproduction is production that reconstitutes in one cycle the elements necessary to continue production in substantially the same form during the next cycle. These elements comprise the human and material inputs, i.e., the workers and masters of the production process and their skills, the raw materials and tools they need in order to be able to produce, and the social relations that combine them in the production process. In simple reproduction there is no necessary and cumulative expansion in the scale of production, though there are variations in output such as, for example, are attributable in agriculture to the weather or natural calamities, and there is no transformation of the structures of production. The cycle reproduces itself, especially with regard to social relations, without fundamental change.

Four modes of social relations of production, all originating in the precapitalist era of simple reproduction, survive in social formations characterized by dynamic development, whether of the capitalist or redistributive types. These are subsistence agriculture, peasant-lord agriculture, the primitive labor market, and household production. As social formations evolved from simple reproduction to capitalist or redistributive development, these four modes of social relations of production became subordinated to other modes. Their changed place in the total configuration of production relations was reflected in differentiations within each of these modes, though the basic structural form remained constant. Novel forms adapted to the dominant patterns of production relations have come into existence alongside the residual forms descending directly from the mode's origins.

### Subsistence

The subsistence mode is the oldest form of social production. It comprised the earliest forms of hunting and gathering and of settled cultivation in small self-sustaining communities. Work in these communities was ordered by kinship. In Polanyi's sense, production relations were embedded in social relations of a kinship or lineage kind. In such communities, certain people have authority over production and to an extent over the distribution of the product, but these people cannot be held to constitute a dominant class. Authority relations are particularized within families and lineages. There are inequalities in that some family units produce more or consume less than others, but these inequalities are not the systematic distortions of distribution effected by a class structure; they are the consequence of age distributions or the incidence of ill health in particular families or such causes. The mode may, indeed very often does, produce a surplus that is redistributed in some manner within the community, e.g., to sustain those who do not produce enough for their own families and as gifts to symbolize the authority of community leaders, but the surplus is not accumulation for expansion.[1]

The term *natural economy* has often been used to designate production systems of antiquity and of some of the more isolated communities studied by anthropologists in recent times. There is little enough of this natural economy left in the world of the late twentieth century. Indeed, a noted anthropologist has castigated his discipline for contributing to the notion that there exist peoples "without history," whereas from the fifteenth century virtually all peoples, primitive or otherwise, have been unable to escape the impact of expansive political, economic, and cultural forces.[2] Though touched by these global currents, some residues of natural economy remain in villages producing primarily for their own consumption.

Such residues constitute one part of the production presently in the subsistence mode. Production here uses primitive technology. Work is allocated according to customary roles under the authority of spirit medium or elder. Custom requires community solidarity in planning production and in sharing the scarce means of biological survival. Household production is collectively constrained by taboo and sanctified by ritual. The social relations and beliefs of the community determine how and when production activities take place. The political, social, or religious hierarchy—all virtually the same—does not, however, take a predominantly economic form, separating rich from poor. All share pretty much the same precarious material conditions.

The term *subsistence* applied to this kind of production refers to self-sufficiency of production, *not* to the level of consumption. Peasants and other poor people in societies with large markets may be able to consume only at a "subsistence level," i.e., at a level barely adequate to sustain life, but are not for that reason considered to be in a subsistence mode of production relations. The distinguishing characteristic of subsistence producers is that they are substantially outside the monetized economy and the networks of commodity exchange.

One scholar of economic anthropology has described the hunters and gatherers as "the original affluent society," not for their abundance of possessions but for the extreme modesty of their needs. In this respect, settled communities of subsistence cultivators differ only in degree. All such communities tend to produce less than they are capable of producing and dispose of more leisure than they would enjoy if they had used their labor power to the full. "The world's most primitive people have few possessions, *but they are not poor* . . . Poverty is a social status. As such it is the intention of civilization."[3]

Production by the family unit in practice places limits on efficiency. Tools are of a kind that can be used by one person or a small group, and in general, skill is more important than tools in productivity. (There are limits to what can be achieved by greater skill, but no such limits to the potentialities of technology.) The more labor available to the family unit, i.e., the higher the proportion of able-bodied members, the less intensive its work. Since production is mostly for direct consumption, the quantity of produce sought by the family unit is determined by its biological needs for survival and reproduction and does not need to exceed them. Excess production makes some contribution to the survival of the whole community by providing a reserve to supplement shortfalls in the less productive family units. It may also constitute a reserve available for legitimating leadership in the community through the practice of gift giving. (The economic relationship of giver-receiver consolidates the political relationship of leader-follower.)[4] But by and large there is little incentive to produce much more than is needed for the family itself.

The residues of natural economy are only one form of contemporary subsistence production. Another form consists of family cultivation of plots that are too small to provide for the sustenance of the family, and so some family members, usually adult males, will have to seek wage employment in some other mode. They may migrate temporarily to work in mines or industries or on plantations, bringing back to the family unit the additional income required to maintain the family. Subsistence of this kind is very largely emptied of the traditional ritual that contributes so much to the social equilibrium of the natural-economy community. It is therefore internally weaker.

An analyst of this contemporary form of subsistence production that coexists and interrelates with other modes of social relations of production describes the problem of rational choice from the perspective of the extended family household:

> Productive labour on the farm is but one aspect of a multitude of possible alternatives that the household actively pursues for its livelihood. The relative importance of direct farming depends, of course, on many local circumstances. The commitment may range from exclusive dedication (when no other alternatives are available) to a complementary activity (albeit a strategic one) when other alternatives are present ... At the level of subsistence living, a mistaken decision may make the difference between survival and starvation. The ... household's margins for economic manoeuvre are slim, and the risks loom large.[5]

In the perspective of the economy as a whole, subsistence production of this contemporary (as distinct from the residual) type constitutes a subsidy to the other, adjacent modes of social relations of production in which members of the subsistence household participate, e.g., as temporary migrant workers. The subsistence mode constitutes a labor reserve and a cost-free means of reproducing a labor force for these other modes.[6] Furthermore, such subsistence settlements are also vulnerable to the land hunger of more powerful outsiders. Subsistence farmers are easily displaced with tacit or open official support when others want to take over land for commercial cultivation.

### Peasant-Lord

The peasant-lord mode, by contrast with the subsistence, is the result of a class structure. A dominant class extracts surplus from a subordinate class of agricultural producers. This dominant class looks after the reproduction of the social relations of the mode but takes no part in agricultural production. The dominant class acquires its position from military power, religious sanction, or the power of money through peasant indebtedness. This pattern of production relations was characteristic of precapitalist civilizations, i.e., collectivities organized on a larger scale than the small subsistence communities. The existence of some kind of state is the principal feature distinguishing a class-ordered from a kin-ordered production system.[7]

The historical origins of peasant-lord production were many and various. Power relations in old-regime Chinese agricultural production were based on a combination of private property in land and a state administration supported by taxation. The Chinese gentry official class had the dual base of land ownership plus tax revenues available to those who acceded to official status through the examination system. Gentry-officials owned most of the productive land closest to the main urban centers and lived mainly as absentee landlords whose estates were worked by peasant tenants. The officials were not, however, completely separated from the land but were linked through clan connections with the rural areas. Tenant farmers working these estates constituted a substantial proportion (perhaps one third) of the population. More than half of the Chinese population was composed of small-holding peasants, cultivating the less good land farthest from the urban centers, and these bore the heaviest tax burden. Usury was widespread, and so a nominal peasant owner was often in reality the tenant of a moneylender. Peasant insurrections, such as those that preceded the imposition of Manchu rule in the seventeenth century, signaled the effective limit of extraction from the rural population under this system.[8]

The salient characteristic of the Islamic pattern of the same period was urban dominance based on the extraction of a surplus from agriculture. Direct links between lord and peasant such as existed in China through the absentee gentry's relationship to clan and land were lacking.[9] Nomadic warriors and Arab merchants were the twin agents of the expansion of Islam. The warrior class disdained agriculture as did the merchants. They were too turbulent a group to provide a secure basis for the ruler's power, and so Islamic rulers typically relied on an elite guard of non-Islamic slaves who acquired considerable privileges within the state. Islamic doctrine denied private property and vested all property in the Caliphate, though this theoretical principle was never consistently applied. Generally, the conquerors confirmed the tenure of the peasants, protected them against local landlords (who would be rivals in extraction), and required delivery of taxes to the state. The tax revenues went in large measure to the urban-based military class—consisting of both Arab nobles and non-Islamic praetorian slaves. The towns were centers for the consumption of what was extracted from rural production.[10]

European feudalism was another source of the peasant-lord mode. In some parts of western Europe (England, Spain, and northern France), there had since the fourteenth century been a trend toward medium-sized holdings cultivated by successful, independent peasants. In southern Europe, where there was less incentive to agricultural specialization, the dominant trend with the erosion of feudal services was toward sharecropping (mezzadria in Italy and métayage in southern France). In eastern Europe, the trend from the sixteenth through the eighteenth centuries was toward an increasingly repressive manorial serfdom. More centralized absolutist monarchies in both western and eastern Europe disciplined the nobility and brought them into a more direct dependence on the state while placing the burden of taxation on the peasantry.[11]

In Japan, during the same era, a fief-type relationship governed landholding, in which the obligation of military service was a condition for enjoying the fruit of the land, as in western feudalism. The system went through evolution in significant respects, without fundamentally changing, during succeeding centuries. The warrior class of samurai that clustered about the magnates and the Shogun became progressively bureaucratized, detached from the land, and educated (a parallel to the emergence of the *noblesse de robe* and service nobility in Europe). The weight borne by the peasantry seems over time to have lightened in the aggregate—whereas some two thirds of the peasant product was extracted by the feudal class in the sixteenth century, this seems to have declined to 30 to 40 percent during the Tokugawa period (seventeenth to nineteenth centuries).[12]

Yet another source of contemporary peasant-lord production relations was the *encomienda*, the right granted by the Spanish crown to Spanish landowners in Hispanic America (and comparable arrangements in Brazil) to extract labor services from the indigenous population. This novel form of compulsory labor went through various modifications—labor services were replaced by the exaction of tribute from the indigenous people, or forced wage labor was substituted for either of these forms. Whatever the precise form, indigenous labor was not "free" in the sense of suffering only the coercion of the market but was compelled by the conqueror's law with the sanction of physical or military force. Originally, this variant of labor control had been justified as a means of Christianizing the Indians. It had been applied initially in the mines, whose produce was the main early export of the American colonies. Later the practice was extended to secure labor for grain production and cattle raising—tasks requiring a somewhat higher level of skill than for the production of sugar and cotton. Alongside the *encomienda*, other forms of coerced labor also existed in Hispanic America, such as a form of debt peonage on haciendas. This latter form served the relative self-sufficiency of a local dominant landowning class rather than the demands of an overseas market, but it was consistent with the milieu in which the *encomienda* was the model form.[13]

The salience of money power in peasant-lord production relations is of more recent origin, arising usually in situations in which there is both a disintegration of dominance based on military or religious authority and an impact of national or world markets on agricultural production. Peasants who cannot meet their own needs for reproduction have to borrow, and merchants who control the trade in the peasants' produce come effectively to control their land and labor.

Several common features run through these diverse origins of peasant-lord production. The subordinate class—the peasants—are bound legally or in practice to the land they till. Their only alternative is flight with the risks that entails. They have no mobility within the mode. Extraction is either directly by or on behalf of a class that does not participate itself in agricultural production—"directly by" in the case of landlords or moneylenders, "on behalf of" in the case of taxation that serves primarily to sustain a dominant nonagricultural class. Members of the dominant class have incentives to acquire control over more land and labor but have little incentive to produce more efficiently. Consequently, they do not accumulate for investment in productive innovation—or if they do, then they shift themselves and their land and labor into another mode of production relations.

Today, in the grain-producing regions of Asia and Latin America, the produce of peasant cultivation is traded, often at some distance from its source. Peasants pay taxes and serve as soldiers in national armies. They are, in short, linked into national and often international exchange relations and political power structures. A dominant class—the "lords"—commands the link, a class for which peasant labor provides material support and the basis for political power.

In this study, the term *peasant* is restricted to agricultural producers who produce a surplus that is appropriated by a dominant class; these peasant agricultural producers have access to land but not effectively to markets, and in practice they are not free to move elsewhere or to escape the domination of their "lords." Subsistence cultivators are excluded from the definition because they do not produce surplus to any significant extent, farm laborers because they are wage workers who have no durable access to the land they till, small holders because they have access to and depend on markets.

In this peasant-lord mode, primitive technology and low productivity prevail, as in the subsistence mode, but peasants and their family units are subject to an economic-political hierarchy, a direct domination, that is not characteristic of the subsistence mode. The lord extracts a large proportion, often in excess of half of the peasant's production. Not only are peasants virtually bound generation upon generation to their land (this in practice is the case of subsistence farmers too), but also and more importantly, they are bound perpetually into their subordinate relationship to the landlord who extracts the surplus from their labor.

The economic power of the dominant class can hardly be distinguished from its political power. The secular state has generally left the dominance of the landlord class over the peasant unimpeded. The state does not formally enter into the relationship between lord and peasant except to enforce property rights (which favor the landlord), to extract some of the product as taxes (thereby supporting a political structure in which the landlord's influence has been paramount), and perhaps to influence the level of prices (which in practice concerns the landlords' power relations with urban clients and consumers rather than with peasants).

While the term *lord* has a connotation suggestive of European or Japanese feudalism, or of the agrarian bureaucracies of other past civilizations, it is used here in a wider sense to cover all forms of domination over peasant producers, many of which in contemporary times lack any "noble" quality. It can refer, for example, to a case where poor peasants deprived of sufficient land and other resources to ensure their own survival fall under the control of a large landowner, or of a moneylender, or of a merchant trading at a distance in the peasant's produce (e.g., in the rice trade). The peasant then works in conditions determined by this new lord, who also determines the return the peasant receives from his labor.

Like the subsistence mode, the peasant-lord mode has also become vulnerable to external pressures. For long its mainstay was the social and political power of the lords, which enabled them to forge alliance with other powerful classes. During the second half of the twentieth century, this alliance has been weakening and pressures from the peasantry have been growing.

The traditional legitimacy of peasant-lord relations, founded on the feudal notion of reciprocal obligations and services, has been undermined. The authority of the lords and their ability to extract now almost everywhere rests on violence and repression of peasant troublemakers by illegal methods tolerated and overlooked by the state. There has, however, been a growth of peasant-based insurgency—late twentieth-century revolutionary movements have nearly all been in peasant societies, from Algeria through southern Africa, to Indochina and Central America[14]—which manifestly increased the costs to states and allied classes of supporting landlord dominance. Furthermore, peasant-lord cultivation has been challenged by capitalist entrepreneurs as being economically inefficient. Agribusiness and commercial farmers want to clear lands of peasant settlement to cultivate with modern technologies for regional and world markets. Former allies of the landlords have become more inclined to abandon landlord claims or to facilitate buying the landlords out and encouraging them to invest in other, more efficient forms of exploitation.

*Primitive Labor Market*
    The primitive labor market, like the peasant-lord mode, is traceable to the *ancien régime*. The term *labor market* in that historical context is an anticipation, since one cannot speak of the existence of a market for labor power before the capitalist era. Two phases must be completed before one can properly speak of the existence of a labor market: first, some people must become detached from the social relations governing production, such as subsistence or peasant-lord relations, so as to be available without attachments, and second, the practice of exchanging labor power for money in such a manner as to provide a mechanism for determining the price of labor power must become common. The first phase was accomplished in precapitalist times. The second was not. Hence, one can speak retrospectively of the existence of a primitive labor market in much the same way as Marx spoke of primitive accumulation of capital forming the basis for later capitalist development.
    Fernand Braudel has pointed to a structural constant of all the preindustrial societies of the old regime, including all those mentioned as sources of the peasant-lord mode: the existence of a whole sector of population for whom society provided

no place and who were known variously as the poor, beggars, and vagabonds—the masterless men of seventeenth-century England and the boat people of south China. In Europe, the poor became noticeable from the economic revival of the twelfth century and thenceforth remained a factor in the social order. Their numbers varied but were always considerable, in the England of the Stuarts being estimated at from one quarter to one half of the total population. From among these people could emerge a sort of nonsociety, given to spontaneous violence, arousing fear and apprehension on the part of the established orders, but in general controllable with the application of a minimum of force because they utterly lacked cohesion.[15]

In the world of the old regime, such people on occasion were caught up in ideological movements of millenarian eschatology that challenged prevailing orthodoxies. Where this happened, it often detonated a violent social and political explosion. In times when economic changes accelerated misery and insecurity, mystical millenarianism could for the disoriented and uprooted poor become a powerful social myth giving them at least a momentary cohesion and canalizing their energies in a revolutionary direction. Such movements severely shook up existing social structures and undermined their ideological foundations without actually transforming them.[16]

Since the primitive labor market stands outside ordered society, it remains extralegal. Relations between the mode itself and the established society that has engendered it are characterized by violence or deception, and relations within the mode, by charisma or domination. There is little scope for institutionalization or for the emergence of a class structure. To the extent that attempts are made to establish institutions among people in this mode, or that class consciousness and organization appear among them, these would be indications of a shift out of the primitive-labor-market mode into another mode.

The primitive labor market today is predominantly a phenomenon of poor and newly industrializing countries of the Third World. It is peopled by former peasants who have been forced out of or escaped from the peasant-lord relationship or by those who have left subsistence cultivation to become landless laborers. Some may exist as casual wage laborers in agriculture, but most leave the rural areas and abandon the use of agriculture-related skills. In the urban environment, they are fit for only unskilled jobs, since whatever skills they possessed have become irrelevant. The supply of such labor far exceeds the demand for it, which accounts for most of the unemployment—open or disguised—in the Third World.

The numbers in the primitive labor market rise in proportion to the social dislocations of the country. They are greater in countries experiencing economic growth than in poorer, undeveloped countries. The size of the primitive labor market underscores the polarization of rich and poor in the process of economic growth. Generally speaking, as subsistence and peasant-lord modes contract, the primitive labor market grows.

People in the primitive labor market are mobile, but choice of employment and individual bargaining power are in practice denied them by the overabundant supply of labor. Initially, they have no collective power. They also have little cohension among themselves, and typical earnings come from one-time transactions with people outside the primitive labor market—hawking an object, shining shoes, watching an automobile. Relations that are not cumulative do not lend themselves to an adjustment of relative power.

Two kinds of relationships are characteristic of the primitive labor market. There is the relationship of the primitive-labor-market producer with someone outside the mode who purchases his or her services, and there is the relationship within the mode between the producer of the service and a boss who exploits, protects, and ensures access to income-earning opportunity to the producer. The prostitute serves as paradigm. On the one hand, there is the prostitute-client relationship, on the other, the prostitute-pimp relationship.

The state does not regulate the work relationship of the first type (with a client outside the mode), or if it does try, it is almost totally ineffective. The state, indeed, intervenes among the populations of the shantytowns, bidonvilles, favelas, or barrios, where the mass of primitive-labor-market workers live, only through police action to protect established society from contamination. Occasionally, the most visible evidence of the primitive labor market—the beggars and street hawkers—are rounded up and expelled from sight, as, for example, when some conference of foreign dignitaries is in the offing.

An analogue to the primitive labor market also exists among the "inner city" dwellers of the urban centers in some highly industrialized countries, although here, by contrast with the poor countries, the state does intervene to regulate the poor and provide a modicum of support for them.[17]

The existence of the primitive labor market offers some advantages to established society—chiefly cheap domestic services and the downward pressure on wages that arise from a massive "reserve army of labor." The visibility of the primitive labor market is an ever-present warning disciplining the employed worker. This mode also seems to pose a threat to the security of established society, less in reality than to the awakened fears of the richer and more secure. The consequence is repression, legal and illegal—the right-wing military coup and unrestrained activity of the death squads.[18]

Participants in the primitive labor market are highly insecure and in this lies the origin of the second type of relationship (with an exploiting-protecting boss in the mode). Primitive-labor-market producers have lost the protection of such social cohesion as may have existed in the rural communities whence many of them came. Often their status is technically illegal in the view of the established society within which they exist, since they are not supposed to be where they are. Many are illegal immigrants, for example. Even where this technical illegality does not apply, people in the primitive labor market tend to be victimized rather than protected by law enforcement.

In such conditions, they try to see to their own security and defense outside the laws of established society. Frequently the bonds of tribe, caste, religion, or ethnicity form a basis for organizing collective self-defense. The sense of obligation to members of the extended family is often appealed to but frequently found wanting. Sometimes security and advancement is pursued more successfully through newly created "families" of gangs and criminal organizations that give their members and those they protect a form of power at the margin of the alien society within which they exist and with which they must come to terms. Millenarian religions also offer compensation for the loss of community solidarity.[19]

The consciousness of the primitive labor market oscillates between a pragmatic instrumentalism—doing anything to procure the requisites of survival—and a holistic commitment to the illusion of a new collective life. Instrumentalist behavior is conducive to clientelism. Politicians can gain votes from them, and they, in turn, can extract some concessions from politicians, e.g., to keep the bulldozers away from their lean-tos or to run a source of electric power into a squatter's settlement. Millenarianism, membership in criminal "families," or participation in revolutionary groups demand holistic commitment and lead to ultra-authoritarianism among primitive-labor-market people. This in turn lends itself to manipulation of them from outside. The subjective consciousness of the mode is characterized by ambiguity and dependence—oscillating between acceptance and revolt, between passivity and self-defense.

### Household

Household production gave a name to economics (from the Greek *oeconomia*, meaning householding or production for one's own use). In its origins, household production merges with subsistence agriculture in a single mode of social relations of production. Indeed, it may be considered as derivative from subsistence production. However, in the contemporary world, household production must be thought of as a distinct mode of social relations of production that is the principle means of sustaining and reproducing the human species and thus the labor force. It survives alongside all other modes, and because of its reproductive functions it is the underpinning of all other forms of production.

The household mode is that most deeply embedded in social custom, most difficult to conceptualize as a mode of *production* relations. The stresses and changes it has undergone under the impact of other modes of production that have drawn off labor from the household are experienced as transformations in the family, as challenges to deeply ingrained psychological attitudes and norms of behavior, as crises of familial authority and sexual relations, rather than as changes in a mode of production. Like the subsistence mode, there is no class structure in the household mode. Authority inheres in the social relations of the patriarchal family, and production is determined by a sexual division of labor consecrated by myth.

Household production includes childbearing and child-rearing, the preparation of food, cleaning and washing, the making of clothing and repair and maintenance of clothing and household articles, gardening and small plot cultivation, etc. It also includes management of family income and resources. All this is production for direct consumption. The tools and raw materials used in it are for the most part obtained and paid for outside the household, but no monetary value is placed on household production itself. For this reason, it has been ignored by statisticians and economists—it does not get into the national accounts.[20] Yet household production is vital to the survival of the family and to the support of the other modes of production the household indirectly serves. Household production reproduces the labor power expended by these other modes.

If, in modern societies, collective production processes have been very largely subjected to rational analysis and negotiation among the interests involved, household production remains for most people governed primarily through the realm of myth. The explanation doubtless has to do with the fact that most of the work is done by women and seems to involve common understandings of the relationship between the sexes that transcend production.

The tenacity of myth has sustained an otherwise battered and beleaguered institution. Full-time housewives are a small minority of household producers in the world today. More representative is the woman who works in some other mode, e.g., as peasant or as enterprise-labor-market worker, and who in addition is expected to attend to household tasks and to bear and raise children. The family of man, wife, and children hired as hands by the nineteenth-century cotton mill owner and paid a family wage such that its survival was conditional upon all members' working was at the same time a household producing unit in which the wife, already full-time employee, was principal household producer. Rarely can the energies available for household production have been so close to extinction.

In advanced industrial societies, other modes gnaw away at household production without ever eliminating it. That goes for socialist, as well as capitalist, societies. Innovations in consumer products reduce the requirements of household production or increase its productivity, while opportunities for women's employment outside the household reduce the amount of time available for household tasks. These tendencies undermine further the valuation of household production, the incentive to engage in it, and the level of skills conventionally associated with it. In consequence, wage rates paid in commercial activities analogous to household work (cleaning, food preparation, and the care and education of children) are among the lowest.

Insofar as the household has been emptied of its productive function, its often troubled emotional core is left more fully exposed. The household remains, however, the producer of last resort. When unemployment rises, production functions are forced back upon the household. It becomes the buffer for economic crisis to the extent that its emotional resilience can stand the strain.[21]

# CHAPTER THREE

# CAPITALIST DEVELOPMENT

Capitalist development is a process that was put together gradually over a period of some five centuries, beginning in western Europe from the fourteenth century, before it became, in the nineteenth, a coherent expansive force on a world scale. This expansive force at the mid-nineteenth-century point was in its competitive phase. From the late nineteenth century, capitalist development entered a new, monopolistic phase. Each of these phases was associated with new modes of social relations of production.

## COMPETITIVE CAPITALISM

Debates continue about when, during that long period from the fourteenth to the nineteenth centuries, capitalism actually became the dominant organizing force of economic life. The issues revolve principally around the question of the essence of capitalism. Those who define capitalism primarily in terms of exchange relations and the accumulation of capital through trade tend to place the origins of the capitalist era toward the beginning of the period. Those who consider the essence of capitalism to be an organization of production designed to generate the expansion of capital have to place it toward the end of the period.[1] The latter position is more consistent with the approach of the present study. In part 2, the emergence of a new form of state—the liberal state—will be brought to the fore as the critical factor in the breakthrough of capitalist development.

Two modes of social relations of production became of special importance in the transition from the old regime of tribute-extracting land-based class power to an economy driven forward by capital accumulation in the hands of expanding entrepreneurs and investors. These modes were self-employment and the enterprise labor market. Self-employment is the condition of the independent small-scale producer using his own and his family's labor with means of production in his own possession for the purpose of marketing his produce. Self-employment thus went hand in hand with the early progress of commodity trade. In the enterprise-labor-market mode, production is by wage labor unprotected or unregulated either by the state or by the collective action of workers. It is production by workers who do not possess the means of production and whose labor power is available on an open or "pure" labor market.

## Self-Employment

Small, independent producers existed in all the old-regime societies, along with a degree of commodity trade in basic necessities. In old-regime China there were small cultivators and artisans, and in the old-regime Islamic societies, a flourishing artisan production. Merchants accumulated wealth by trading in commodities produced by artisans and farmers, although they did nothing to change the methods and organization of production, but the accumulation of mercantile wealth was recurrently checked by the dominant land-based military and bureaucratic classes as a possible rival to their power.[2] It was in western Europe, however, where the growth of independent farming and artisan production reached a scale sufficient to become the basis for an alternative organization of economy and society. The determining factor in the development of independent farming was the success of peasant resistance to attempts by the feudal nobility to extract more and more of their produce. As a result of this resistance, obligations of personal service by peasant to lord were progressively commuted to payments in kind, payments in kind to payments in cash, and total rent paid to the feudal class was gradually reduced. Western Europe became populated in the main by small holders who marketed part of their production, some of whom were tenants paying rent and some freeholders, all of whom paid taxes to a state that constituted the continuing dominance of the nobility.[3] Opportunities for peasant resistance were enhanced by several factors: the demographic decline of the fourteenth century devastated the peasantry as the most numerous class (the Black Death) and made labor scarce; autonomous towns provided a refuge and an alternative life for peasants; and mercantile capital, ensconced in the towns, counterbalanced the land power of the nobility, breaking or limiting their monopoly of power in society. These factors encouraged the growth of independent farming and artisan production. They led to a transformation from peasant-lord to self-employment production for a substantial part of the western European rural population.

Today, the self-employed are a large and varied category of producers. The category includes the family farm (probably the largest single group in it), independent artisans, small shopkeepers and itinerant peddlers, professionals and independent consultants, artists and writers, etc. The term *self-employed* is used in this study to cover only individuals (or family units) who are engaged on a fairly regular and stable basis in producing goods or services for sale. Excluded are the casual transactions that take place in the primitive labor market discussed in chapter 2.

Self-employment is a dependent mode that exists within the interstices of larger scale production. Self-employment depends in the first instance on the existence of a market for the goods or services provided, and the existence and nature of that market is conditioned by the dominant modes. Self-employment operates in the residual spaces left by the dominant modes. It provides some services in a capitalist society that big organizations find too costly, e.g., the corner variety store that stays open at night when the supermarket is closed. It has also been found to be a flexible and efficient means of handling the problem of production and distribution of certain categories of consumer goods and services in redistributive central planning. There has been a revival of self-employment activity for this reason in post-Mao China, and such activities have remained significant in Poland. Self-employment is not a form of capitalist production insofar as it does not involve the employment of hired labor. Profit in the market is achieved by self-exploitation on the part of the self-employed producer rather than by extracting a surplus from employees.

The social relations of self-employment, apart from this internalization of self-exploitation, are those involved in the market—with suppliers of inputs, with customers, and with competitors. The self-employed are also and increasingly involved in relations with the state, which extracts through taxation and regulates production and markets. Some of the most acute disputes with the state have involved taxation, the state endeavoring to block tax evasion by ever more detailed reporting requirements while the self-employed enjoy greater flexibility in reporting income than businesses or salaried employees (who are sitting targets for the tax collector).

Apart from a limited range of highly prestigious occupations, mainly those in the liberal professions, most forms of self-employment are precarious in the long term. For those who are successful, self-employment verges toward the enterprise-labor-market mode. The successful producer will hire workers and expand production when he finds a propitious market. More likely for large numbers of people, self-employment declines into a form of disguised wage employment. The service provided may be of a kind that a big business would find costly to provide by itself by labor paid according to its own wage levels and protected by health, safety, and social security legislation applying to its own workers, and so it subcontracts to an "independent" contractor who may have no other "client."

Small farming is a particular case of the precarious status of the self-employed. Often land reforms have been carried through with the aim of "land to the tiller," i.e., to give small farmers firm legal title to their land. Very often these reforms have not been accompanied by measures to prevent the market from subsequently undermining this aim. Consequently, small farmers become indebted and either lose their land or lose control of production to others. This leads either back to a new form of peasant-lord control by moneylenders or grain merchants or forward toward consolidation of holdings for capitalist farming with innovations in technology and use of hired labor. The alternative course offered by historical example is that of land reform carried through by a revolutionary regime as in Russia, which passed through a transitional stage of small farming into total collectivization of agriculture.

Confronted with this instability, the self-employed have tried to stabilize their situation by collective action. The steps taken to defend their prized independent status often mean adopting some of the features of big organizations. Such forms of organized defense include cooperative purchasing and marketing groups, cartels that fix common work-rules and rates, syndicates that bargain with suppliers or purchasers, and political and economic action directed toward influencing public opinion or the state (e.g., shopkeepers' strikes, farmers' disruption of commercial or tourist traffic by blocking highways, etc.). Organizations and actions limited to particular occupations are the most typical. However, with a self-image of rugged individualism in a society perceived to be increasingly bureaucracy ridden, the resentments of the self-employed have exploded at times into right-wing populist movements of which *poujadeisme* in France is the typical instance.[4]

*Enterprise Labor Market*

Like self-employment, wage labor existed, though on a small scale, in old-regime societies. In Japan, for instance, especially during the eighteenth and early nineteenth centuries, some independent farmers rose to a position of relative wealth. Less fortunate peasants with very small holdings fell under the control of usurers, often rich peasants; and this new class of rich peasants brought industry into the villages, *sake* brewing and silk manufacture for example, and thereby escaped the control of guilds and used the labor of the depressed stratum of poor peasants that had fallen under their control.[5]

Again, it was in western Europe that wage labor grew to a scale where it could become the basis for a different organization of the economy. The attraction exerted by the towns drew in a new category of cheap labor displaced from rural areas, which enabled manufacturers to locate outside the area over which the town guilds had jurisdiction—a development that heightened class conflict within the extended urban area.[6] The transformation of wage-labor commodity production into capitalist development proceeded along two routes. On one route, the successful individual producer expanded from self-employed artisan production to the use of hired labor in larger scale manufacture. On the other route, merchants who had accumulated working capital and who knew the markets for manufactured goods and raw materials "put out" the manufacture of these wares to cottagers in suburban and rural areas.[7] These cottagers shifted gradually in status from self-employed workers dealing with a single client to become de facto piece workers earning a wage.[8]

During the seventeenth century this change in the mode of manufacture accompanied and facilitated a shift in the location of industry away from the old industrial centers of northern Italy and Germany and even from France toward newer centers emerging in England, Sweden, and Switzerland. It broke the control of the old crafts and the guild-dominated towns over industry and made possible a rapid increase in industrial production under more concentrated commercial and financial control before the introduction of the factory system.[9]

Self-employment and even the employment of wage labor are not inherently capitalist in the sense of being necessarily bound up with or exclusively associated with the capitalist mode of development. As has been pointed out, they came into existence before the capitalist mode of development. In western Europe, their existence was a necessary condition for capitalist development to take place. It was not, in and of itself, a sufficient condition. In other places, independent producers and wage-labor production became segments within an economy that remained dominated by tributary relations between peasantry and a ruling class.

The conjunction of four factors enabled the transformation from simple reproduction to capitalist development to take place in western Europe. These four conditions were (1) accumulation of capital in the hands of people who would invest in the expansion of production for the market (as distinct from old-regime states and ruling classes that invested in territorial aggrandizement to extend the sphere of feudal agrarian relations), (2) expansion of the market for basic necessities of life to the point where production for exchange supplanted production for use, (3) creation of a market in land by "freeing" land from entailments and the whole range of feudal restrictions and concurrent obligations, and (4) enlargement of the market for labor by separating an increasing proportion of workers from the means of production and allowing wages to be determined by supply and demand.

The first two conditions were attained in England during the eighteenth century. This was the first country in which a national market became a reality. Internal barriers to the movement of goods were substantially removed. So were residual medieval guild-type restrictions on production and obstacles to the transfer of people from agricultural to industrial pursuits. Thus grew a broadly based, effective demand for the essentials of life—food and textiles for clothing. Market-oriented landowners and industrial entrepreneurs innovated production methods to meet this demand. Capital accumulated in the West Indian sugar and slave trade flowed into this development of production through the expansion of banking facilities, and those in whose hands capital accumulated acquired the political influence necessary to ensure that the state through its domestic and foreign policies maintained and extended the conditions for capital accumulation. Market-oriented production could now grow on the basis of an expanding internal market, and industries grounded in this market expanded even more rapidly as suppliers to the outside world. (By contrast to the English case, the Dutch merchant oligarchy for long dominated the world market in long-distance trade and became wealthy commercial and financial intermediaries without ever being able to base their economic growth on a large domestic market and industrial development. Capital accumulation alone did not give the Dutch sufficient staying power. Through aggressive trade wars and protectionism the English fostered the basis for their ultimate industrial and commercial triumph.)[10]

There was much greater resistance to the two remaining conditions—creation of markets in land and in labor. The resistance of established landholding classes to unrestricted sale of land was overcome in western Europe only in the aftermath of the French Revolution. But the most difficult condition of all was the creation of a labor market. The historical experience of the human race suggests that a free labor market was a most unusual and unnatural phenomenon. What the classical liberal political economists represented as consistent with the laws of nature has never been so regarded by historical societies. As Polanyi argued, the free market in labor was a utopia that was brought for the first time into existence in England in the early nineteenth century by the intervention of the state, which revoked the policy continuous from Elizabethan times of supporting the poor in the rural areas.[11] It was only during the nineteenth century in England and in western Europe that state policies contrived to turn the displaced poor into a supply of undifferentiated labor power. Thus was a long-standing practice of wage labor expanded into the mode of social relations of production of the early factory system—the enterprise-labor-market mode. The social history of the period that followed can be seen as the natural reaction of social forces striving to counteract, tame, control, and in some measure, to humanize this artificial creation.

By the first half of the nineteenth century the four previously specified structural conditions for the transformation of the production relations characteristic of late feudalism in northwestern Europe had been substantially completed.

Somewhat analogous developments have taken place in other agrarian-based societies—in eastern Europe and Mexico during the first part of the twentieth century, and in countries of north Africa, Asia, and Latin America during the last half of the twentieth century. The conjunction of peasant pressures, often in an organized political form, with state-enacted measures of land reform has aimed to expand the sphere of self-employed smallholder cultivation. Typically, such land reforms have resulted in a partial redistribution of land to independent farmers through a breaking up of big estates, followed by a reconcentration of land in the hands of some of the more successful farmers and the failure of others, who become a labor pool. The mechanism for this reconcentration has generally been indebtedness—the result, a growth of enterprise-labor-market production in agriculture and a movement of failed self-employed to seek wage work in urban areas.[12]

During the first decades of the nineteenth century, industrial production continued to grow but still mainly in the form of cottage industry coordinated by commercial capitalists through the putting-out system. Even by 1848, there were still relatively few real proletarians in Paris in the sense of wage workers in large-scale factory production. The cities of Europe were still peopled—as regards the working classes and the poor—very largely by self-employed, small-scale handicraft producers and small shopkeepers and by a marginal population of uncertain and unstable occupations in the primitive labor market. Factory production in the enterprise-labor-market mode had appeared but was still of limited extent, existing mainly in cotton textiles in England and to a lesser extent in the north of France and the Low Countries. In this sector, the traditional craft skills of self-employed artisans were being steadily undermined both by the introduction of new machinery and by the increasing employment of children and women, as well as of unskilled male laborers, as operatives. Both putting-out and early factory production were carried on in this way with a labor force of increasingly indeterminate skills recruited through the labor market. The state protected the employer's freedom to contract and penalized attempts at collective self-defense by workers.

During this formative phase of the industrial system in England, it was difficult to distinguish employed from unemployed by any objective and durable characteristics. In Marx's terms, the proletariat was hardly distinguishable from the reserve army of labor. Frederick Engels, in his description of the condition of the working class in England in 1844, wrote:

> Thus the working-class of the great cities offers a graduated scale of conditions in life, in the best cases a temporarily endurable existence for hard work and good wages, good and endurable, that is, from the worker's standpoint; in the worst cases, bitter want, reaching even homelessness and death by starvation. The average is much nearer the worst case than the best. And this series does not fall into fixed classes, so that one can say, this fraction of the working class is well off, has always been so, and remains so. If that is the case here and there, if single branches of work have in general an advantage over others, yet the conditions of the workers in each branch is subject to such great fluctuations that a single working-man may be so placed as to pass through the whole range from comparative comfort to the extremest need, even to death by starvation, while almost every English working-man can tell a tale of marked changes of fortune.[13]

During the second half of the nineteenth century, by contrast with the first half, a growing distinction within the working class can be observed with increasing clarity, a distinction between a more established category of industrial workers and another category less established or more precariously connected to permanent industrial employment. The more established generally possessed a higher degree of industrial skills and had more stable jobs. The nonestablished were less skilled and had less employment stability. The dramatic growth in population and the population shift from rural to urban areas that occurred in late nineteenth-century Europe accentuated this differentiation.

When the migration crossed national boundaries, it added visible ethnic identification to the social differentiation of the emerging distinctions within the working class. Workers of the older native stock tended to become more established, as the newer immigrants to the towns swelled the ranks of the nonestablished. The migration of Irish workers to the industrial northwest of England gave an early instance of ethnic appearance for a work-based social differentiation. Subsequently, the United States in the twentieth century came to provide the foremost example of overlap between the established-nonestablished differentiation and successive waves of migration. Established workers were from the older stock of Yankees, German, Scandinavian, and Irish, while recent immigrants from south and central Europe and blacks from the southern United States staffed the new mass production industries based on semiskilled labor.[14] In the post-World-War-II period, more blacks, Hispanics, and women entered the U.S. labor force as successors to the earlier waves of immigrants.

Today there are many workers employed in enterprises such as factories, stores, or plantations, in nearly all countries, whose conditions of employment are not materially influenced by trade unions or government regulation. Insecurity of job tenure, low skills, lower pay than that of established workers, and frequently, membership in a group suffering adverse social discrimination characterize these nonestablished enterprise-labor-market workers' situation.

Broadly there are two types of nonestablished worker. The first type are employed—when they are employed—in medium to small private enterprises. These enterprises are the successors to the small factories that launched the Industrial Revolution in Britain in the early nineteenth century. Latterly, they have been exemplified by the rural textile mill, the Manhattan sweatshop in the needle trades, the Hong Kong electronics component factory. Small-scale industries survive to form what John Kenneth Galbraith called the competitive sector of industry, which exists alongside the large scale monopoly sector of advanced capitalist countries.[15] They have also multiplied in some newly industrializing countries of the Third World. The lower productivity of their technical processes is compensated by the lower wages and greater malleability of their workers. The practice still prevalent in construction in some countries, where a gang boss recruits and pays his own workers to carry out a specific job of work for an all-in price, also falls into this type.

The second type of nonestablished worker is employed in big industry in semiskilled jobs. (The term *semi-skilled work* is a euphemism describing an operation for which a worker can be trained in anything from a couple of days to a couple of weeks.) In this form, the entreprise labor market is included within the big corporate monopoly sector of industry. Here established and nonestablished workers are institutionally separated in a variety of ways. The established may be unionized and the nonestablished lack unions; or the two groups may have different unions; or where they nominally have the same union, it will protect the established more effectively than the nonestablished. The two groups have different income levels, different expectations of job security, different levels of health and safety protection, often different legal status (e.g., *gastarbeiter* versus national). The nonestablished workers in big industry include immigrant workers employed on a full-time basis, temporary workers such as office overload staff, and employees of enterprises to which big industries subcontract certain tasks like cleaning and certain kinds of maintenance performed on the big industry's premises.

This second type does not conform strictly to the pure labor market, because state regulations do impinge somewhat on the terms of employment affecting some jobs. The distinction holds, however, in that protection is always less effective for the nonestablished worker. His or her employment is more precarious in every way. Poor protection shades into no protection for the many nonestablished workers who are in "black," illegal, or undeclared work entirely outside the state's official cognizance or regulation.[16] This second type of enterprise-labor-market mode is becoming more important than the first type, especially in the industrially more developed countries.

The social relations of the small enterprise have an ideological importance beyond their economic significance. They are represented as embodying the ideals of entrepreneurship and free enterprise. Small-enterprise employers also sometimes claim to have a close, nonconflictual, sometimes paternal relationship with their workers. In some cases, enterprises do maintain steady jobs for at least a core of old hands. High turnover and unstable employment is, however, endemic in small enterprises because of fluctuations in their markets. This very narrowly limits the real possibility of long tenure, which would be the aspect of paternalism most meaningful to workers.

Efforts by the state to extend more impersonal forms of protection into the employment situation of nonestablished workers may be thwarted by employers who are suspicious of, and hostile to, trade union growth, and these employers may also enjoy the complicity of some workers for whom maximizing individual earnings is a more salient goal than class solidarity. If the participant in the primitive labor market is a lumpenproletarian, the small-enterprise worker is often a proletarian who has yet to make collective efforts to improve things. Individual survival rather than class solidarity is uppermost in his or her mind.

In the second and growing type of enterprise labor market—the nonestablished worker within big industry—the ideological rationales of small industry are totally irrelevant. The milieu of big industry is a powerful stimulus to the awareness of relative deprivation. Since the basis for institutional segregation of the nonestablished is often in nonproduction-related characteristics—principally ethnicity and sex—it is not surprising that these characteristics become the focus of protest. The civil rights movement for black people in the United States and the feminist movements in many countries have taken up the cause of these groups of nonestablished workers. Such action has sometimes spilled over into trade unions, transforming an initial hostility or aloofness towards nonestablished workers into efforts to organize them and to promote solidarity between established and non-established. Such efforts are, however, very largely dependent on a favorable economic environment and are placed under considerable strain or reversed by large and growing unemployment, which hits the nonestablished most severely while encouraging a more self-protective attitude on the part of the established.

Enterprise-labor-market production, and self-employment relations, have also not only continued to exist but have also been actively revived and encouraged in the redistributive development of centrally planned economies. This fact underlines that there is nothing inherently or exclusively capitalist in these modes of social relations of production. During early phases of redistributive planning there was, indeed, a tendency to regard these forms of production relations as residues of capitalism to be superseded by large-scale collective organization of production. This attitude has generally been set aside with the accumulation of experience in planning. Small, independent enterprises, both individual self-employed and those employing a few wage workers, have become more prized by planners as relatively efficient and flexible ways of meeting many basic needs of the population. Planners then turned from discouraging and restricting these modes of production relations to regulating them and including them in their planning as regards both allocations of inputs and anticipated outputs.

### Bipartism

A third mode of social relations of production appeared with the consolidation of the capitalist mode of development in industry—bipartite relations between organized workers and employers. Its emergence has to be situated in the context of the changes in the nature of the labor force mentioned in connection with the enterprise-labor-market mode—the differentiation between established and nonestablished workers.

Trade unions took root among the established workers, based usually upon the skilled occupations, and unions were but the centerpieces of a broader labor movement that included political parties supported by workers in the main industrialized countries. The new political importance of this upper layer

among the working class brought a response from politicians and
the state in the form of legislation extending the vote to them,
conferring legal status upon trade unions, requiring certain minimum standards in conditions of industrial employment, and
introducing social insurance.[17]

Union recognition was secured first by the early established workers in the form of craft-based organizations. Successive waves entering the labor force as semiskilled, nonestablished
workers created pressures for the extension of bipartite relations
to these groups. The advantages of possessing greater resources
gave skilled workers the edge in developing effective trade union
organizations.[18] The semiskilled followed behind. As they in turn
developed organizational capacity they altered the organizational
basis, the strategy, and the aims of trade unionism. The work on
which these later waves of workers were employed was of a
different character—fragmented tasks coordinated by an industrially engineered process. The skilled trade gave way gradually
to the industry as a basis for union organization. Control of jobs
(which made sense for skilled workers) took second place to
wages and working conditions as bargaining issues. Political action became a more salient part of union strategy.[19]

An ideological and an organizational distinction accompanied this gradual separation between the two categories of
labor. The ideological distinction was symbolized by the break
between Marx and Bakunin. Orthodox Marxists thenceforth saw
in the established worker the proletarian type who embodied the
contradiction to the highest development of productive forces
under capitalism. They often disdained the nonestablished and
marginals as a lumpenproletariat unsuitable to be the basis for
revolutionary action. Bakunin and his emulators, up to and including Frantz Fanon, on the contrary, saw the marginals as
among the most exploited, *les damnés de la terre,* and for this
very reason more disposed to be fully committed to revolutionary
action than what they perceived to be a coopted aristocracy of
labor. Lenin in attacking the labor aristocracy as the betrayers of
the working class, inclined more to Bakunin than to Marx. *Tiers-
mondiste* populism continues the same current of revolutionary
ideology, while radical Marxists like Rosa Luxemburg and An-

tonio Gramsci remained more consistent with Marx's view of the working class.[20]

Organizationally, the distinction was between trades unionism, initially craft-based unionism, and the larger, looser forms of organization associated with semiskilled, nonestablished workers. In North American experience, the Knights of Labor and the Industrial Workers of the World appealed to the nonestablished workers, as did the industrial unionism of the Congress of Industrial Organizations at its origins in the 1930s. The trade unionism of established workers became the preeminent form of working-class organization in northern Europe, whereas a form of syndicalism took root in southern Europe (especially Italy and Spain) in areas of lesser industrial development where an established working class had not yet become so fully formed and so clearly differentiated from the more marginal or nonestablished workers.[21]

Craft-based trades unionism and forms of political action leading in the direction of social democracy were dual expressions of the institutionalization of conflict achieved by established workers through the evolution of bipartite social relations of production in the industrially most advanced areas from the late nineteenth century. Worker-employer conflict became institutionalized when the trade unions of established workers were recognized and accepted as legitimate and came to perform regular functions in industrial relations. Institutionalization of conflict is the product of hegemony—concessions can be made to the unions within bipartism without disturbing the ultimate control of the hegemonic class.[22]

By contrast, syndicalism never acquired such legitimacy. Ideologically, it remained as a challenge to the foundations of social dominance and organizationally it never acquired the positions of strength and leverage within industry that would enable it to become a stable bargaining partner with management. Syndicalism and anarcho-syndicalism remained forms of consciousness of workers in an enterprise-labor-market mode of social relations of production—a challenge to the continuance of this mode but not of itself an adequate force to transform the mode. Wherever, as in the case of the CIO, an essentially syndicalist movement, using syndicalist weapons like the sitdown strike or plant occupation, did acquire positions of strength within industry, it tended to embrace bipartite social relations of production, to work toward established status for its members, and to change its ideology in the process.

A condition for bipartism is a rough balance of strength between labor and management. Too great an imbalance favoring management would remove the incentive to negotiate and presage a return to enterprise-labor-market conditions. Historically, how has such a balance come about? By a combination of working-class pressure through the formation of effective trade unions and action by the state both to encourage union organization and provide it with a legal framework. The further question is: why should the state have taken such action? The answer: because the people in control of the state perceived the opportunity of strengthening their political base by attracting worker support without antagonizing other politically important elements.

Working-class pressure became effective first during the nineteenth century in western Europe in the form of craft-based associations that could influence the supply of skills in the labor market. These were local groups linked in loose national networks built up through the movement of craftsmen in the practice of their trades. The importance of the working class as a political force is associated especially with the emergence of industrial unionism from the late nineteenth century. Industrial unions tended to be more centralized, with larger top-level bureaucratic structures. They had a greater propensity to exert pressure on the state both directly and through political parties controlled or influenced by labor.

Government responses to legalize union activities and encourage collective bargaining came in Britain in 1867, in France in 1884.[23] The new legislation resulted during the following decades in substantial increases of union membership. The counterpart to acceptance by the state of the legitimacy of trade unionism and collective bargaining was acceptance by labor of the capitalist social order as the legitimate framework within which labor could act to advance its own interests.

Worker organization, in turn, tended to stimulate employer organization, leading to the creation of employer associations for purposes of negotiations with unions, or at a minimum, to a coordination of bargaining strategies among individual employers confronting a single trade union. National practice varied in regard to the level at which negotiations would take place.[24] In the United States, the enterprise remained the bargaining unit, whereas in European countries, the practice of industry-level and national-level negotiations developed between strongly centralized worker and employer organizations. Even where bargaining was at the enterprise level, however, the goal of the trade union was to establish a precedent for subsequent application in other enterprises in the trade or industry. Some countries have recognized this in their legislation, which provides for the extension of collective agreements to enterprises other than those directly covered by negotiations. Bipartism thus has a built-in spread effect toward equalizing conditions in the occupations covered by its negotiations. This, in turn, facilitates mobility of workers within the same occupation. Unions gain control over access to jobs, over the supply side of the labor market, and to some extent over the workplace. The worker, for his part (and in bipartism is has usually been a "him" and not a "her"), identifies primarily with his skill or occupation and with his union rather than with the enterprise. In the course of a working lifetime, he may be employed in a number of enterprises, conserving all the time his status in his occupation.

The role of the state in the creation of bipartism cannot be underestimated. The state did not merely respond to worker pressures. The state often facilitated trade union organization and put pressure upon employers to come to terms with unions. Nowhere was this clearer than in the United States, the last of the major industrial countries to equip itself with trade union legislation. The 1930s New Deal administration of Franklin Roosevelt was the turning point for bipartism in the United States. The craft-based trade unions of the American Federation of Labor (AFL) had been much weakened by the depression, and the AFL leaders had been consistent supporters of the Republican Party. Through section 7A of the National Industrial Recovery Act and especially through the Wagner National Labor Relations Act of 1935, the government placed the weight of legality behind the union movement and behind collective bargaining as the manner of settling disputes, and it protected union organizers against harassment by employers. A new union movement, the industrial unions of the Congress of Industrial Organizations (CIO), proceeded to organize the largely immigrant semiskilled workers of the mass-production industries, long ignored by the established native-stock craft-union leadership of the American Federation of Labor. In the years that followed, the union movement grew from less than 3 million members in 1933 to more than 8 million in 1939 and became part of the political coalition put together by the Roosevelt Democrats.[25]

Under bipartism, the state's role, though fundamental, has nevertheless been limited. It has sought to bring about a balance of forces in industry between workers and employers and to ensure that peaceful means are used for the settlement of industrial disputes.[26] The state has sought, in other words, to institutionalize labor-management conflict. It has not itself intervened directly as a party with an interest in the specific outcomes of these disputes. (Where the state does this, it transforms bipartism into tripartism.) In the bipartite mode, the state typically provides a legal framework for negotiations, and it administers minimum labor standards, which are of direct consequence mainly to workers outside the bipartite sphere. Indirectly, state labor administration safeguards the bargaining strength of unions. State regulation puts a floor under conditions of unorganized workers outside the bipartite sector, sometimes extending to them the minimum conditions gained by workers through bipartite negotiation. Labor legislation thereby limits the impact that a pool of unorganized workers might otherwise have in enhancing the power of employers in the bipartite sector. Legislation may also require employers to negotiate with unions "in good faith."

Agreements reached between unions and employers do not systematically take account of interests beyond those of the parties directly concerned. They are not concerned with public policy and public policy is not concerned with them.

Although created by capitalist development, bipartite production relations need not be considered to be necessarily confined to that mode of development. Of course, the fact that no case can be cited of bipartism within redistributive development creates a certain presumption against this possibility. However, some critics from within redistributive systems have foreseen the possibility of the growth of more transactional, bargaining types of relationships in these systems without their becoming capitalist.[27] The possibility must remain open; bipartism could conceivably become part of the panoply of redistributive development just as self-employment and enterprise-labor-market production relations have now found an accepted place there.

## MONOPOLY CAPITALISM

The monopoly phase of capitalist development begins with the long depression of 1873–96. Its salient characteristics have been (1) the concentration of capital into large corporate units; (2) the growth of a dual structure of economy in the industrialized countries distinguishing large-scale and small-scale enterprises, or monopoly and competitive sectors; (3) increased importance of the role of banking consortia and states in bringing together the amounts of capital necessary to fund large-scale industries; (4) increased concern of states not only for raising the capital for industry but also for ensuring the conditions in which production and capital accumulation can continue without disruptions, i.e., specifically concern for maintaining adequate levels of investment and employment and for the balance of payments; and (5) an international division of labor brought about by capital in the most industrialized countries investing in complimentary and subsidiary production in less industrialized countries.

This phase has brought into existence several new modes of social relations of production. The emergence of a monopoly sector made it possible for some of the larger enterprises to sponsor enterprise corporatist relations for a relatively privileged segment of their labor forces, those for whom it became capital's interest to provide quasipermanent tenure. Such favored employees came to enjoy conditions of employment analogous to those of civil servants. The new role of the state as an active agency of economic policy in liberal, parliamentary, pluralist polities also led toward tripartism—in which the state takes on the role of consensus shaper, associating capital and organized labor in the framing and execution of economic policy. In late industrializing countries that did not have a firm liberal, pluralist foundation of polity, the state assumed a more authoritarian role and imposed a framework of collaboration upon capital and labor—state corporatism. These tendencies can be perceived clearly from the 1920s. They revived and became more widespread during the years of economic expansion following World War II. Wherever they appeared, enterprise corporatism, tripartism, and state corporatism coexisted with other, older modes, the enterprise labor market, self-employment, household production, and bipartism. The new modes associated with monopoly capitalist development became, however, dominant within the social formations where they appeared in the sense that they characterized the leading sectors of the economy, and the other modes assumed a subordinate relationship to them.

## Enterprise Corporatism

A primary condition for the existence of enterprise corporatism was the large-scale undertaking. The long depression beginning in 1873 brought about the bankruptcy of innumerable small enterprises and set in motion a process of industrial concentration in all the countries of advanced industrialism. The corporation emerged as the dominant form of organization of the means of production. With the corporation went the bureaucratization of management, the development of what Reinhard Bendix calls "internal bureaucratization" to distinguish it from the "external bureaucratization" that represents an extension of state control over industry.[28] Internal bureaucratization involved delegation of authority, and technical and administrative specialization of functions, the distinction of "staff" and "line," and the emergence of what John Kenneth Galbraith called the "technostructure."[29]

The corporate form of organization and its internal bureaucracy came to adopt a distinctive form of ideology. Its essential feature is the social integration of the corporation as a productive community. In its Japanese form, this ideology appears as a continuous development within a nonconflictual concept of production relations. In the 1920s, the largest companies in the heavy industries, the zaibatsu, offered a stable and privileged position to their permanent employees, and this model of relations was reconstructed during the Korean War boom of the 1950s to provide the bureaucratized corporate welfare of lifetime commitment employment to the established industrial workforce in Japan.[30] In its American-European form, the ideology of enterprise corporatism appeared as an alternative to bipartism issuing from the initiative of employers. The scientific management of Taylor was one critical step in a process of eliminating the worker's residual autonomy in production and concentrating control of work performance with management. The industrial psychology of Mayo, following Taylorism, attempted to reconcile the semiskilled workers to the diminished condition in which "scientific management" had placed them.

Bipartism moderated and regulated conflict by institutionalizing it. Enterprise corporatism denied the legitimacy of conflict, representing it as a mere misperception of interests on the part of workers (who mistakenly thought they wanted more money when what they really needed was more satisfaction in their work) and a deficiency of manipulative skills on the part of management. The doctrine of Mayo and his followers has been of practical benefit to numerous exponents of industrial psychology who have become consultants to managements and organizers of training programs for middle management; as Bendix points out, it "has found only limited acceptance in managerial practice, but . . . its contribution to managerial ideology has been pervasive."[31]

The American-European ideology of enterprise corporatism, originating as an antiunion reaction to bipartism, moved a stage further in the later twentieth century toward attracting trade unions away from bipartism into a symbiotic relationship with corporate management. The ability of large-scale enterprises, public or private, to grant a privileged position to preferred segments of the workforce exerts a power of attraction on unions. A tendency toward plant-level negotiations, reinforced by techniques like productivity bargaining, whereby management gains back from unions control over the production process in return for wage concessions, and also by forms of worker participation in management that encourage an enterprise consciousness, can all attract workers away from solidarities based on occupation or industry or the labor movement as a whole, in order to focus their interests and loyalties on the corporation, the source of their well-being. Thus, through a different historical route, a structure similar to the enterprise unionism of Japan took shape. Both are encompassed within the twentieth-century mode of enterprise corporatism.

Enterprise corporatism maintains stable employment conditions for established employees. The central core of IBM employees, civil servants of modern states or international agencies, and lifetime employees of big Japanese industrial and banking groups are not much concerned or affected by fluctuations in the supply of and demand for labor on the open market. Their concerns are career prospects, seniority rights, fringe benefits, and pension entitlements.

In the enterprise corporatist mode, the enterprise is the basic unit of employer-worker relations, as in the enterprise labor market, but the employment instability of the enterprise labor market has been reduced, and employment security and the welfare of workers and their families is ensured by the employer. The corporatist concept implies a contrived harmony of interests between workers and management—or at least attitudes and behavior on the part of both that are consistent with this notion of harmony. Management orients the loyalties of established employees to the enterprise. Of course, big corporations also employ nonestablished workers who are excluded from the regime of enterprise corporatism.

The primary condition for enterprise-corporatist relations is a substantial concentration of industry into large-scale units—private or public corporations. The quasi-monopolistic position enjoyed by the corporation enables the employer to guarantee security of tenure to the employee and to introduce measures to gain the employee's personal identification with the goals of the enterprise. The high cost of capital equipment and risk of loss from stoppages of work make it in the employer's interest to provide the favorable conditions. The large corporation can master its own environment and plan for a long time span, and this allows it to gain control over product markets and over its labor force.

Enterprise corporatist management is professional in all aspects. In labor relations it establishes an impersonal, bureaucratized internal welfare management that is infinitely more effective than the personal pseudopaternalism claimed by some small enterprises. Personnel management gives emphasis to the psychological, family, and social aspects of the worker's life in responding to pressures for improvements in wages and working conditions. Its target is the worker as a whole person, and it forges a multiplicity of links binding him or her to the enterprise—health benefits, privileges that come with seniority, pension rights, and so forth.[32]

Corporate management and the political elite are close to one another, and corporate and state policy are closely aligned on trade, financial, and industrial questions, but the state does not intervene significantly in labor matters within the corporation. State intervention in the labor field rather concerns workers in other modes whose material conditions are less favorable than those of workers under enterprise corporatism. Enterprise corporatism tends to outbid state regulation as regards employment conditions. In countries where enterprise corporatism is well established, the state leaves corporations their full autonomy in dealing with labor matters.

In some cases, the security and welfare provided by the corporation act as a deterrent to the formation of unions. In others, unions or staff associations complement management by performing personnel and welfare functions and by handling individual grievances. Trade unions, where they exist in enterprise corporatism, function primarily as enterprise unions. They concentrate on protecting and enlarging the advantages of established workers within the large undertakings. They ignore in substance the issues of concern to nonestablished workers or to the unemployed outside the corporation.

The union-management relationship in enterprise corporatism is symbiotic rather than adversary. Symbiosis does not exclude conflict about some issues of concern to workers in the enterprise, but it is a conflict carried on within an overriding common interest in the well-being of the enterprise. Enterprise corporatist unions may, for example, dispute with management over the size of employer contributions to a supplementary unemployment benefit fund but adopt a common front with the employer in resisting the imposition by the state of antipollution devices or health hazard warnings to protect the public. Corporations are to be thought of as coalitions of interests, among which unions and staff associations are included, engaged in playing a positive-sum game with each other. The other face of this moderated rivalry within the corporation is exclusivity toward outsiders.

*Tripartism*

In the most industrially advanced countries, where bipartism had already developed in the late nineteenth and early twentieth centuries with solidly organized movements of established workers, the increased intervention of the state in national economic management tended to transform bipartite relations in the direction of tripartism. The state now was not merely concerned to provide a framework for orderly settlement of issues between employers and workers but also took a hand in shaping these settlements and bringing about more cooperative labor-management relations. Tripartism was a further development in the same hegemony that had generated bipartism. The state's definition of national economic policy conformed to the conceptions and interests of the dominant employer class while it encouraged concessions such as would retain the acquiescence of the articulate class of established workers. But the increased complexities of national economic management after World War I now required greater state intervention. Governments were no longer prepared to leave wages and employment questions entirely to the interaction of employers and unions.

As a consequence, corporatist structures grew within the state, and the line between state and economy, state and civil society, became blurred. Ministries of industry encouraged the development of industry organizations and established regular links with them; ministries of labor did the same with trade unions. Regular contacts and the performance of functions within an expanded state machinery bound employer and worker organizations more closely into the state. Such developments were taking place in the industrialized countries of western Europe from the early postwar period.[33] In the United States, initial tendencies can be observed in the Hoover administration's move to bring business into closer consultation with government and were accelerated with the New Deal.[34]

The origins of tripartism lay in the mobilization of labor and capital for war effort in all the major industrial powers during World War I. In England, the oldest industrial power, the temporary truce in class conflict so impressed some leading civil servants that they drew up plans for an international organization to perpetuate and promote the association of labor with capital and government—a proposal that became the International Labour Organization under Part XIII of the Treaty of Versailles in 1919. This reflected a recognition on the part of government leaders that union contributions to the war effort earned labor a right to be consulted by the state on policy matters concerning labor, a right that corresponded to labor's effective position of collective power in society. It also reflected a concern that, lacking such hegemonic consciousness on the part of the state leadership, Bolshevism would provide an alternative and more threatening model for labor. As the leading trading nation, Britain might have been disadvantaged in world markets if a peacetime prolongation of tripartism were to have the effect of raising labor costs. Hence the concern of British officials to internationalize the experiment.[35]

Tripartism in the interwar period was a mixed success. British practice in fact reverted to bipartite confrontation. It was in Germany that the impact of early tripartism was greatest. The war economy persisted into the postwar period most of all in this country because of the twin pressures of the burden placed on German industry by reparations obligations and the close proximity of the Bolshevik menace. Employers in big industry perceived the utility of allying with unions to secure government defense of the interests of their industries. The alliance preempted a more radical revolutionary development in the labor movement and won industrialists government support during a phase of political preeminence of the Social Democratic Party in the immediate postwar years. It also fueled galloping inflation, for both capital and unionized workers had the joint power to protect their profits and earnings through government operation of the printing presses for money, while other elements of the population, the future clientele of Naziism, lost out. Labor's relative strength waned in the late 1920s, to collapse altogether in the 1930s with the arrival of the Nazi regime.[36] Tripartism had served to confine labor's demands to what was acceptable to capital during the postwar crisis when labor had political and economic opportunity, but it had not delivered any lasting gains to labor.

In the United States, the early New Deal was inspired by the tripartite concept. General Hugh Johnson, President Franklin Roosevelt's National Recovery Act administrator, was much influenced by his World War I experience in mobilizing industry. Schlesinger (1960) cites Johnson's reflection after the war: "If cooperation can do so much, maybe there is something wrong with the old competitive system."[37] The NRA achieved a temporary mobilization of Americans for economic recovery in the *élan* of a new administration during the crisis years 1933–34. Its impact faltered before the hostility of employer interests. The lasting structural effect of the New Deal was the erection with governmental support of trade union countervailing power.[38] A transitory tripartism relapsed into a strengthened bipartism. Tripartism received further impetus during World War II in the Western powers, where organized labor was brought into a variety of boards and agencies whose aims were the maintenance of production for the effective prosecution of the war effort. Wartime experience was consolidated in the post-World War II institutions set up in Western European countries to associate the economic interests with national economic policymaking—national economic and social councils advisory to governments, planning commissions, and so forth.[39]

When, during the 1960s, concern to limit inflation took the place of an earlier preoccupation with reconstruction in the priorities of these countries' governments, the incentive to strengthen tripartite structures was increased. Even in the United States and Canada, where organized labor was politically weak relative to labor in northern European countries and free-enterprise ideology was more resistant to market-constricting collaboration, tripartism was invoked as an instrument for putting incomes policies into practice.

Thus, through this whole period beginning after World War I and continuing into the aftermath of World War II, tripartism made appearances in the industrially advanced capitalist countries. It became a significant mode of social relations of production, more significant at some times and in some countries than others. Tripartism coexisted with other industrial modes, principally enterprise corporatism, bipartism, and the enterprise labor market, where and when it appeared as the overarching mode of dealing with limited but crucial issues. Tripartism thus became an option in advanced capitalist countries, sometimes practiced, sometimes advocated as a way out of crisis.

In the tripartite mode, government plays an active role interacting with industrial management and trade unions. Whereas in the bipartite form, government confines itself largely to facilitating and encouraging union-management bargaining, in the tripartite form, government is directly interested in influencing the outcome of this bargaining and so becomes a party to it. This substantive concern of government arises for two main reasons. One is that government is itself a large employer, and the terms of employment in the state sector are bound to be influenced by decisions of unions and managements in the private sector. The second reason is that wage settlements in the private sector affect the attainment of the economic and social goals of public policy.

Tripartism attempts to institutionalize decision making among the most powerful group interests in those areas of public policy upon which labor relations have a bearing, e.g., prices, incomes, investment, the level of employment, and the balance of payments. Tripartism flows from a recognition by government that public policy in these areas can work only with the compliance of the powerful corporate and union interests, and it arises only in a political culture that rules out direct government control over these interest groups and requires that compliance be secured by persuasion.

A certain kind of political culture is, indeed, a condition for tripartism, one in which the state is regarded both as the instrument of civil society and at the same time as the agency for harmonizing civil society's divergent interests. Government is thought of both as the channel for procuring satisfaction for separate interests and as a force constraining these interests toward reconciliation.

There are, however, conflicting principles of interest representation within the state. The more traditional principle is territorially based representation of electors through parliament. The alternative principle is one of economic interest groups that cut across the territorial subdivisions of the state. Tripartism erects the second of these principles—which is the less legitimate of the two in the Western liberal political tradition—into a more or less institutionalized decision-making process. Tripartism thus contradicts the conventional notion that public policy is to be defined by representatives of the people rather than by interaction of economic interests. However, the incapacity of parliaments to deal effectively with the complex issues of economic policy in a modern state has generated legitimacy for the sectoral interest-bargaining approach. Elected legislatures nevertheless remain in the background, and the executive of government can always appeal to the public and its representatives as a means of disciplining recalcitrant economic interests and thus can exert pressure on these interests toward reconciliation and conformity. Tripartism, accordingly, can be regarded as a corporatist form of decision making within a polity that retains at least the potentiality of parliamentary control and accountability.

Tripartite corporatism presupposes two political conditions. One is a certain level of strength of the working class expressed both through strong trade unions and a strong political party. The other condition is the existence of capitalist hegemony, i.e., an acquiescence by organized labor in the continued organization of the economy through the capitalist mode of development and recognition by capital that this acquiescence must be acquired through some concessions to labor. Where labor has been politically weak and inarticulate, tripartism has had no durable basis, as in North America. Where capitalist hegemony has not been accepted by major labor organizations, e.g., in the cases of the French CGT and the Italian CGIL and the Communist parties of both countries, tripartism has perforce been limited to those labor elements who do, with correspondingly limited effect.

## State Corporatism

State corporatism was the other new mode to appear following World War I, first with fascism in Italy and subsequently in other countries of relatively late industrial development—in Portugal, Brazil, and Spain during the 1930s. State corporatism is an attempt by political leaders to create the organization of a modern industrial state in conditions where the organizational base among employers and workers has not successfully evolved in the direction of bipartism. This has been characteristic of late industrializing countries in which the dominant employer class in industry has not been able to achieve a social hegemony. In such cases, workers' organizations typically are either weak or are of the syndicalist type. They represent a *prise de conscience* on the part of workers who in terms of their actual production relations remain in the enterprise-labor-market mode of social relations.

The Italian case was the first and illustrates the principal characteristics of state corporatism. As Antonio Gramsci reflected, the northern Italian industrial bourgeoisie had never been able to establish its hegemony over the whole of Italy. In place of hegemony, there was the *trasformismo* of Giolitti and the Liberals, the construction of coalitions of sociopolitical forces. When the bourgeois order was threatened during the aftermath of war by factory occupations in the north, land occupations in the south, and the revolt of agricultural wage laborers in the Po valley, *trasformismo* did bring about a temporizing truce but one through which the dominant classes lost confidence in the regime. Industrialists in particular saw in the violence of the fascist squads the means of putting in place a state that would discipline the workers. The Liberals shared the aim but lacked the means, i.e., the ability to use force. Liberals and industrialists eased Mussolini's way to power and sought to ensure that fascism would in fact serve the goal they both had in mind. For this Mussolini would have to suppress the more disruptive elements of fascism, those that continued to see it as a revolutionary and anticapitalist movement. Some of these disruptive elements were in the syndicalist unions that had joined fascism. A few industrialists like Giovanni Agnelli of Fiat even preferred to deal with communist unions rather than the fascist syndicalists. Mussolini, in putting into place the Ministry of Corporations, did in fact eliminate the syndicalist elements, just as he sidetracked the violence-prone squadrist elements.[40] Fascist corporatism imposed the state's order upon large-scale industry, an order within which the state ceded authority in the enterprise to management. In the depression years of the 1930s, the state's order-preserving function extended to the creation of a large parapublic industrial sector. The state through fascism assumed the tasks that a non-hegemonic bourgeoisie could not perform on its own.

State corporatism has been an alternative route, divergent from bipartism, in the transformation of the enterprise labor market. With bipartism, an emerging procedural consensus allows for the institutionalizing of industrial conflict, but where no such consensus is attainable, and conflict remains acute and polarized, the state, through an imposed corporatism, uses its force to compensate for society's lack of hegemonic consensus.

Under state corporatism, the state imposes authoritatively upon industry an organization of formal representation for employers and workers intended to maintain order, to regulate working conditions, to promote social harmony, and to eliminate conflict. In Bendix's terminology, this is a form of external bureaucratization. The name "state corporatism" has not traveled widely since World War II, no doubt because of its erstwhile association with fascism, but the essence of the type has become prevalent in many of the late industrializing countries of Asia, Africa, and Latin America.

State corporatism might be defined as that form of corporatism in production relations in which the power of the state, in the hands of a political leadership, predominates over both management and labor without their being any effective counterweight through parliamentary control or accountability. This mode of social relations of production accordingly is to be found in countries where liberal political institutions and competitive party politics have been suppressed or are only formal and where semiautonomous organizations of employers and workers exist or are created under state tutelage. Leadership in these organizations is usually conditional upon loyalty to the ruling political party or the government leaders.

There is no effective delegated bargaining under state corporatism. Both worker and employer organizations seek satisfaction mainly through direct relations with officials either of the state bureaucracy or of the ruling political party. Ideologies of state corporatism place high value on peaceful labor relations as being in the national interest. Although industrial conflicts sometimes arise, they can be and usually are limited or repressed by the political leadership.

State corporatism has never been extended to the whole of a national economy. Usually it has been confined to large-scale industry. State corporatism has typically been conceived by the political leadership as a control mechanism to prevent opposition to its authority from arising within industry, not as a means of mobilizing the working class. State corporatism is significant for what it excludes: usually most of the national workforce in the enterprise labor market, small farming self-employment, and peasant-lord agriculture. State corporatism is essentially a preemptive political form of social control.

The three modes characteristic of the monopolistic phase of capitalist development—enterprise corporatism, tripartism, and state corporatism—are peculiar to that phase of development. They are means of organizing the commanding heights of the economy in the hierarchical ordering of modes of social relations of production characteristic of that phase of capitalist development. All three imply significant involvement of the state in leading the developmental process. Enterprise corporatism appears to exclude the state, since relations at the point of production are between enterprise management and a relatively privileged cadre of employees. Yet enterprise corporatism involves a close relationship between corporate management and state economic agencies in the organization of the economy. It is this relationship that creates the conditions in which corporate planning is motivated to stabilize employment conditions for these employees. Enterprise corporatism implies a pyramidal structure of economy and society in which corporate management relates to state economic policy at the top level, key employees have a special relationship to corporate management at the next level, and subordinate modes of social relations of production service the corporations at the lowest level. In both tripartite and state forms of corporatism the state participates directly and the more favored segments of the labor force have access to decision making at the peak—in the one case through pluralistic bargaining, in the other through a bureaucratically imposed subordination. But neither tripartism nor state corporatism touches the whole economy directly. Both are superstructures under which subordinate modes—enterprise labor market, self-employment, household, in particular—perform subordinate functions, transferring surplus to the dominant modes.

# CHAPTER FOUR

# REDISTRIBUTIVE DEVELOPMENT

The redistributive mode of development came into existence through the second Russian revolution, during the 1930s. The first, or Bolshevik, Revolution of 1917 stands historically in line with the European upheavals beginning with the French Revolution of 1789 that overthrew political structures of the old regime. In the years following 1917, the Bolsheviks struggled to maintain and consolidate their political hold over the territories formerly ruled by the Czars and to protect their power from foreign intervention. They had no clear program for the reconstruction of society and economy. They reacted to situations created by revolutionary developments while carrying on a debate about the proper policies for a socialist revolution. They first supported worker soviets that took control of enterprises, then brought them under party and state control. They nationalized industrial property to forestall speculative transfers of ownership and then placed the former owners in charge. They tried to satisfy peasant demands through redistribution of land, then imposed compulsory deliveries of agricultural produce as a war measure, and subsequently, when the war crisis diminished, encouraged private farming and marketing through the New Economic Policy.[1]

It was only in the late 1920s and during the 1930s that the new mode of redistributive development took shape in the second or Stalinist revolution. Its concerted features were collectivization of agriculture and a drive for rapid industrialization directed and coordinated by central planning. Two distinctive modes of social relations of production were generated through this developmental effort: the communal mode, applied in agricultural production, and the central planning mode through which industrial production was organized. Central planning, in this historical context, has two meanings: one is the fixing of priorities and production strategies and the allocation of production means for society as a whole; the other is a way of organizing production through a hierarchical command structure that in practice applied mainly in large-scale industry. In the first sense, central planning is the form of organization of the redistributive mode of development. I shall henceforth call this aspect redistributive planning. In the second sense, central planning is a mode of social relations of production, and I shall henceforth confine the term to that meaning.

The mode of development pioneered by the Soviet Union in the 1930s was subsequently applied with variations in China, when the Chinese Communist Party established its control over the mainland after World War II, and in North Korea and countries of eastern Europe that fell within the Soviet sphere in the same period—and subsequently in Cuba and Vietnam. Where redistributive development practices have been transplanted, it is often difficult to distinguish practices that are inherent in the mode of development per se from those that are derived specifically from the circumstances of the Soviet experiment in the 1930s. The coercive-repressive features associated with the collectivization drive and mobilization against perceived military threat, which are to be ranged in the latter category, left their imprint upon the institution and practices of redistribution in the Soviet Union and therefore upon the form in which these institutions were exported to other countries.

The redistributive mode of development has not been limited to the two modes of social relations of production just mentioned—the communal and central planning modes. At various phases and in different countries, other social relations of production have been either tolerated or encouraged as adjuncts of redistribution. Self-employment has continued on a substantial scale in farming, crafts, and distribution. Georgian farmers bring their produce to Moscow to sell on the free market. China in the 1980s has made it a national policy to encourage farming by contracts with individual households, bringing self-employment within the framework of redistributive planning. Similarly in countries of eastern Europe that have moved far in the direction of large-scale organization of agricultural production for grain and other major crops, intensive household agriculture remains more effective for vegetable and poultry production and has been encouraged and incorporated within national redistributive planning. In some redistributive formations, e.g., Poland and Yugoslavia, the enterprise labor market continues to exist both in farming and in small enterprises such as hotels and restaurants; and in post-Mao China the revival of small enterprises employing a few workers has become national policy as a means both of expanding employment and providing more effectively some basic necessities to the population. There is no necessary contradiction between individual enterprise, whether in self-employment or enterprise labor market form, and redistributive planning. Indeed, planning has incorporated individual enterprise within its calculations.

In addition to these legally recognized activities are the extralegal or illegal operations of go-betweens and fixers who are able to circumvent the bottlenecks arising within the redistributive planning process by securing needed inputs for enterprises or procuring other favors within the dispositional powers of the redistributors.

Altogether, these officially encouraged, tolerated, and outright illegal but persistent forms of individual enterprise constitute what has been called a "second economy" of considerable proportions that coexists symbiotically with central planning and communal social relations and may be regarded as a support for and lubricant of redistributive development.[2] It would be wrong to see this as resurgent or incipient capitalism. There is no expanded reproduction within these collateral self-employment and enterprise-labor-market forms of social relations and no accumulation of the capitalist type. They provide an outlet for the enterprise of some individuals and help to overcome some of the administrative inadequacies of the central planning system.

The distinction between communal and central planning

modes of social relations of production arises from the key initial problem confronted by redistributive development: how to overcome the agricultural gap. Redistribution has not evolved out of capitalist development—it is historically an alternative route to expanded reproduction. Capitalist development, which emerged first, confronted the same problem at an earlier stage—it raised productivity in agriculture and thereby both displaced part of the agricultural work force and produced enough food to sustain a growing urban and industrial population. In England, the agricultural gap was bridged by a sequence of events, from the enclosures of commons and the innovations of improving landowners in the eighteenth century to the repeal of the corn laws of 1846, which consecrated a policy of cheap and abundant food supply.

Redistributive development was adopted by revolutionary regimes seeking to catch up with this early capitalist development by overcoming the agricultural gap more rapidly through planned measures. They would use the coercive force of the state where capitalist development was born of the coercive force of the market and property law. The method adopted was collectivization of agriculture through which the state envisaged it would have more control over production and could introduce changes in the technology and scale of production on the model of the most developed capitalist forms of agriculture, e.g., the big farms of the midwestern plains of North America. Since redistributive development was undertaken in poor countries lacking agricultural capital equipment, there would have to be a transition period during which labor-intensive cultivation would proceed within larger scale organizational forms of a collective kind pending the gradual mechanization of production. During this transitional phase, it would not be possible to redistribute on the scale of society as a whole.

The theory of "socialist primitive accumulation" associated (in a relatively benign form) with the Soviet economist E. Preobrazhensky and practiced (in a much more coercive form) by Stalinist collectivization, recognized that during the initial stage of redistributive development, agriculture would have to supply the surplus for development, that agriculture would be relatively more exploited. Accordingly, during this stage, redistribution in agriculture would take place within the collectivized producing units (collective farms), which would in addition be required to deliver a surplus to the state for the sustenance of the nonagricultural population and for general accumulation. Supposedly, this extracted surplus would be gradually compensated by an increasing supply of manufactured goods and capital equipment for the agricultural collectives. In the long run, it was envisaged that conditions for agriculture would be assimilated to those of industry; the duality of production organization between central planning (industrial) and communal (agricultural) modes would be eliminated and with it the distinction between workers and peasants. The communal mode was thus in concept transitional.

Both communal and central planning modes of social relations of production contain two categories of personnel: direct producers and redistributors. Within the subordinate communal mode, redistributors organize production within each unit (collective farm, commune, or village—whichever is the accepted accounting entity), are responsible for deliveries to the central redistributors in the central planning mode and arrange for distribution of the residual product within the unit according to accepted principles (so much reserved for seed for the new crop year and for general purposes and the rest distributed to individuals or families according to established criteria). Within the dominant central planning mode, redistributors attempt to increase the amount of product that can be redistributed for the social formation as a whole by extracting from the communal mode, as well as by increasing the surplus produced directly within the central planning mode itself. Some will go into general accumulation, some will be returned to the communal mode, some will be made available for general consumption.

## Communal

Communal forms of production in centuries past have preceded Soviet and Chinese revolutions. They resulted in enclaves within societies constituted in regard to their production relations on quite different bases. Communal experiments in these contexts took the forms either of withdrawal and anticipation of an alternative form of society contrasting to the ambient society or else of a higher form of social experience to which all could not aspire but which embodied ideals that all could in some lesser measure accept. Various millenarian cults, utopian communities, and hippie communes are examples of the first. Medieval monasticism and the Israeli *kibbutzim* are instances of the second. Sometimes enclave communalism became an antecedent and prototype for communal agriculture introduced by the state as an aspect of redistributive development strategy for a whole society—the kind of communal social relations that have made the greatest impact during the twentieth century. In Bulgaria, for instance, a small part of the nation's agriculture was organized in cooperatives before the Communist takeover after World War II, and these cooperatives provided a precedent for the introduction of collectivization on a national scale. Such a transition from enclave to society-wide communalism has, however, been a rare phenomenon and one entirely dependent on a political revolution through which redistributive development is instituted as national policy. On its own, enclave communalism has not had notable results in transforming societies. The production features of enclave communalism have more generally either disappeared or adjusted to the norms of society.

Collectivization of agriculture, through which the communal mode was instituted in the Soviet Union, China, and Eastern European countries, came as a second phase of agricultural revolution, succeeding a land reform phase directed against former landlords, which led initially to a redistribution of holdings rather than to collective ownership. Subsequent collectivization required a combination of coercion and ideological conversion and involved a disturbance of routines of cultivation that adversely affected output for some time. The previously existing dominant modes of social relations of production in agriculture were displaced by the two phases of revolution: peasant-lord relations by the first land reform phase, and enterprise-labor-market relations (prosperous independent farmers or kulaks employing wage labor) by the second collectivization phase. As noted, however, some elements of the self-employment mode continued to exist as handicraft workers and artisans, both fixed and itinerant; farming of private plots by collective-farm families; and local free markets for items of popular consumption. Indeed, a very substantial part of the vegetables, poultry, and pork consumed by both rural and urban populations in redistributive formations was produced and distributed through the self-employment mode. Official toleration of its continued existence was in some measure a recognition by the redistributors of the trauma caused the rural population by collectivization.[3] The survival of self-employment was a fallback position for rural people who had become at least partially dependent on commodity exchange but who had not acquired confidence in the ability of collectivized agriculture to satisfy their basic needs.

Chinese communalism, like its Soviet predecessor, was imposed upon the rural villages from without by a victorious revolutionary movement. In the Chinese case, by contrast to the Soviet, this movement had a care to build support within the villages by mobilizing more deprived elements of the village under the tutelage of the Party. Collectivization could thus proceed by a dual pressure from without and from within the village, both coordinated by the Party cadres. Chinese collectivization was thus more reliant upon the use of ideology and persuasion and less exclusively reliant upon direct coercion than Soviet collectivization was. Furthermore, extraction by the state during the process of collectivization was relatively less heavy than in the Soviet case. These factors may have in large part accounted for the greater speed with which collectivization occurred in China and the lesser degree of open violence associated with it. Collectivization took all of ten years in the Soviet Union, from 1929 to 1939, by which time independent farmers and unorganized domestic workers had been reduced to only 2.6 percent of the population. In China, 90 percent of all rural households were incorporated within advanced or higher level agricultural producers cooperatives (APCs) during the space of only two years, 1955–56.[4] It would be difficult, however, to differentiate the human costs of the two transformations. Millions died in the Soviet Union, some in the massive transportation of kulak families to northern Siberia and the East and many more in the famine of 1933–34. Millions more died in China in the famine years of 1959–62 brought about by the combination of natural disaster with the human disorganization wrought by the excessive speed and incompetence of cadres during the Great Leap Forward.

The long-term gamble of the revolutionary leadership in initiating collectivization was that the creation of larger units would make it possible to produce more efficiently with fewer workers. In China, an inspirational ethic was viewed by the Maoist leadership and cadres as a substitute for nonexistent capital—the opportunity to invest a surplus of human effort over what was required for bare survival in the construction of works that would result in long-term productivity gains. In the short run, however, communal production, because of the organizational confusion and coercion involved in its introduction, proved to be less efficient. In the Soviet Union, the leadership maintained the coercive course. In China, the communal experiment oscillated between extremes of collectivism propagated by mass mobilization campaigns and retreats to reliance upon material incentives. It was difficult to maintain the inspirational ethic over long periods, especially in cases of poor local leadership and organization.

The revolutionary leadership is confronted by a major dilemma in the pursuit of its aim of using communalism as a transitional means of accumulation intended to raise the general productive level of society. If they extract too much, they risk the destruction of agriculture. If they extract too little and give precedence to the problems posed in the agricultural milieu, they risk inability to pursue accumulation for industrial development. The Soviet leadership chose the first horn of this dilemma; the Chinese, the second.

The communal mode, given precedence in state policy, may tend to become stabilized and to develop a social structure that impedes its transcendence by a universalized central planning mode. The problem of accumulation is at the heart of this tendency. The logic of communalism is redistribution of the producing unit's produce among members of the unit. If a large part of the product is extracted by the state without appreciable compensation, communal organization will be perceived as merely a form of exploitation and will acquire no legitimacy. If, however, a large part of the local product is not extracted, socialist primitive accumulation (to use Preobrazhensky's term) will not occur. In a predominantly rural social formation in which industry by itself can contribute only modestly to accumulation, the

goal of economic and social transformation will indefinitely re-
cede. A formation in which the communal mode became dominant in policy, as well as large in size, might come to resemble
the preindustrial agrarian-bureaucratic formations of the old regime. Social groups would emerge within them with an interest
in preserving the communal structures. The revolutionary Party
would either defeat these groups and maintain the thrust of transformation or be itself transformed into something like the old-
regime type of bureaucracy.

The inequalities inherent in communal production abet
this tendency to stabilization of the mode. Those producing units
with the best land and the most productive labor get richer while
those poorer in land and quality of labor get poorer. Within
producing units, families with more healthy working-age members thrive better than those with more dependents and less
healthy members. Those in charge of organizing a unit's production are most likely to give opportunities to the most productive
teams or family work groups, with consequentially increased
returns to these groups. Such tendencies toward increasing inequalities could be counteracted only by determined, conscious
policy on the part of the redistributors, which implies the maintenance of a revolutionary tension in the relations between redistributors and the most efficient producers. These relations
tend, however, to become stabilized at the local level by the
development of patterns of reciprocity within the redistributive
system—exchanges of favors, services, and loyalties—that maintain a redistributive pattern creative of inequalities. "The back
door" is the Chinese expression for such extralegal but widespread inequality-maintaining relations of reciprocity.

The tendency toward a conservative stabilization of the
communal mode would be offset if the mode were maintained
in effective subordination to central planning. Political and ideological direction from the center would have to keep up the
struggle against the practices mentioned and prevent their institutionalization. Parallel tendencies develop, however, at the center, giving rise to a struggle between the revolutionary Party's
cadres and the administrators of redistribution, the planners and
bureaucrats. The latter are by their functions inclined to favor
methods that enhance production and output and to be skeptical

about ideological mobilization that is disruptive of work routines. The former, in line with their revolutionary role, have stressed equalitarianism, even when it became detrimental to incentives to produce. Mao fought to keep the tendency toward bureaucratic stabilization in check and to maintain the supreme control of revolutionary ideologues. Under his successors, the revolutionary mobilization associated with the Cultural Revolution has been condemned, and the two components of the central leadership—political elite and economic managers—achieved a balance in status and influence. Both components agree in maintaining the directing function of central planning over the social formation and the long-term goal of transforming the communal mode.

During the 1980s, the communal mode has been in retreat in all the redistributive formations. In the Soviet Union and countries of Eastern Europe, the stage of transcendence is at hand. Few practical differences remain between agricultural and industrial conditions of employment, although agricultural workers and their families still generally have somewhat fewer opportunities for mobility and advancement. Production is increasingly organized on a large scale in agroindustrial complexes encompassed within the central planning mode of social relations. In China, where legal distinctions between workers and peasants remain significant (e.g., workers are entitled to subsidized rice while "peasants," many of whom are working in rural industries and not in the fields, are not), agricultural production is now for the most part achieved under a system of contracts with individual households. The household-contract system is a way of incorporating self-employment and some forms of enterprise-labor-market employment within redistributive planning. An individual may contract with the local economic unit (brigade) to produce a certain quantity of a crop on land provided by the brigade. Certain inputs and services, e.g., fertilizers, harvesting equipment, and help, may be provided by the brigade. The contractor bears the risk and can sell surplus product at a preferential rate.

The incidence of the communal mode in China has shifted away from agriculture (now mainly in the self-employment mode) toward some forms of small-scale industrial production and services that are organized in collectives or cooperatives. Generally speaking, two kinds of collectives now exist. There are "bureau collectives" or enterprises directly responsible to the bureaus or departments of provincial and municipal governments in which conditions of employment are becoming increasingly similar to those of state enterprises. In other words, they have become assimilated to the central planning mode. There are also smaller and more informal collectives that retain more of the features of the communal mode, especially in redistributing to members the results of the unit's production. These small collectives are being encouraged to give employment to school-leavers in urban areas awaiting job assignment in the central planning sector. Similar collectives of the communal type organize rural industries intended to facilitate a shift from agricultural to industrial occupations without precipitating population movements. The communal mode thus remains as a significant auxiliary to the central planning mode, although the extent to which surplus is extracted from it by the central planning mode is less clear than formerly.

### Central Planning

Central planning represented a transformation, not of the evolved modes of production relations such as existed in northwestern Europe and North America (bipartism and enterprise labor market), but of a quite distinctive pattern that still bore the marks of eastern European manorial serfdom. The Russian industrial bourgeoisie was a subordinate class, dependent on the support of the Czarist administration and controlled by the Czarist bureaucracy, a case of what Bendix calls "external bureaucratization."[5] Peter the Great had allowed ascription of serfs to industrial enterprises as part of his policy of promoting industries useful to the state. This transplanting of serfdom from agriculture to industry had been designed to overcome a prevailing shortage of labor. Although by the nineteenth century, factory workers had become nominally free, they continued to exist in conditions reminiscent of the manor. Employers frequently built barracks to house them and attempted to regulate all aspects of their life in a quasi-military pattern—"necessity and tradition gave to labor relations the character of a household discipline."[6]

Nothing like the established labor force of western Europe had emerged in Russia; the factory worker remained semirural, moved to and fro between town and country, and maintained a family link to the rural scene while being in urban employment. The government was the absolute authority over industry, and government used this position to grant the employer within the factory an absolute control over the worker.

When a more permanent category of workers began to take shape in the 1880s, and thus formed a body receptive to doctrines of protest, nascent organizations among these permanent workers were penetrated by Czarist police agents whose "police socialism" competed with the socialism of opponents of the regime, though it was able to attract little in the way of concession from the political authorities. Thus external bureaucracy controlled or attempted to control both management and workers in Russian industry. Central planning under the Soviet state came as a change in external bureaucracies and in the aims of external bureaucracy rather than as a novel imposition of external control over industry.

Central planning did bring about one more fundamental change, and this was in the work ethic. The coerced-labor tradition derived from manorial serfdom assumed no positive motivation on the part of the worker, whose efforts were thought to be provoked by fear of external sanctions. (By contrast, the consciousness of at least the more established segment of the British working class was influenced by the legacies of craft pride, the Puritan notion of individual responsibility, and the prevailing nineteenth-century idea of individual striving for success.) Lenin clearly seized the point that a requirement for the success of a revolutionary state would be to encourage an internalizing of the work ethic on the part of the Russian masses—the people must "learn to work" and the Soviet government must teach them. Hence the apotheosis of work in early Soviet literature.[7] The people would learn to work if they understood that the goal of the external bureaucracy was their own welfare—that the bureaucracy was the virtual agency of their collective self. This ideological revolution joined an inner force to the external directive of planning to make this a fundamentally new form of production relations.

Successful central planning depends on the existence of a large, technically sophisticated, and competent bureaucracy. These conditions are fulfilled only in societies that have carried through a political and social revolution to the stage of firmly establishing a new state and that have a sufficiently broadly based educational system and adequate scientific and technical cadres. It is hard to imagine central planning in a less developed society. Stalin's revolution put in place a new elite of administrators and planners, a new intelligentsia of working class origins loyal to Stalin's leadership, displacing both "bourgeois experts" and "old bolsheviks" of the generation that had made the revolution. This new elite learned on the job, making some horrendous mistakes but gradually consolidating their positions.[8] With time, the Soviet educational system selected and trained their successors. If Soviet-style planning faltered after a few years in the Chinese People's Republic, it was in part due to a suspicion that the Chinese planners, especially those in the Manchurian region, had links of loyalty to the Soviet Union and in part also to Mao's perference for ideological over administrative methods of control, but it was in large part due to the lack of a sufficient breadth of scientific and technical cadres in China during the decades following the installation of the People's Republic.[9]

There is a question of whether or not labor markets exist under central planning. The concept of a labor market is, of course, anathema to Marxism. It would be more fitting to speak of greater and lesser degrees of occupational mobility. Workers in the Soviet Union, since the labor law reforms of 1956, have been free to change jobs, and enterprises are free to compete for labor. Wage differentials rather than administrative assignment became the principal method of labor allocation. Enterprise-related benefits and workers' acquired rights are, however, a deterrent to movement, and managers may have great difficulty in dismissing workers. High mobility and high employment turnover are characteristic of the lowest skilled—the Soviet equivalent of nonestablished workers—but not so much of skilled workers. Indeed, it is frowned upon as a sign of irresponsibility. ("Flitters" are in the same category as habitual drunkards.)[10] The Soviet problem has been one of efficient allocation of skilled manpower in a condition of overall shortage. Enterprises are tempted to hoard labor. All-union agencies to organize labor allocation on the style of Western national employment services were created only in the 1960s. In China, the disposition to regard employment as permanent for a lifetime is even more ingrained, though the post-Mao leadership has been concerned to introduce more flexibility into labor allocation.[11] The "iron rice bowl" or permanency of job tenure has met increasing criticism in the official media and yet endorsement of the goal of greater flexibility in manning recoils before the prospect of dismissals for redundancy. Workers can still be removed only for grave fault of a virtually criminal kind. Employees in the state enterprises still expect to enjoy the right to transmit their job on retirement to a suitably qualified family member.

Accumulation organized through redistributive planning has gone through two historical phases. These are closely related to the external links of the redistributive social formation. The first phase was that of the industrialization drive, the Stalinist phase of the 1930s, in which the goal of rapid accumulation was reinforced by the perception of imminent external military threat. Heavy industry and defense were the priorities. These were built on the only available model—existing capitalist industry. Consequently, the organization of production and the hierarchy of command within capitalist production were reproduced within the social relations of central planning, although there was little direct economic relationship through exchange of products between capitalist and redistributive economies.

The second phase came when the limits to the initial accumulation process were reached, i.e., when capital-broadening or the extensive pattern of adding new productive units of the same kind with the same labor-output ratios ran up against labor shortages and technological backwardness. From the late 1950s and early 1960s, the search for capital-deepening or more technology-intensive development began in the Soviet Union. This has involved an increase in the scope and volume of economic links with the external world both to acquire and introduce new technologies developed in advanced capitalist formations and to earn the foreign exchange required to pay for these technologies. A further factor accentuating the expansion of external economic links has been the inadequacies of agriculture, in which a proportionally large part of the working population (more than 25 percent) is engaged but which has been deficient in grain production, necessitating large foreign grain purchases. This second phase in the accumulation process of redistributive planning has, if anything, strengthened the resemblance in the organization and hierarchy of production between advanced capitalist and redistributive social formations.

The development of the productive apparatus of central planning produces a form of social stratification based very largely on economic status and education. At the top are the redistributors, divided between political elite and planning technicians. Next down is the level of direct economic management (direction of enterprises and enterprise trade union and Party sections). Below them is a layer of middle management and lower level supervision, expanding under central planning, just as it has also expanded in the capitalist modes of social relations. Next are skilled engineering and technical workers; and below them are the semiskilled and unskilled. There are differences in prestige and status in the last category; workers in distribution are less well regarded than those in industry, and agricultural workers remain relatively underprivileged.[12]

A central and critical question about redistributive social formations is whether this social stratification has produced a class structure. The stratification produced by the organization of production under central planning is not in and of itself a class structure. It is rather a hierarchy of command determining differential access to resources that, if it were to become stabilized and reproduced among the same social groups, could turn into a class structure or structure of status groups. This would happen if people from the same social groups, in successive generations, were to occupy the same positions in the hierarchy—the children of agricultural workers having little option but to become agricultural workers and those of top management becoming, more than likely, members of top management. Such a tendency is offset by a merit-based educational system, which is the principal medium for reproducing the command hierarchy. The openness of educational opportunity is counteracted by two factors: one is ideological conformity, a characteristic of most educational systems, which tends to exclude or sidetrack those with deviant

opinions, but probably more effectively so in formations dominated by an ideologically sensitive Party leadership; the other is
the skewing of educational opportunity in favor of the children
of the more educated and higher placed, which comes about
partly through the motivation and support of educated parents
and partly from the advantages highly placed parents can procure
for their children through the informal exchanging of favors characteristic of redistributive systems. Thus there is a potentiality
for the reproduction of social groups having different degrees of
social power.

What these groups are, where the lines of cleavage are
drawn between them, and what possibilities of alliances exist
among groups are more difficult questions of a subjective kind
touching attitudes and behaviors. It would seem that during the
most recent phase of development, a technological and humanistic elite with a status legitimated by education has achieved an
identity distinct from the Party political elite. Within industry,
the official trade unions have promoted a corporative association
of management and skilled workers based on enterprise-related
benefits and loyalties. The line of cleavage has come between the
skilled and unskilled workers—the former more closely linked
to the enterprise by length of tenure, fringe benefits, and social
activities (including participation in trade union and related activities), and the latter more frequently changing jobs, nonparti-
cipant in enterprise and community activities, and including
those officially frowned upon as social deviants. This cleavage
corresponds to that in the advanced capitalist formations between
established and nonestablished workers.

The strategy of the political elite has been (1) to neutralize
the technological elite by according it recognized status and privileges, (2) to obstruct a coalescence of technological and humanistic elites and to marginalize those elements of the humanistic
elite who manifest dissidence, and (3) to court the loyalty of
skilled workers and the intermediate layer of supervisors by
emphasizing the corporative aspects of industrial organization
and extending privileges and benefits to the upper stratum of
manual workers.

# EPILOGUE TO PART I

Part 1 has focused on existing modes of social relations of production as they originated within different development processes—capitalist and redistributive—and as they subsequently evolved. It has dealt only by implication with the configurations of modes, in which some modes are dominant and others subordinate, that have been typical of different phases of these development processes. The outlines of some such configurations can now briefly be indicated.

Competitive capitalism, as it emerged in mid-nineteenth-century Britain, was characterized by the enterprise labor market in factory production, flanked by a substantial self-employment mode in farming, craft production, and small shops. The self-employment mode was not directly subordinate to the enterprise labor market but contributed to the growth of the latter insofar as prices for wage goods produced by self-employed were kept low, thereby helping to keep wages low and enhancing the profits of enterprise-labor-market employers. More directly subordinate were the labor reserve constituted by the primitive labor market (with its downward pressure on wages in the enterprise labor market) and the household mode that sustained and replaced the wage workers of the enterprise labor market.

When labor later became more differentiated by skill, the bipartite mode emerged among established workers in the new engineering industries that led the second wave of capitalism's advance. Higher profit margins in these newer industries plus labor's gains in relative social power through unionization ensured better conditions for workers than in the enterprise-labor-market industries of the earlier phase, which were experiencing declining profit margins.

With the advent of monopoly capitalist development, economies bifurcated into monopoly and competitive sectors, the latter taking on a subordinate and dependent role. The new modes of social relations of production characteristic of the monopoly sector—enterprise corporatism and tripartism—occupied dominant status along with the bipartite mode. The enterprise labor market now took two forms: a residual small-business form and the novel form of nonestablished labor employed in monopoly sector enterprises alongside the established labor of the dominant modes. The primitive labor market diminished in importance within advanced capitalist social formations, although it gained renewed importance as a labor reserve in late industrializing countries. This international availability of cheap labor could be an incentive to shift certain labor-intensive manufacturing processes away from the advanced formations or alternatively to employ immigrant workers. Self-employment also diminished in relative importance and became an alternative to the residual small-business enterprise labor market as a subordinate mode providing services for the personnel of the dominant modes and some inputs to dominant-mode production. Household production continued its reproduction of the labor force.

Redistributive development began with a duality of central planning and communal modes—the latter being placed in a planned subordinate relationship, transferring surplus to the dominant mode. Thenceforth, different patterns of change have characterized the Soviet Union and Eastern Europe, on the one hand, and China, on the other. In the first, the communal mode has become assimilated progressively to the central planning mode; in the second, the communal mode has been largely dismantled in agriculture and replaced by a form of self-employment. Self-employment has been a healthy survival in the Soviet-type formations, and forms of enterprise labor market have also been revived in China within the framework of redistributive planning.

Configurations in late-industrializing capitalist formations have differed from the competitive-to-monopoly capitalist pattern of development in the now advanced formations. Bipartism never struck firm roots. The initial effects of the forcible creation of labor markets in what is now called the Third World has been the phenomenal growth of marginality—what in this study is called the primitive-labor-market mode—and also the appearance of enterprise-labor-market conditions where industry has been established. The enterprise labor market has rarely been a stable and durable mode of social relations of production in Third World countries, at any rate in the larger sectors of industry. In the longer term, the development of production relations in the Third World has been determined largely by two factors: one, the reproduction of advanced capitalist models under the influence of the agencies of external economic penetration; the other, the efforts of local political elites to gain greater control over local economic growth.

Enterprise corporatism was brought into the industrial enclaves of the Third World by the multinational corporations that had pioneered its formation in Japan, Western Europe, and the United States. It presented to the corporations the advantages of cultivating a privileged, permanent labor force, and of maintaining a relatively secure and steady supply of raw materials and other inputs for final processing.

State corporatism has been the characteristic response of Third World political elites to foreign economic penetration. By taking control over local industrial labor, these elites both limit the risks of opposition to their rule among a stragegically placed element in the local population and also gain leverage in relation to foreign investors. Tripartism has been preached by international agencies (like the ILO) that have been under the substantive control of advanced capitalist countries, and its forms have been adopted by a number of Third World countries, but the inadequacy and lack of effective autonomy of the existing organizational base in both labor and management mean that in practice formal tripartism often becomes substantive state corporatism. Thus, under late twentieth-century conditions, the enterprise labor market in Third World countries, while substantial in middle- and small-scale production, has tended to become subordinated either to state corporatism or to an enterprise corporatism imported by multinational management and unions in the larger production units.

Turning from configurations of modes to the overall trends in the growth and decline of individual modes on the world scale, I find it difficult to arrive at quantitative estimates of changes. Trends may be hypothesized from evidence about events, in the absence of reliable aggregate figures. A long-term decline in the peasant-lord mode may be assumed. Indeed, the incidence of violence on the world scale since the mid-twentieth century has been in areas of peasant agriculture—evidence in part of the struggles accompanying the break-up of the mode. Subsistence in relatively isolated communities has virtually ceased to exist and now takes the adapted form of labor reserves and household cultivation's providing an off-season support for migrant wage workers, especially in Africa. The primitive labor market, as noted, has grown to large proportions in some Third World countries. A plausible hypothesis is that the primitive labor market—or its equivalent, often called marginality—grows most rapidly with the early stages of capitalist development. It is largest as a proportion of the total labor force, not in the poorest or in the richest countries, but in those simultaneously undergoing transformations in agriculture (consolidation of medium-scale market-oriented farming and large-scale agribusiness) and expansion of industrial production. The combination of continuing increases in the size of the working-age population, reduction of employment in agriculture, and slower creation of jobs in industry and modern-sector services yields a growing pool of unemployed and underemployed.

Central planning has grown steadily in the redistributive formations; and in the more advanced capitalist formations, enterprise corporatism, together with the new forms of enterprise labor market (migrant workers, temporary and part-time casual employment, and extralegal "underground" work), has led the pace. In late industrializing Third World formations, state corporatism and the enterprise labor market have expanded. Self-employment is also thriving, most of all, ironically perhaps, in the redistributive formations. Household production, though deprived of much of its traditional content in some of the advanced capitalist formations with the progressive commodification of the household, remains everywhere the basis for reproducing the work force.

In summary, part 1 has considered the characteristics of the different modes of social relations of production observable in the world today and the distinctive capitalist and redistributive development processes, each associated with particular sequences of configurations of production modes in dominant-subordinate relationship to one another. Causal questions have so far not been raised: What occasioned particular modes of social relations of production to come into existence? What explains the manner in which specific combinations of modes are put together and maintained in relationship to one another?

To be sure, the notion of distinctive development processes—capitalist and redistributive—suggests a functional logic in the interrelationships of production modes. Functional logic describes the fit among the modes, their mutual adaptation and reinforcement. But functional logic does not explain origins or transformations. When we ask such questions, we are led to examine the role of the state. Different forms of state have been the creators of new modes of social relations of production and have acted as coordinators and regulators of configurations of modes. States have chosen or endorsed developmental processes and created the conditions in which these processes could unfold. States are not, of course, all-powerful. In production matters, as in political-strategic matters, states are limited by the world system, by the structure of world political economy. It is to these matters that I turn in part 2.

# Part 2

# States,
# World Orders,
# and Production
# Relations

New modes of social relations of production become established through the exercise of state power. States also make the choices for societies in regard to their modes of development. The actions of a state in these matters are, in turn, conditioned by the manner in which the world order impinges upon the state. Thus any attempt to explain the transformations of production relations must refer to states and world orders. These are the propositions to be examined in part 2.

It has already been suggested that the general concept of the state is of limited usefulness in accounting for state actions and that in order to comprehend the real historical world it is necessary to consider distinctive *forms of state*. The principal distinguishing features of such forms are the characteristics of their historic blocs, i.e., the configurations of social forces upon which state power ultimately rests. A particular configuration of social forces defines in practice the limits or parameters of state purposes, and the modus operandi of state action, defines, in other words, the *raison d'état* for a particular state. The notion of a form of state implies that during certain periods of history some states are based on comparable configurations of social forces and animated by a similar *raison d'état*.

My concern is principally with the ways in which states determine the organization of production, if not directly then by fixing the framework of laws, institutions, practices, and policies affecting production. In various ways, states give preeminence to particular modes of social relations of production. They also facilitate the formation of dominant-subordinate configurations of modes of social relations of production and thereby influence the process of accumulation that takes place through transfers of surplus from subordinate to dominant modes.

The state is the agency that can activate and channel the potentialities of a social formation either toward maintaining the existing social order or toward bringing about a new order. Once an equilibrium between state and society has been established, the state draws resources from the society and uses these resources to maintain and reproduce the society. During periods of upheaval or social revolution, when an emerging historic bloc challenges and displaces the established historic bloc, a more active and innovative capacity of the state becomes apparent in production relations as in other aspects of social existence.

Social revolutions are not to be understood as exogenous events that burst in upon states. They are transformations within the state itself, displacing one form of state with another. These changes take shape through political activity—the formation of new political organizations or parties that prove capable of mobilizing sufficient material and ideological force to effect this displacement. The first thesis to be examined in part 2 is, then, that the formative phases of production relations are determined by transformations in forms of state that are by definition accompanied by the displacement of one historic bloc by another and of one *raison d'état* by another.

The organization of production is only one consequence of a particular *raison d'état*—and not the aspect that has hitherto drawn the attention of commentators on *raison d'état*. The conventional meaning of *raison d'état* has been the understanding and pursuit of a particular state's interests in relation to other states. This conventional meaning must be brought into relationship with the derivative meaning discussed here—its application to production. The internal and external applications of *raison d'état* are coherent and indivisible. There is a practical connection between the effort of a state to organize its society and its effort to maintain itself and pursue its goals in the interstate context.

*Raison d'état* and the modern state system emerged together in fifteenth- and sixteenth-century Europe. Not that other parts of the world at other times have not known dispersions of power among rival centers. Chinese, Islamic, and early American civilizations experienced alternating phases of centralized power and of fragmented contending powers. The fourteenth-century Arabic Islamic philosopher-statesman Ibn Khaldūn[1] reflected on this alternation in the configurations of power, as did his contemporary Chinese theorists of politics. They could explain it in terms of the relative weight of urban or nomadic elements or the level of tolerance of the peasant base of society for exactions by the dominant classes. The novelty of the European developments of the fifteenth and sixteenth centuries was the founding of a state system in a context of economic changes that accumulated wealth in centers that ultimately were able to transform that wealth into a capitalist development process—a process that spread from its points of origin in Europe over the whole world.

The state system provided a framework within which that process engendered a world economy, developing and functioning according to its own dynamic. Initially, during the age of mercantilism, that world economy was constrained within political boundaries laid down by states through national monopolies and trade restrictions. By mid-nineteenth century, with the sponsorship and political support of the single most powerful state, the world economy achieved autonomy, such that its own laws began to constrain state policies, particularly through the workings of international finance centered in the City of London. In the mid-twentieth century, a further stage was reached in which production became organized on a transnational scale, and international production, as well as international finance, presented constraints on and opportunities for states. During this century, the relative weight of Europe receded, the center of world power shifted from Atlantic rim to Pacific rim, and Europe, the originator of the process, became a subplot in a global drama.

From the nineteenth century, world order has to be defined in terms of the duality of interstate system and world economy.

If, internally, the state-production relationship is to be seen as shaped by the nation's historic bloc, externally the state (including its relationship to production) is constrained by world-order pressures. These are expressed in military and financial forms and in dominant-class links with external classes. Such factors influence the composition of historic blocs, and through them the parameters circumscribing state policies relating to production.

In focusing on the transformations in forms of state that bring about changes in production relations, we are led to discover the relationships between changes in forms of state and changes in the structures of world order. The second thesis to be enunciated in part 2 is that there is a parallelism between the two, that the emergence of new forms of state is associated with changes in the structures of world order and that these parallel changes have been mutually reinforcing. Both kinds of change—in forms of state and in world order—have to be taken into account to explain changes in production.

In examining changes in world order, the alternation between hegemonic and nonhegemonic structures is of particular significance. The hegemonies of the Pax Britannica and the Pax Americana both constituted interstate systems that gave free rein to the expansion of the world economy. The most perceptible constraints on internal state-production relations came from the world economy. In the intervening nonhegemonic and more turbulent structure, the interstate system reasserted itself so as to subordinate and control world-ecomony influences. Recent scholarship has been divided on the question of the relative weight to be given to states and world economy. The modernization theories popular in North America in the 1960s considered political systems independently of each other as evolving from archaic to modern forms divorced from the context of the world economy. These theories underestimated the external constraints on state formation. At the same time, by positing one outcome—the pluralist, industrial, market-oriented, modernized state—they became an ideology of the world economy. Dependency theories, on the other hand, originating in Latin America and popularized more broadly in the 1970s, put the whole weight on the world system, regarding states and national societies as merely playing out roles assigned to them by their place in the system. These theories underestimated the indigenous capacity to bring about changes in relative power and in forms of society. Here I am suggesting that the relative weight of internal and external factors, and the nature of these factors, is not constant but is conditioned by the prevailing structure of world order.

Three successive structures of world order are examined in the following chapters as a framework for considering transformations in forms of state and consequential shifts in the patterns of production relations. These are (1) the coming of the liberal international economy (a period that can be roughly dated 1789–1873), (2) the era of rival imperialisms (1873–1945), and (3) the neoliberal world order (post World War II). In the third structural phase two ongoing processes call for particular comment, one affecting the world economy, the other the interstate system: the internationalizing of production and the internationalizing of the state. Each successive structure of world order was characterized by the emergence of new forms of state, new historic blocs, and new configurations of production relations. The task of part 2 is to suggest explanations for the connections between these changes.

The ultimate purpose of these historical reflections is to see how far the relationships they reveal can be helpful in understanding events affecting world order, states, and production relations that have occurred since the early 1970s. These questions are to be considered in part 3.

# CHAPTER FIVE

# THE COMING OF THE LIBERAL ORDER

The modern state emerged through the fifteenth and sixteenth centuries in Europe out of the decadence of the medieval universalistic institutions of Empire and Papacy. An international milieu composed of states was fully formed at the time of the Peace of Westphalia, which brought a close to the Thirty Years' War in 1648. Throughout the eighteenteenth century the modus operandi of this congeries of states—the balance of power and mercantilism—became routinized practice such that it could be understood as a system, as a definable structure of world order. This system was severely shaken by the wars of the French Revolution and Empire, which became the catalyst for subsequent change in the world order. The attempt by the victorious coalition to restore the eighteenth-century system at the Congress of Vienna in 1815 gave way gradually to a new world order grounded in the liberal principles of political economy espoused in Britain. From the 1840s, these principles were institutionalized in British practice and subsequently emulated by other major powers. A state system in which Britain played the central role became the underpinning of an expanding world economy. This world economy functioned through private agencies, centered mainly in the City of London, that were symbiotically related to the British state and to the Europe-centered state system. The coming of this liberal world order was the culmination of the first major transformation in state structures, historic blocs, and modes of social relations of production to have left its traces in the present.

## THE MODERN STATE AND EIGHTEENTH-CENTURY STATE SYSTEM

The fourteenth century inaugurated a long period of turbulence in Europe that can be traced to a reversal of the economic and demographic expansion of the previous two centuries. As the bioecological current ebbed, punctuated by famines and plagues, the dominant feudal classes struggled over control of stagnant or declining resources. Conflict between lords and peasants intensified, as did conflict among the lords themselves. The interclass struggle moved toward different outcomes in eastern and western Europe. In eastern Europe, peasants suffered the increasing repression of the so-called new serfdom. In the west, peasants gained significantly in independence, though they remained the sole economic support of the dominant class. The intraclass struggle among the nobility was gradually, through the sixteenth century, brought under control by national monarchies in western and northern Europe. These monarchies formed the nuclei of the modern states. In them lay the origins of the state and state system as we know it.

In the realm of ideology, the revival of models of classical antiquity strengthened the secular spirit against the supranational claims of divine and natural law, and in art and architecture gave expression to the form of a new territorial power. In an age when religious symbolism served to justify wars, religion was converted from a principle of universal solidarity to become the unifying public ceremony of a single state. The doctrine of *cujus regio, ejus religio* was enunciated in the Peace of Augsburg of 1555 and reiterated in the Peace of Westphalia in 1648. The revival of Roman law consecrated the authority of the state, an authority proclaimed also in the new political theory of sovereignty.[1]

The unified expression of the state was *raison d'état,* a

concept that came into existence with the state itself. *Raison d'état* was understood as a political logic that dictated what specific acts were necessary to create and maintain the state internally in the face of threats to the unity and strength of the state and also to defend and advance the interests of the state externally. *Raison d'état* dictated that Henry of Navarre forsake Protestantism for the Catholic religion in the interests of the French state and that Emperor Ferdinand II arrange the judicial murder of his general, Albrecht von Wallenstein, last of the great independent military entrepreneurs, whose troops then came under Austrian state command. The specific interests of particular states superseded universalist notions of natural and divine law as the ultimate criteria of action.[2]

The consequence for Europe as a whole of the coming into existence of a number of centralized territorial powers was the emergence of the balance of power as a regulating mechanism among states. A balance-of-power system came into being among the Italian states of the fifteenth century at a time when Italy was relatively free from foreign intervention. Turbulence had engulfed the lands of potential intruders. Italians innovated and developed the techniques of statecraft and diplomacy, the tools of *raison d'état*. Italy's respite came to an end on the threshold of the sixteenth century when France, Spain, and Austria intruded into the peninsula.[3] With the defeat of Emperor Charles V's dream of a reunified Christendom, the balance of power became a European balance.

The interstate system of old-regime Europe, as it reached maturity in the eighteenth century, has been perhaps best described by Albert Sorel.[4] No remaining concept of public law effectively circumscribed the behavior of states, no real residue remained of the medieval ideal of *res publica Christiana* supreme over territorial rulers. No principle outside of the state could be affirmed by which to judge a state. No practices of intercourse among states, such as the inviolability of embassies, were sacred. Their observance depended ultimately on enforcement by individual states. Nor were general ideas concerning the proper constitution of states taken seriously. Ideological or constitutional criteria were foreign to the thought of the eighteenth-century statesman. Differently constituted states existed—republican, aristocratic, and monarchic—but the only test of their status in the system was their power to compel recognition on the part of other states. Ideological affinities played no part in diplomatic practice. The solitary goal of a state was its own conservation and aggrandizement. Other states might weaken a rival by fomenting internal conflicts and revolutions. Indeed, the European states generally welcomed the French troubles of 1789 as a weakening of a powerful member of the state system. Aggrandizement was limited by the system itself. Here Sorel epitomizes the balance of power:

> . . . tous les puissants sont d'accord pour ne permettre à aucun d'entre eux de s'élever au-dessus des autres. Qui prétend à la part du lion, voit ses rivaux se liguer aussitôt contre lui. Il se forme ainsi entre les grands Etats une sorte de société en participation: ils entendent conserver ce qu'ils possèdent, gagner en proportion de leurs mises, et interdire à chacun des associés de faire la loi aux autres. C'est ce qu'on appelle la balance des forces ou l'équilibre européen.[5]

The eighteenth century gave us the pure form of the balance of power system just as the nineteenth gave us the pure form of competitive capitalist economy.

The impetus to centralize authority under national monarchs was political and military in origin. Reaction against feudal disorder was furthered by developments in military technology. The firepower of cannon, the planning and execution of fortifications, and the effective use of disciplined infantry required central direction, professional attitudes, and sustained finance. The unruly and unreliable feudal levy was replaced by a force officered by nobles who had been transformed into state servants, and it was manned by mercenary troops drawn mainly from the more remote and marginal regions of Europe (Switzerland, Scotland, Ireland, Albania, etc.) Mercenaries employed directly by states (and no longer, as in earlier times, by independent military entrepreneurs like Wallenstein) presented the advantage that the dominant class of the centralized kingdoms could maintain military force without having to arm their own peasantry. The state and the professional permanent army came into existence together.[6]

This military-political innovation had economic consequences. The need to mobilize resources for warfare brought the
state into the performance of new economic functions. Medieval
monarchs, when they wanted to make war, borrowed from merchant capitalists and hired mercenary commanders who raised
their own troops. Kings either squeezed sufficient revenue out of
their nobles, prelates, and townspeople, or they defaulted and
tried to coerce their creditors. The new states had to be put on a
more stable financial basis in order to sustain permanent military
forces so as to stay in the interstate game of power.

The new states confronted a fiscal crisis in the seventeenth
century, and their success or failure in dealing with this crisis
foreshadowed the rise and decline of powers. Spain's inability
to put state finance on a sound basis despite the asset of new-
world treasure heralded that country's loss of the first position
in Europe. The English civil war and constitutional struggles of
the seventeenth century were about fiscal control—Crown versus
Parliament. And the fact that the English state was able to establish an unequaled reputation for fiscal management gave Britain
the edge over France in their eighteenth-century wars. Britain
could raise the funds for war more readily than any other state.[7]

State managers sought to encourage the inflow of specie
through trade and the production within the nation of materials
and equipment needed for war. Overseas explorations, coupled
with European advances in military technology, opened the possibilities for colonization. States sought to establish and protect
monopolies in trade, access to resources, and colonial settlement
as adjuncts to their domestic sources of power. Mercantilism is
the name given retrospectively to a series of such ad hoc measures
intended to enhance state power in relation to other states. The
national debt, an invention of the seventeenth century, put the
relationship between central political power and merchant
wealth on a businesslike basis that, in turn, required regular tax
revenues.[8]

The intentions of seventeenth- and eighteenth-century
states in the realm of economic interventionism far exceeded
their capabilities and results. State administration was minuscule
where it was most effective, as in England, and encumbered by
the practice of sale of offices and the wastefulness of tax farming

where it was more extensive, as in France. The events leading up to the revolution in France were triggered by the impending collapse of state finance.[9] Nevertheless, through a variety of mercantilist measures, states nurtured the accumulation of merchant wealth and the expansion of manufacturing. Mercantilism had economic consequences in society beyond its limited effect in enhancing state power.[10]

The historic blocs of old-regime Europe can conveniently be discussed in terms of two types. Ludwig Dehio analyzed the politics of power in Europe since the sixteenth century in terms of two kinds of state: the continental power state, of which, first, Spain, then France, and then Germany were exemplars, and the insular state, exemplified in succession by Venice, England, and the United States.[11] To these two political concepts correspond two patterns of historic bloc.

The French monarchy of the seventeenth century is the archetype of the continental power state in the era of absolutism. The term *agrarian bureaucracy* expresses the relation of state to social formation. The dominant class—a combination of the old *noblesse d'épée* and the newer official-professional *noblesse de robe*—derived its power from the land through a mixture of rents paid directly to landlords and tax money owing to the state but in practice sustaining its retainers in the noble class. This tribute was borne exclusively by the peasant base of society.[12] Peasant-lord relations of production were in slow transformation toward household farming, a process that would be completed only by the Revolution's abrogation of feudal obligations and the establishment of the peasantry as self-employed smallholders. The agrarian bureacracy also fostered some wage-labor-employing industries of interest to the state.

The insular state derived its power from trade, and its historic bloc reflected the relative strength of mercantile wealth. The quasi-insular Dutch Republic became the center of a world trading system under the shadow of Spanish continental power. Its merchant oligarchy was protected by an alliance with regional nobility. By the first decade of the seventeenth century, the Dutch had secured independence from Spain and had assured the survival and growth of the nascent world economy. The fully insular English state shared with the Dutch an interest in the growth of the world economy, but it was a rival to the Dutch for dominance in that economy. United against Spain, or against France, when these powers threatened the heart of commercial empire, the Dutch and English fought each other at sea when the continent was quiescent. During the second half of the seventeenth century, England displaced the Netherlands as the center of the world economy and maintained that place through the nineteenth century. Mercantilism, by creating a national market that could sustain the expansion of English trade, gave England the advantage over Amsterdam, the last of the great city-based commercial systems.

As in the Netherlands, mercantile interests were preeminent in England in determining state policy from the time of the civil war; they achieved osmosis with land-based wealth and together created opportunity for the development of manufacturing. Manufacturing in England depended less on state support and monopoly privilege than industry in France did and more on the availability of accumulated wealth for investment, the availability of labor for employment, and the existence of the broadest national market in which to realize gains from sale of product. In England, a peasantry had been all but eliminated, independent farming and larger scale improved agriculture flourished, and occupational specialization or division of labor had advanced further than on the continent.[13]

The old-regime historic blocs engendered contradictions that ultimately brought about changes in forms of state, production relations, and the interstate system.

First of all, through mercantilist policies, states assisted the accumulation of private wealth. At the same time, the commercial interests entrenched in mercantilism, as well as those of the state itself, were resolutely opposed to the further steps necessary to emancipate wealth for capitalist development. These further steps would be to transform land and labor power into commodities and to remove mercantilist restrictions on the market when they became an impediment to capital accumulation. This contradiction was foremost in the insular-mercantile state.

In the second place, the production basis of the agrarian-bureaucratic state was becoming less secure. Peasant-lord relations had been much eroded, but the surplus on which the state and dominant class rested was still extracted almost exclusively from the peasantry. State power rested on an increasingly resistant base. The mercantile-insular state had been more successful in shifting the economic basis of state and dominant classes onto surer grounds. The peasant reaction to the initial stages of the French Revolution shattered an overstrained historic bloc.

Thirdly, the historic bloc had little depth in the population. The *raison d'état* of the agrarian-bureaucratic state by the eighteenth century had become primarily the logic of a court in its military-political relations with other courts; that of the mercantile-insular state, the logic of naval power permeated with commercial instinct. Both neglected the internal logic of state power, the assurance of the political support or acquiescence for governmental powers, such as had been of preeminent concern in the formative phases of the European states. A *raison d'état* truncated of its internal dimension could be only dimly aware of the fragility of its domestic base, unprepared for the storms that would shake it. The French state was unaware of the dangers it unleashed in convening the estates general. The British state was better able to repress popular disaffection in mobilizing against the revolution in France, but it too was surprised by the depth of popular movements.

A fourth contradiction concerned the world order of the old regime. A balance of power activated by the particular and conflicting interests of states was, during the eighteenth century, challenged in the realm of ideas by a new secular universalism that conceived of a rational state-supported world order governed by rules. The eighteenth-century philosophers, as an American scholar has written, were engaged in reconstructing the heavenly city of St. Augustine with rationalist materials.[14] Immanuel Kant argued that a world order founded on the rule of law must be based on component units respectful of the rule of law. Political economy meanwhile was rediscovering the laws of nature in economic processes, laws that were a manifestation of divine Providence's beneficence to mankind—or rather the beneficence of that secularized Providence, variously called the Invisible Hand (Adam Smith) or the Ruse of Reason (Hegel). An organization of perpetual peace was the political condition for a wealth-of-nations vision of world economy. Neither was consistent with the existing political-economic world of balance of power and mercantilism: both had a strong appeal for the bourgeoisies, whose further strengthening seemed to be held in check by the historic blocs of the old regime.[15]

## THE ABORTIVE
## RESTORATION HEGEMONY

Albert Sorel interpreted the post-Napoleonic settlement of the Congress of Vienna in 1815 as an attempt to reintroduce universalist principles of public law into a state system that before the Revolution had been activated solely by the pursuit of individual state interests. This, he argued, could be understood only as the collective response of the victor powers to the upheaval of the Revolution and the spread of its ideology across Europe.[16] Henceforth, the internal dimension of politics, the relationship of government to people, would necessarily form part of the management of interstate relations. Europe was not only a state system; it was now also to be perceived as a social order. To the victors, defense of the social order would become intimately linked with the maintenance of the balance among states.

From this point of view, the Grand Alliance put together to bring about the defeat of Napoleonic France was a peculiar coalition comprising insular-mercantile Britain and the absolute monarchies of the east—Russia, Prussia, and, at the end, Austria. It was a coalition of nascent capitalism with the new serfdom against the regime that had struck a deathblow to the principles and legal basis of feudalism in western and southern Europe.

French conquest had done much to stimulate the spirit of national resistance within the various eastern elements of the coalition, but in a real sense the success of the struggle against Napoleon was an economic achievement. British subsidies financed the allied armies. Napoleon had understood the economic threat and tried to counter it by denying British commerce access to Europe. He thought that he had succeeded and that Britain had reached the limit of her resources in 1814. In that year, however, Britain was subsidizing armies of 150,000 in each of her major allies. She had, in addition, 225,000 soldiers in her direct pay—only 70,000 of whom were British, the rest being hired from foreign powers. The payment of British subsidies was somewhat eased by the opening of northern Europe to British trade that the advance of the allied armies made possible.[17] The continental power state, even as transformed and modernized by Napoleon, proved less effective than the insular-mercantile state in mobilizing the economic sinews of war.[18]

The ideological basis for the post-Napoleonic settlement sprang from the mind of Talleyrand. In defeat, France had few bargaining counters. Talleyrand's achievement in regaining recognition of France's great-power status came from his ability to use rational argument from accepted premises as his weapon. The principle on which he grounded his argument was legitimacy. Concerning his goals for France and for Europe at the Congress of Vienna, he wrote in his memoirs:

> Le premier besoin de l'Europe, son plus grand intérêt était . . . de bannir les doctrines de l'usurpation, et de faire revivre le principe de la légitimité, seul remède à tous les maux dont elle avait été accablée, et le seul qui fût propre à en prévenir le retour.

Talleyrand went on to say that legitimacy was not to be understood merely as the conservation of the power of kings, ". . . il est surtout un élément nécessaire du repos et du bonheur des peuples." Legitimacy could be monarchic or republican, hereditary or elective.[19] In Talleyrand's concept, legitimacy meant, not so much a return to the older order for its own sake, as the search for a basis of consent in a war-weary world. Tranquility (repos) takes primacy over happiness (bonheur) in its justification, though the one may be held to lead to the other. A usurper power, because it was not legitimate, was a fearful power—frightened itself of is own illegitimacy and causing fear in its subjects and its neighbors—a power that in its fear was repressive and aggressive. As a usurper, Napoleon was incapable of making peace. Only the restored Bourbons could make peace for France, but the restored monarchy, Talleyrand proposed, should be constitutional, not absolute. Necessary change could flow from the principle of legitimacy. For Europe as a whole, the settlement should undo the effects of conquest and return to regimes and boundaries that could be justified by recognized precedent and in public law.

Legitimacy was more than a diplomatic ploy designed to maximize the influence of a defeated great power, though in this it eminently served Talleyrand's purposes. It was also a political doctrine of broader import. But it was a political doctrine only partially developed, presented in universal terms that left obscured the shakiness of its foundations in early nineteenth-century societies. It was a doctrine applied to the European superstructures that the European societies, in full mutation, could not for long sustain.[20]

The British government, secure in its own legitimacy, had the least use for the doctrine of legitimacy. For Lord Castlereagh, the British foreign secretary, the doctrine was a mere expedient. The British were, however, firmly convinced of the need to return to a general system of public law in Europe.[21] It was the theory, not the practice, of legitimacy that British diplomacy disdained.

The Russian Czar Alexander I embraced the doctrine with more enthusiasm, giving it his own interpretation. Alexander's position illustrates the divorce between doctrine and social basis at its most extreme. The autocrat of all the Russians professed liberal ideas and was, indeed, looked to by liberals in western Europe as the hope for a new order. Professions of liberalism mingled in his words and actions with repressive authoritarianism. Harold Nicholson (1947) drew this portrait:

> What Metternich described sententiously as the "periodic evolutions of the Tsar's mind," were none the less sincere phases of conviction. What renders his policy so difficult to interpret is that, although he would oscillate wildly between a given theory of action and its opposite, he sought always to remain constant to his word; and since the promises that he had made when under the influence of one set of theories were irreconcilable with the needs imposed upon him by another set of theories, he often tried, in almost pathetic confusion, to carry out the recently discarded and the recently adopted theory at one and the same time. As these successive impulses were contradictory, a marked impression of inconstancy and dissimulation was conveyed.[22]

Alexander was a schizophrenic and an idealist. His schizophrenia only underscored the idealism of his politics. Politics was the will of the ruler, disconnected from the material conditions of power. Insofar as that will was confused and contradictory, its disjunction from reality became the more evident. In Alexander's initiative, the principle of legitimacy became the Holy Alliance, a personal compact of monarchs binding themselves mutually to sustain each other's rule in accordance with the dictates of Christianity. Castlereagh, no idealist, regarded the Holy Alliance as "this piece of sublime mysticism and nonsense."[23] Its political effect was entirely reactionary, serving as the pretext for joint actions to suppress liberal movements in western and southern Europe.

Castlereagh, in line from his mentor Pitt, had during the wartime period associated the reconstruction of Europe with the idea of a collective guarantee by all the powers, and principally by the Great Powers, to the whole of the peace settlement embodied in one general treaty. By the time this idea had evolved in the Czar's mind into the Holy Alliance, Castlereagh's thinking had moved in a different direction. He envisaged a permanent system of conferences through which the powers combined in the Alliance could make by consensus the necessary adjustments to the European order. For Castlereagh, however, this system should deal only with strictly diplomatic questions and not involve itself in the internal political structures of states. "[N]othing," he wrote in a cabinet memorandum on the occasion of The Conference of Aix-la-Chapelle in 1818, "would be more immoral or more prejudicial to the character of government generally than the idea that [the] force [of the Alliance] was collectively to be prostituted to the support of established power without any consideration of the extent to which it was abused."[24] He reiterated these warnings when, in 1820 and again in 1822, the Czar was threatening military intervention in Spain on behalf of the Alliance to repress a revolution against that country's monarch.[25] The Russian autocrat-idealist persisted in trying to mobilize governments and opinion to defend the immutable principles of Christianity against the evil specter of Jacobin revolution. The arch-Tory pragmatist struggled to preserve a mechanism for negotiating consensus that would at the same time allow for the possibility of change. The first presupposed a consensus that did not exist, and the mechanism envisaged by the second was becoming all the time further from reach because of mutations in the relationship of governments to people that made consensus harder to achieve. In western and southern Europe, the historic blocs of the old regime had been only partially restored. They were, during the decade following the restoration, challenged and reshaped by emerging counterhegemonic forces. Diplomacy could not create a hegemony that had insufficient basis in society. By 1822, the negotiating mechanism of the Alliance nurtured by Castlereagh had ceased to be an effective instrument of European collective will.

## THE EMERGENCE
## OF THE LIBERAL ORDER

The liberal state and the liberal world order emerged together, taking shape through the establishment of bourgeois hegemony in Britain and of British hegemony in the world economy. Britain's ability to manage the balance of power was the link between the one and the other. For the new form of state to become consolidated, a period of security and freedom from external intervention was required. The balance of power provided this respite.

From at least the time of the Seven Years' War (1756–1763), British policy had not only recognized the balance of power as a fact of diplomatic life but had also used it to keep the European powers divided so as better to extend British commercial and imperial interests beyond Europe.[26] Napoleon had destroyed that balance and had organized the continent under French suzerainty. Britain's insular position and supremacy at sea together with Russia's expanse of land and abundant manpower became the basis of a coalition that ultimately overturned French dominance. In 1804, Pitt, responding to an overture from the Czar, drew up a memorandum concerning postwar European reconstruction that was founded on the idea of the reestablishment of the balance of power. Castlereagh, sharing and continuing Pitt's conceptions of European order, pursued this goal in shaping the postwar settlement. The victors were agreed to combine against a revival of the threat of European domination by France, yet in the interests of balance, French power had to be maintained at a level of rough equality with the other great powers. Further-

more, in the perspective of Britain, safeguards would have to be
taken against the potentiality of Russian dominance. For this
reason, it was an important consideration of Castlereagh's policy
to strengthen central Europe—Prussia and Austria—as a counterweight to both France and Russia.[27] Britain for her part sought
no territorial gains in Europe, only the independence of the Low
Countries from control by any other great power and their close
alliance with Britain. The balance of power was thus the keystone
of British policy.

In elaborating this policy, Castlereagh was the embodiment of the fully autonomous state. He worked as much as possible in private, informing his cabinet colleagues as little as possible and concealing from Parliament everything he could. A
leading member and sometime parliamentary leader of Tory-
reactionary cabinets led by Lord Liverpool and the Duke of Wel-
lington, he had no regard for public opinion and steadfastly
refrained from any attempt to inform or arouse opinion to support
his policy. He did not even have any personal confidants. He
made foreign policy for Britain in the way that seemed right to
him with few constraints placed upon him by Cabinet or Parliament.[28] Yet Castlereagh's policy conformed perfectly to the interests of British economic expansion and the British bourgeoisie—
despite the facts that his coolness toward liberal democratic
movements abroad was at odds with an increasingly isolationist
and liberal-sympathizing British opinion; that he was remote
from the world of commerce and finance; and that there was a
lack of understanding of the balance of power on the part of the
commercial community.

In the first place, the maintenance of the balance of power
in Europe had resulted in an overwhelming preponderance of
British strength in the rest of the world. Britain's trade had become oriented increasingly toward Europe, South America, and
the United States, and proportionately less toward the British
empire. Formal empire mattered less than freedom of commercial
access to all countries. The balance of power in Europe left Britain's "maritime rights"—its freedom of navigation and claim to
the right of visit and search of all shipping, in other words its
unchallengable naval supremacy—intact. Pitt and Castlereagh
secured naval bases across the world's oceans but were prepared

to compromise on the question of colonial possessions if it would help secure a proper balance of power in Europe. Castlereagh was ready to grant commercial recognition to Spain's South American colonies, as a first step to ensuring access to British merchants, while deferring political recognition. The second step, political recognition, was taken by his successor Canning, who also opened the way for the enunciation by the U.S. President of the Monroe Doctrine, which in practice guaranteed South America's openness to British economic penetration. In commercial matters, whether in South America or Europe, Castlereagh sought openness for all countries, not special advantages for Britain. In this, he left behind eighteenth-century mercantilism for nineteenth-century free-trade conceptions. In an open trading world, it was clear that Britain's industrial and financial lead gave her a decisive advantage over all other powers.[29]

In the second place, the balance of power, by ensuring Britain's security from a European threat without requiring a military presence in Europe, was a relatively cheap foreign policy in financial terms. During the war, Castlereagh had used Britain's financial capability generously to political advantage. Payments to the allies had taken the form of subsidies rather than loans.[30] However, the financial effort had been considerable for Britain and proved to be the factor that imposed the most serious constraint on the government's foreign policy in the postwar period. The government had financed the war by borrowing from the Bank of England, a private chartered institution empowered to manage the public debt and to issue banknotes. During the war, conversion of banknotes into specie had been suspended (thereby preventing conversion of privately held government debt into gold) and an income tax introduced. With peace, the income tax was abolished, but the government was reluctant to return to specie payment so long as it had to raise more bank loans to carry the public debt, and almost two thirds of public expenditure was for service on the national debt. Commercial interests, articulated notably by David Ricardo, demanded a return to a gold-exchangeable currency as a necessary foundation for world trade, and to achieve this, draconian steps to retire the debt. Tory country gentlemen, on the other hand, enjoyed the inflationary effect on agricultural prices of a paper currency freed from the discipline of gold. Commercial interest and sound money prevailed. It was a young Tory, Robert Peel, initially predisposed to the agricultural interests, who chaired the commission that prepared the return to specie payments in 1819 (the year in which Ricardo purchased for himself a seat in Parliament).[31] This decision marked the limits imposed on state policy by Britain's international commercial position.

In the third place, by preventing Holy Alliance interventionism, the British balance-of-power policy removed external obstructions to the bourgeois-liberal transformations of western European states in the 1820s and 1830s, as well as to the independence (and commercial opening) of South America from Spain and Portugal. The balance of power operated in such a way as to allow emerging social forces to develop and to bring about political changes.

Castlereagh conducted foreign policy as an aristocrat conscious of serving the interests of the insular-mercantile state. He did not self-consciously serve a class interest. A class-based foreign policy was, however, articulated in England by the doctrinaires of laissez faire. Richard Cobden challenged the concept of the balance of power and favored a cheap foreign policy based on disarmament and free trade. The Manchester School saw the world market as the primary criterion of policy. The possibility of commercial access to the whole world took precedence in its thinking over Britain's formal empire, and it perceived sound gold-exchangable currency as the linchpin of the world trading system. These ideas were naturally combined with a sympathy toward liberal and nationalist movements seeking to remake states abroad. As a consequence, British radicals espoused a contradiction in foreign policy, favoring proliberal or pronationalist interventionism ideologically but rejecting military expenditures on economy grounds. The economy horn of their dilemma easily took precedence over the ideological, and the issue was resolved in the radical consciousness by the myth of a free-trading world in which force had ceased to be necessary.[32] The aristocratic managers of foreign policy maintained a more realistic equilibrium. They practiced a policy of presence in Europe, but one designed to preserve the balance of power, not to dominate politically. That balance could be preserved so long as the continental powers remained of roughly equal strength, and Britain could play the part of manager of the balance so long as her strength, and particularly her financial capabilities, were greater. This policy was consistent with the commercial aims of the new bourgeoisie, even if some of its spokesmen found it uncongenial. The balance of power was the practical nineteenth-century substitute for the organization of perpetual peace, which eighteenth-century political economy posited as the foundation for a division of labor that would increase the wealth of nations.

Castlereagh's successors continued the substance of his policy while altering its ideological coloring and its style. Canning and, later, Palmerston invoked liberal sympathies for revolutionary movements in Europe and took an open stand against the Holy Alliance when it fitted their purposes, but they kept the balance of power at the center of their foreign policies and never allowed ideological bias to dictate action. Castlereagh, for his part, had no sympathy for revolutionary movements and opposed Holy Alliance initiatives almost apologetically, never seeking to arouse, let alone defer to, public opinion. The practical results were similar.[33] The need to mobilize public and parliamentary support for foreign policy was, however, a new reality of the nineteenth century. Castlereagh's lack of perception of this need was the principal defect of his conduct of foreign policy.

The liberal world order, like the liberal state, posited a separation of politics from economics, together with a fundamental compatibility between them. The free-trading world economy was understood to be the condition for the wealth of nations; this was the domain of industrial, mercantile, and financial operators. The responsibility of the state and the state system was to ensure the conditions for this open world economy while refraining from interfering with the operations of these economic agents. This was the meaning of "liberal" as attached to the terms *state* or *world order*. Liberalism had a circumstantial connection with political pluralism and parliamentary government in the British case. Regimes in other countries proved capable of achieving the same balance between economy and politics under authoritarian auspices. Both were "liberal" in the sense discussed here.

In the British case, politics, and especially foreign policy, remained preeminently the domain of the aristocracy; economics was the sphere of the bourgeoisie.[34] Aristocratic managers understood that the limits within which they must manage were fixed by the conditions necessary for bourgeois economic expansion. This shared understanding, and the aristocratic-bourgeois division of labor, constituted the bourgeois hegemony in Britain, the basis in turn for British hegemony in world economy.

The Restoration doctrine of legitimacy was powerless to stop the social forces encouraged by two decades of ferment all over Europe. Those social forces—the rise of the bourgeoises and the revolt of the young intellectuals—could successfully challenge old-regime historic blocs because the balance-of-power system prevented any international concentration of force against them. "Legitimacy" in its turn became illegitimate.

Before 1830, the Restoration powers tried but failed, largely because of British objections, to give effect to a mutual commitment among governments to defend established regimes. After 1830, international rivalries among the powers were too great to permit even an attempt at collaboration against internal threats. Changes of regime did come about in France, Belgium, Portugal, Spain, Italy, Greece, Poland, and the Ottoman Empire. These changes generally favored the installation of liberal states. They did not go so far as a democratic breakthrough. Democracy remained anathema to established authorities, a threat to both property and power, to both economy and polity. In 1848, the liberal revolutionaries faltered before the implications of democracy, and the failure of these revolutionary movements strengthened this fear of democracy on the part of the ruling groups and those benefiting by their rule. The very fear of democracy acted as a moderating factor in international relations. The powers were constrained not to act forcefully against one another lest they thereby open the way to revolutions.[35]

These conditions made for a prolonged internal and international equilibrium of forces favorable to liberalism. These conditions came to an end during the last decades of the nineteenth century when governments perceived the potentiality of nationalism to establish a bridge of solidarity between government and people. Democratic forces, assuming the forms of rival nationalisms, disrupted the liberal equilibrium and enabled states once more to challenge one another without fear of nourishing internal dissensions. International conflict was facilitated by domestic unity and helped to generate it.[36]

The liberal era thus permitted both the transformation of states toward the liberal form and the expansion of the world economy in relatively peaceful conditions. The key to the first was Britian's management of the balance of power and to the second the omnipotence of British sea power.[37]

## THE LIBERAL STATE

The emergence of the liberal form of state, as of any form of state, can usefully be looked at in two different perspectives. One is to treat the form as an ideal type, specifying its properties and considering how far the particular historical state approximates them. The ideal type gives a functional view of the state in relation to society and economy. It posits certain activities on the part of the state in order to produce certain results for society and economy. But it cannot explain how that particular form of state came to exist or how it may change. The other perspective addresses directly the explanation of the state's existence; in it the state is perceived as the product of political struggle. This second perspective is concerned with the making of the historic bloc. The two perspectives are not alternatives but complementary. The ideal type may serve as an approximation for the project of an emerging historic bloc or as a shorthand for the hegemonic ideology of an established historic bloc.

The ideal-typical view of the liberal state can perhaps best be represented by combining the ideas of the classical political economists with the measures instituted by the reform movement in Britain and in other countries in the early nineteenth century. Adam Smith constructed a theory of civil society on the basis that a natural harmony would result from the freedom of individuals to pursue their own particular interests. State interventions would only impede this natural harmony and reduce the general welfare. Implicit as conditions for the wealth of nations were domestic and international freedom for economic agents and the removal of the threat of violence within and among states.

Ricardo and his followers took a somewhat less optimistic view of civil society. They recognized more explicitly the existence of conflicts of interest between capitalists and workers, and between both and landlords, but they also agreed that state interventions would make things worse rather than better. Despite this generally negative view of the state, however, there were certain indispensable functions the state should perform in order to enable civil society to maximize wealth.

In the first place, the state had the task of removing the existing obstructions to economic freedom inherited from feudal and mercantilist practices. There was a long list of these: laws of succession and entail that inhibited a market in land; privileges granted by the state to monopolies and corporations; laws entrenching guild regulation of production; statutes of apprenticeship and Elizabethan labor statutes that regulated recruitment of labor and wages; protective measures like the Corn Laws; and the whole mercantile system designed to maintain a favorable balance of trade, restrict colonial commerce, and produce a stock-piling of bullion. The reform movement in Britain brought about the dismantling of all this legislation. The only relic of a former plethora of price controls, the assize of bread, was repealed in 1815 on petition of the London bakers. In the same period, the Elizabethan labor statute and the apprenticeship laws (except as regards seafaring) were also repealed. Mercantilist protections, more firmly entrenched by politically powerful interests, took longer to remove, but by the 1840s the Corn Laws, the sugar preference protecting the West Indian planters, and the Navigation Acts were repealed. In France, the guild system was abolished as one of the acts of the Revolution in 1791, although in central and northern Europe control of guilds and corporations over entry into artisan production remained strong up until the second half of the nineteenth century. Freedom to enter and practice any trade was established in Austria in 1859, and in the German Empire by 1869, contributing to a lingering hostility toward liberalism among formerly protected artisans.[38]

A second function of the liberal state, beyond the dismantling of existing obstructions, was to establish the conditions for free markets in goods and labor. Mercantilist policy had paved the way in Britain by making the largest national market the prime explanation for Britain's lead in manufacturing. The French Revolution resulted in the dismantling of internal obstructions to commerce. The German zollverein completed unification of a large economic space in 1834. Thenceforth, the process of market enlargement proceeded internationally: first, unilaterally in the tariff reductions of Sir Robert Peel's budgets in the 1840s; later, through the elimination of restrictions on the major international waterways, e.g., the Danube (1857) and the Rhone (1861); and then by the negotiation of a series of commercial treaties for tariff reduction and the extension of the most favored-nation principle, beginning with that between Britain and France in 1860.[39]

The creation of an unregulated labor market bore more directly upon the social relations of production than the free market in goods did. In England, the poor law, since the reign of Elizabeth, required each parish to care for its own poor. The intention was to limit the dangers of vagrancy by ensuring that the poor were stabilized in their own localities under the supervision of local landed authorities in their capacities as justices of the peace. In the late eighteenth century, this practice had been expanded by the justices of the peace of Speenhamland into a system subsequently extended throughout England that guaranteed a basic income to the poor out of the rates paid by landowners, an income linked to fluctuations in the price of bread.

This practice, born of the paternalism of precapitalist society, resulted in a distortion of the allocation of labor in an emerging capitalism. Adam Smith, Malthus, and others attacked it as obstructing the free movement of labor and contributing to overpopulation in rural areas. One result was that low wages paid by some landlords to their agricultural laborers were subsidized in the form of outdoor relief financed by all the ratepayers. Another was the general demoralization of agricultural laborers, who became permanently dependent on poor relief.

Poor law reform became a major objective of the liberal reformers, a reform carried through by Parliament in 1834 with the enactment of the new poor law. The principles on which the new law was based were, first, the abolition of outdoor relief in favor of confining relief to the workhouse, and second, the making of workhouse conditions a sufficient deterrent so that any work available on the labor market would be preferred to relief. These changes in practice reflected a change of attitude toward poverty—toward regarding poverty as a matter of personal rather than community responsibility. The new system did away with maintenance in parishes of origin or settlement and thus encouraged mobility of labor throughout the country as a whole (particularly migration from the south to the northern manufacturing centers). The primary consequence of the poor law reform, apart from reducing the fiscal burden of poor relief for the ratepayers, was to create a nationwide labor market. This was complemented by the repeal of the old legislation affecting wages and apprenticeship, so that the state both created the labor market and refrained from intervening in the arrangements made by employers with workers.[40] The state also obstructed workers from combining collectively to influence the labor market on the presumption that the labor market is strictly an interaction of equal individuals.[41]

A third state function was to ensure the soundness of money. Mention has been made above of the suspension of gold convertibility during the Napoleonic wars and the controversy preceding the resumption of specie payments in 1819. Government manipulation of the value of money pits the interests of some economic groups against others. Agricultural producers were happy under the suspension of convertibility; the fund holders, or those who had lent to the government, demanded a return to gold. The return to specie payment was much criticized as sacrificing the producers to nonproductive groups. Liberal doctrine, particularly as urged by Ricardo, sought to remove the state from active manipulation by making the state responsible for ensuring strict application of the gold standard. This was achieved by the Bank Act of 1844, which separated the Bank of England's function of issuing currency from its banking functions and tied currency issue by statute to gold. This arrangement survived well into the twentieth century.[42]

A fourth function, which seems to contradict the principle of abstinence from intervention on the part of the liberal state, was the specialization of functions and centralization of state power. In fact, there was no contradiction, since to allow the market mechanism to function without disturbance required the sanction of coercive force, and to ensure this force was not to be used in particular interests but to defend the system as a whole required the creation of a specialized state apparatus. The decades during which the liberal state was built up were decades that saw a wide-ranging reform of government at all levels and the expansion of the public service.[43] A new mobile police force was established in Britain in 1829 under direct control of the Home Department, first in London, then extended elsewhere in the country.[44] The administration set up to manage relief under the new poor law, by forming unions of parishes, introduced a new and more centralized basis for other functions of local government. A Municipal Corporations Act provided the basis for middle-class control over urban local government.[45] Fiscal reforms also enhanced state power. As tariffs were reduced in the interest of free trade, this source of government revenue had to be replaced. The income tax, previously only a wartime expedient, was introduced on a permanent basis by the government of Sir Robert Peel in 1842. Government expenditures in Liberal Britain at that time were four times those of Czarist Russia.[46] The liberal state was not a weak state. It had acquired capabilities far beyond those of the old-regime state.

A fifth function of the liberal state was in the area of mobilizing capital. It involved both direct investment by the state and the provision of legal arrangements that encourage private capital formation. Adam Smith recognized that the state could properly produce some public goods essential to the working of the market that would not be privately produced, e.g., roads and harbors. His only qualification was that in doing this the state should simulate the market as far as possible so as to provide only what would be used widely and at a reasonable cost. The era of the liberal state saw the expansion of public postal, railway, judicial, and educational systems. Private capital formation was encouraged by legislation limiting liability through joint-stock and corporate forms of business enterprise. The corporate form lost its erstwhile character of public monopoly to become an organization of capital for private purposes free of state control.[47]

Adam Smith posed very clearly the issue of the autonomy of the state. He was highly suspicious of the motives of merchants and capitalists when they began to involve themselves in state policy. This led, he perceived, to demands for special privileges and protections that would distort the proper functioning of the market. He thus rejected in advance the instrumentalist view of the liberal state, in which the state is the mere vehicle through which various organized interests of civil society interact and reach compromises among their divergent goals.[48] Smith's analysis enhances the view that the coincidence of political pluralism with the liberal state is fortuitous, a matter of circumstance—and indeed a circumstance carrying with it some risks to the purity of the liberal form. Enlightened authoritarianism might be an equally valid and possibly less vulnerable mode of government for a liberal state. Historical experience has given both variants.

Here it becomes desirable to abandon the functionalist perspective so as to examine the processes of political struggle through which liberal forms of state came about. The British case has long been considered the model of liberal development. The French bonapartist state, as a more authoritarian instance of state autonomy, and the United States, as an instance of a more instrumental liberal state, offer points of comparison.

Recent work of British historians has stressed the political character of popular struggles during the late eighteenth and early nineteenth centuries. These struggles were concerned essentially with the line between access to and exclusion from power in the state. The agricultural and manufacturing laborers, and the skilled artisans and domestic putting-out workers were, of course, excluded; but so also was the middle class, including the entrepreneurs in burgeoning but politically unrepresented manufacturing towns. The existing state was perceived by the excluded as an agency through which the power-holding groups could engross land through enclosure bills, protect themselves by passing corn laws, and reward themselves as fundholders through such measures as the return to specie payment in 1819. The conflict was pictured by the opposition as one between the producing classes (both workers and middle-class manufacturers) and the idle classes who drew income but did not work.[49]

For the workers, the employers were "middlemen," intermediate between themselves and their oppressors who controlled the state. Up to the 1830s, the critical point in the evolution of the struggle was about how the middlemen would align themselves. Briggs (1960) has written: "The Whigs wished to hitch the middle classes to the constitution to prevent a revolution: a section of the extreme radicals wanted to associate them with the working classes to secure a revolution."[50]

Among rural laborers there occurred a spontaneous movement of revolt born in resentments against pauperization and increasingly restrictive applications of poor law maintenance, which burst into machine-breaking and incendiarism in the "Swing" riots of 1830. These riots took on the aspect of a nationwide movement. They were forcibly repressed, with sentences of death and transportation, leaving smoldering, spasmodic violence in the English countryside during the following decades, until the emergence in the 1870s of agricultural trade unionism. In this early nineteenth-century revolt, the rural working class never linked up with manufacturing working class discontent.[51]

Mobilization of manufacturing workers took place alternately through Chartism and Owenite trade unionism. Trade unionism grew apace during the years of economic growth when employment levels were relatively high (1832–36). This was not the collective bargaining craft unionism of the late nineteenth century, pursuing incremental goals. It was a movement of big unions that envisaged a radical transformation of production from the rule of employers to worker control through cooperative associations. The movement failed from its own internal divisions and from resistance by employers and local authorities. The downturn in the economy with rising unemployment that followed during years of extreme privation for the working class from 1837 into the 1840s rechanneled worker protest into the more overtly political form of Chartism. Chartism aimed at changing the state by gaining representation for the working class through universal manhood suffrage, annual parliaments, equal electoral districts, and the abolition of property qualifications for members of Parliament.[52]

The Whig reforms enacted by Parliament during the early 1830s brought the middle class into participation in the state. These reforms also had the effect of dividing middle-class from working-class opposition. The working classes remained excluded. They now perceived the state as an oppressive apparatus intended to maintain a dictatorship over workers on behalf of the owners of capital, a vision that replaced the view of the state as the agency of landlords and fundholders—the idle classes—enriching themselves at the expense of the productive classes. Now the "middlemen" had aligned themselves with the old oppressors to bring about a more direct polarization between their combined force and the excluded majority of working people.

Specific reform measures reinforced this image. The Reform Bill of 1832 gave the middle class representation in Parliament, but the property qualification excluded the working class from the vote.[53] The Municipal Corporations Act of 1835 put local government into the hands of the employer class. The new police system and the coercive measures undertaken in Ireland in 1833 seemed like the construction of a coercive state apparatus that could be used to repress workers. The refusal of Parliament to provide relief for the distressed and starving handloom weavers, leaving them victims to market forces, and the poor law reform of 1834, which transformed the old sense of a right to assistance into a form of compulsion to work for low wages, showed clearly the purposes for which state power would be used. The rise and fall of Owenite trade unionism and the flaring up and remission of Chartism were manifestations of worker response to this class polarization of society during the initial phase of formation of the liberal state.[54] The Chartists, anticipating Marx, argued that labor was the source of all value, that manufacturers were robbing workers of a part of their just return for their labor, and that the employer's ability to exploit in this way was abetted by state measures that created a "reserve army" of labor.[55]

The Anti-Corn Law League was the principal agency of middle-class mobilization during the period following the Whig reforms of the 1830s. It maintained the distinctive pursuit of middle-class policy aims once the bourgeoisie had secured admission to representation in the state. There were also attempts both on the part of League members and on the part of some Chartist radicals to build an alliance between worker and middle-class activists on the basis of opposition to the landed interest's stake in corn-law protection. These efforts foundered as the opposition between manufacturers' and workers' interests became increasingly manifest, state power being used by the one against the other. Furthermore, the solidity of the landed interest was

breached. Many larger landlords had no special interest in the
corn laws, which were defended with most determination by
tenant farmers. The Tory Sir Robert Peel, himself representative
of a new alliance between land and manufacturing capital, sponsored repeal in 1846.[56] Richard Cobden, the principal activist of
the League, saw this as a decisive bourgeois victory. In a since-
famous letter to Peel, he wrote:

> Do you shrink from governing through the bona fide represen-
> tatives of the middle class? Look at the facts and can the country
> be otherwise ruled at all? There must be an end to the juggle of
> parties, the mere representatives of traditions, and some man
> must of necessity rule the state through its governing class. The
> Reform Bill decreed it: the passing of the Corn Bill has realised
> it.[57]

Peel did not, however, perceive the event in the same way.
He saw repeal as resolving an issue that had become extremely
divisive, pitting middle class against gentry, and workers against
both. Where Cobden was calling for a middle-class dictatorship,
Peel became the architect of a new hegemony. Repeal removed
an obstacle to the aristocracy's regaining its status as Britain's
natural leaders. It also removed the principal reason for the political mobilization of the middle class, enabling it to return
without distraction to its preordained activity of making money.
The alienation of the workers was another matter. An aristocratic
governing class running the state in accordance with the requirements of the liberal economy could also make some concessions
to workers without undermining the basis of bourgeois order.[58]
As early as 1815, Peel had introduced a factory act with the
support of Robert Owen. In 1847, an act limiting the working day
to ten hours was passed and within a few years made effective.
Though no political concessions were made to Chartism, coercive
repression of the movement ceased. It withered and died during
the 1840s.

The British liberal state as consolidated under Sir Robert
Peel was autonomous; it brought order and regulation into business activity through the Bank Act and the Companies Act of
1844, and the income tax put state finances on a sound basis. It
was hegemonic in bringing to a close the era of greatest class

conflict. Conflict was not eliminated but diffused. Revolt in the countryside never passed beyond the level of individual acts of violence. Employment picked up with economic expansion, and a "new model" unionism of skilled artisans, which accepted the existing production relations as a basis for improving their members' positions, disarmed middle-class fears of rebellion. The hegemony was a bourgeois hegemony under an aristocratic governing class. This hegemony reached from the center of the state into local government. The manufacturing boroughs, as noted, were securely in the hands of the manufacturers.

In the rural areas, the new poor law administration had brought about a compromise among the Tory paternalism of the squirearchy, continuous from Elizabethan times; the capitalist character of farming, which employed a wage labor force; and the manufacturers' needs for an open labor market with a mobile reserve pool of labor. Local peers and gentry took a leading role in the early boards of guardians set up under the new poor law. The "Swing" riots left both a conviction of the need to reestablish order and labor discipline and a sense of the need to show some small measure of compassion for the laborer's plight. The boards of guardians enjoyed a certain flexibility in applying the rules concerning entitlement to relief. As the threat of disorder receded, peers and squires left the task of active management to tenant farmers without thereby losing control.[59]

This hegemonic social order remained in place until the end of the century, when a further phase of legislation began the process of transformation that culminated in the welfare state of the post-World War II period.

Marx's analysis of the bonapartist state formed in France following the revolution of 1848 presents certain points of structural similarity and also of contrast to the British experience. In both cases, the liberal economy became the basis for public policy, and the state became strong and centralized. However, in France no hegemony was achieved as in Britain.

The proportions of the different classes made a marked contrast between the two countries. Small-holding farmers were preponderant in numbers in French society, whereas wage labor was prevalent in Britain both in agriculture and in manufacturing, which was much more developed than in France. The removal

of residual feudal obligations by the revolution of 1789 in France
had turned self-employed small-holder farmers from a revolutionary into a conservative social force. Marx perceived that
though these small holders constituted a class because they
shared a common material situation, they had not achieved any
community or political organization that could express their common class interest.

> They cannot represent themselves, they must be represented.
> Their representative must at the same time appear as their mas-
> ter, as an authority over them, as an unlimited governmental
> power that protects them against the other classes and sends
> them rain and sunshine from above. The political influence of
> the small-holding peasants, therefore, finds its final expression
> in the executive power subordinating society to itself.[60]

Here, Marx has identified a more general phenomenon, in more
recent times often characterized as populism, whereby a social
group that has not achieved any effective and autonomous articulation of its interests responds to the appeal of an authoritarian
leader.

Another distinction between the British and French cases
was the relatively greater size of the state bureaucracy in France.
This is something France inherited from the old regime, which
was further developed by the Revolution and Empire and again
by the Second Empire. It meant that very many families, particularly of the petty bourgeoisie, were directly dependent on the
state for their material welfare. The state machinery itself had a
greater formative impact on society in France than in England as
a force both of attraction and of coercion.

At the same time, society was more polarized in France as
a consequence both of the cleavages brought about through revolutionary experiences and the lesser development of capitalist
production. The wage workers, especially those of Paris, had
played a decisive role in the revolutionary movements of 1830
and again in 1848. They were, however, a minority in an urban
population composed in its majority of self-employed artisans
and petty bourgeois shopkeepers. The bourgeoisies of agriculture,
finance, and manufacturing had, following the setback they suffered by the proclamation of the worker-dominated "social re-

public" in the first revolutionary thrust of 1848, regained control thanks to the support of the small-holder mass of the population outside Paris and the separation of the urban petty bourgeoisie from the workers. The social republic gave way to the bourgeois republic. The cleavage between them was wrought in blood during the June Days of 1848 when thousands of workers were slaughtered by troops in Paris and thousands more transported afterward. Thenceforth, a weak labor movement in France identified itself with the radical revolutionary republican tradition; conservative France united the surviving old-regime elements of society with the bourgeoisie of the emergent liberal economy. Each segment of France lived in fear and distrust of the other. This cleavage was strengthened after the downfall of the Second Empire by the even greater butchery that occurred in the repression of the Paris Commune (1871).

Uncertain of their ability to give secure and continuing political leadership in a coalition of conservative forces, the French bourgeoisie in 1852 abandoned their own parliamentary parties and placed their political fate in the hands of Bonaparte and the army. The bonapartist regime was a form of state power that could enforce order within which the bourgeoisie could get on with their business of making money. (The event created a precedent. The post-World War I Italian bourgeoisie in similar fashion abandoned the Liberals and placed its fate in the hands of Mussolini.) The coming of the bonapartist state signified a failure to overcome the basic cleavage in French society and the failure of the French bourgeoisie to achieve a hegemony. The state machine, staffed by petty bourgeois bureaucrats and the army, had to substitute for the kind of hegemony achieved in British society.

Though the French state had great powers of attraction and compulsion, it presided over a society beset by contradictions. The bonapartist state became the virtual representative of conflicting class interests. It represented the bourgeoisie by enforcing the rules of liberal economy—and the era knew no alternative economic system. But Bonaparte was also the representative of the small-holding mass of the population and of the lumpenproletariat he had organized as his political fighting force. He exhibited also an unrequited desire to become the representative of the workers (he legalized strikes in 1864). It required a permissive economy and a permissive world order for such a state to be able to give payoffs to this variety of divergent interests. The economy was indeed expansively permissive through the duration of the Second Empire; the regime collapsed just before the onset of the late nineteenth-century long depression. World order ceased to be equally permissive with the coming to power of Bismark in Prussia in 1862 and ultimately with France's defeat by the Hohenzollern Empire in 1870.

As Marx observed, Bonaparte broke the political power of the bourgeoisie in order to protect its material power, but in protecting its material power, he generated the bourgeoisie's political power anew.[61] In the successor regime of the Third Republic, a petty bourgeois governing class continued the task of protecting the bourgeois economic order.

The Third Republic, traumatized by the repression of the Paris Commune, was no more able than Bonaparte was to bring the workers within a hegemonic order. The labor movement in France, weak as it was, maintained its fundamental rejection of the bourgeois order. The bourgeoisie for their part maintained a defense of the absolute rights of property, unwilling to share power in industry with a movement that rejected the legitimacy of ownership. Thus, even after the legalization of trade unions in 1884, industrial relations in France remained characterized by state interventionism. Employers were disinclined to negotiate with workers who challenged their rights. Confronted by impasse and possible violence in the event of industrial disputes, the local prefect would intervene, sometimes at the instance of the workers' leaders, to bring about a settlement. The state maintained its autonomy, acting to restore peace and orderly production rather than as enforcer of the particular interests of employers in industrial disputes. In so doing, the state maintained an order that favored employers over workers.[62]

The United States during the nineteenth-century liberal world order maintained a state that was relatively undeveloped in relation to civil society. Struggle over the state was a struggle among divergent class interests to use the state for their own protection and for the advancement of their particular interests. The interests of the growing manufacturing economy of the Northeast conflicted with those of the plantation economy of the

Old South. Distinct from both were the interests of small-holding farmers in the North and the New West. These various interests used the machinery of government to their own ends where they could but were not overly constrained by it. Local and state governments directly invested in or guaranteed loans for the construction of canals and railways that would serve the needs of capitalists. The tariff, a matter of controversy between the protectionist manufacturers of the North and the free-trade planters of the South, became in its details the creature of innumerable particular manufacturing interests. The issue of cheap versus sound money pitted farmers against manufacturers, and farmer resistance obstructed the creation of a national central banking system until the twentieth century. The greatest resource at the disposal of governments was public land, and the issue over whether this should be held as a reserve for the future or distributed liberally to able-bodied citizens, thereby strengthening the farmer interest, was another major contention.[63] In short, government was an opportunity of plunder in somebody's interest. At the same time, government did not impinge much on the actions of citizens by comparison with European usages of the time. It did little to regulate business, whose standards were free-wheeling, especially in the post-Civil War era, when business and government corruption merged in Mark Twain's "gilded age."[64] The private justice of vigilantes went uncontrolled, and capitalist barons maintained private armed forces to defend and extend their property. By no stretch of the imagination could one speak of an autonomous state in nineteenth-century America. State autonomy, insofar as it now exists in the United States, was the creation of twentieth-century wars and the Great Depression.

Nor can one speak of a hegemonic society in nineteenth-century America. The Civil War (1861–65) was precipitated by an alliance forged in the Republican Party of tariff and homestead, of northern capitalist and western farmer, against the power formerly wielded by southern planters through the Democratic Party. Three modes of social relations of production, each with a distinct geographical base, competed for supremacy. The balance tipped against the slave economy of the planters and gave the upper hand to the wage-labor economy of the northern capitalists, but the self-employed farmers remained a constraining force obstructing a full-fledged bourgeois hegemony.[65] The farmers won a victory in the Homestead Act of 1862 for the granting of western land freely to settlers. In practice, the operation of the act worked in the interest of large land speculators, but the small-settler movement continued through the century as a political and economic force. This movement drained a potential wage-labor force away from the manufacturers, but the manufacturers were compensated by the Immigration Act of 1864, which gave federal authorization to the importation of working people under terms of contract analogous to the indentured servitude of colonial times. Western farmers did provide markets for manufacturers, and farmers also helped to sustain the ideology of free enterprise and freedom from governmental controls.

If the western frontier delayed the proletarianization of the United States, wage labor did nonetheless become the preponderant form of economic activity by the late decades of the nineteenth century. Conflict between labor and capital, unmediated by state intervention, was widespread and violent in the 1870s and 1880s. This reached a point of crisis in the 1890s, when capital decisively defeated labor and began to bring about a new organization of production—an organization that displaced the old agglomeration of skilled workers in factories by a fragmentation of the work process coordinated under managerial control.[66] It is on this basis that U.S. capital built its hegemony in the twentieth century. State autonomy, regulating this capitalist development, came with the New Deal during the Depression of the 1930s.

## CONSOLIDATION
## OF THE LIBERAL WORLD ORDER

The economic processes given free rein by the institutionalizing of liberal principles in early nineteenth-century states enjoyed a period of expansion from the 1840s to the 1870s. It was a period of growing prosperity for the more advanced economies and of optimism in the continuity of expansion in manufacture and trade. Transport improved within and among countries. New sources of energy and raw materials were opened up in response to the appetites of industry. Increased mining of gold, together with increased circulation of paper currencies and the introduction of new techniques of credit, expanded the money supply and stimulated economic activity. New methods of finance, notably the joint-stock investment bank, facilitated the mobilization and channeling of capital.[67]

The liberal world order was the creation of an expansionist society, British in the first instance and European in the following instances—*les bourgeois conquérants*.[68] Expansionism took the forms of trade, emigration, and capital investment. The movement was aided and abetted by state actions, notably by Britain. There was a certain consistency in the variety of methods used by the British state to promote this expansion: formal intervention and political control where necessary, but where possible, informal and less costly arrangements that would leave enforcement of the rules in the hands of reliable local governments.[69] Britain promoted, recognized, and protected the independence of Buenos Aires and Brazil in the early years of the century and secured favorable commercial treaties that the new governments were relied on to enforce. India, however, which became the key to the British payments system, giving Britain a favorable balance to offset its deficit with Europe and the United States, was managed directly and in accordance with mercantilist practices. In small states, where local governments proved less reliable, Britain intervened forcibly, e.g., to protect bondholders' interests in Guatemala and Colombia in the 1870s. Overseas territories controlled by European settlers could, however, be relied on to conform to the economic requirements of liberal world order with a measure of self-government. These instances suggest the variety of state policies and political responses to a single expansionist movement of global reach.

The world of liberal states was a hierarchical order. Britain was its center: the principal trading nation, principal source of capital for the rest of the world, principal enforcer of market rules, and preserver of the military balance. Other European countries—France, Germany, the Low Countries—formed an inner circle of participants in industrial growth and trade expansion. Protectionist at the outset, the governments of these and other European countries became converted to the principle of free trade during the peak years of liberalism. From 1860 through the two following decades a series of trade treaties reduced tariffs among the major trading nations (except for the United States). International trade and payments were further facilitated by the gradual acceptance of the gold standard by all these nations from the 1870s up to the outbreak of war in 1914. These were, however, the years during which the liberal era passed its peak and entered a phase of closure. Protectionism, never abandoned by the United States, revived in Germany, Italy, and France during the 1880s and 1890s.

Politically structured global economic expansion had an impact on both production relations and forms of state in the penetrated areas.[70] The initial effect of commercial penetration by British or European commercial expansion was to put pressure on local tributary or peasant-lord production methods to yield more surplus that could be exchanged for goods produced by enterprise-labor-market relations in the expansive country. Throughout the nineteenth century and well into the twentieth these precapitalist production relations were linked into worldwide capitalist exchange relations. Surplus extraction was intensified in peasant-lord cultivation without any basic change in production relations. In other places, changes in production relations did come about. Slave production of cotton in the southern United States gave way to enterprise-labor-market plantation production after the Civil War. In Egypt, demand for cotton by British and European mills led to a concentration of land into large holdings and the ruin of peasant agriculture.[71] In India, the imposition of direct British rule during the nineteenth century, and the application of British contract and property law that this involved, transformed land into absolute property and made it a marketable commodity. Concurrently, the ruin of Indian artisan textile production by the importation of British cotton textiles created a mass of unemployed laborers.[72] Enterprise-labor-market production emerged in India in these conditions in the forms both of plantation wage labor producing raw cotton and of a new indigenous machine cotton textile industry. Indian cotton textiles, along with Indian opium, were exported to China, offsetting China's export of tea. Extraction of raw materials sought by British and European industry was achieved by the implantation of foreign-controlled enclaves of mining and plantations in parts of Africa. These enclaves required a labor force, to secure which local state action was necessary. Sometimes such state action took the form of direct coercion, i.e., forced labor, and sometimes the indirect method of imposing a head tax, which would make it necessary for at least some members of a community to earn a wage in order to pay the tax. Some areas of the penetrated regions came to serve as catchment zones in which labor contractors would recruit a supply of migrant wage workers (mainly young males) while another part of the population (women, children, and elderly) continued through subsistence production to reproduce a wage-labor force available for temporary export.[73]

Thus the penetrated areas of the liberal world economy were transformed in their production relations. In this process, local state machinery, both colonial and formally independent, was likewise transformed. The state developed its capacity to protect the growth of the liberal economy through a mix of direct coercion, tax policy, and property law. The state also mobilized finance for investment in transport and communications facilities. Thus, the functions of the liberal state were exported from the expansive countries to the penetrated countries. In penetrated regions, old hegemonies were challenged, but rarely could it be said that new social hegemonies were established under bourgeois leadership. Typically, state machines intervened to enforce an order that would permit these changes in production and exchange relations to continue. In penetrated countries from the Mediterranean through Asia and Latin America, local bourgeoisies acted as agents or intermediaries for capital from the expansive centers. European economic penetration was encouraged and protected by local authoritarian regimes, as well as welcomed by these comprador groups.[74]

Toward the external world, the liberal state in the penetrated country had the function of adjusting the local to the world economy. Sometimes this function was freely accepted, sometimes forced upon it. British naval power enforced mercantile access and financial contracts where necessary, but most frequently coercion was not necessary. States were glad to have access to British capital and technology for their countries and were ready to adopt the rules and practices of the liberal order as their own guidelines.

The stability enjoyed by the liberal state and world order during the mid-nineteenth century (roughly 1848–1873) can be attributed principally to three factors: (1) class conflict in the expansive center was not polarized—the bourgeoisies had ceased to be a revolutionary force since the old-regime aristocracies had learned to rule in their interests, and the workers had not yet become a coherent challenge; (2) the economic boom of 1848–1870 sustained governments and undermined revolutionary hopes; and (3) the managers of the world economy in the City of London and European *haute finance* moderated adverse effects of recurrent payments deficits in the penetrated zones of the world economy by providing a flow of new capital.

Underlying this stability were the contradictions inherent in the liberal system that would ultimately challenge and transform it: (1) the self-regulating market, as Karl Polanyi pointed out,[75] by undermining the traditional social fabric and leaving many people vulnerable to unemployment and starvation, provoked a reaction of social defense through factory laws, social insurance, trade unions, and political action by labor; (2) the hierarchy of the world economy generated inequalities that became more entrenched, thereby demonstrably falsifying the formal equality of market relationships; and (3) the maintenance of conditions for continuing capital accumulation came to conflict with the requisites for legitimating the liberal order in broad public support, e.g., through the unemployment-creating and income-reducing consequences of deficit-country adjustments under the gold standard.

## ANALYTICAL PROPOSITIONS CONCERNING THE TRANSFORMATION OF FORMS OF STATE AND WORLD ORDERS

This review of evidence relating to the coming of the liberal order enables us to return to some general analytical propositions about the transformation of forms of state and world orders and the impact of such transformation on production relations. These propositions may serve as heuristic guides for the examination of subsequent history.

First, the form of state is the product of two configurations of forces: one, the configuration of social classes within a historic bloc; the other, the permissiveness of the world order.

The aristocratic British governing class recognized that Britain's world power depended on its commerce and manufacturing and was therefore prepared to govern in such a way as to allow the bourgeois economy to flourish and expand. The middle class was sufficiently politically mobilized to specify and demand policies in its interests and to take control of municipal governments in its particular areas of implantation. Aristocratic paternalism, together with economic growth, made possible sufficient concessions to workers to keep the peace so that repression, an ever-present possibility, was rarely resorted to.

The economic and naval power of Britain enabled it to lead an alliance to victory in the Napoleonic wars, thereby securing the military-political conditions for continuing economic supremacy. Britain's manipulation of the European balance of power secured a permissive environment for western European countries to adopt liberal forms without risk of intervention from old-regime restorationist powers.

Second, class struggles leading toward a transformation of states take a political form, i.e., they are struggles about the inclusion or exclusion of social groups from access to political decision making. The outcomes of such struggles are influenced by a variety of factors, including relative numbers (determined by the extent of development of particular modes of social relations of production), self-awareness of groups, geographical concentration or dispersion, effective organization and leadership, and access to existing forms of state power (both carrot and stick, services and coercion).

Third, class conflict in the formation of new historic blocs can lead either toward states that are autonomous in relation to civil society or toward states that are the mere instruments of divergent social forces; with regard to the former, the autonomous state may rest on a hegemonic society, or it may bind together a society in which no hegemony has been achieved. The British case showed an autonomous state in a hegemonic society; the French, a powerful state holding together a nonhegemonic, polarized society; the American, a weak state struggled over and used in their respective interests by conflicting social forces.

Fourth, the state gives a legal-institutional framework for the economic practices of the economically dominant class, i.e., the class that sets the pattern for the development of production relations. The autonomous state, whether in hegemonic or non-hegemonic societies, stands over this class to regulate its activity in a manner consistent with the economic project of the class as a whole, not responding to particular interests of elements in this class. The weak state that becomes the creature of particular interests is unable to achieve this level of disinterested regulation. The interaction of particular interests in this case is closer to the Hobbesian state of nature.

Fifth, the legal-institutional framework set up by the autonomous state creates the basis for the social relations of production, laying down the conditions for the development of the dominant mode of social relations of production and for the subordination of other modes to the dominant mode. State legal and institutional reforms dismantled the old economic and social protectionism and established labor markets. This, together with legal-institutional inhibitions to combinations of workmen, made the enterprise labor market the dominant mode of social relations of production of early capitalism. In France, small-holder production was subordinated to the dominant sector of manufacturing and large-estate agriculture employing wage labor through the mechanisms of banking and mortgages, as well as by a change in the terms of trade detrimental to agriculture (late-nineteenth-century decline in agricultural prices). In the penetrated economies beyond Europe, peasant-lord production was linked into exchange relations with enterprise-labor-market production, and exploitation of peasants was intensified to provide more raw materials. Subsistence production became a labor reserve for enterprise-labor-market production.

Sixth, a world hegemonic order can be founded only by a country in which social hegemony has been or is being achieved. The expansive energies released by a social hegemony-in-formation move outward onto the world scale at the same time as they consolidate their strength at home. The French Revolution gave birth to a hegemonic project that reorganized Europe before it was defeated by a combination of external forces. The defeat left France in a condition of polarization: conservative forces reasserted themselves and came to outweigh the continuing revolutionary thrust, which remained present but frustrated. The British victory opened the way for the consolidation of bourgeois hegemony at home and its expansion to found a liberal world order abroad.

Seventh, the hegemonic order both domestically and on the world scale separates economics from politics. The political foundations of hegemonic economic order are so taken for granted as to be practically ignored. Politicians learn to observe the distinction between economics and politics in their political practice. This observance sustains the economic order by confirming the predictability of its rules and practices. The British government, for instance, continued to honor its financial obligations to the Russian government during the Crimean War. The duality of economic and political rationalities was not unaccompanied by sentiments of disdain and resentment. Disraeli described the international bankers somewhat disparagingly as "mighty loan mongers, on whose fiat the fate of kings and empires sometimes depend."[76] The prominence of Jewish families in international banking was reflected in antisemitism among the aristocratic political class—a phenomenon distinct from the populist antisemitism and racist doctrines that became tools of political mass mobilization in the later nineteenth and twentieth centuries. The fact that the separate claims of the economic order were observed despite political inconvenience gave the world order a kind of autonomy in relation to national interests similar in kind to the autonomy of the state in relation to particular dominant-class interests.

Finally, hegemony, though firmly established at the center of the world order, wears thin in its peripheries. Actual revolts provoked by economic penetration arose in the peripheries, and the use of coercion was much more evident in these areas. Lands peopled by non-European populations experienced violent reactions to the penetration of European capitalism—there were colonial risings in India in 1857–58, in Algeria in 1871, and in Egypt in 1879–1882, and the Taiping rebellion in China (1850–1866) was the most extensive social movement of the nineteenth century.[77]

# CHAPTER SIX

# THE ERA
# OF RIVAL
# IMPERALISMS

The years from the Universal Exhibition of 1851 in London to that of 1866 in Paris can be seen as the apogee of the liberal era. The decades that followed witnessed regression from the principles, practices, and institutions of liberalism. Historians in retrospect have noted a rupture in continuity during the period from the 1870s to the 1890s. The discontinuity marks the decomposition of one fully formed structure that coherently linked world political economy, forms of state and production relations, and the emergence of the elements of a new structure in process of formation in which all of these elements were to become transformed. It was, in Geoffrey Barraclough's words, one of those "moments when humanity swings out of its old paths on to a new plane . . ."[1]

## THE TRANSFORMATION
## OF THE WORLD POLITICAL ECONOMY:
## THE END OF HEGEMONY

To begin with, a change in the relative power of states altered the way in which the interstate system functioned. In Europe, the start of the period saw the consolidation of a unified Germany, which in limited wars had defeated first Austria (1866) and then

France (1870). Paris and Vienna, hitherto foci of the European balance, yielded precedence to Berlin. A united Italy under Piedmontese leadership entered the balance. Britain withdrew from an active presence in Europe with the death of Palmerston and the triumph of Cobdenite ideology in foreign affairs. British liberals looked to free trade to maintain peace and Conservatives' preoccupations lay overseas rather than in Europe. Both agreed to a benign neglect of the European balance of power.

That balance was not ended following 1870 but was transformed. A number of powers still remained effectively in the European system, sufficiently equal in strength that no one could dominate the others. (Bismarck, after his success over France, proclaimed Germany a satisfied power, thenceforth intent on maintaining the balance, not suppressing it.) However, from the 1870s there began a new phase of alliance building that by the 1890s, had led to a polarization of Europe between the Triple Alliance (Germany, Austria, and Italy) on the one side and a Franco-Russian alliance on the other. When Britain reentered the European political system after 1900, it was as a member of the alliance with France and Russia. The balance of power had by then come to an end.[2]

The rising power of Germany in Europe and relative decline of Britain and France were items in a larger agenda. Europe's world dominance was in relative decline as non-European powers claimed status in world politics. The United States emerged from its Civil War as a power that by the end of the century would stake out claims in the Pacific and in World War I decide the outcome in Europe. The Meiji restoration made Japan into a new power that was brought into the world system by the Anglo-Japanese alliance of 1902. Japan then proved its status by the dramatic defeat of Russia in 1904–5.

Sensing that a shift was taking place from a European to a world political system, Germany, flush with new preeminence in Europe, sought to gain the status of world power. In this ambition, Germany was encouraged by Britain's disengagement from European politics and by the emergence of the new non-European powers, foreshadowing a dispersion of power at the global level. Germany's bid took the form of a direct naval challenge to Britain, the building of a fleet that could seek a decision in the North Sea, and thereby open Germany's way to the world overseas. This action convinced Britain that Germany had become its number-one enemy and that the full resources of diplomacy and military strength should be directed to circumscribing that challenge.[3] Britain accordingly came to terms with Russia, removing from contention Anglo-Russian imperial rivalry in Asia; entered into alliance with France; and strengthened bonds with the United States. It took two world wars finally to defeat the German thrust to world-power status before the world political system once again, after 1945, became restabilized in a new configuration.

The logic of interstate power relations was but the outer skin of the onion. The underlayers explained the rupture in world politics—the end of the European balance of power and of British world hegemony, and the shift from a European to a world system in which neither balance of power nor hegemony could be reestablished. First of these underlayers was the continuing and uneven spread of industrialization. Industry was the basis of military and naval power. Britain's lead had been overtaken by Germany and the United States. France had developed more slowly. Japan began a drive to industrialize after Commodore Perry's squadron in Tokyo Bay had demonstrated Japan's vulnerability to western intervention. The relative pace of industrialization in different countries determined their military-political potential. Weapons costs, reflecting new technologies, became so expensive that only the front cluster of runners in the industrialization race could afford power status, and positions within this cluster were likely to change as the race went on. Britain's launching of the *Dreadnought* in 1906 gave the Royal Navy an instantaneous advantage over the German fleet, but it also, by rendering virtually obsolete all warships built before 1905, wiped out Britain's long-term lead and gave Germany, with its up-to-date industrial capacity, the opportunity to compete on a more nearly equal basis. Steel production was the best single indicator of industrial power, and hence, of military potential. By 1893 Germany had passed Britain in steel production. As early as 1890, the United States had already taken first place. The monopolistic position of Britain in industrial power during the midcentury period gave place at the end of the century to a competition of industrial powers among which Britain was in many ways the least dynamic.[4]

This competition for power required states to promote their own industrial bases. Two consequences for state policy directly followed: a revival of protectionism and an expansionary thrust for markets and colonies. Protectionism can be looked at from two perspectives. In one, it is the result of pressures from particular interests to use the state for their own benefit. It has been argued that landed interests identified with old-regime aristocracies led the revival of protectionism in the late decades of the nineteenth century.[5] At the same time, the owners of emergent industries challenging British dominance, together with workers in these industries, supported protectionism. In another perspective, states concerned both with enhancement of their own military strength and with the need to bond the social classes of a growingly complex society into loyalty to state goals perceived protectionism as an instrument to these ends. The French return to protectionism seemed to conform to the first perspective. French economic interests had resented Napoleon III's move to free trade, an initiative by the state intended as a stimulus to efficiency and modernization. These interest-group pressures gained their ends in the Méline tariff of 1892. In Germany, the second perspective had doctrinal legitimacy from Friedrich List and the Historical School in the notion of the state's responsibility to orchestrate an organic development of state, economy, and society.[6] In Japan too, the state supervised the development of industry while protecting the homeland against foreign economic penetration. Even in Britain, free trade doctrine was challenged when Joseph Chamberlain launched his protectionist program in 1885, though it was not until World War I that import duties, and subsequently, imperial preferences became state policy. The British state, close to the financial interests of the City, retained a lingering allegiance to the liberal economic policies of its hegemonic past. Britain's rivals had no such inhibitions.

A complex of factors encouraged the overseas expansionism of the "new imperialism" in the last two decades of the nineteenth century. Prominent among these was state concern to safeguard industrial growth. Domestic markets were alone insufficient to absorb the products of national industries. Raw materials had to be procured abroad. Outlets for surplus capital were sought. Industrial growth was necessary to sustain the fighting capabilities of states. Naval bases were required to give those capabilities global reach. In actual fact, colonial acquisitions of the late nineteenth century did not bring notable economic benefits. The principal states, not their respective colonies, remained each other's best customers. Nevertheless, the incentive to expand was irresistible. It was rationalized and publicized by ideological forces—Christian proselytizing, *la mission civilisatrice*, and racial supremacy doctrines.

All the major powers, the United States and Japan, as well as Britain and the European powers, joined in. From 1871 to 1914 there was peace in Europe, but rivalry shifted to Africa, the Far East, and the Pacific. The greatly augmented hiatus in power between the new industrially based states and the nonindustrial world beyond invited domination over the latter, and the perception that the frontier of preindustrial lands was closing, that a finite area remained to be brought under the control of the industrial states, incited preemptive action to secure even zones of marginal economic or military interest. The western European powers partitioned what was left of Africa during the 1880s and 1890s. China's weakness and supposedly vast internal market beckoned, and only the presence in the region of other rivals—Russia, Japan, and the United States—preserved that country from a similar fate.

Peeling off yet another layer of the onion, industrialization had brought about major changes in the structure of societies that had consequences for the nature of the state. During these years, the balance shifted from rural to urban society in the industry-based powers. Between 1870 and 1900, the population of Europe doubled, increasing by one hundred million. During the same period forty million emigrated, mostly to the Americas. The principal impact of the quantum jump in population was, however, in Europe's urbanization. In the overseas countries of immigration too, population rose fastest in the cities. By 1850, when the liberal form of state was becoming well established, only in Britain was urban population greater than rural, and factory workers remained a minority in the whole population. Paris in 1848 was a city populated mainly by artisans and other self-employed workers. The liberal state ruled over a population in which the old solidarities were being destroyed, releasing individuals and nuclear families for employment by manufacturers. Political protest during this period, though acute—consider the Chartist rebellions in England—could be mastered by state power. When, during the last decades of the century, the majority of the population became concentrated in towns, and when people were brought into durable, compact groups in the factories and in the urban areas where workers lived, political action became more feasible and more threatening to the liberal order. The spread of literacy, the emergence of a popular press, and the formation of mass-based political parties of socialist allegiance enhanced this probability. States now confronted strategically located, cohesive population groups with very explicit social grievances, against whom repression could at most be only a partial response—a phenomenon generally identified as "the labor problem."

The state's predicament was rendered easier to resolve by other tendencies in economic and social organization that simultaneously fragmented and divided the workers. These included the growing concentration of capital (accelerated by the long depression beginning in 1873) and increasing application of science and technology to large-scale industrial organization, which tended to separate workers into established (more educated, more skilled, more permanent) and nonestablished (less educated, less skilled, less steadily employed). The former had the resources to develop the organizations of a new labor movement—trade unions, workers' educational institutions like the mechanics' institutes, cooperatives, and political parties. The latter were less able to articulate their demands in a coherent manner. The state could selectively respond to the established workers by giving them a place in the political system, providing some state support or legitimacy for their organizations, and encouraging them to look to the state for protection. Various measures were steps along this road: the British factory acts, Disraeli's extension of the franchise to include the skilled workers, legal recognition of trade unions, Bismarck's social insurance, and (especially following World War I) immigration restrictions to protect national labor markets.

Symbolic of this restructuring of state-society relations

was Bismarck's initiative to enter into secret discussions with Ferdinand Lassalle, the leader of the principal organization of German workers of the early 1860s. The common ground of the two protagonists was a perception of the state as the shaper of society. Bismarck sought worker support for the military and for territorial aggrandizement by the state in return for state action to improve workers' conditions. Lassalle's responsiveness foreshadowed European labor movements' future behavior, in departing from the appeal made by Marx and Engels in 1848 for the international unification of worker action against states. Bismarck was the first statesman of a major power to use effectively the popular force of nationalism to bridge class antagonisms in common loyalty to the state and its foreign policy goals. The formula was nationalism, protectionism, and welfare. Leaders in other states adopted the same course. The trend of the late nineteenth century was well expressed by Carr: "The socialization of the nation has as its natural corollary the nationalization of socialism."[7]

The merger of nationalism and welfare was in the first instance an initiative from above, a preemptive stroke by state mangers aware of the disruptive potential of the social forces generated by urbanization and industrialism. Marx published the first volume of *Capital* in 1867, but he was by no means unique in perceiving the contradictions of industrial society. Joseph Chamberlain addressed the issue of unemployment in Birmingham and launched an attack on the laissez-faire system in 1886. The Fabian Society was founded in 1884. In England as in Germany the first initiatives came from above. In Germany, these social policy initiatives proved for a time sufficient to enable Bismarck to suppress the socialists. In Britain, worker franchise, enacted in 1867, made little distinctive impact on the political system until the end of the century. In addition to measures of social protection for workers, the social dimensions of imperialism may have retarded the independent articulation of worker demands—as one German scholar has expressed it "diverting attention away from the question of emancipation at home towards compensatory successes abroad."[8]

Nevertheless, past the turn of the century, the pressure for welfare began to well up from below through the political participation of workers. During the years before 1914 the germ of the modern welfare state was visibly at work. The Liberal party victory in Britain in 1906 inaugurated a series of social reforms and was accompanied by the first appearance of a significant number of Labour Party members of parliament. In the United States, the successes of the Progressives in federal and state elections marked an interlude of concern with social policy in the Hobbesian social struggle for economic survival and aggrandizement. In Germany, the Social Democrats scored a major victory in the elections of 1912, becoming the largest single party, though short of a majority in the Reichstag. World War I mobilized all social forces behind the nation-state, and in so doing reaffirmed, in a context of enlarged political participation, the supremacy of the Bismarckian union of nationalism and welfare over class conflict.[9]

Beneath this process of sociopolitical restructuring manifested in all the industrial powers, yet another and deeper layer of reality has been revealed through the study of long waves in economic history. The long depression from 1873 to 1896 marked the end of one such long wave. Many small businesses failed, and capital became more concentrated in large concerns. The depression was the threshold between competitive and monopoly capitalism. The nineteenth century had been a period of more or less steadily declining prices, punctuated by a few sharp hesitations or reversals, as the productivity gains of the first industrial revolution affected a widening range of commodities, initially in manufacturing, then, after a revolution in international transportation and agricultural machinery, in food production. By the late decades of the century, the last returns were being wrung out of the industrial innovations put in place during the first industrial revolution. This was a principal explanation for the relative decline of Britain, the power that had the most extensive stock of obsolescent means of production, in terms both of installed physical plant and of the capacity to generate knowledge and attitudes conducive to future growth.

The years from 1896 onward saw the start of a new wave. The technology of a second industrial revolution had been pioneered and was ready for expanded application—the technology of steel, electricity, organic chemistry and synthetics, and the internal combustion engine. An investment boom in the new industrial processes was facilitated by an increase in the money supply from the boom in gold mining at the end of the century. The trend in prices reversed and inflationary pressures appeared. World War I gave further impetus to industrial growth.[10]

The weakness of most theorizing about long waves has been the economic determinism it tends to assume. Human trajectories are reduced to histories of technology and prices, explained by the occurrence of clusters of technological innovations, which themselves remain unexplained. It is more consistent with the approach of this book to posit a social dimension to the invention and selection of technologies. Technologies are means of solving social problems of production. Those who have the most social power can determine which problems merit solution and which of the available means are most appropriate to their interests.

Following this line of reasoning, the widespread application of a cluster of new technologies at the beginning of a long wave would be preceded by the putting into place of social relations capable of exploiting these technologies, or what a U.S. scholar has called a new "social structure of accumulation."[11] The installation of such a new social order of production would come about as the outcome of struggle among social forces. It would be conditioned by existing power positions but not entirely predictable or determined. The turning points in history are thus not to be explained by the impersonal movements of prices or sequences of technological applications but rather in terms of the changes in social relations that make these possible.

Such a restructuring of social relations in production was undertaken under the aegis of capital in large-scale industry during the 1880s and 1890s in the more advanced industrial countries. At the point of production, the most important change was a transition from the workshop to the assembly line. It completely changed the nature of work, the qualifications required of workers, and the method of control over the work process and led, in the longer run, to new modes of organization and political behavior of workers. In the larger context of society, these changes brought about a concentration of capital into large firms capable of innovating new technologies, a growing distinction between monopoly and competitive sectors of capital, and a change in the relationship between state and capital, the state playing an increasing role in the new social structure of accumulation. The growth in the state's role was not steady and continuous. It moved by fits and starts, in one area and then another, under pressure of events moving forward on a broad front, then for a time in repose or retreat. World War I precipitated a rapid advance; the postwar years, relaxed effort or withdrawal; the depression years, rearmament and World War II, a new thrust forward.

The work of Frederick William Taylor at the Bethlehem Steel Company in the 1880s is symbolic of the changes introduced by management in the organization of production. The pattern affected, however, all the industrial societies.[12] Its essence was to take the control and pacing of work out of the hands of skilled workers, to fragment work into a number of simple operations that could be performed by unskilled persons, and to recombine these fragments into a process controlled and paced by machines. As profit margins narrowed in the late stages of the industrial cycle, management had a strong incentive both to compress labor costs in production and to minimize labor's control in the production process. Taylorism (in the broad sense in which that term has come to be used)[13] achieved both goals. It was a clear case of technology designed and used as an instrument of social struggle—one that greatly strengthened management's power over labor and thereby set the stage for a new expansion of investment.

The new workers of mass production industries—called "semiskilled" or in French *ouvriers specialisés* (O.S.) because they could be trained for their jobs in anything from a few hours to a few weeks—were a different breed from the old skilled workers. They came in the new demographic wave, uprooted from rural society or from foreign lands. They did not suffer a degradation of trade skills or loss of autonomy to their craft organizations, as the skilled workers had. Their strength lay in their numbers, which gave them leverage on governments insofar as they could act collectively. They learned also that if individually or in small groups they could make no impact on the machine-regulated production process, collectively they could bring it to a halt. The new work process encouraged mass-based

industrial unions that would enter the political process to influence governments and legislatures. The new unionism appeared
in Britain and western Europe before World War I; it appeared
first in North America in the general labor movements of the
1880s and early twentieth century but acquired durable organizational strength there only through the industrial union movement of the 1930s.[14]

The state had little directly to do with the restructuring of
social relations at the point of production. Mass production with
semiskilled workers was an innovation of capital. The state's
support of this phase of restructuring was indirect, through its
encouragement of investments in industries that would enhance
national power. Soon, however, the state had to confront the
social and political consequences of this restructuring at the point
of production. In Britain and western Europe, the confrontation
began in the years before World War I as mass-based political
parties and mass-based unions first pressed their demands upon
the political system. World War I enabled governments to re-
channel these popular pressures into conflicting national causes.
States acquired experience in coordinating industrial production
for their war efforts; at the same time they had to take account of
worker requirements in order to retain loyalty. The state had to
offer the goal of a postwar world to which workers could join
their hopes. Out of this experience came two related projects:
national economic planning, or state capitalism, and corporatism,
or the alignment of worker with employer interests in harmo-
nized state policy. These two projects joined with a third, the
social protection initiated by western states from the 1880s, to
become the interrelated features of a new welfare-nationalist form
of state, a compound of nationalism, social security, planning,
and corporatism.

Tripartism was the form corporatism took in the evolved
industrial states of western Europe. It was a development out of
the bipartite production relations that had grown up under the
liberal state when the state gave legal recognition of the right to
organize trade unions and for unions to bargain collectively with
employers. Tripartism gave an institutional shape to the state's
recognition of its own stake in the regulation of industrial conflict

and in the outcomes of negotiations. It also implied a recognition that the state would need the collaboration of both unions and employers in order to define and attain policy goals.

Tripartism at its origins, and even in its fullest development, covered no more than a part of national production; it covered only workers in large-scale industry. Even in the leading industrial countries on the eve of World War I—on the eve, that is, of the first experiments with corporatist organization on a national scale—large-scale industry employed fewer workers than small-scale enterprises of the family-firm type whose social relations were in the enterprise-labor-market mode. Agriculture occupied a substantial proportion of producers in western Europe (though relatively fewer in Britain). Self-employed shopkeepers and artisans were numerous, as were employees in commerce and administration. Domestic household production accounted for a much larger range of goods and services than is the case in the same countries in the late twentieth century. Nevertheless, though the tripartite sector covered but a relatively small portion of the total productive effort of society, it covered that portion most vital to the state. The state could safely leave the other modes of social relations of production to their own devices; it seemed compelled to try to guide social relations in the leading sector.

The countries that rivaled Britain in the second industrial revolution, in the new long wave that began at the turn of the century, shared many of the characteristics of the ideal-type welfare-nationalist state. For these, the reputed advantages of backwardness proved real.[15] They were able to invest in the latest technologies and to begin the new international competition on conditions more nearly equal than prevailed when Britain led the first industrial revolution. They all experimented with various forms of tripartite corporatism.

Other countries lagged behind. To remain without a strong industrial base, however, not only implied an acceptance of lower standards of national material well-being; it also meant exposure to the threat of foreign intervention and control. The condition of the interstate system heightened state security concerns. The liberal state, in its basic political-economic (not political-constitutional) form, was sustained by the hegemonic liberal world order. Interventions could, where necessary, ensure observance of the rules of that order. The dispersion of power and absence of rules in the era of rival imperialisms precluded any such conformity. Both the attempted restoration of liberal order through the League of Nations and the attempted foreign interventions to subvert the Bolshevik Revolution in Russia failed. States had more freedom of internal management in a more anarchic system, provided they were able to muster sufficient internal strength in their economies and in their public's sentiments.[16]

In this world context, two alternatives to the tripartite corporatism of the welfare-nationalist state were mapped out by states whose industry lagged behind the new leaders. Bolshevik power gave birth to central planning, a mode of organizing non-capitalist redistributive development. Fascism, first in Italy, later in other countries of southern Europe and beyond, offered in state corporatism a "catch-up" model of capitalist development. These alternative models were perceived as ways to accelerate industrialization, to preserve a country's independence, and to raise its power status in an unstable and potentially threatening world system.

The era of rival imperialisms divides into three phases. From the 1870s to the 1890s, the power structure, practices, ideology, and institutions of the liberal era became weaker, challenged not by a coherent alternative world order so much as by similar but conflicting national ambitions. In forsaking world order, state leaders focused on bridging the chasm of class antagonism to consolidate loyalties to the national order; hence, the beginning of a transformation from above in the construction of social and welfare policy. From 1900 through World War I, forces at the base of society became more articulate; the initiative in social policy was no longer from above but now from below; the state succeeded through wartime mobilization in reconciling the new pressures with national unity behind state goals. From 1919 to 1945 came a phase of building new historic blocs as the foundations for quite different developmental trajectories with tripartism, state corporatism, and central planning as their principal modes of social relations of production.

The different forms of state and of production relations

they spawned emerged in reaction both to developments within societies (urbanization and the new social structure of accumulation) and to the transformation of the interstate system (demise of hegemony and of the balance of power in the confrontation of rival imperial ambitions). In this reshaping of social institutions and practices, the preeminent role of the state and the forcing ground of war cannot be denied. This is proclaimed as obvious in the histories of Bolshevism and fascism. Democratic constitutionalism may be less disposed to accord preeminence to the same forces. Nevertheless, reflecting on the end of this era in World War II, the British *Civil History of the War* stated:

> There existed, so to speak, an implied contract between Government and people; the people refused none of the sacrifices that the Government demanded from them for the winning of the war; in return, they expected that the Government should show imagination and seriousness in preparing for the restoration and improvement of the nation's well-being when the war had been won.[17]

This restates Bismarck's strategy in mid-twentieth-century terms. The contract now extended beyond state-guaranteed social security to include state involvement in production relations and in the maintenance of economic growth.

## THE WELFARE-NATIONALIST STATE

As for the liberal state, two distinct approaches can help toward understanding the nature of the welfare-nationalist form of state, one a functional modeling of its different aspects, the other a genetic explanation in terms of the struggle of social forces that gradually produced this form of state.

The term *welfare state* did not come into common use until after World War II, even though elements in its composition had been apparent since the late nineteenth century.[18] To my knowledge, the term *welfare nationalist state* has not been used hitherto and serves here to characterize a historical structure that can be recognized even if it has not yet acquired a conventional name. The welfare-nationalist state was not built according to a comprehensive plan. It was built step by step in reaction to a sequence of events. In different countries, variations in aspects of this general form are attributable to national cultures, traditions, institutions, and political and social practices.

The necessary point of departure is to recognize that the welfare-nationalist state was a transformation of the liberal state in which the essence of the liberal state as guardian of the market and of the principle of private (or nonstate) property in the means of production was preserved.

However, the state supplemented the market-sustaining functions of the liberal state with new functions intended to compensate for the negative effects of the market on significant numbers of citizens. Unemployment, occupational injury, extended sickness, and old age were recognized by the state as social contingencies that the free play of the market would leave many people unable to cope with on their own. Some citizens, the incapacitated and handicapped, might never have the opportunity to participate fully in market-regulated activity so as to support themselves. In time, purely market-oriented activity came to be recognized as having some negative effects for the whole of society such as excessive atmospheric pollution and depletion of natural resources. In all of these respects, functions were attributed to the state for the protection of individual citizens and of the whole of society.

Recognition of social contingencies implied an abandonment of that element of liberal ideology which attributed social distress to personal failings. These afflictions were now perceived as resulting from impersonal economic processes. Unemployment was produced by the industrial process itself, not by the indolence of individuals.[19]

Step by step with the building of welfare-nationalist-state institutions went an increasingly profound knowledge of economic and social processes and a search for ways in which the state could influence or control these processes. The observation that there were regular recurrent cycles in economic activity, phases of investment and labor absorption followed by phases of stagnation and unemployment, led to speculation about the causes of these cycles and thus to the identification of remedies through which the state could act to moderate or counter these cycles. Concern to correct the market's social defects thus moved toward a project for regulating the market itself, for making the state into the market's tutor while at the same time preserving the market's preeminence in the economy.

Of all social contingencies, none has greater consequence for the mass of citizens than unemployment or the threat of unemployment. No factor has been more central to the design and development of the welfare-nationalist state. Understanding of the various causes and types of unemployment came slowly over time. Joseph Chamberlain, politically rooted in the industrialist class of Birmingham, recognized unemployment as a social problem (rather than an individual failing) during the depression of the mid-1880s and proposed municipal works as a means of tiding over honest workmen who had been affected. Such a measure tended, however, in practice to help seasonal or casual laborers who had never had regular employment rather than those for whom Chamberlain had intended it. The British Unemployed Workmen Act of 1905 still conceived the cure for unemployment as temporary relief works.[20] Inadequate as was the prescription, the act did cross an ideological threshold by implicitly recognizing the right of a man to expect work and the obligation of the state to try to ensure that he got it. Still, the means of achieving a satisfactory level of employment was not well understood. William Beveridge, in his 1909 report, took a forward step by distinguishing underemployment from unemployment (the former endemic, the latter cyclical) and recommended a complex of measures, including public works, labor exchanges, and a higher school-leaving age, combined with industrial training, as measures to deal with these different kinds of unutilized working capacity.

During the interwar period, when unemployment remained an intractable problem, a further aspect began to be understood. One part of British society (in the midlands and south) was relatively prosperous with new expanding industries, while another part (the north and Wales) remained depressed amid declining industries. Long-term structural unemployment required remedies different from those for cyclical unemployment resulting from fluctuating demand. The depression of the 1930s stimulated analysis of the phenomenon of mass unemployment. Keynes' *General Theory of Employment, Interest and Money*, published in 1936, focused attention on the need to maintain high levels of investment and of aggregate demand in order to have full employment.[21] States could do this, Keynes' analysis suggested, by direct investment in public works and by transferring money from the rich to the poor, who were more likely to spend it than to save it. Social programs could thus be seen not merely as measures of compensation for the ill-effects of impersonal economic forces, but as built-in stabilizers for the economy, which, in times of economic regression, would raise the level of demand and restimulate growth. It remained only to discover once again in the late 1930s the most effective corrective to a sluggish economy: preparations for war and war itself.

The central issue of unemployment, the most politically dangerous of social contingencies, thus provides a thread connecting all the major innovations of the welfare-nationalist state: social insurance, relief works, public investment and the creation of a state sector in the economy, the organization of the labor market through employment services and other agencies, the expansion of education and the linking of education and training to employment, measures to protect and/or aid in the transformation of declining industries, measures for the development of depressed regions, and still others. All of these measures impinge upon one another in their effects; their use requires coordination, in other words, planning.[22] Planning in the welfare-nationalist state meant that the state attempted to reconcile and make compatible its goals of economic policy—to make some determination, for example, of the acceptable mix of unemployment, inflation, and balance-of-payments deficit and to select a mix of instruments appropriate to this determination. The fact that both the desirability of goals and the acceptability of policy instruments were swayed by political pressures did not diminish the necessity for planning. They only underlined that planning is never simply a matter of rational choice; it is rational choice superimposed upon bargaining among interests. Of course, the ideological heritage of liberalism inhibited many politicians from using the name "planning" for this activity of the state. The activity often went unnamed or else described by some euphemism (like "medium-term programming" or "conjunctural policy"), but was nonetheless present. Planning came about not by design but as practical necessity.

There is a functional relationship between economic nationalism and market-correcting planning. National planning requires control over economic effects originating abroad and thus to a degree either the defensive isolation of national economic space or aggressive external expansionism. The latter extends the national economy's access to foreign resources while ensuring that the countries providing these resources are brought within the orbit of the national economic plan either as colonial appendages or as client states. The promotion of social welfare, which is the legitimating function served by economic planning, in this way became implicated in economic nationalism and imperial expansionism.[23]

There were, however, practical limitations to the planning of welfare-nationalist states. The state retained the liberal notion of the market as the basic determinant of the economy. In the long run, the market would determine what was to be produced. The state's role in planning was to correct some politically and socially disastrous consequences of the market, while continuing to acknowledge the preeminent role of the market in capitalist development. Reinforcing this functional principle of the welfare-nationalist state's relationship to the economy was the practical political fact that democratically elected governments cannot plan beyond their term of office and the organizational fact that administrative implementation of policies is modified in practice by pressure of clients served or regulated by bureaucratic entities. The state reacted to the market; it neither replaced the market nor subordinated the market to politically determined goals.

With this essential qualification, the state's role in the economy was considerable. It made a major investment in the material infrastructure of transport and communications. It made even greater investment in human resources—in health and housing and in education. The right to a basic standard of physical well-being and the right to learn, i.e., to equal opportunity, became recognized principles of the state. One of the principal advantages that the late-nineteenth-century newcomers to the industrialization race—Germany, the United States, and Japan—

had over Britain was the rapidity with which they built merito-cratic, scientifically oriented higher educational systems upon a base of universal literacy.[24] Furthermore, states contributed heav-ily to the growth of knowledge with industrial applications through funding research and development. National security considerations were the main stimulant here, but radar and elec-tronics, nuclear energy, and space research had civilian industrial spinoffs. States also set up labor exchanges and other services for the management of manpower. In all these ways, states contrib-uted to the development of the productive forces of societies by making investments that market rationality alone would have neglected.

The state's role in accumulation extended beyond these services. Tariffs and subsidies were time-honored methods of state aid to private accumulation, but many states now acquired direct ownership of substantial segments of national economies. The expansion of the state sector was more haphazard than pre-meditated.[25] Frequently it happened as the ultimate means to save an unprofitable industry, especially if this could be justified on national-interest or national-security grounds, and to protect the jobs of its employees. In some cases, expropriations were the political consequence of war, e.g., as in the Austrian state's ac-quisition of former German industries and industries taken over by Soviet occupation, or the acquisition of Renault by the French state. In a few cases, states have invested more deliberately in advanced technology in order to establish a position in the na-tional interest. Whatever the historical explanation for the growth of the state sector, it has taken a place alongside monopolistic and competitive sectors.

This threefold division of monopoly, competitive, and state sectors gave the welfare-nationalist state leverage to promote the organization of the economy. State and market are coordi-nated by consensus, not by authority. The state provokes and distills consensus among the most powerful groups (industry and trade unions) because their acquiescence is necessary to the im-plementation of policy. If they must acquiesce in order that pol-icies be carried out, they must also be consulted and participate in some way in the formulation of these same policies.[26] The existence of a large state sector, combined with the economic

expertise available to the state and the administrative and enforcement services of the state, give the leverage necessary to set
the consensus-seeking process in motion. Despite constitution-
ally enshrined principles of territorial representation and parliamentary or legislative decision making, welfare-nationalist states
moved gradually in the direction of functional representation
and corporatist decision making as regards those aspects of policy
most closely related to production. Corporatism was expressed
through a variety of institutional experiments and practices, all
having tripartism as their common feature.

Ideological consensus is a necessary underpinning for corporatism. A certain tension of conflicting interests is inherent in
the postliberal pluralism of the welfare-nationalist state, but for
corporatism to work this tension must be containable within a
commitment to seek a modus vivendi among the rival interests.
Conflict has to be thought of in terms of the division of shares
and of distributing obligations and responsibilities and not as a
matter of fundamental antagonism. This desirability of finding
ground for agreement arises in a context of constraints imposed
by alien and impersonal forces: on the one hand, the external
constraints of the world economy; on the other, the internal
constraints of inflation, employment levels, rates of profit and
propensity to invest when these are thought of as the outcome of
impersonal economic laws. The assumption is that the parties to
corporatist decision making perceive these forces in more or less
the same way. They accept the rationality of the market and the
laws of economics derived from it as part of the natural order.
Nationalism brings them to coalesce in dealing with the external
forces, and hegemonic economics is their basis for consensus in
dealing with the internal constraints.

Public education, which in one aspect is an investment in
raising the level of productive forces, in another aspect is an
investment in conformism. One function of education is to
heighten the critical faculty, but this affects a relative few. For
the majority, public education creates a basis for acceptance of
the established social order as a technically complex system
intelligible to officially certified specialists. This disposition is
reinforced by other agencies forming opinion—the press, radio
and television, and advertising. Cumulatively, these influences

generate a picture of public policy as a problem in engineering, a problem of technical means, not one of moral choice. It is assumed that there are no fundamental issues concerning the nature of the state. What the state has to do is determined by impersonal forces to which an agreed-upon rational response is possible. The state's task is not perceived as involving a conflict between alternative visions of the future. Alternative societies are deemed to be "unrealistic." Politics therefore becomes management and is depoliticized. Party conflict is over the choice of the best team of managers, all of the contenders being likely to carry out the same set of rationally dictated policies. Corporatism in its origins was a challenge to the ideologies of both liberal self-regulating market and Marxist class struggle—an ideological alternative. Corporatism triumphant, through its depoliticization of the state, mystified its ideological character as pragmatism and technical problem solving.[27]

The welfare-nationalist state carried through a fiscal revolution. In Britain, total expenditures by all levels of the state in 1905, represented less than 10 percent of GNP. In 1959, this had risen to somewhat less than 30 percent.[28] State expenditures were playing a major redistributive role. This redistribution was not uniformly in a rich-to-poor direction. Private corporations benefited considerably by subsidies and state purchasing. Professor Titmuss has demonstrated that the redistributive consequences of social services can benefit the bureaucracies of these services more than those who are to be served.[29] Redistribution through the welfare-nationalist state reflects the relative political power of the major organized interests—the military-industrial complex, the trade union movement, the welfare bureaucracies, and private insurance—and the state's need for legitimacy in being seen to respond to the problems of influential groups.

Alongside this redistribution through the state budget, corporate welfare schemes burgeoned. Ranging from stock options for senior employees to fringe benefits negotiated by trade unions, corporate welfare strengthened corporatism among the top third of society who participated in it. Enterprise corporatism symbiotically related the most favored in production relations to the larger group covered by tripartism. The material interests and loyalties of these people were focused on the corporations and trade unions that secured these benefits, and the state encouraged the process by exempting contributions to corporate welfare from taxation. Thus the welfare-nationalist state tended to develop a two-tier structure—a relatively privileged corporate welfare system supported by the state for the top level and a basic social security administered by the state for the rest.

The growth in the volume of state expenditures and correspondingly in taxation meant that the old division in society between those who paid taxes and received directly no benefits and those who received public assistance but paid no taxes was very largely eliminated. In its fully developed form, most citizens paid some taxes to the state and most participated in some direct benefits, though in different ways and to different degrees. State budgets in becoming larger also became more rigid and difficult to modify, because entitlement to benefits was fixed by legislation, and contracts with private corporations, e.g., for the delivery of arms systems, were large and of long duration. In a period of economic growth, state revenues would rise sufficiently to carry the state's financial obligations, but in a period of prolonged stagnation or declining growth, the state's payment obligations would increase while its revenues decreased. The welfare-nationalist state was constructed to revive or sustain growth in a market-led economy. Fiscal crisis would in turn be compounded by rigidities obstructing readjustment of production. As social benefits increased the proportion of the individual worker's income received from the "citizen wage," i.e., the total of benefits received as of right through legislative entitlement, in relation to the employment wage, the "reserve army" effect of higher unemployment was reduced. The liberal method of readjustment by lowering wage levels and facilitating reorganization of the labor process was thus hindered. Prolonged recession would test corporatism's ability to find alternative means of reviving industrial activity.

The functional coherence of the welfare-nationalist form of state is perceptible only as the outcome of a long period of development. To present the state in this way conveys an illusion of teleology—either a teleology of conscious purpose, the gradual construction of a preconceived plan, or the teleology of an unconscious historical determinism. Neither can be justified. The welfare-nationalist state was the outcome of struggle among social forces in the course of which new historic blocs took shape. The histories of Britain and Germany illustrate the process.

The first measures of social protection taken in the late decades of the nineteenth century were initiated from above by governments representative of ruling classes continuous from the old regime. These measures responded to a perceived threat from below. The Paris Commune of 1871 made a profound impression on governments all over Europe as the image of what this threat could become: the people in arms engaged in violent overthrow of established order.[30] This unforeseen consequence of the Prussian armies' quick victory over France underscored Bismarck's conviction of the need for a preemptive stroke of policy to give some measure of satisfaction to workers so as to attach their loyalties to the state and to forestall the appeal of socialism. That Bismarck's mind was already alive to the problem was demonstrated by the conversations he had initiated with Lasalle as early as 1863. Concrete measures of social insurance were not enacted in Germany for another decade, but the rulers' minds were already fully alerted to the problem.

In Britain, revolt on the scale of the Paris Commune appeared somewhat less threatening. In 1867 the franchise had been extended so as in practice to bring skilled workers into participation in the electoral process. The decision was analogous to the inclusion of the middle classes in 1832, an expression of confidence on the part of the ruling groups that these workers were now secure against revolutionary temptations.[31] The 1880s were, however, troubled times in British society. Output dropped in the depression and labor disputes increased. In 1885 there were riots in London and some of the provincial towns. Birmingham was particularly hard hit, and Joseph Chamberlain, a leading figure among the industrialists of that city, articulated a new, radical program. In the years that followed, Chamberlain came to represent the tendencies making for the welfare-nationalist state—a combination of imperialism, protectionism, and social reform. He led a breakaway from the Liberal Party that linked up with the Disraelian tradition of social reform in the Tory party. Chamberlain's impact on policy was profound, even though he was never able to break through the class barrier of

Tory aristocratic governance to achieve the status of first minister. Bismarck and German policy were strong influences in his thinking at a time when German models were shaping thought in Britain over a wide range.

As mayor of Birmingham, Joseph Chamberlain came forward with measures to counteract the unemployment of the mid-1880s; he also undertook slum clearance and workers' housing construction. In Parliament, he was successful in securing a workman's compensation law in 1897. He raised the issue of old-age pensions, inspired by the German old-age insurance law of 1889, though the enactment of this measure was deferred by his imperialist commitment to Britain's involvement in the Boer war. Chamberlain's social-policy initiatives were, in the paradoxes of politics, brought to fruition by the Liberal government that took office in 1905, culminating in the old-age pension act of 1908 and national health insurance act of 1911.[32]

Just as Germany, during these years, was striving to overtake Britain in naval construction, so Britain was attempting to catch up with Germany in social protection. Welfare and warfare were the twin dominant concerns of the state in both countries, and both concerns were structurally linked in the evolving *raison d'état* of the ruling groups with the existence of a labor problem.

The manner in which that problem was manifested among the working classes differed in the two countries. It is probable that the failure of bourgeois revolution in early nineteenth-century Germany left the way open for social democracy to combine the demands for political and social rights into a single opposition movement. The concern of the ruling groups to forestall this opposition could explain why the construction of the welfare state began earlier in Germany than in Britain despite the latter's much longer industrial history. In Britain, political rights were extended gradually to workers, but a political labor movement was slower to develop and did not become the real parliamentary opposition until World War I. Reform initiatives sprang from the minds of perceptive ruling-class politicians and were shaped by the researches and writings of civil servants and of reformers like William Booth, Seebohm Rowntree, Charles Booth, Sidney and Beatrice Webb, William Beveridge, and the Fabian Society. The phrase "We are all socialists now," attributed to the Liberal politician Sir William Harcourt in 1889, stands as a reflection of the consciousness of at least those members of the ruling class most sensitive to the labor problem. It can be juxtaposed to the lament of the upper class Fabian reformers in 1896: "The difficulty in England is not to get more power for the people, but to persuade them to make use of the political power they have."[33]

Although hardly visible at all at the national parliamentary level, working class participation in the administration of welfare had begun at the level of local governments, where, since the urban franchise of 1867 and rural franchise of 1884, workers had been elected to county and borough councils. This experience gained by worker representatives at the level of government closest to the reality of welfare problems would be important for the future development of the welfare system. However, in Britain at the turn of the century, as in Germany, welfare measures were enacted for the workers, not by them.[34]

In France and the United States, state intervention in the social policy field was less in evidence. Alone among the European states, France was ruled by a nonaristocratic class. A petty bourgeois political class manned the apparatus of the state and political parties, leaving the grande bourgeoisie of finance and industry their economic freedom. The electoral predominance of the rural small holders and urban artisans and petty bourgeoisie precluded the expression of a strong socialist movement, and the labor movement, rooted in craft traditions, espoused an antipolitical syndicalism that rejected the state instead of seeking to use it. The issues of the time were ones of political ideology rather than welfare. When some social measures were initiated through the participation of the socialist Alexander Millerand in the Waldeck-Rousseau government in 1899, these were criticized by other socialists.

The other major country to have had no aristocratic governing class was the United States. Here the progressive movement of the first twentieth-century decade gave vent to an appeal for state intervention in the economy. Such intervention was, however, conceived as regulation of economic agents so as to equalize conditions for strong and weak in the marketplace, not as compensation for the socially undesirable effects of the market. Antitrust and monopolies regulation epitomized the progressives' approach, but no state of the union established unemployment insurance until the Wisconsin measure of 1932, and social security came on the political agenda only with the New Deal.

During the years before World War I, the working classes in Britain and Germany ceased to be purely latent forces whose autonomous action ruling groups tried to forestall by preemptive reform. They became active, organized social forces capable of changing existing political structures. In Germany, this transformation took effect through the rising strength of the Social Democratic Party, which gave a firm organizational, political, and cultural identity to the working class and its affiliated social groups. In Britain, the transformation was less firmly anchored in a single organization, more diffuse; it found expression partly in the growing strength of the Labour Party, but most of all in a worker movement that challenged both capital and the existing trade union leadership on the industrial front. The great strike wave of 1911 began in the seaports among unorganized, unskilled workers. The movement radicalized the old centers of union strength—coal, cotton, engineering, shipbuilding, and railways—and spread to hitherto nonunionized industries. It was sparked by the decline in real wages that had followed upon the general rise in prices touched off by the increasing world gold supply, but the majority of strikes were less about wages than over issues connected with the right to organize and conditions of work.

The goals of the movement were hardly precise; it was a welling up of protest, not a strategically planned campaign; yet ideologically it bore a certain resemblance to the syndicalism whose practice had been theorized in France as a direct challenge to the rule of capital within industry. Syndicalism had, however, entered upon its historical moment of contradiction. Looking backward, syndicalism had been the practice of skilled workers, seeking to maximize their own control over the labor process and ultimately to supplant the owners of the means of production so as to create producers' self-government without benefit of the state. Looking forward, the unskilled workers who were taking initiative in the labor movement—workers who had been recruited into industry by capital's restructuring of the labor process through the long depression—would come to seek their salvation through industrial unions and political action directed toward the state. At this historical moment, however, the one certainty was the fact of worker revolt. British industrialists, already conscious of their declining world supremacy, were frightened.[35]

Initially, the war resolved these fears. It generated a nationalist unity transcending class struggles in both Britain and Germany. World War I marked a transition from state interventions in particular aspects of economic activity—with tariffs, subsidies, colonial expansion, and measures of social protection for workers, as instances—to state direction of whole national economies through the mediation of businessmen and with recurrent concern for the loyalty of workers.

Germany took the lead in recognizing that the war would in the last analysis prove to be a struggle of economies and that therefore the economy must be managed and directed by the state toward the priorities of war. In August 1914 a war materials department was set up to coordinate private business under state direction, with the businessman Walter Rathenau at its head. England followed; in May 1915 a ministry of munitions was created, and by 1918 it had become the country's largest employer. (A similar ministry was created about the same time in France with the socialist politician Albert Thomas at its head— a token of concern to consolidate worker backing for the production effort.) Further extension and centralization of economic controls in Britain followed the political crisis of December 1916, when ministries of food and shipping took over all aspects of supply and imports, coordinated within a small war cabinet. The experience of economic planning of these years left a deep impression on many of the participants. Even in the United States, a far less comprehensive experience with war planning left an ideological legacy to the New Deal.[36]

As the war went on, class tensions reappeared. Although in August 1914, the Social Democratic Party representation in the German Reichstag had decided to vote war credits, within a year there existed a vocal antiwar opposition within the party even at a time when German armies seemed to be prevailing in both Russia and France. In 1916, there were serious strikes on the Clyde and in Wales and sporadic disruptions elsewhere, less explicitly directed against the war than signaling workers' alienation from their rulers' sense of national goals. The revolution in Russia aroused panic in the ruling circles of all the belligerents, a fear that their own troops and workers might also prefer peace to the continuing slaughter. During 1917, there were major strikes in Berlin and Leipzig, and, following the Brest-Litovsk *diktat* in January 1918, strikes of German munitions workers, coinciding with Ludendorff's final offensive in France. When the London Metropolitan Police went on strike during the summer of 1918, a rumor spread that the British army was affected.[37]

If the German High Command sought armistice in the autumn of 1918, it was to prevent its army from disintegrating as the Russian army had before it, to forestall enemy occupation of Germany, to be able to obstruct Bolshevik revolution in Germany, and to conserve the armed forces as a factor in Germany's uncertain political future. The specter of Bolshevism sweeping through central Europe was equally agitating to the Allied governments. What had happened in Russia and might well happen in central and even western Europe remained a persistent underlying concern of all parties to the Versailles peace negotiations.

The resurgence of class tensions undermining nationalist unity in the belligerent powers was, however, contained. It was contained through a new coalition of social forces, the germ of a new historic bloc, a conflictual tripartite entente of state, industry, and trade union leadership.

In 1917, Labour Party representatives were brought into Britain's coalition government. As the price of participation, the Ministry of Labour was created. In response to the strike wave of the previous year, a committee of Parliament under the chairmanship of J. H. Whitley framed proposals for an organization of industry under Joint Standing Industrial Councils providing equal representation for employers and trade unionists. These councils were to be complemented by works committees, one to each factory. The Whitley Councils proposal sought to meet several concerns. One was for the perpetuation and institutionalization of wartime experience in the settlement of specific industrialization issues—wage rates, working conditions, technological change, etc. In this respect, the Whitley proposals could be seen as a recognition by Parliament of labor's right to collective bargaining—recognition, in effect, that the working class had attained a collective strength sufficient to compel acknowledgment of this right by employers and the state. A broader goal of the Whitley proposals was, however, to found a new structure of production relations upon class collaboration. In this concept, the councils would become a constitutional starting point for industrial governance to be elaborated by future practice.[38]

Whitley councils were set up by mutual agreement in industries with newly organized trade unions. They were shunned by unions in the already strongly organized industries, e.g., mining, railways, and transport. Only a small number of works committees were set up, and these were created by employer initiatives aiming at a worker-employer community in which unions would play a less adversarial role.[39] When, early in 1919, the British government faced the prospect of a paralyzing strike in the key industries, Lloyd George called a National Industrial Conference that attempted to deal both with the material wages and hours issues and with longer term institutional questions. The postwar slump, however, disciplined worker militancy, and the government largely ignored the recommendations of the conference. In 1921, the trade union members resigned.

In Britain, the state took the lead in promoting a corporatist structure for industry. In Germany, the employers took the initiative at a time when the state was disintegrating. In the impending chaos of defeat, industrialists discounted the discredited military and civilian bureaucracies and the inarticulate middle classes as valid allies. Perceptive industrial leaders saw their salvation in alliance with trade union leaders, especially those in heavy industry. There was some objective basis for the alliance in the fact that workers' real wages had grown along with company profits in war production. Both would have a stake in maintaining high exports and both could turn the inflation that had begun with war financing to their benefit. An alliance with the trade unions would give industrialists some leverage with a Social Democratic Party strengthened by Germany's defeat and with Allied Powers endorsing the notion of democratization of erstwhile monarchic-military political structures. The mining industry's Hugo Stinnes negotiated an agreement with Carl Legien of the SPD-affiliated unions to set up a pyramid of joint labor-management arbitration committees known as the *Arbeitsgemeinschaft*. This institution, though set up without state participation, was recognized in the early decree legislation of the revolutionary regime that assumed political power in November 1918.

Parallel with this employer-union initiative was the growth of the works councils movement, i.e., organs of worker representation within particular factories. Such bodies had been recognized as "Worker and Employee Chambers" under a wartime law of 1916. Contrary to the British case, where works councils had been envisaged in the original Whitley proposal but rarely set up as a general practice, in Germany (and also in Italy after the defeat) works councils became a mode of worker representation distinct from trade unions and, in the perception of some union leaders, rivals to the unions.[40]

The increase in working-class strength brought about through the war was thus countered in both Britain and Germany by initiatives from the state in one case and from employers in the other toward a corporative governance of industry. These initiatives were at least partially successful, but they did not in any way meet the demands for economic reorganization to which some elements of the labor and socialist movements were attached. On the one hand were the advocates of guild socialism in England and of the ideas of Karl Korsch in Germany. These had affinities with syndicalist thought and envisaged the self-government of industries by workers organized on a corporative basis—corporatism without capitalists and with the state playing a minimal role. The works councils movement fitted in with this approach. On the other hand were the advocates of a more technocratic state socialism. The terms *socialization* and *nationalization* confused both approaches.

In both countries, the issue of nationalization was decided in the coal industry. The provisional revolutionary government in Germany proclaimed the principle of coal industry socialization at the end of 1918 and set up a committee to examine how to go about it. The proposal that emerged envisaged a supervisory organ on which company directors, workers, consumers, and the state would be represented. Ultimately a compulsory Coal Association was set up on which worker and consumer representation was ineffective and real power rested with the employers. It became little more than officially consecrated cartel.[41]

In Britain, confronted by demands for worker control in the mines, which had been taken over by the state during the war, Lloyd George appointed a royal commission to study the matter. The chairman of the commission, Mr. Justice Sankey, rather unexpectedly sided with the workers and came out for nationalization with worker control. Lloyd George, politically aligned with capital's opposition to nationalization, at first temporized, then proposed an alternative to nationalization in which the industry would be concentrated into large corporations with vaguely empowered joint labor-management conciliation boards. Meanwhile, he tested the solidarity with the miners of other sectors of the labor movement and the degree of commitment of the workers to nationalization. It developed that the miners were not supported by the Trades Union Congress and that the workers were more concerned about the bread-and-butter issue of wage rates that would be paid once the mines reverted from state control to private ownership. (Since 1917, when the mines were unified under state control, all miners were paid on the same rate scale where previously under fragmented private ownership, small marginal mines had paid less than others.) The prospect of a nationwide worker mobilization behind the demand for nationalization had passed.[42]

The corporatist experiments of the late wartime and early postwar periods in Britain and Germany were responses by state and employers to a worker offensive. The offensive was, however, diverse in its objectives—torn between the aims of worker control, nationalization with planning, and immediate material gains—and divided in its leadership. By late 1920 and early 1921 its force was spent and there was very little to show for it. No nationalizations. Few significant gains in material conditions. An increase in unemployment. And the loss by the working classes of the crucial political influence they had possessed in the immediate aftermath of war. In 1920–21, the working classes snatched defeat from the jaws of victory. Thenceforward, they were on the defensive, in retreat. As the working classes weakened, so did the interest of state and employers in corporatism. The Whitley councils all but faded away by 1921.[43] In Germany,

works councils remained as an institutional bridgehead gained
in the offensive, but works councils were not necessarily agencies
of worker control; they could and did just as well become organs
of enterprise corporatism (as those British employers who had
favored them surmised). Yet the corporatist model had entered
into the consciousness of employers, union leaders, and state
officials. It would be revived as state policy in the crises of
depression and war during the 1930s and 1940s when the acquiescence of the working classes had once again to be sought and
obtained.

The corporatist experiments stimulated by World War I
were manifestations of the solidity of European bourgeois society
and of its resiliency in responding to the pressure of social demands unleashed in the postwar demobilization—compounded
in the German case by the collapse of the state. Antonio Gramsci
was later to explain the contrast between the success of revolution
in Russia and its defeat in the West by the differences in the state-
society relationship:

> In Russia the State was everything, civil society was primordial
> and gelatinous; in the West, there was a proper relation between
> State and civil society, and when the State trembled a sturdy
> structure of civil society was at once revealed. The State was
> only an outer ditch, behind where there stood a powerful system
> of fortresses and earthworks: more or less numerous from one
> state to the next, it goes without saying—but this precisely
> necessitated an accurate reconnaissance of each individual
> country.[44]

The war of maneuver, successful in Russia, could not
achieve victory in the West. There a war of position would have
to be fought by the workers to establish their own hegemony in
civil society, creating their own "powerful system of fortresses
and earthworks" before they could durably take control of the
state. The workers lost in the postwar West because the bourgeoisie was hegemonic—it had the effective leadership of the other
classes, including the leading elements of the working class itself.
Corporatism was the bourgeoisie's hegemonic response to the
worker challenge, and it waned as the worker challenge ebbed.

Tripartite corporatism did, however, become institutionalized at the interstate level during the brief moment of corporatist experiment in postwar Europe. In the peace negotiations at Versailles, a British initiative produced the International Labour Organization (ILO), which consecrated tripartism as a world model of industrial organization. The first director of the ILO was Albert Thomas, a French socialist who had been minister of munitions in Clemenceau's wartime government. His appointment was an expression of the same desire on the part of the ruling groups to secure worker collaboration in the conversion to peacetime industry as had given substance to the British proposal for an ILO. One of the first concerns of the British and French leadership in the new ILO was to bring postwar Germany and Austria into the organization, so as to confirm tripartism's status as an acceptable model.[45]

After World War I, the economic primacy of the market reemerged and wartime planning was dismantled. Yet two decades of inflation followed by restabilization, endemic unemployment followed by mass unemployment, and brief recovery followed by stagnation and depression undermined credibility in the ability of the market to satisfy the needs of society. Corporatist literature burgeoned, and economic revisionism reached a pinnacle in Keynes' *General Theory* published in 1936. Such theorizing was more reflective of the demise of liberal hegemony than indicative of the pursuit by states of coherent policy alternatives to liberalism.

More influential than theory were the facts of the post-1929 depression and the *sauve qui peut* international economic environment it generated. States struggled to defend their national economies as best they could with a series of ad hoc measures. In market-led economies, i.e., those industrial powers other than the Soviet Union and Nazi Germany, there were many state interventions but no overall plan with consistent goals. A state's competitive position in international trade was most often the controlling factor in state intervention. Tariffs, devaluations, quantitative import restrictions, and other forms of protectionism were adopted by all; and states also sought to make protectionism work in the absence of market discipline by taking steps to enable their industries to produce more efficiently. In Britain, the state encouraged the reorganization of industries, often a euphemism for concentration around the biggest enterprises, and initiated a permanent process of interaction between industry representatives and state managers. Few gestures were made during the interwar period in the direction of the unions, much weakened by unemployment and the shift in the balance between new and old industries.[46] In some of the smaller European countries heavily dependent on foreign trade for the maintenance of their living standards, there were greater achievements in labor-management agreement. Industrial peace treaties were concluded in Norway in 1935, Switzerland in 1937, Sweden in 1938.[47] In all industrial countries, the experience of mass unemployment during the 1930s rekindled political demands that the state extend its responsibility for welfare to a commitment to achieve full employment, though practical advance in this direction awaited economic recovery through war.

World War II revived the practice of planning and gave it the clear goals that had been lacking, eliminated unemployment, built upon the existing state-business relationships, and gave labor access to government.

Britain can be taken as the paradigm for the welfare-nationalist state as it became fully developed through World War II. Samuel Beer has pointed out that the critical moment in forging the new collaborative relationship between labor and the state was 1940, i.e., the start of the organized war effort, and not 1945, i.e., the election of a Labour government. Labor's organized strength in the economy made it indispensable that the state secure labor's acquiescence in directing the economy toward national goals. The syndicalist thesis giving priority to power in production was thus validated before the achievement of electoral success.[48]

Subsequently, trade union power in production became a constraint upon the development of socialist planning. In 1940, the unions accepted compulsory direction of labor by the state and a ban on strikes. To retain a semblance of their collective-bargaining rights, the unions had rejected wage-fixing by the state. After the war, the unions opposed an extension of government controls by the Labour government, seeking to return to full collective bargaining and free movement of labor. This was the principal reason for the government's shift from direct physical planning to the use of indirect levers on the market. Wage policy remained a crucial element in any form of planning, however, and the government recognized that no wage policy would work without union concurrence. In 1948, the government reached agreement with employers and unions whereby the unions would observe wage restraint in return for an assurance of a reduction in profits, a continuance of food subsidies, and a policy of full employment. The agreement lasted until 1950 when price increases consequent upon devaluation of the pound eliminated one key element in the bargain. Wages began to rise sharply through trade-union action in 1950, and businesses relaxed the limitations on dividends.[49]

This British experience illustrated both the new balance of social forces in the state and the constraints imposed upon the welfare-nationalist state by its very structure. The working class, beaten into retreat following World War I, had during World War II acquired through the trade unions an apparently entrenched position in the state. Union leaders had access to government at the highest levels and to all agencies of the state in which they had an interest. Thenceforth, government would have to take labor, as well as business, into account in framing state policy. However, in a polity based on a continuing negotiation among powerful interests, government was limited in the powers it could use. Unions, no less than employers, imposed constraints upon economic planning by the state.

Government was in many ways dependent on interest groups for information and advice. It relied on these same groups to give effect to the policies agreed on. It could not, accordingly, act against the veto of any powerful group. Government could influence the evolution of an oligopolistic market through the use of its fiscal and monetary levers to the extent that consensus could be maintained among the powerful economic and social forces. Government could also exert influence because of the size of the state sector of the economy (which made the government itself a particularly weighty interest in the negotiation, though one among several). But the government could not dictate, or if it were to try to dictate, could not enforce. Moreover, consensus was relatively difficult to reach and maintain in the absence of war.

The primordial character of this task of negotiating economic and social consensus induced a similar pattern of behavior in both major political parties. Labour and Conservatives might have different styles and appeal to different constituencies among the voters, but on the substance of policy they came to differ very little. Both were committed to the welfare state, to Keynesian management of a market economy, and to the consultation of organized interests in the making of policy, i.e., to a corporatist form of polity. Both conceived their range of action as limited to a reactive form of economic management, responding to the consequences of the market—to inflation, unemployment, payments deficits, and falling exchange rates—but both unable and unwilling to envisage an economic planning that would supersede or subordinate the market. The corporatist structure of power within the state reinforced by ideology determined this limitation in capability and intent. The welfare-nationalist form of state created tripartism, and tripartism in turn limited the scope of action of the state.

Corporatist forms of organization were revived, not only in Britain but also in other countries of advanced capitalist development, through the mobilization of government-business-labor collaboration during World War II. Corporatism was subsequently embodied in some of the postwar institutional and constitutional settlements in western Europe. These took a variety of specific forms: the representation of economic interests in the Economic and Social Council and the *Commissariat général du Plan* in France; the Social and Economic Council and the Foundation of Labor of the Netherlands; the National Economic Development Council and its sectoral "little Neddies" established by the British Conservative government of Harold Macmillan in 1961; the labor market organization of the Scandinavian countries; the formal interest representation within the Austrian state and its more informal counterpart in Switzerland.[50] The United States, reluctant latecomer to corporatism in the 1930s, beat a retreat in the postwar period, though it did, in 1973 under President Nixon, experiment unsuccessfully with corporatist methods of wage and price control. These post-World War II institutionalizations of corporatist machinery occurred, however, after changes in the structure of world order had already begun to place demands on states different from those that had led to construction of corporatism in the first place. This threshold of the post-World War II era is, accordingly, a suitable point at which to contemplate the contradictions of the welfare-nationalist form of state.

Corporatism, which aims to transcend class conflict, produces a pattern of cleavage between those who are included and those excluded from the corporatist sector. It attempts to stabilize this cleavage by granting to the corporatist sector—to large-scale business and officially approved trade unions—a monopoly of the resources of organization and of access to political authority. It alienates the excluded and leaves large numbers available to be mobilized by a revival of class-based solidarities. Class-based cleavages are obscured by corporatist organization and ideology but can resurface when corporatism appears to some of the included workers as an unrequited concession to capitalist interests and gives them cause to merge their opposition with the discontent of the excluded.[51]

The inequalities of the corporatist form of polity are many, but their expression is muted. Tripartism institutionalizes the inequality between the relatively privileged established workers who are included in the corporatist sector and the other modes of social relations of production—enterprise labor market, self-employment, and household production, for instance—which are excluded and are subordinated to the tripartite mode. There is an inflationary bias to the Keynesian demand-management mechanism of economic regulation, and the more powerful groups—big business and trade unions—can protect their interests in a situation of rising prices while the weaker cannot. Inflation thus becomes a mechanism for disguising a redistribution of wealth favoring those included within the corporatist sector, disadvantaging those excluded.[52] In the political bargaining process that yields general acceptance for the state's welfare programs, benefits are granted to those not in social need, e.g., children's allowances to middle- and upper class families, in order to gain political support for benefits to those who do need them. Politics thus skews redistribution through the state budget in a regressive manner that in practice favors the welfare bureaucracies and the middle classes more than the poor. A hierarchy of

levels of welfare emerges: at the top, those protected by enterprise-related benefits additional to those benefits universally
available through social security; below, the dependent clients
of the welfare state. Some of the latter, like old-age pensioners,
are sufficiently numerous to be courted by politicians. Others
constitute a category of more or less permanently unemployed
who might pose a threat to the social order. The corporative state
avoids this danger by ensuring that these groups remain fragmented and depoliticized.[53]

Richard Titmuss, philosopher and analyst of the post-
World War II British welfare state, expressed his critical disillu-
sionment with the extent to which a welfare state had been
achieved when he put the question: Who disposes of the social
surplus? In the emergence of a corporatist pressure-group polity
as the manipulator of welfare systems, he perceived the distortion
of the idea of a society organized to create social equity. He saw
that powerful and very largely unaccountable interest groups
were coming to have a preponderant influence over the disposition of the social surplus. The alternative he advocated was state
ownership and state economic planning by publicly accountable
representatives.[54] Yet the practical prospect of achieving Titmuss'
preferred state has been negated by the politics of the welfare-
nationalist state.

The economic management record of the welfare-nationalist form of state has not been notably successful. Its economic
interventions were incapable of pulling the industrial nations out
of the Depression during the 1930s. Attempts at incomes policies
in the postwar period—a carryover of welfare-nationalist state
practices—were likewise ineffective. Military Keynesianism in
World War II worked better than civilian Keynesianism. The
welfare component of the state proved to be dependent on the
nationalist component. This lack of success in peacetime economic management must be perceived as a counterpart to the
limitations tripartism placed on the scope of the state's economic
initiative. Being restricted to a reactive role in relation to the
market, the state lacked the ability to conceive and carry through
an organization of production and distribution that would replace
the market. It could tinker or "fine tune"; it could not design.

Finally, the accumulation process was threatened by being

restricted to the national economy. This was tragically apparent in the beggar-my-neighbor climate of the 1930s. Accumulation could be extended, it seemed, only by imperialistic expansion and war, or else, possibly, within a new world hegemony in which national economies were once again, as in the mid-nineteenth century, subordinated to a world economy in which a world process of accumulation could proceed. The ineffectiveness of welfare-nationalist state policies opened the question whether Keynesianism, which had been tried with only limited effect on the national level, might not be more effective on the world level as a regulative mechanism for a world economy.[55] But this speculation implied a different form of state and a different world order.

## THE FASCIST
## CORPORATIVE STATE

Fascism was born in Italy when capitalist corporatism failed to become established after World War I. Fascism spread in Germany and central Europe during the economic collapse of the 1930s when the capitalist corporatism that had become established there failed to contain the social and economic crisis. In Germany, fascism substituted one form of corporatism for another—it displaced an autonomously generated capitalist corporatism by an authoritatively imposed state corporatism.

In functional terms, the fascist state was a distortion of the same development that produced the welfare-nationalist state. The two forms of state had similar economic functions but different social and political bases. Both forms of state, quite independently of their professed ideological aims, reacted against the social consequences of market dominance, particularly unemployment. Both acted to maintain, revive, and expand the capitalist production process and, though in very different ways, to bring about labor peace.

Fascism in Italy in the mid-1920s followed economic policies analogous to those of conservative governments in other European countries. It espoused liberal laissez-faire, monetary stabilization, and a high exchange rate. Mussolini's actions in revaluing the lira in 1926 mirrored Winston Churchill's revaluation of sterling in the previous year. Later, following the examples of Britain and the United States, Nazi Germany abandoned an international monetary standard to construct the tightest of all the economic blocs into which the world economy fragmented. Fascist Italy clung to the gold bloc with France, Belgium, the Netherlands, and Switzerland until that remnant of an earlier international monetary order dissolved in the later 1930s. Both Italian and German fascists practiced fiscal conservatism.[56]

Under fascism, however, these economic policy objectives were pursued in a context in which both parliamentary accountability and the institutionalized forms of labor-management conflict had broken down. They broke down as both cause and consequence of the advance of fascist power itself. The dominant economic classes lost confidence in the ability of their own political parties to secure the industrial order that was a condition for profits. Fascist preeminence in the practice of illegal violence convinced them that only the fascists could restore and guarantee this order. Fascism accomplished this through an imposed state-corporatist system in industry. Strikes were abolished and strict labor discipline enforced. Workers were given some access to political power as a channel for resolving grievances. An ideology of enterprise community, betriebsgemeinschaft in its German form, was proclaimed. Although in theory the worker-employer community was one of reciprocal obligation subordinated to an overriding common obligation to nation or state, in practice it was biased in favor of the employer. The rights of management became supreme in the workplace.[57]

To achieve their goals, the dominant economic classes connived to create a power they could not themselves control. The fascist rulers had their own goals, and they would use industry instrumentally to pursue these goals. They did not hesitate to intervene in the economy by securing the voluntary acquiescence of businessmen if possible but using force if necessary. A "command economy" was superimposed upon the economy dominated by corporate monopolies. Yet if the capacity to apply direct instrumental power lay with the fascist rulers, structural power remained with the dominant economic class. The fascist rulers' ability to attain their goals depended on the economic strength of the industrial system, which the dominant economic class controlled. In that sense, the fascist rulers had to and did serve the interests of the industrial system and its monopolists. Fascist economic intervention in practice strengthened the industrial combines and enhanced their ability to make profits.[58]

Fascist economic management was effective in reducing unemployment, raising industrial output, controlling wages and prices, and introducing technological innovations. In these respects, by placing German and Italian economies on a war footing before World War II, fascism anticipated the revival that the war brought to the economies of the emergent welfare-nationalist states. Yet state intervention and the considerable expansion of state ownership accomplished under fascism never aimed at or approached the coherence of an economic plan conceived as an instrument for transforming economy and society. The fascist state's economic goals remained specific and relatively short range.[59]

If functionally the fascist state appears as a distortion of the welfare-nationalist state with a more authoritarian political base, the importance of fascism lies precisely in the genesis of that political base. In this genetic perspective, fascism appears not just as a historical aberration of welfare-nationalism but as a type that may be replicated under certain conditions.

Probably no one achieved a clearer understanding of fascism in its origins than Antonio Gramsci. He saw, experienced, and struggled against its birth in Italy in the post-World War I period. He distanced himself from some of the simplistic explanations of the Comintern, such as those that identified fascism with monopoly capitalism and with social democracy. Confined in a fascist prison, he reflected on the historical specificities of Italy, western Europe, and Russia in an attempt to understand the conditions for fascism and its meaning.

Among these conditions, Gramsci listed three: first, an emergence of popular forces that had hitherto not participated in political life, but in a manner in which these forces had no coherence, leadership, or direction; second, an alienation from the political system of the petty-bourgeoisie or middle classes, particularly those employed in the state bureaucracy or of the milieus furnishing state officials; and third, a polarization of employers and workers and their respective allies such that neither side could effectively lead and society appeared to be headed for a catastrophic conflict. Under these conditions, parliamentary institutions, which function effectively only to the extent that the real forces in society are mediated through them into acceptable compromises, become paralyzed. The alienated middle classes, disillusioned by the conventional political process, support those of their number who use illegal violence to gain control of the streets. The popular classes, lacking an effective political organization, are unable to resist but are sufficiently aroused to provoke petty-bourgeois violence. A caesarist solution—the man of destiny—imposes itself between the antagonistic forces. Caesarism produces order, but it freezes conflict without resolving the issue between the antagonistic social forces.[60]

Caesarism becomes the instrumentality of a "passive revolution", i.e., of an attempt to introduce aspects of revolutionary change while maintaining a balance of social forces in which those favoring restoration of the old order remain firmly entrenched. Italian fascism sought to modernize capitalism along American lines but shrank before the implications of market freedom as the avenue toward industrial concentration, shrank particularly before the threat of unemployment this approach would involve. Instead, fascism sought to introduce modernization and concentration within the framework of a state corporatism in which the traditional economically dominant classes would be preserved, including the rentier class and the clientelism of the mezzogiorno. Fascist corporatism represented therefore a passive (and in Gramsci's view ineffective) modernization of capitalism. The basic antagonisms of capitalism were suppressed, not overcome.[61]

Gramsci's analysis highlights key factors in the rise of fascism in both Italy and Germany. In both countries, fascism presented some of the aspects of a revolutionary movement but was ultimately eased into power by the dominant economic and social groups with the connivance and support of their foreign counterparts. In Italy, the factory and land occupations of 1919–20 so shocked the industrial bourgeoisie and the landlord class that they were ready to abandon their traditional parties (and a political system of coalitions known as *trasformismo* geared around the liberal center) for a fascist solution. The Liberals themselves were prepared to view fascism, in Charles Maier's words, "as a regrettably cruder but muscular wing of liberalism."[62] The violence of the fascist squads may have been regrettable to Liberals and their erstwhile industrialist backers, but violence clinched the argument that only Mussolini could restore order. Mussolini's own declaration of affiliation to economic liberalism before his accession to power gave assurance sufficient for the bourgeoisie to discount the radical rhetoric of fascist syndicalism. Petty-bourgeois fears and the backing of industrial and landlord interests gave fascism an electoral success at the expense of the traditional liberal center. The path to governmental power was prepared by the former ruling groups, but it was preceded by a symbolic reminder of the revolutionary pretensions of fascism and of its ultimate foundation in violence—the march on Rome. Once he enjoyed a monopoly of state power, Mussolini domesticated the squadri and demobilized the syndicalists. Both retained only a marginal utility as levers he could use when necessary to influence the old dominant classes and the organized employers.[63]

The same combination of street violence with petty-bourgeois alienation gained electoral support for National Socialism in Germany. But Hitler's real strength lay not in electoral success but in the conviction of the dominant groups that only the Nationalist Socialists could protect their interests in a situation of increasing mass unemployment and ineffective legal institutions. It was, in fact, after the National Socialist vote had fallen in the November 1932 elections that army (Hindenberg), aristocracy (Papen), and Ruhr industrialists (Thyssen) allowed Hitler to form a government. The Nazi radicals were purged in bloodier fashion than their Italian counterparts on the night of June 30, 1934, half a year after Hitler's accession to power.[64]

In his comparative study of France, Germany, and Italy in the 1920s, Charles Maier discerned a common pattern of change in political structures from the emergence of a working-class challenge in the immediate postwar years to the recasting and restabilization of the bourgeois order in the mid-1920s.

> What permitted stability after 1924 was a shift in the focal point of decision making. Fragmented parliamentary majorities yielded to ministerial bureaucracies, or sometimes directly to party councils, where interest-group representatives could more easily work out social burdens and rewards. This displacement permitted a new compromise: a corporatist equilibrium in which private interests assumed the tasks that parliamentary coalitions found difficult to confront.[65]

Fascism played a role of maintaining bourgeois order in two distinct stages. In the first stage, fascism was decisive only in Italy; in the second, in both Germany and Italy.

In the early 1920s, the Italian bourgeoisie was unable through its own means (political parties and economic power) to exorcise the demon of popular rebellion and the challenge to property. Fascism acted in place of the bourgeoisie through a combination of state corporatist industrial structures and liberal economic policies. In Germany during the same period, the working class was divided and the industrial bourgeoisie was able to come to an understanding with one section of the working class in order to suppress the other. Indicative of this understanding was the action taken by the Social Democratic minister of defense Gustav Noske in January 1919 to call in the anti-Bolshevik Free Corps of demobilized army officers, to crush a left-wing labor movement in Berlin. The German industrial bourgeoisie was not alone in its effort to build a basis for understanding with moderate elements of the political and trade-union wings of the German labor movement. The Allied governments were preoccupied that Bolshevism might spread in the wake of Germany's military defeat. The German general staff remained intact as a result of the armistice and able to back this effort. Field Marshal von Hindenberg entered into a compact with Friedrich Ebert, then leader of the Social Democratic Party and later the first president of the Republic, to fight Bolshevism. Thus, with the collaboration of a part of the German working class through its political and trade-union representatives, a new institutional structure was put in place within which a capitalist corporatism could become the focal point for decision making. Fascism was unnecessary to the recasting of the bourgeois order in Germany at this stage and remained unimportant. The division within the German working class lasted, however, to weaken its capacity for resistance when later the fascist threat became real.[66]

This came about during the second stage with the onset of the Great Depression of the 1930s. Capitalist corporatism in Germany proved incapable of containing that crisis. Those within the corporatist compact—industrialists and employed workers—could defend themselves, but those excluded—the unemployed, small businesses, and fixed-income people—became increasingly numerous, alienated, and susceptible to the anticapitalist rhetoric of National Socialism. German fascism came to power as a movement against capitalist corporatism. It used power to establish state corporatism. Italian fascism, with state corporatist structures already in place, made the transition to the second phase without a break in institutions.[67]

By following Gramsci's cue that we should look at the formation of historic blocs in order to understand the foundation of different forms of state power, fascism may be considered as one possible outcome of a crisis of hegemony.[68] Fascism takes power when the industrial bourgeoisie through its normal political parties and modes of influence has been unable to contain the rise of a popularly based but insufficiently coherent challenge. The bourgeoisie has either not attained or is in danger of losing its hegemony, and no counterhegemonic power based in the working class is able to displace it. This is a situation that, as mentioned above, Gramsci suggested is ripe for caesarism. But he was quick to add that the charismatic man of destiny is only one form of caesarism. Another form, which perhaps strains the roots of the word but not the concept as Gramsci presented it, is a parliamentary type of equilibrium between balanced but opposing social forces.[69]

A social formation in which such an unresolved polarization of social forces exists may alternate between two forms of state: an authoritarian repressive form that emerges out of acute social conflict and a more relaxed cartel form of state that maintains the stakes of the principal contending social forces during a phase of relative truce. Italy has exemplified both models in the *fascismo* of Mussolini and the *trasformismo* of Giolitti. Indeed, fascism when it came to power incorporated the praxis of *trasformismo*. Mussolini's first government was as broadly comprehensive a coalition of existing parliamentary fragments as Giolitti ever could have mustered.[70]

Fascism has come to power in situations of acute polarization of an apparently irreconcilable kind such as arose in the agricultural and industrial revolt in Italy in 1919–20, during the Popular Front and civil war in Spain in the 1930s, and during the Greek civil war after World War II. Similar crises of hegemony have been recurrent in late-industrializing countries in the post-World War II period, including some in Latin America, where capitalist production had become implanted but the national bourgeoisie had been no more successful in establishing hegemony than the Italian had in the post-World War I era. Italian fascism created the prototype of the authoritarian fascist state and elaborated and institutionalized state corporatist social relations in production. The Argentine, Chilean, and Uruguayan military-bureaucratic states of the 1970s and 1980s are its latter-day manifestations, Franco's Spain and the Greece of the colonels having passed in the interim. The Italy of Christian Democracy, post-Franco Spain, the Greece of Caramanlis, the Portugal of the post-carnation-revolution period, all exemplify the cartel state.

Fascist authoritarianism freezes class antagonisms under a cloak of populist nationalism backed by repression of dissent. It gives the petty bourgeoisie possession of state jobs, turns a blind eye to landlord violence and protects the agricultural interest, continues the state role in capital accumulation, and compensates repression of industrial labor protest by according a certain status in the state to official organizations of established industrial workers. The cartel state allows more freedom of expression and some mobility in interclass relations. Struggles can be more open so that the balance of class forces can be tested. At the same time, this conflict is very largely institutionalized and takes place within the state, which remains the structure through which contending classes get their payoffs. Unions may be able to demonstrate an increase in strength and in allegiance among workers (as in Italy during the "hot autumn" of 1969) and thereby claim and secure a strengthening of their institutional position within the state (control of the labor ministry, more secure status within enterprises). But maintenance of the cartel state depends on moderation in the level of conflict; any return to total and irreconcilable conflict would threaten a reversion to authoritarianism.

The cartel state appears to effect a transformation of state corporatism into tripartism. The directing role of the state is, indeed, dismantled and more initiative allowed to autonomous labor organizations. The state, however, maintains much of the mechanisms of control over unions that could be invoked in emergency, and unions continue to direct their action toward the state. Strikes are more political than economic, leading to state intervention in the negotiating process. Thus corporatism at the national level remains, though the state's role in it may be more muted than in the authoritarian phases.

For the critical differentiation between fascism and the more benign form of cartel state, the decisive factor must be found in fascism's disposition to violence. Petty-bourgeois shock troops and street gangs furnished the human material for violence, but the disposition itself seems to lie deeper than class structure in the human psyche. In this respect, Gramsci separated himself from the limited class analyses of fascism made by other marxists during the years marxism was dominated by the Comintern. As early as 1921 he wrote in the *Ordine Nuovo:*

> It has now become evident that fascism can only partly be assumed to be a class phenomenon, a movement of political forces which are conscious of having a real goal: . . . it has become an unleashing of elemental forces within the bourgeois system of economic and political government, which cannot be braked: fascism is the name for the profound decay of Italian society. . . .[71]

He went on to explain fascism as the result of a low level of culture ("Italy is the country where mothers bring up their children by hitting them about the head with a clog") in specifically national terms. Others have been impressed by the ubiquity of the phenomenon. Wilhelm Reich, for instance, saw fascism as the unleashing of a normally subconscious layer of character,

which consists of "cruel, sadistic, lascivious, rapacious and en-
vious impulses" and which has been generated by the experience
of authoritarian repression in childhood. This layer of character
he saw as something characteristic of the great mass of mankind,
not limited to any national cultures. Normally this irrationally
aggressive layer is overlaid by a conscious personality restrained
by norms of civility. Reich perceived the attraction of fascism for
the petty bourgeoisie as deriving from a character structure
shaped by the authoritarian family. When these strata of society
are placed under dire stress in which their status appears to be
threatened, hidden wellsprings of violence become revealed. The
character structure shaped by authoritarian repression expresses
this violence in a typically fascist form.[72]

## THE REDISTRIBUTIVE
## PARTY-COMMANDED STATE

The fascist corporative state deviated from the welfare-nationalist
form of state in becoming a framework for the continuation of
capitalist development where bourgeois hegemony was either
absent or had broken down. A quite different mode of development was initiated by the state that took form following the
Russian revolution. This was a redistributive mode development
carried on under the leadership of a revolutionary party with a
monopoly of state power.

The redistributive Party-commanded form of state did not
evolve out of a transformation of the liberal state. In the two most
significant cases—the Soviet Union and China—the form
emerged out of the crisis of old-regime agrarian-bureaucratic
states.[73]

In Czarist Russia, private industry was introduced and
encouraged under state tutelage and for purposes of the state (e.g.,
producing military supplies). In that respect, Czarist industrialization was analogous to the mercantilism of the seventeenth-
century French monarchy. The social relations of production in
industry were initially adapted from the peasant-lord pattern of
serfdom, though following the ending of serfdom and the initiation of reforms such as those of Stolypin in agriculture, the Czarist

state acted to create an enterprise-labor-market mode of social relations in both industry and agriculture.[74] This had, however, been only partially achieved when the state collapsed.

Imperial China suffered the implantation of enclaves of foreign capitalism on its coastline, and republican China fostered capitalist development from its coastal base. Here, too, capitalist production and enterprise-labor-market social relations had only a limited impact when the state collapsed and the protoliberal experiment ended.[75]

In some of the eastern European states where redistributive Party-commanded states were installed after World War II under Soviet political-military dominance, capitalist organization of production and the modes of social relations of production—enterprise labor market, bipartite and tripartite—associated with them were more developed, as was the self-employment mode among the small holders of their agrarian sectors. In these cases, the new form of state was imposed by external intervention with a modicum of internal support and cannot be considered as an endogenous transformation of the preexisting national state. In still other cases, Yugoslavia and Indochina, the redistributive Party-commanded state was founded after a successful peasant-based revolutionary struggle.

Virtually all the historical evidence thus suggests that this form of state inaugurates an alternative to the capitalist process of accumulation fostered by the liberal state and that it does not presuppose any initial liberal phase.[76] Just as the liberal state created the enterprise labor market, so the redistributive Party-commanded state created central planning and also, as a transitional mode of social relations of production, instituted the communal organization of agriculture. The historical fact that the redistributive Party-commanded state constitutes, so to speak, a separate track does not exclude that, once established, it can be a model to be propagated in social formations with a capitalist and liberal-state past either by force or conceivably by emulation.

The Soviet state came into existence in a hostile world and had from the beginning to defend its existence. One current of revolutionary thinking envisaged the Bolshevik seizure of power in Russia as but a first step in a world revolutionary process and that, indeed, the success of the revolution could be assured only to the extent that it spread from Russia to the capitalist nations. These expectations were set back when revolution was forestalled in defeated Germany by the coalition of capitalist, social-democratic, and military forces with the backing of the Allied powers. Then the new Soviet state had to fight a war on its own territory against counterrevolutionary forces reinforced by foreign military intervention. Success in this defensive effort led to a pause in the revolutionary process—the New Economic Policy.[77] The isolation of the Soviet state in a world in which bourgeois order had been reestablished in western Europe left "socialism in one country" as the only independent option open to it.

The defeat of intervention gave the Soviet state a respite, but for how long? The League of Nations could only appear to the Soviet leaders as a hostile alliance, though one that lacked coherence and effectiveness. The greatest guarantee to the Soviet state lay in the divisions among the capitalist powers, not in their tolerance of a communist power. Revolution had been possible to achieve in a backward, peripheral economy, but to sustain that revolution the Soviet state would have to be able to modernize its economy rapidly enough to match the military capabilities of the most advanced capitalist powers before they attacked again. The imperative placed upon the new state by the condition of the world system was industrialization and militarization.

This imperative shaped the nature of the regime. The collectivization of agriculture and the construction of the central planning system did not come into existence in utopian fashion as the conscious realization of an intellectually determined model. The structure emerged as the consequence of a series of political decisions shaped by social and economic realities and taken under the stress of acute political conflict. The internal debate during the 1920s was overshadowed by the issue of how most effectively to prepare for the expected attack from the capitalist world. Those like Bukharin who advocated "snail's pace" industrialization so as least to disrupt a possible peasant-worker alliance had to confront the charge that this strategy would leave the Soviet state vulnerable to the external threat. Forced collectivization was justified as the only way to expand agricultural production rapidly and at the same time free up a labor force for industrialization. Draconian enforcement of labor discipline was justified as necessary to adjust an industrial labor force of ex-peasants to factory work. In short, the coercive and repressive characteristics associated with Stalinism flowed with a certain logic from the Soviet state's vulnerable position in a hostile world system. To its supporters, the justification of this phase of forced draft development was the ability of the Soviet system to survive under the German onslaught during the Great Patriotic War and to emerge as one of two superpowers in the postwar world.

The other great redistributive system, that of China, began its course in a similar world-system context. When the Commu-nist forces occupied the coastal cities evacuated by the retreating Guomindang armies and proclaimed the People's Republic in 1949, Mao Zedong offered a place in the new order to the national bourgeoisie. This offer envisaged the maintenance of the trade links between the Chinese coastal cities and the southeast-Asia region in which the coastal-city bourgeoisies had been the inter-mediaries. China was, however, immediately confronted by a U.S. blockade and threat of U.S.-supported invasion from the Guomindang forces in Taiwan. Soviet alliance and the introduc-tion of the Soviet planning system for the development of Chinese heavy industry was the only remaining option consistent with building up China's capacity to defend the new order. When this option was taken, the alliance with the national bourgeoisie be-came meaningless. Shanghai and the other coastal cities were brought within the scope of the central planning system.[78]

In the post-Stalin years, the position of both the Soviet Union and China changed within the world system. Mutual nu-clear deterrence gave a certain stability to U.S.-Soviet relations, a situation that became mutually recognized in the more relaxed relationship that followed the test ban treaty of 1963. During the post-Stalin years the internal development of the Soviet economy required a shift from the extensive pattern of development fol-lowed under Stalin to an intensive pattern that could sustain growth now that labor reserves had become fully employed. The only source of growth now would be new capital and technology and the quickest way to obtain this seemed to be through in-creased economic intercourse with the capitalist world. Internal and external factors combined to favor detente.

China at the same time appeared to its leaders to be in a most vulnerable position. During the height of Soviet-Chinese cooperation, the Soviet Union had agreed to assist China in the development of a nuclear defense capacity. Now in the context of detente leading up to the test ban treaty, in which both superpowers accepted the principle of nuclear nonproliferation, the Soviet Union renounced this agreement. Relations between Chinese and Soviet communist parties had also become embittered: in 1954 the Chinese leadership purged the directors of Manchurian heavy industry and the central planning mechanism, suspected of being a Soviet bridgehead within China, and in the summer of 1960 the Soviet technicians were withdrawn from China. Meanwhile U.S. hostility and the threat from Taiwan continued to menace China. The Chinese leadership reacted with a dual thrust toward autarky: continued priority for the development of an independent nuclear military capability plus a shift from Soviet-style heavy-industry-based development to a gamble on internal self-reliance. The internal development strategy had profound implications for production relations. It, in effect, staked everything on the ability of ideological mobilization through communalism to create by human investment the new capital and the technological innovation required to sustain China's inward-oriented development. China was successful in developing its nuclear capability. It was not successful in achieving sustained growth through full and effective utilization of its vast manpower.

By the late 1970s the world system entered another phase. Both capitalist and Soviet economies encountered severe problems of maintaining growth, and their mutual political relations became more hostile. The United States began to revise its heretofore consistent anti-Chinese stance to perceive in China a useful counterweight in the east to the Soviet Union. The new post-Mao Chinese leadership was at the same time determined to change the internal development strategies based on self-reliance in order to place the emphasis on the modernization of Chinese industry and the raising of agricultural production. The new development strategy, by its insistence that improvement of productive forces had priority, implied both a drastic change in production relations—notably a shift from ideological mobilization to material incentives—and a need to expand economic relations with the outside world in order to import technology. Now, however, the outside world meant the capitalist world economy.[79]

The manner in which the world system has conditioned the development of production relations in redistributive systems through the mediation of the redistributive party-commanded state underlines the dilemma of revolution in backward, peripheral economies. If one were able to abstract the world system from development processes, there would be nothing inherent in redistributive development that would tie it to the authoritarian and repressive features associated with Stalinism. It should be possible to sift out what is essential and lasting in central planning as a system of social relations of production from what is transitory and conjunctural, to see it as a dynamic and evolving structure not irrevocably bearing the stigma of its Stalinist origins. It is, however, impossible to abstract the world system in the case of a backward, peripheral country. Severance from the world system through revolution exposes such a country to intervention and destabilization. It can gain a sense of security only by rapid industrialization such as would give the country the military strength to survive. The paradox of this necessity is that in order to industrialize rapidly the revolution must adopt the same kind of industrial technology and organization as is used in the more advanced capitalist countries and must thus forgo the possibility of pioneering new forms of social organization of production consistent with the goals of revolution. The implication, in other words, is that the opportunities for revolutionary development in backward, peripheral countries are severely limited.

Things would be otherwise if revolution were to occur in the most advanced industrial society. Such a revolution would be less constrained to retain the models of social organization prevailing in competing powers for the simple reason that its own productive forces were already the most developed. The paradox in this case is that, being the most developed, more resources are available for alleviating the causes of revolution and so revolution is least likely to occur there. Juxtaposition of these hypothetical cases—one technologically backward, the other advanced—suggests, however, that prospects for internal changes in social organization may be enhanced as the technologically backward redistributive society succeeds in raising the level of its productive forces. This is perhaps the strongest argument in support of the declared aims of the present Chinese leadership. This leadership takes the position that China's productive forces must be improved before significant further advances can be made toward more collective forms of life and work. The question that remains to be answered is whether growing links to the world capitalist economy designed to facilitate the development of productive forces will in themselves restrict or divert such advances in a capitalist direction even if the level of productive forces is raised. Will these links undermine the redistributive character of the regime and assimilate it to a market-oriented world economic order?

The redistributive party-commanded state fuses politics and economics into a single process. The functional outline of this form of state economy is given in chapter 4, i.e., the role played by the state in coordinating three modes of social relations of production: central planning, communal and self-employment modes (with in some cases the addition of enterprise-labor-market production). It is, however, important to consider how functional relationships may be changing, and it is most difficult to form an accurate and up-to-date picture of the internal developments that are transforming redistributive systems.

Gramsci's analogy from wars of movement and wars of position is apposite to conceptualizing this transformation. Revolution in Russia succeeded, Gramsci argued, as a war of movement. The Czarist state was strong in its coercive powers until these succumbed in military catastrophe, but it had no firm base in civil society. It was possible for a determined revolutionary party to destroy such a state in a rapid war of movement and then to make a new state that would mold an amorphous society in its own image. The Russian case could not, Gramsci continued, be transposed to western Europe, because there even the collapse of a regime, e.g., Hohenzollern Germany, would leave behind solid bulwarks of economic and social power. Any revolutionary group that seized power in such circumstances would confront organized forces that would soon bring it down. In this case, the necessary revolutionary strategy was the war of position—slowly but surely to build up a class-based counterhegemony in civil society until the conquest of power in the state became a feasible goal. Gramsci, in other words, was thinking about the prospects for a socialist transformation of societies permeated by capitalist institutions and social relations in a way that Czarist Russia and prerevolutionary China were not.[80]

The state founded in a war of movement is, in substance, the centralized disciplined party organization that proceeds to insert itself into the inherited mechanisms of the prerevolutionary state and to create new institutions and instruments for reshaping society. The revolutionary party dominates the disarticulated remains of prerevolutionary social structure in a directly dictatorial, nonhegemonic manner. It attempts to draw certain social elements into its orbit in a preferential status (urban manual workers, rural poor peasants), but the party itself has not been built upon the broad support of an existing social class that through the party extended its social hegemony over other social classes. The party substitutes for a class-based social hegemony and uses organization and ideology as the means of establishing a broadly based mass support.[81]

The initial revolutionary seizure of power—the war of movement—is thus followed by an extended social "revolution from above." In the course of this effort, the party-state (1) maintains and renews a disciplined cadre; (2) removes coercively or by attrition the social authorities (notables, the wealthy, experts) of the old regime, thereby creating space for replacements recruited for their loyalty to the new order; (3) uses ideology as a tool for reshaping attitudes toward work, social relations, and polity; and (4) creates the economic-material base for new state power. During the phase of primary accumulation, in which the economic, as well as the social, bases of a future society are to be laid, the party's focus is on struggle against the residues of old social classes and against the emergence of new social groups that could challenge or undermine its leadership.

The most interesting and difficult questions concerning the development of redistributive social formations concern the reemergence of civil society following this initial phase of primary accumulation and "revolution from above." Social categories are shaped by the new political and production organizaton: the top party-political leadership; the leading cadres or heads of enterprises and other productive units and of the various levels of economic and social bureaucracies; the scientific-humanistic elite; the much larger category of degree-holding intelligentsia who staff the middle levels of state, party, and economic organizations; the established skilled workers and technicians; non-established workers; richer and poorer peasants. As this new structure of social categories becomes a relatively stable configuration, the party-state has to take it into account in its task of directing the development of the economy. The war of movement must accordingly give place to a war of position. The party, in advancing its policies, will rely on the support of some social groups more than others.

The essence of Stalinism, the "revolution from above," was that the top party-political leadership monopolized power and prevented the other categories from acquiring any separate sense of identity or any legitimacy of their own, distinct from the legitimation of political orthodoxy conferred by the political leadership. The post-Stalin era saw the emergence of both the "leading cadres" and the scientific-humanistic elite as distinct social forces. Some critical observers from within the system perceived a "historic compromise"[82] through which the political leadership recognized the existence of these social forces, and they in turn acknowledged the hegemony of the political leadership.

Hegemony is, of course, a different thing from dictatorship. The hegemonic political leadership has to take account of the distinctive interests of the social forces on whose acquiescence its exercise of power in a measure depends. One factor favoring the continued hegemony of the Soviet political leadership group is its ability to mobilize the support of the upper level of established workers, the engineering-technical personnel (ITRs) who have been the dominant element in the Soviet trade unions and close to management. An ideological consequence of the leadership's reliance on this support has been a propensity to encourage populist, manualist, antiintellectual sentiments that can have the effect of isolating manifestations of deviance among the scientific-humanistic elite. Socially, this support relationship could lead toward the consolidation of a labor aristocracy enjoying corporatist relations with management and dominating over any tendencies toward deviancy from a subproletariat of nonestablished workers. Speculations can be raised about whether analogous tendencies are at work in post-Mao China.

To the extent that this analysis is correct, the party has lost something of its erstwhile character as a mechanism for enforcing discipline and uniformity, to become somewhat more of a channel of communications among and an *encadrement* for the now more identifiable groups associated in the exercise of power. The party can, perhaps, no longer be identified so exclusively with the political leadership. Once a substitute for civil society, the party may now be experiencing something of the diversity of a reemergent civil society.[83]

The relationship between party and society could move in different directions. The labor revolt in Poland in August 1980 that led to the formation of *Solidarnośc* showed that the strategy of the political leadership to seek support among the established workers and thereby to marginalize the humanistic intellectual opposition might not succeed and that other alignments within evolved redistributive societies are possible.[84]

In the Polish case, the political elite was in danger of becoming marginalized by a coalition of workers and intelligentsia in which the divisions between skilled and unskilled, rural and urban, mental and manual seemed to have been very largely bridged. The Polish case is certainly untypical in outcome but may not be untypical in terms of the social groups available for coalition. Recognition of the existence of identifiable social groups within industrialized redistributive social formations gives a basis for reasoning about alternative futures for these formations.

The most conservative vision of the future—and perhaps the most likely prospect—is for a continuance of the peaceful coexistence of a political leadership and a technological-humanistic elite, the former ruling, the latter managing. This outcome would be reinforced by a reform of the official trade unions reinvigorating corporatism in industry and an improvement of efficiency and reduction of corruption in planning and administration with the use of more sophisticated methods, including computers. A variant of this strategy, favored by some members of the technological elite, would give greater place to market mechanisms. These are intended to make the allocation process more efficient, not to open the way for a transformation of redistributive into capitalist accumulation. There is no clear pattern of support or opposition among social groups for the market orientation. Some enterprise directors may support it and others be concerned that it would make their work more precarious. Workers may be indifferent or worry lest the market orientation extend to the staffing of enterprises, thereby undermining the job security that is guaranteed under existing practices.

More radical directions of change could attack the organization and hierarchy of production by challenging what Rudolph Bahro calls subalternity, essentially the reproduction within redistributive social formations of the command structure of capitalist industry. One such line of attack envisages worker self-management at the enterprise level. This could lead to a weakening of central redistributive functions and a growth of autonomous self-regarding enterprises. Another radical—one might say utopian—challenge envisages a strengthening, not a weakening, of political Party control over the redistributive process, but with a revitalized, nonbureaucratic, democratically reponsive Party.[85]

The contradictions or problems inherent in this form of state can be put under four headings:

First, there is a contradiction between the social goals of emancipation on which the legitimacy of the regime rests and the dictates of the world context, which tend to maintain its extractive (high redistributive accumulation) and repressive character.

Second, and closely related to the first, is a contradiction between the command hierarchy and alienating character of work in industry organized on the same pattern as capitalist production and the expectation of new nonalienating working relationships kindled by revolution.

Third, the rationality of central planning is limited by inefficiencies, but changes in central planning might well lead to lower rates of redistributive accumulation. For instance, to seek greater efficiencies by giving greater scope to market mechanisms might encourage corporative engrossment of earnings with the result that less would flow into central redistribution. Alternatively, rank-and-file responsive planning would challenge the hierarchical basis of established state power and would probably also lead to lower central accumulation.

Fourth, the reemergence of civil society after an initial phase in which the Party has an exclusive initiative in reshaping society requires that a modus vivendi be reached between state structures and emergent social forces. This concerns particularly the relationships between Party elite, technical intelligentsia, humanistic intelligentsia, and workers.

## FURTHER ANALYTICAL
## PROPOSITIONS

The questions discussed in this chapter enable us to add to the analytical propositions concerning the transformation of forms of state and world order presented at the end of chapter 5. Many of the changes considered in the present chapter are further evidence of those propositions, particularly as regards the political form of class struggles (second proposition), the formation of new historic blocs (third proposition), and the creation of new frameworks for production (fourth and fifth propositions). The experience of the era of rival imperialisms added particularly to our understanding of world-order structures. To the eight propositions of chapter 5, the following may now be added.

Ninth: the transformation of a historical structure of world order is a complex process involving simultaneously (1) change in the relative powers of the principal states, (2) uneven development of productive forces leading to a new distribution of productive powers among social formations, (3) changes in the relative power of social groups within social formations and the formation of new historic blocs, and (4) the formation of a social structure of accumulation, i.e., the putting into place of new social relations of production and new mechanisms of capital accumulation through which economic growth is able to continue and increase.

Tenth: such transformations may be in the direction either of a unified and consensual, homogeneous, hegemonic order or toward a fragmented and conflictual, heterogeneous, nonhegemonic order. The hegemonic order tends to limit forms of state to those that are compatible with the prevailing social structure of accumulation. The economic-productive structures of social formations are made compatible with the hegemonic world economy even though state-political structures may differ. The differences among the latter are such as to ensure the compatibility of the former. The nonhegemonic world order, because of the fragmentation of power that prevails within it, permits the emergence and development of forms of state and of social structures of accumulation that are not compatible with any single preeminent form of world economy.

Thus—consistent with the ninth proposition—the last decades of the nineteenth century witnessed a simultaneous pattern of changes that cumulatively transformed the social structure of accumulation (and with it the typical modes of social relations of production) of the liberal era and brought into existence a nonhegemonic world order. The welfare nationalist form of state evolved out of the liberal state as an adaptation both to the nonhegemonic world order (its nationalist aspect) and to the new internal relationship among social forces (the welfare aspect). Fascism was the most extreme manifestation of aggressivity in interstate relations during the era of rival imperialisms. Where the welfare-nationalist state was a continuation of bourgeois hegemony internally adapted to a nonhegemonic external world, fascism expressed a rupture of internal hegemony—a state based on domination in the service of which it was able to mobilize barbaric propensities latent in all populations. Fascism represented, however, continuity in the structures of accumulation—indeed a tightening of these structures by assimilating them through state corporatism to the mode of domination established in the state. The establishment of revolutionary redistributive regimes initiated an alternative social structure of accumulation to that linked with the emergence of the welfare-nationalist state. The decentralization of power in the world system—consistent with the tenth proposition—was sufficient to preclude the suppression of this alternative at its origins and thus to enable the revolutionary regimes to survive. But the competitive nature of power in the world system did constrain the way in which redistributive development took place. This way was not freely chosen but dictated by the desire to achieve the most rapid increase in productive forces so as to enhance the regime's survival capacity in a conflictual world.

# CHAPTER SEVEN

# PAX AMERICANA

World War II was the final paroxysm of a long time of troubles. Out of it emerged a new hegemonic era in which the United States assumed the same kind of leadership that Britain had exercised during the mid-nineteenth century. The term *superpower* entered the political vocabulary to signify the distance separating both the United States and the Soviet Union from other major states in the system. No balance of power in the conventional sense was possible—only condominium or bipolarity. The institutional framework for condominium was prepared in the design of the United Nations Security Council. Although the fiction of a balance-of-power world was preserved in the designation of five permanent members, there was little doubt but that two (the United States and the Soviet Union) were determining and the other three (Britain, France, and China) present in acknowledgment of their historic status. The rule of unanimity of the permanent members, embodied in the right of veto, signified the hope for condominium. That hope was short lived. Polarization quickly became the postwar pattern. The United States took the initiative to construct an open world political economy, exclusive of the Soviet sphere, in which Western Europe and Japan and what came to be known as the Third World were all to be incorporated. The redistributive systems of the Soviet Union and China at first continued a separate existence, later to become involved in some tentative controlled links with the U.S.-led world economy.

The present chapter is concerned with the structure and

mechanisms of this hegemonic world order: the Pax Americana. In reference to proposition nine enunciated at the end of chapter 6, the new hegemonic order was brought about through a change in power relations among the major states, reflecting a decisive shift in their relative economic-productive powers—a change that gave the United States an opportunity for unquestioned leadership outside the Soviet sphere. The putting into place of the new order involved the transformation of state structures— the emergence in the countries of more advanced capitalist development of a neoliberal form of state attuned to the hegemonic order and in peripheral economies of forms of state geared to the linking of these peripheral zones to the world economy.

It did not, however, bring into existence a new social structure of accumulation. Basically the same structure of accumulation remained in place that had emerged out of the long depression of the late nineteenth century at the beginning of the era of rival imperialisms. The new hegemonic order enabled this structure of accumulation to work for a time with maximum effectiveness as a global system. The question whether its potentialities have been exhausted and whether the accumulation process is entering a phase of restructuring must be linked to the question whether or not the Pax Americana has come to an end.[1] Here I am concerned with the anatomy and physiology of hegemony—with the forms of state and configurations of social forces that have sustained global hegemony and with the processes of internationalizing of production and internationalizing of the state that have bound these forms of state and social forces into a total system. In part 3 I turn to consider the economic, political, and social forces generated within the Pax Americana that could lead to its transformation.

## GLOBAL HEGEMONY

Although there was considerable activity of planning for postwar political and economic organization among the allied powers in the later phases of World War II, what eventually came about was not clearly envisaged during this planning phase. The allies of the United States were concerned to avoid a U.S. relapse into isolationism such as followed World War I and were disposed to make concessions to encourage U.S. commitment to an active leadership role. Both U.S. and allied planners were aware that the U.S. economy that had fueled the war effort could be kept running at capacity when the war ended only if the United States were able to continue a huge export surplus for a number of years. Such an export surplus would also be the means of reequipping the economies of war-devastated countries (and in the longer run, which then preoccupied few people, of developing economically backward countries). It was by no means clear, however, in what sort of world order these objectives of U.S. participation could best be accomplished.

The experience of the Depression of the 1930s left a legacy of opposed policy orientations in all the major capitalist countries, including the United States. On the one hand were those who saw salvation in the return to an open liberal world economy by breaking through the barriers and controls erected during the Depression years. On the other hand where those who had acquired experience with the planning techniques developed through the Depression and war; these people had more confidence in conscious state policy than in the invisible hand of the market to achieve the social goals to which governments were now obliged to be sensitive—above all the maintenance of reasonably high levels of employment and social security.

In the United States, Wall Street and the State Department represented the former, the U.S. Treasury, with its New Deal heritage, the latter. In Britain, the Labour Party and the trade unions, with their commitment to full employment and the welfare state, recognized that government must be prepared to use controls in pursuit of these goals. On the right, the Beaverbrook press defended imperial preferences as the bastion of British world power. Thus elements of both left and right in Britain saw salvation in the preservation of national economic autonomy. The City of London represented, like Wall Street in the United States, the internationalist option. Lord Keynes, the chief British negotiator in the conclusion of the postwar international economic settlement, thought both sets of goals might be reconciled. The Clearing Union he proposed would have preserved national autonomy in economic policy so that governments could pursue full employment and welfare, and it would have required substantial commitments by states to international cooperation both in the creation of credit and in avoidance of measures that would export deflationary pressures. Keynes' aims were shared by the U.S. Treasury negotiators: they wanted a scheme that would be internationally expansionist while at the same time preserving a directing role for the state in the economy. But influential forces in Congress, as well as some in the executive, were wary of substantial financial commitments by the United States over which the United States would not have full discretionary control.

The history of international economic institution building after World War II traces the victory of the liberal internationalists over the proponents of state capitalism.[2] The way in which the International Monetary Fund's modus operandi was put in place in March 1946 gave the Fund powerful leverage over economic policy in deficit countries. Where Keynes had defended the principle of unconditionality in drawing rights on the Fund so as not to compromise a government's ability to pursue expansionist policies internally, loans would in fact now be made conditional upon the adjustment of national economic policies to favor a return to payments equilibrium, and this would most likely require debtors to abandon expansionary measures for full employment. Even though the Fund did not begin to operate for some years thereafter because of the onset of the Cold War and the exceptional measures taken by the United States for European recovery, the future policy lines for the world economic system were made clear at that time.

The principal instrumentality through which the United States shaped the postwar world economic order was the Marshall Plan. The concept of multilateralism was embodied in the provision that the countries receiving Marshall funds should agree among themselves through the Organization for European Economic Cooperation on the distribution of these funds. They would also through this agency develop a practice of mutual negotiation over the framing of national economic policies. Common policy conceptions envisaging movement toward a more integrated multilateral world economy consistent with U.S. policy could thus be put into effect. The Marshall Plan led Western

Europe progressively toward trade liberalization and exchange convertibility, basic conditions for the coming into effect of the open economy envisaged in 1946.

There was a transition period, roughly from 1946 to 1958, during which the major participant states other than the United States adjusted their own structures and their national economies to the requisites of the new world order. The Marshall Plan provided the incentive to join the new economic order and allowed time, as well as funds, through which the adjustment could be made. Opposition from less competitive protection-oriented industries was moderated in a climate of economic growth; the Korean War boom, for instance, facilitated restructuring in the steel and coal industries—industries that in other circumstances might have been successful in demanding protectionist policies.[3]

The Marshall Plan extended beyond influencing state policies right into the conscious shaping of the balance among social forces within states and the emerging configuration of historic blocs. Trade unions in Germany were reconstructed after the war under U.S. influence with leadership favorable to the new political-economic orientation. In France and Italy, U.S. influences were instrumental in splitting off minority groups from the majority communist-sympathizing trade-union movements—secessionist movements that were ready to support the Marshall Plan orientation. These minority trade unions were accorded access to the governments of their respective countries, while the majority trade unions, opposed to Marshall Plan policies, were excluded from consultation. U.S. business and labor-management relations practices were exported to Europe in a drive to raise productivity. Informal U.S. initiatives supported the formation of a European movement of influential private individuals that through various European channels, carried forward the project of European unification based on liberal economic policies and support of the Atlantic alliance. This unofficial grouping—and its successor, Jean Monnet's Action Committee for the United States of Europe—became potent channels of influence on national governments in Western Europe.[4] At the political level, the strong communist parties in both France and Italy were excluded from the internal coalition-building process. The leftward thrust of European and British politics, pronounced in the immediate postwar years, was stemmed. The Marshall Plan was able to bring about a center-right orientation in the domestic politics of Western Europe during the 1950s and 1960s that provided the political basis for the building of neoliberal states.

By 1958, the Western European governments, their economies fully recovered, were able to make their currencies freely convertible. Six of these countries joined in a common market and seven others in a free-trade association. These steps signified the readiness of the Western European countries to participate without basic reservations in the U.S.-sponsored world economic order. In 1960, the coordinating agency for economic policies of the Western European countries—renamed as the Organization for Economic Cooperation and Development (OECD)—was expanded to include the United States, Canada, and Japan. All the major capitalist countries thereby signified their commitment to the new world order.

U.S. initiative, based on that country's economic and military preponderance, thus led the Western European countries and Japan toward a world economy with free access to raw materials; free movement of goods, capital, and technology; and the elimination of discrimination in economic relations. In such a world economic space, capital accumulation could transcend national limitations. Only the Soviet sphere remained outside this design.

The new world economy grew very largely as the consequence of the U.S. hegemonic role and the global expansion of U.S.-based corporations. U.S. hegemonic actions included the Marshall Plan and extensive military expenditures abroad (notably in Korea and Indochina, the Indian Ocean, and the Persian Gulf). U.S. corporations moved capital on a large scale, particularly into Europe. These two factors created a large and accumulating U.S. payments deficit.

Initially, the flood of dollars stimulated economic growth in Europe and elsewhere. From the 1960s, it created inflationary pressures. From the mid-1970s, the dollar flow continued as the world economy was stalled in prolonged recession. Burgeoning unemployment coincided with continuing inflation as Keynes' "liquidity trap" reemerged.[5] Only the U.S. government might have been able to control the deficit, but it was a convenience to

U.S. world policy that foreign firms and governments were ready to accept and hold dollars. Seigneurage of the world's money gave the U.S. government unlimited credit abroad to pay for its foreign expenditures without having to compensate by liquidating U.S. assets and increasing taxes on U.S. corporations and citizens.

The U.S. public debt became a world debt as an increasing proportion of it was held by foreigners. The more dollars foreigners held, the more they became hostage to U.S. hegemonic policy. Some countries had specific interests implicated in the dollar outflow. West Germany agreed to accept more and more dollars in order to maintain a U.S. military presence in Europe. Arab countries accumulated big dollar balances by increasing the price of oil, which was denominated exclusively in dollars. U.S. policy makers were able to ignore the admonitions of some foreign governments that they should control the deficit and adopted an attitude of benign neglect.[6] The international financial institutions—the International Monetary Fund and the World Bank— behaved as accessories to U.S. policy.

The new hegemonic order was held in place by a configuration of different forms of state whose common feature was the role each form played in adjusting national economic policies to the dynamics of the world economy. The central premise of hegemonic order was that the world economy is a positive-sum game in which some businesses and some national economies may benefit more than the others but in which all have the opportunity to gain. The ideology derived from this premise represents the highest interest of all countries as being to faciliate the expansion of the world economy and to avoid restrictive national measures of economic policy that would be in contradiction in the long run with world-level expansion. The international institutions of this world order—principal among them the International Monetary Fund—were able to use both incentives and sanctions to secure compliance on the part of the more reluctant governments and disabled national economies.

Two principal forms of state constituted the most active participants in the world economy that emerged following World War II. The neoliberal form of state managed those national economies with the most highly developed productive forces—the countries that formed the OECD. A distinctive form of state became characteristic of late-developing peripheral economies that we can call the neomercantilist developmentalist form of state. Historically the neoliberal state was a transformation of the welfare-nationalist state in which an internal bourgeois hegemony was preserved. The functions of the state became adapted to the different world context—the transition from a rival-imperialisms to a hegemonic world order. The neomercantilist developmentalist state followed the prototype of prewar Italian fascism. It initiated capitalist development as a passive revolution within an authoritarian framework under state leadership for lack of any established bourgeois hegemony.

Beyond these two forms of state that played a major role in the new world economic order, two other forms of state established a more tenuous link with it. They are of quite different kinds.

One category would more accurately be described as various forms of protostate, i.e., political structures that try more or less successfully to monopolize the capacity for exercising political force within the national territory but have not acquired either a firm social basis of consent or the administrative capacity to formulate and apply effective economic policies. Some of these protostates are conservative structures continuous from former colonial administrations or from monarchic or oligarchic regimes that had formally independent international status. Some are best described as lumpenprotostates that manifest bizarre forms of arbitrary rule resting on the violence of armed thugs over an inarticulate majority of the population.[7] Others are protorevolutionary states that have more or less radical goals of social transformation but that are so weak relative to the outside world that their societies and economies are penetrated by external counterrevolutionary forces.[8]

The world economy does not depend to any significant extent on the protostates—although some contain mineral-exporting enclaves that supply world-economy industries. Although the vast majority of their populations are engaged in agriculture, these countries often do not grow enough food to feed their people. They import food and equipment from a world economy to which they are marginal, and they borrow from its public and private lending institutions. The primary concern of the world-economy managers with reference to these protostates is to prevent the situation within these countries from deteriorating to the point where it might constitute a political threat to the world order on which the world economy is based. This objective is pursued by a combination of foreign loan consortia that establish a collective world-economy management of the national finances of some protostates; IMF-imposed stabilization programs that direct economic policies; United Nations and bilateral administrative aid, advice, and support; World Bank programs to promote agricultural self-help and employment on labor-intensive projects; and bilateral military counterinsurgency aid.[9]

The other category of states consists of the redistributive systems that have established links to the world capitalist economy without thereby becoming an integral part of that world economy. During the 1960s, detente brought with it an increase in economic exchanges between the Soviet sphere and the capitalist economies of the OECD. From the late 1970s, the new Chinese leadership manifested a desire for increased economic links. The problem for the redistributive system is to be able to draw specifically desired benefits from relations with the world economy without losing control of the direction of its own development. By contrast with the functional role of the neoliberal and neomercantilist states in relation to the world economy, redistributive states maintain priority for their own autonomously determined developmental goals and seek a modus vivendi with the external world economy. They do not subordinate their own national economies to a development dynamic determined by the world market.

## THE NEOLIBERAL STATE

The welfare-nationalist state was built to protect the national economy from outside influences and to enhance national power in relation to rivals. The neoliberal state sought its security as a member of a stable alliance system and its economic growth as a participant in an open world economy. Its task was to adjust the national economy to the growth of the world economy, to faciliate adaptation rather than to protect existing positions. The term *neoliberal* is more appropriate than the term *liberal*, evocative of the nineteenth-century situation, because the new form of state had to pursue its course in conditions created during the intervening era. It had to take account of a more complex situation in three main respects.

First, the state itself had become an economic actor playing a direct role in the accumulation process by undertaking tasks not profitable for private industry and by coming to the financial aid of private industries in various ways (subsidies, price supports, tax abatement, etc.). Second, the state had taken on a political responsibility to cushion vulnerable social groups when the market threatened to penalize them—at least those groups that had some political clout (labor, farmers, small business, the unemployed). Third, the structure of the economy was not the market of anonymous equals pictured in nineteenth-century ideology but a segmented structure in which concentrations of capital in an oligopolistic sector coexisted with a competitive sector of smaller scale businesses reminiscent of the nineteenth-century doctrine and with the state sector. The oligopolistic sector was open to the world market, and the other two sectors were conceived as playing supporting roles. The world market had become a realm of competition among unequal giants capable of manipulating demand and of mobilizing varying degrees of economic power and political influence. The neoliberal state mediated between an oligopolistic world market that dictated the policy priorities and domestic groups that had varying claims on its political allegiance. The mediating role justified transitional exceptions to the pure doctrines of liberalism. Such exceptions take the form of adjustment assistance or temporary import restrictions to cushion the negative impact of the world market on particular sectors while encouraging a restructuring of the national economy in the direction dictated by world market tendencies.[10]

The neoliberal state inherited from the welfare-nationalist state the institutions of corporatist government-business-labor coordination and the tools of Keynesian macroeconomic demand management. In appearance there was virtually nothing to distinguish the neoliberal from the welfare nationalist form. The difference emerged in the goals pursued, in the uses to which the structure was put.

Fiscal policy, because of the large proportion of national income that passed through the state budget, was the principal regulator of the economy and stimulus to growth. Governments used demand management to pursue expansionary policies in time of recession. With incomes widely distributed, demand could be kept high and investment encouraged. Moderate inflation was a modest price to pay. Differential rates of inflation and their effects on the balance of payments did, however, put a strain on the exchange-rate stability, which was a central feature of the world-economy system established at Bretton Woods. Consequently, governments of the major countries were recurrently confronted with a conflict between international commitments to maintain exchange stability and domestic political commitments to avoid the unemployment that would result from slower growth. The outcome for the neoliberal state was what came to be called "stop-go" economic management—alternating phases of expansionary and restrictive fiscal and monetary measures geared to the evolution of the balance of payments, i.e., dictated by the rhythm of the world economy. The United States, because of its role as coiner of the world's money and its imperial position abroad, for long managed to avoid the constraint of stop-go. This constraint caught up with the United States evenutally in the long downward slide of the dollar during the administration of President Carter. Britain experienced the constraint much earlier. West Germany and Japan minimized the constraint through export-oriented policies with undervalued currencies and effective restraint on rising wage costs.[11]

Superficially the causes of inflation lie in the relationship of money to goods. Within particular societies, however, this relationship has to be explained at a deeper level in terms of the political decisions dealing with the issues of capital accumulation, investment, unemployment, and growth. These political decisions, in turn, are influenced by the level and nature of social conflict prevailing. Britain and Italy have had higher levels of class polarization and conflict than West Germany and Switzerland, and correspondingly higher levels of inflation.[12] The neo-

liberal state has tried to moderate the inflationary bias inherent
in its own structure through the use of its corporatist framework
for policy making.

Demand-pull inflation could be regulated directly by the
state through fiscal and monetary policy. But it became apparent
that the demand-pull was only part of the problem. Cost-push
inflation was another matter. It arose from the ability of big corporations to pass on to the general public through administrative
pricing the costs of wage settlements reached with their trade
unions. Wage and price controls would be one conceivable response to this kind of inflation but a response inconsistent with
the corporative theory of policy making. Incomes policies became
the preferred method—a consensually reached agreement on restraint by unions and corporations with regard to wages and
prices. Incomes policies became the principal objective of social
contract or general consensus among the most powerful economic interests and government within the neoliberal state.

Incomes policy had meaning within the framework of the
welfare-nationalist state as one element in a comprehensive national economic planning. In this context, agreed restraint in
respect of incomes would be a counterpart to an agreed policy
regarding accumulation and investment geared to maximizing
output, welfare, and employment. Incomes policy in the context
of the neoliberal state had a quite different significance. Here
incomes policies were geared to the balance of payments, themselves the consequences of a world accumulation process over
which national policies had little or no control. With capital free
to flow within a world economy, there could be no guarantee
that incomes restraint in one country would be followed by
investment in its national economy.

During phases of expansion, when labor markets were
tight and unions might expect to gain higher wages, workers
would be subject to wage restraint. During phases of recession,
unions could gain little in any case. To workers it seemed there
was no evident predictable quid pro quo for wage restraint. Furthermore, the general rule advocated for incomes policies was
that wage increases should keep in line with increases in productivity. That in effect meant the existing distribution of income
between labor and capital would be maintained. So long as na-

tional economies were growing, this freezing of income shares between labor and capital might be acceptable to unions. It strengthened corporatist tendencies in union leadership and undermined union combativity and class consciousness. As Charles Maier wrote: "The concept of growth as a surrogate for redistribution appears, in retrospect, as the great conservative idea of the last generation."[13]

Moderate levels of inflation were the consequence of corporatist tripartite economic management. Such inflation was the price paid by the neoliberal state for the moderating of social conflict among the most powerfully organized economic and social forces. Moderate inflation had a redistributory effect favoring both corporations and established labor though disadvantaging unorganized groups excluded from the corporatist compact. Higher levels of inflation had, however, a contrary effect. At a certain threshold the stimulus to growth turned into a disincentive to invest and a consequential downturn in growth. A series of factors could combine to reverse the growth trend: inflation led to trade deficit and pressure on currency exchange rates; monetary restrictions, i.e., higher interest rates, intended to combat both inflation and exchange depreciation, inhibited investment while raising the cost to capital of debt service; unions would press harder to maintain the inflationary incomes expectations of established workers, narrowing capital's profit margins and creating further disincentives for investment. This negative spiral did not materialize until the mid 1970s. The neoliberal state worked well enough during the long postwar phase of eco nomic growth. It proved unable to cope effectively when inflatio1 combined with surplus capacity and unemployment.

The world economy was the external constraint upon the neoliberal state. Whereas the welfare-nationalist state had sought to create its own protected autonomous sphere within which national goals could be pursued, the neoliberal state flourished or languished with the world economy. The major capitalist states, foremost among them the United States, could exert some influence over the world economy. They had differing conceptions of their roles in this respect. The United States and Britain generally espoused the "pure" concept of neoliberalism: primacy to the world market and acceptance of international interdependence with a minimum of direct state involvement in industrial decisions and a restricting of state action to the use of macroeconomic instruments of fiscal and monetary policy. In Japan and France, the state played a more active role closely coordinated with big national capital in investment and trade policy. West Germany and some of the smaller European states manifested something of a compromise between these two variants: commitment to liberal competition policies in the world-economy sphere combined with domestic welfare protection.[14]

The Bretton-Woods institutional structure for the world economy began to work according to its basic constitution only in the late 1950s. European and Japanese recovery were conditions for its coming into effect. By the early 1970s its rules concerning gold parity and fixed exchange rates ceased to be operable and were abandoned, though the institutions continued as a framework for applying the residue of the system and for exploring the possibilities for a reconstructed monetary order. The ability of the United States to dominate world-economy arrangements had been weakened with the revival of Europe and Japan. Henceforth, a series of issues beset the economic relations of the major capitalist powers: exchange-rate policy, interest-rate policy, the surveillance of international indebtedness, access to markets, and protection of market shares. There seemed to be no longer any effective overall means of regulating the world economy. Though neomercantilist tendencies appeared during the 1970s and 1980s, these took the form of state involvement in a struggle for world-market shares, not the carving out of separate economic spheres. Countries could not secede from a system to which they were bound in a web of reserve holdings, foreign indebtedness, foreign investments, trade outlets, and political and military commitments. The neoliberal state had become tributary to an uncontrolled world economy.

From the mid-1970s the world economy ceased to be an engine of growth. For the neoliberal state, a principal consequence of this slump was a growing fiscal crisis. The gap between state expenditures, including service on enlarged public debts, and state incomes became an acute problem with the prolonged economic downturn. Statutory-entitlement payments for social security rose and state revenues declined as a result of the depressed economy. The countercyclical remedy of deficit financing seemed likely only to accelerate both inflation and stagnation by driving up interest rates through increased government borrowing while deterring new investments. The limits of conventional macroeconomic techniques of cyclical adjustment seemed to have been reached.

The limits of tripartite corporatism were also tested. The neoliberal state endeavored to maintain a coalition of powerful economic and social forces—oligopolistic business and those elements of the labor movement disposed to work with government and business in a consensual economic policy. The basis for agreement in such coalitions included support for welfare programs, an understanding attitude by union leaders toward balance of payments considerations and the need to keep export industries internationally competitive. Union and business bureaucracies had a mutual interest in the institutionalization of conflict in industrial relations procedures. Dramatization of issues dealt with through these procedures enabled business to pass on higher labor costs to the public in the form of price increases and enabled union leaders to reassure rank-and-file members that their interests were being defended. Governments could offer union leaders the symbolic benefits of access to the highest level of state and the appearance of participation in at least certain spheres of public policy.[15] They also in North America and more reluctantly in Japan opened the state sector to unionization, something that had already happened in most o the European countries.[16] Business gained the aura of politica and union backing for its own expansion.

The mutual benefits available through the tripartite coalition were most apparent in times of economic expansion. Economic stagnation brought out the underlying conflicts of interest. The testing ground lay in attempts to implement incomes policies—the ultimate form of tripartism and the occasion of its breakdown.

The Beveridge package of welfare state policies prepared for Britain during World War II included wage restraint as a quid pro quo for full employment.[17] The same reasoning gained acceptance in trade union circles in other countries, more especially when social-democratic parties were in government and seemed more likely to deliver on wage restraint's counterpart. In practice, however, investment policies were largely inoperative, price controls proved ineffective, and improvements in the employment level appeared to depend on external events over which governments had little or no control.[18] In such circumstances, incomes policies became a trap for the labor leaders who participated in them. The symbolic accolade these leaders received from government for their public-spirited deference to the "national interest" had to be balanced against loss of support among union members when real wages declined. Union leaders who refused to be involved in incomes policies—the French CGT and the Italian CGIL, for example—were less compromised vis-à-vis their own rank and file.[19] Participating union leaders were threatened when rank-and-file movements challenged existing officeholders and effective bargaining power shifted toward the shop floor.[20]

The world recession that began in 1974 beleaguered and ultimately routed tripartite incomes policies in neoliberal states. In Britain, the Wilson and Callaghan Labour governments negotiated a "social contract" with the unions and employers in 1975. It first resulted in a reduction in real wages and then dissolved in industrial confusion, which abetted the election of the Thatcher government in May 1976. In West Germany, the less formalized practice of "concerted action" between business and labor leaders who accepted the rationale of defending industry's export position, which had been difficult to maintain following 1974, came apart in the strike wave of 1978–1979.[21] In the United States, President Nixon introduced a negotiated and mandatory incomes policy accompanied by price controls during 1973 as part of a package of measures addressed to the international position of the U.S. economy. Subsequently, labor's reluctance to participate made incomes policies politically unlikely and labor's relative weakness made them unnecessary to government and business.

In France and Italy, where labor movements had been split and weakened in the postwar period as a result of Marshall-Plan activities,[22] social protest concentrating in the trade unions reemerged during 1968–69. Governments in those countries, confronting the economic crisis of the 1970s, had to deal with strengthened labor movements. In France, an incomes policy was applied by direct government controls in 1976.[23] In Italy, the *compromesso storico* in which the Communist Party (PCI) for a short time gave support to a center-left government, may be considered a functional equivalent for an incomes policy, since Communist participation provided a measure of restraint in union demands. The unpopularity of the *compromesso storico* among rank-and-file union and party members and its connotation of sharing responsibility without substantial compensating influence ensured its end and the return of PCI and unions to opposition. Even in Sweden, where national-level bargaining has taken account of public interest considerations, this practice was severely shaken by the strike wave of 1980.[24] All of these events confirm that the limits of tripartite corporatism within the neoliberal state had been tested and reached during the recession period following 1974. Tripartism was tending to revert to bipartite confrontation.

Various factors have played a role in the incentive to negotiate tripartite incomes policies and the relative success such policies have had. Where trade union movements have been strong and broadly based in the labor force, there has been a strong incentive on the part of governments and capital to involve them in incomes policies. High dependence on exports—and particularly the perceived need to maintain competitiveness in manufactured exports on world markets—is another powerful incentive. Conversely, a high level of class conflict prevailing in a society is an obstactle to the achievement of incomes policies. A further factor that, in at least some cases, has facilitated the conclusion of tripartite arrangements is presence in the government of social-democratic or labor parties with links to the trade unions. Incomes policies were for a time most successful in countries like the Netherlands and the Scandinavian countries, where labor has been strongly organized and recognizes the country's high dependence on maintaining a competitive edge in export markets. Class conflict has been muted in these countries by the practice of corporative public policy making. In the Scandinavian case, the long-term presence of social-democratic parties in government has certainly provided a propitious climate for tripartism, although in the Netherlands this has not been a significant factor.[25] In Britain, although the strength of the trade unions has constituted an incentive to government to attempt incomes policies, class conflict and a disposition of labor to discount the imperative nature of maintaining export competitiveness have made incomes policies harder to sustain. In the United States, trade unions have been relatively weaker and less imbued with class consciousness; they have been ready at times to take a pragmatic if skeptical approach to wage and price guidelines. In France and Italy, trade union movements have been either too weak to be an *interlocuteur valable* (the case of the minority unions) or too opposed on class grounds to want to participate (the case of the majority unions).

Apart from formal tripartite incomes policies, a practice of informal corporatism has also developed. The general model of this type consists of a close interrelationship between central agencies of government and the management of big corporations at one level and a cooperative pattern of relations between corporate management and the core established workforce of these corporations at a second level. Management is the hinge between core labor and government, and government is the hinge between corporate management and the world economy. This pattern has been characteristic of Japanese labor-management-government relations. It has also emerged in French practice, and some aspects of the model have been evident in West Germany and the United States as well.

The two-tier structure of informal corporatism corresponds to the internationalization of the neoliberal state—a process to be discussed below. The primary function of the neoliberal state—adjustment of the national economy to world-economy trends—involved a restructuring of the hierarchy of agencies within government. The welfare-nationalist state brought into prominence agencies concerned with national economic planning and associated corporative arrangements: planning bureaus, ministries of industries and labor, all with links into the client groups of the national economy. The neoliberal state gives priority to those central agencies of government that act as links between the world economy and the national economy: finance ministries and treasuries and foreign trade and investment agencies, functioning in close coordination with the offices of presidents and prime ministers. The earlier structures of national corporatism are not displaced; they are just subordinated, becoming instruments of policies transmitted through the world-economy-linked central agencies.

The French case, though untypical in its relative clarity of form, serves to suggest an ideal type of the two-tier structure of informal and formal corporatism. Two patterns of linkage between the state and industry became superimposed. One pattern was the formal structure of institutionalized corporatism, which connects the ministries of industry and labor with business trade associations and trade unions respectively. The principal task of this structure is to regulate the different sectors of the economy according to general norms. In order to do this, these structures also determine what the relevant facts are on which regulation is to be based; e.g., state agencies and their clients collaborate in the preparation of sectoral statistics.

The second pattern of linkage consists of informal contacts between the upper levels of public administration and the management of big enterprises. In France, such contacts are facilitated by the existence of informal networks among graduates of the grandes écoles who occupy high-level positions in industry, as well as in the state administration. (In Japan a similar function is performed by the cohorts of prestige-university graduates.) This level of interaction is propitious for active intervention by government in the economy, i.e., specific interventions rather than the formulation of general rules. Specific intervention emphasizes the discretionary rather than the normative role of state officials; consequently, routine-seeking bureaucrats of the Weberian ideal type fight shy of it, and this kind of activity tends to be performed by the more "political" officials attached to the cabinets of ministers. Thus a flexible managerial coordination develops between key agencies of the state and the bigger enterprises in both state and private sectors, i.e., between government and oligopolistic capital.[26]

The first pattern of institutionalized corporatism prevailed in France during the years following World War II. The reconstruction of French industry took place under the guidance of the Commissariat général du Plan. This may be regarded as a continuation of the thrust of welfare-nationalist state planning. As the French economy became increasingly open to the world economy, i.e., with the transformation from welfare-nationalist to a neoliberal form of state, the second pattern assumed predominance. The first pattern was not rescinded, but it functioned mainly for the smaller enterprises and to manifest preferred status for the minority trade unions (excluding the majority Communist-sympathizing CGT) that participated in it. Different parts of the state machinery were involved in the two patterns. National-level planning lost most of its initial meaning when the national economy was opened formally to partners in the EEC and when at the same time U.S.-based multinational corporations expanded their investments within the EEC.[27] Government influence thenceforth could be exercised through fiscal and monetary policies and by state influence in financial networks, together with discreet interventions in the ad hoc decisions of big enterprises.[28] These enterprises in effect set the pattern for sectoral development; a few big enterprises could determine the direction for a whole sector.[29] The ministry of finance and the offices of the prime minister and president of the republic were in the position to undertake this kind of intervention and direction of the economy.

In this two-tier corporative structure, trade-union influence was nonexistent in the upper and determining level. Established workers in the big enterprises of the oligopolistic sector are encompassed indirectly through the development of enterprise corporatism.[30] Trade unions have direct access only to the lower and less important level. This level regulates in particular the medium and smaller scale enterprises. It does so in the wake of the key decisions taken at the higher level, which are dictated by world-economy opportunities.

## THE NEOMERCANTILIST DEVELOPMENTALIST STATE

In a number of countries of the Third World, forms of state power exist, even repressive coercive power, that are not sustained in any coherent way by internal social forces and are of only limited effectiveness in controlling external economic and political influence. I have called these forms protostates. The protostate can extract tribute but lacks the capability or incentive to reshape society, and society is neither strong enough nor coherent enough either to manage itself or to fashion a state in its own image. In economic terms, the national market does not contain sufficient effective demand to become a dynamic force, and the existence of an excess supply of labor gives no incentive to stimulate greater efficiency on the part of investors. In political terms, the power holders in the state apparatus can gain enough credit and enough arms from external sponsors not to have to mobilize society so that it will produce a surplus under state auspices. The protostate is symptomatic of an impasse in the relationship of state to society.

A development of state power may overcome that impasse by allowing the state to take the initiative to induce change in economy and society. This initiative may be more or less successful. The attempt may be aborted, or its successes, its consequences, may not correspond to the declared intentions of the state managers. The form of state that thus seizes the initiative is, in the first place, neomercantilist; it seeks to gain control over the instruments necessary to shape the national economy. In the second place, it is developmentalist because it wants to use these instruments to achieve continuous growth and structural change. (Growth is not, of course, identical to development. Growth is reducible to a statistical concept, namely, continuing increase in GNP. Development is a more complex, normative, and telelogical concept, implying changes in the structures of production and the distribution of the product. The initiative of the state envisages both growth and development.)

Neomercantilist aims include control by the state apparatus over access by foreigners to the national economy and the terms on which that access may be granted, e.g., for extraction of minerals, production of agricultural export crops, manufacturing either for the local market or for export. The initiative-taking state extracts rents when it authorizes foreigners to undertake such operations, and in addition it undertakes certain forms of production directly through an expanded nationalized sector. These become more important sources of state revenue than general taxation, and the state comes to control a very large part of the surplus product and of total domestic resources available for investment.[31] In its disposition of these resources, the state is not activated solely by the dynamic of capitalist accumulation; i.e., it is not obliged by its own rules to make a profit. Its investments are determined by political, as well as by profitability criteria. However, the state is not redistributionist in the sense in which central planning is a redistributionist system operating through the state. Neomercantilist developmentalism opens a wide sphere of political appropriation and disposition of resources within an economic system that remains linked with capitalist accumulation at the world level, i.e., through remission of profits by foreign direct investment and by servicing of foreign debt.

Development has thus become conditional upon external capital and technology. The principal determinants of the direction of development, i.e., decisions about what is to be produced and for which markets, are the investment criteria of international capital. The state's role is to maximize its share of the profits to be earned by the nation's participating in world-economy investment and marketing. The state may also exert some secondary influence on development objectives. This influence is, however, nullified at the point where it runs up against international capital's criteria of profitability.

The neomercantilist developmentalist state seeks to increase its bargaining power vis-à-vis foreign capital without breaking with foreign economic dependency. This form of state is the principal agency for transforming classic dependency into dependent development.[32] The state achieves this chiefly through a combination of stricter control over access by foreign capital, increases in the rents extracted from resource exports, support for national capital, expansion of the state sector, and increased foreign borrowing for investment according to state-determined plans. The state sector plays an increasingly important role alongside national private capital and foreign capital. The foreign component shifts away from direct investment by multinational corporations toward an increasing proportion of joint ventures and especially of state-guaranteed loans from multinational banks.[33] The neomercantilist state poses problems for foreign investors because it is more interventionist, but it also offers advantages. The social peace and internal political order maintained by strict state control over labor relations and police and parapolice repression protect foreign investments and safeguard the servicing of debt.

The state that seizes the initiative in the state-society impasse will try to incorporate some elements of society within its sphere, under its direct sponsorship and control. These efforts usually encompass the industrial workers and some parts of the rural population. The attempt to incorporate industrial workers often involves domesticating or replacing any forms of labor organization not controlled by the state. Incorporation of the rural population usually implies setting up new state-sponsored cooperative organizations.[34] Corporatist initiatives of this kind are often undertaken in a time of social crisis either as a preemptive response by the state to the threat that autonomous class-based organizations might gain the allegiance of these social groups or as a means of neutralizing such organizations where they already exist. State-sponsored organizations are also a means of giving the developmentalist program a basis of popular support. Corporatism can result either from the ruler's desire to create a secure base of support for state initiatives or from fear that independent initiatives arising in civil society will thwart state aims. The first leads to a degree of mobilization at state initiative; the second, to a degree of demobilization under state supervision.[35] In both cases, the mobilization of society is partial and controlled.

Social conditions characteristic of Third World countries are in some respects propitious for this pattern of state-dominated organization. Dependent and instrumental attitudes and behavior patterns tend to prevail among newly urbanized populations. Autonomy, whether for individuals or organizations, usually requires a degree of adaptation to the urban-industrial milieu and an accumulation of resources sufficient to give self-confidence. Both conditions are usually missing in Third World urban settings. Reforms designed to benefit urban marginals come more frequently from incorporative initiatives of the state than from the pressure of mass revolt. This tends to confirm the dependent pattern of behavior.[36] Mobilizing experiences in different countries do, however, leave legacies of autonomous organizations, e.g., the Peronist trade unions in Argentina, the tin miners' organization in Bolivia, the APRA-linked unions in Peru. Residues of autonomy may thus persist in uneasy coexistence with the incorporating drives of the neomercantilist developmentalist state.

This form of state creates state-corporatist institutions as its characteristic mode of social relations of production. The organization of industrial production in the peripheral formation is itself conducive to this mode. Typically, there is a dualism of large state- or foreign-owned undertakings and smaller local private enterprises. The big undertakings dependent on export markets and with substantial capital investment have an interest in continuous production that makes them ready to give firm guarantees of employment and to provide a certain training and upgrading for their employees. Their relatively high nonlabor production costs give the employer an incentive to stabilize employment, even for some semiskilled workers, so as not to risk disruption of production. In the Japanese model, such stabilization was achieved through enterprise corporatism, and this tendency was also to be found in some of the enclave enterprises set up by foreign-based multinational corporations before the emergence of neomercantilist states. Neomercantilist states have, however, combated and generally replaced employer-dependent incorporation of workers by state-dependent incorporation. This tendency was further assisted by the international diffusion through the ILO of the practice of legalizing labor relations. Although the ILO favored autonomous trade unions based on the experience of advanced capitalist countries, this idea did not fare well in late-industrializing countries where neither social conditions nor the will of the state gave it much support. It was easy for the state to give newly drafted labor codes a state-corporatist form. Consequently, where states in late-industrializing countries succeeded in taking the initiative, their own wills conspired with both the organization of production and the international milieu of ideas to produce state corporatism.[37]

The origins of the neomercantilist developmentalist state and the pattern of conflict through which this form of state evolved can be described in general terms as the result of (1) the impact of foreign economic penetration and the gradual inclusion of a country within the world capitalist economy and (2) the nature of the local response by social and political forces to this impact.

Opportunities to extract minerals and some agricultural products have loomed large among the incentives for capital in the industrially advanced countries to penetrate into precapitalist, resource-rich zones. Foreign mining or petroleum extraction or plantations recruited a local work force, part of more permanently employed and often unionized workers, and part largely unskilled and continually replaced by migratory movements. Those activities also came to employ some local managerial staff alongside expatriates from the metropole. Locally spent wages provided incomes for small local businesses. At the same time, the growth of industry and of overseas economic relations was accompanied by an expansion of state services, whether through colonial administrations or by sovereign countries; by a continual erosion of primitive agriculture (accelerated often by state policies designed to create a wage labor force, e.g., by direct forced labor or more indirectly by compelling subsistence farmers to earn cash in order to pay a head tax); and by a flow of job-seeking rural emigrants into the cities. Thus foreign economic penetration brought with it a new structure of production relations: enterprise corporatism in the state services and the staffs of foreign corporations; elements of bipartism or tripartism among the skilled workers in the bigger undertakings; an enterprise labor market, partly of the small-business type, and partly of nonestablished workers in big industry; a growing primitive labor market of those displaced from rural modes; and declining subsistence or peasant-lord agriculture.

In such a social formation, a new class structure became apparent, superimposed upon earlier social divisions. A petty bourgeoisie, very largely bureaucratic and consisting of government and big corporation employees but also of small businessmen, and a small organized worker group with notions of labor relations patterned on those of the metropole, jointly acquired the potential to form a nationalist coalition. This coalition, where it was formed, demanded a greater share of the benefits of growth brought about by foreign-induced economic activity, in which its component elements were all directly involved. The enterprise-labor-market workers in big industry, because of their high turnover, and those in small local enterprises, because of patrimonial-type relations with bosses, were less likely to form a class capable of consistent action but were nevertheless capable of explosive spontaneous protests that could be turned to serve the political goals of the nationalist coalition.

In general, the class most capable of achieving a degree of popular cohesion and common purpose around a nationalist program was the urban petty bourgeoisie, composed mainly of government officials, military officers, clerical and supervisory employees of foreign businesses, and indigenous businessmen. The ability or willingness of this rather heterogeneous aggregate to undertake radical social transformation was usually limited by the state's dependence on external supports, e.g., foreign loans, monopsonistic markets for national produce, and military and administrative aid. Petty-bourgeois leaders might use populist slogans to arouse the workers but backed away from more thoroughgoing mobilization of the popular strata.

The social groups upon which such an emergent state based its support were not themselves hegemonic. Nor were the political parties that monopolized participation in such states disciplined monoliths like those that carried out revolutions founding redistributive systems.[38] The state itself was the only basis for the project of an indigenously inspired, populist-flavored, autonomous direction to national development. The petty-bourgeois state managers identified with the state and tended not to think of themselves in class terms. They were, however, dependent on the support of the urban petty bourgeoisie and the urban wage earners. To consolidate their influence over the latter, the state managers introduced state corporatist production relations. This gave the political leadership control over trade unions, which they used to restrict industrial conflict and as a lever in bargaining with foreign investors; they did not pursue full-scale worker incorporation into unions but limited corporative unionization to the key industries.

Populist leadership typically marked the first phase of neomercantilist development. Populism was facilitated by external revenues from foreign loans and sales of resources. These provided the state with the ability to make payoffs to the social groups on which it most depended—the urban middle strata, the armed forces, and state-corporatist workers—as well as provided returns to foreign and national capital. The populist appeal would

soon wear thin as revenues declined—something determined by
the world economy, over which the state managers had no control. Populist leadership was inhibited internally from thoroughgoing mobilization of the whole population because of the lack
of either a firm basis in society or of a disciplined vanguard-party
organization capable of sustaining a long-term dictatorship working to transform society. (The Algerian political cadres in effect
demobilized the peasantry, which had been the basis for the
liberation struggle, and the Peruvian radical military failed to
mobilize either a rural or an urban worker base.) It was inhibited
externally because of its dependence on world-economy sources
for the revenues that made populist policies possible. Populism
in the Third World faltered in the early 1960s and virtually
disappeared as a political basis for neomercantilist development.

 Populism was replaced typically by military-bureaucratic
regimes. Populism's legitimacy rested on evidence of benefits for
at least some of its client groups—an import substitution thrust
in industrial development, job security for state-corporatist workers, subsidized housing for the urban middle strata, etc. The
legitimacy of the military-bureaucratic regime rested on maintenance of law and order among urban populations vastly increased
by internal migrations that had not been absorbed by employment
creation. These regimes also shifted the emphasis in industrialization from import substitution to export promotion. They
worked out a modus vivendi with both foreign capital and national bourgeoisie. The state became more autonomous, more
authoritarian, and even more dependent on world-economy
links. Where populist leadership had a tendency to undermine
the confidence of world-economy managers because of spend-
thrift catering to internal client groups, the military-bureaucratic
leadership offered these world-economy managers greater guarantees of security for their investments.[39]

 The shift from populist to military-bureaucratic leadership
over nonhegemonic societies that characterized neomercantilist
development in the Third World during the Pax Americana has
a clear analogy to the alternation between cartel state and authoritarian state discussed above in chapter 6 in connection with
fascism. Gramsci's analysis of caesarism applies to both.[40] There
is a caesarism without caesar—the assemblage of factions in a

cartel state, each maneuvering for influence within the state apparatus, seeking control over strategic instruments of state (military forces, police, intelligence, development bank, regional power positions, etc.), and cultivating clienteles and support bases in society. There is a caesarism with caesar—now not so frequently the "man of destiny" like Mussolini or Peron, but more frequently the faceless autocrat like Pinochet, the function rather than the personality of repressive power. There are progressive, transformative forms of caesarism, and there are reactionary, stabilizing, and repressive forms. Their common denominator is the external dependency of a passive revolution from above.[41] The ideas and techniques of the developmental process these various forms of caesarism sponsor are taken from abroad. These techniques are welcomed by some segments of society, e.g., state technocrats and some local entrepreneurs, but obstructed by others, e.g., traditional landowners. The developmentalist state mediates among social groups by making the state the arbiter and by suppressing open social conflict. The state does this within its primary constraint, which is the need to adjust its policies to the requirements of accumulation at the world level. Such states appear objectively to be allies, if sometimes querulous allies, of multinational capital.

The failure of populism was in part the result of an inability of cartel states to resolve developmental issues in which social forces were polarized. The state as arbiter could only try to suppress open conflict but proved to be incapable of removing the roots of conflict.

The existence of primitive peasant-lord agriculture was an obstacle to capitalist development in all such countries. When the state came to grips with this problem it attempted to resolve it through land reform, more successfully in the case of some of the smaller countries (South Korea and Taiwan) than in the case of the larger ones. The Mexican land reform carried out by Mexico's early twentieth-century revolution was the first and most revolutionary attempt to deal with this issue; it is now, in retrospect, the classic example of the ultimate failure of an incomplete or insufficiently comprehensive reform.[42] Land distributions to individual families and to traditional indigenous communities insufficiently supported by other measures such as state-supported credit and locally based political power resulted in farmer indebtedness and a return of dominant-subordinate relationships in the countryside and in marginalization of part of the rural population into subsistence farming. Halfhearted land reforms in India and Pakistan generally did not break the local power of landlords.

In Indonesia, the prospect of land reform implicit in President Sukarno's move toward closer alliance with the Indonesian Communist Party in 1965 was countered by a military coup supported by the U.S. Central Intelligence Agency and the massacre of more than half a million people. In Brazil, a tacit division of powers came about from the 1930s between urban-based political parties and rural landlords, which left the latter a free hand in rural areas (rule by local "colonels" or strong men) and resulted in violent repression of recurrent attempts to organize peasant and subsistence farmer cooperation and resistance to landlord power, as in the peasant leagues of the *nordeste* in the 1960s. When the populist president João Goulart seemed to be encouraging a mobilization of peasants, urban workers, and rank-and-file military such as would threaten to upset the balance of social forces in a radical direction, he was removed by a military coup in which covert U.S. encouragement was also a factor.

The political limits of populism were thus manifested by military coup when populist regimes seemed to be turning toward radical popular mobilization. The military regimes that took over proved to be better able to preside over a different direction of change: the removal of obstacles to capitalist development. Military-bureaucratic states expanded the state sectors of national economies; they bargained with multinational corporations and persuaded them to undertake more innovative and developmental activities in the country; they channeled foreign borrowing from transnational private banks into national (public and private) investment projects; and they facilitated the displacement of traditional agriculture, both intensive small-holder farming and wasteful extensive *latifundia* farming, by indigenous green-revolution commercial farming and foreign-controlled agribusiness.

At the lower reaches of the social hierarchies, a new balance of forces was also emerging. Between the abject poverty and social disorganization of the primitive labor market and the closely supervised spheres of enterprise corporatism and state corporatism, the nonestablished workforce of the enterprise labor market grew appreciably. Nonestablished workers consist of distinct segments: green-revolution-promoted commercial agriculture has expanded wage employment in agriculture; small indigenous industries have grown with official encouragement; and larger industries, both national and foreign, employ more nonestablished labor. The latter segment, often working in proximity to the more protected and privileged established workers, are most likely to become a self-conscious and articulate working class. Agricultural laborers, experiencing a growing polarization of rural society, may also become available for protest movements. These newly mobilized workers could become a threat to the stability of domestic politics.

Capitalist development led by neomercantilist states achieved some notable successes during the decade of the 1970s with the stimulus of foreign borrowing. During this decade, the growth rates of countries like Brazil, Mexico, South Korea, and Taiwan measure this achievement. This pattern of development also generated internal social tensions in some of these countries; it fostered widening income differentials between social classes and regions. Foreign-linked firms using high technology enjoyed relatively high profit rates; local enterprises, maximizing their commercial advantage in local markets, had lower rates of profit. Established workers in the state corporatist sector received a certain measure of protection giving them advantages relative to enterprise-labor-market workers and the unemployed. Commercialization of agriculture favored the larger holdings, reduced employment in rural areas, and increased the flow of rural migrants into the primitive labor market of the urban centers. Prices rose during the inflation of the expansionary phase; the most favored groups could keep pace with it, though those outside the corporatist sector were in greater difficulty.

Then at the beginning of the 1980s came the debt crisis.[43] Regimes that had financed their growth on foreign credit were no longer able to meet the interest payments on their external debt. The measures required by foreign creditors as a condition for extending debts included currency devaluations and cutbacks in domestic spending, which had the effect of raising prices of food to the general population, raising prices of imported equipment to local capitalists, reducing government services, and reducing real wages. These measures could only exacerbate the social tensions and inequalities that had been generated during the expansionary stage. The success of dependent development had a social cost.

Would it also have a political cost in terms of the viability of the military-bureaucratic regimes that had led the latest phase of neomercantilist development? Schematically, there seemed to be three possibilities of future political orientation. One was a continuation of military rule maintaining sufficient repression to prevent the increased tensions from exploding into domestic disorder. Another possibility was a radical turn under different leadership toward a more autocentric development. A third was reversion from military rule to the cartel state that would continue the path of dependent development under civilian auspices, gaining in domestic legitimacy what it lost in repressive capability.

Under the military-bureaucratic regime, the relatively more satisfied part of the population acquiesces in repression in order to fend off the threat of revolt from the dissatisfied. In order to maintain this balance of support, the military-bureaucratic regime must be able to ensure continuance of the process of dependent development that sustains the relatively satisfied part of the population—and this means retaining and expanding foreign markets, maintaining a flow of foreign credit, and continuing the growth of export industries. The military-bureaucratic regime may be able to count on external military aid from the principal guarantor of the world hegemonic order. But military aid and the maintenance of a strong domestic repressive capability may not be enough. Dependent development must be perceived to work in the economic sphere, at least for enough of the population to maintain sufficient support for the regime. Events during the early 1980s in Argentina, Chile, Brazil, and the Philippines suggest that some of those middle-strata social groups that initially supported military-bureaucratic government may have withdrawn support and thereby opened the prospect of a transition to civilian rule.

Autocentric development under radical leadership would

imply a return to populism but under very different conditions from those of the earlier phase of populism. To carry through an effective revolution from above, the radical leadership would have to be less timid in its determination to mobilize the whole population behind the development effort, and it would have to do this on the basis of domestic resources, where earlier populism lived off accumulated foreign exchange reserves and foreign revenues. Whereas the earlier populism flourished in a permissive world order, a postmilitary-bureaucratic populism would confront a hostile world order—a foreign embargo of credit and of export markets, together with active military and political destabilization.

The radical alternative presupposes a distinctive economic strategy. Rejecting the illusion of a total severance from the external world economy, the radical alternative nevertheless envisages that internally determined development priorities will dictate how external economic links are to be used. A popularly based development effort would give first place to the satisfaction of human needs. This means primarily increasing agricultural production and expanding employment and thus spreading incomes to create an effective mass demand for essentials. Such a policy is not limited to labor-intensive investments; it could well include some foreign-financed capital-intensive projects designed to produce the inputs to the agriculture production process, for example, fertilizers and farm machinery, as well as capital-intensive production of foreign-exchange-earning exports. But it would be quite different from the production and import patterns characteristic of dependent development toward which the conservative direction of neomercantilist developmentalism tends, i.e., one that features local production of consumer durables for an élite domestic and foreign market.

The radical alternative equally presupposes a certain political base. In Gramscian terms, the war of movement seems unlikely to succeed or to succeed for long where the repressive state apparatus is strong and external destabilization effective. This would be the lesson of the fall of the government of Salvador Allende in Chile. Electoral strength alone is clearly not enough. The radical alternative would have to be based on a long-term war of position building a secure support base within society—

such as has occurred in some countries of the Third World in the course of prolonged wars of liberation. On the assumption that it has been possible to create such a base of support, it is also necessary to foresee how popular pressures can maintain the radical course once state power has been acquired. One thesis envisages the possibility that some forces within the governing populist combination will coalesce with popular forces supportive of the radical economic program and thereby build sufficient political pressure to enhance the influence of this faction with the state. Continuance of the radical reforming thrust would then have to be ensured through the same dynamic repeating itself— some factions within the state always being ready to activate renewed popular pressures.[44]

Hitherto, radical caesarism has been of relatively short duration. The experiences of Algeria just after independence, of Nasser's Egypt, Sukarno's Indonesia, Nkrumah's Ghana, and Velasco's Peru provide a variety of examples to support this proposition. In all these cases, a radical thrust turned after a time in a conservative direction. There are compelling reasons for this. Political cadres hesitate to pursue mobilization lest it get out of hand, and so they come to rely more on police methods to control populations. Foreign borrowing offers an easier way to finance development than extracting capital from the nation's human resources through organizing popular participation in the development effort. The cadres themselves may be torn apart into rival factions competing for the state's resources, giving more scope for private capitalists, who favor and secure more liberal economic policies.

The third possibility—a reversion to a civilian form of cartel state—implies a failure of both military-bureaucratic and radical-populist experiments in a situation where no internal social hegemony has become established. The cartel state would continue the path of dependent development and would doubtless receive external support from the principal capitalist states and agencies of the world economy, which would perceive it as a hope for stability. This state's effectiveness would suffer from its very lack of unity—unity being the corresponding virtue of the military-bureaucratic and radical-populist alternatives. The different components of the cartel take up positions within the

state. Their struggle to capture shares of the rents and other
revenues flowing through the state undermines consistency in
the disposition of state-controlled resources. It may lead to un-
wise investments, to the entrenchment of rival power positions
within the state, and to corruption. State corporatism, for instance, enables established workers in state-sector enterprises to
capture a disproportionate share of income at the expense of
nonestablished workers, unemployed, and rural producers.[45] The
cartel state is the political expression of a stalled passive revolution. The fundamental problem underlying its immobility is
the absence of social hegemony, and that situation can be changed
only through a successful war of position that would result in
the construction of a hegemonic historic bloc.

## THE INTERNATIONALIZING
## OF PRODUCTION

The Pax Americana created a world hegemonic order in which a
*world* economy of international production emerged within the
existing *international* economy of classical trade theory. The
international-economy model connects national economies by
flows of goods, capital, and specie. Where the international-economy model focuses on exchange, the world-economy model focuses on production. It consists of transnational production organizations whose component elements are located in different
territorial jurisdictions.

Each of these transnational production organizations produces for the world market. Each takes advantage of differences
in costs and availabilities of factors of production in deciding
about the location of its component elements.

Knowledge, in the form of technology and market information, is the principal resource in the world economy, especially knowledge in its dynamic form as the capacity to generate
new technologies and to market new products. Money can be
tapped where it is to be found by those who have knowledge
assets, e.g., in local capital markets or in international credit. The
nature of international trade changes. Arms-length intercountry
exchanges are characteristic of the international economy. Intra-

corporate transfers become more important in the world economy.

Transnational production organizations take advantage of the differences between the factor endowments of countries in the international economy, especially differences in labor costs. They internalize these differences, making use of them to minimize overall production costs. The world economy promotes a homogenization of consumer habits, social values, and productive technologies, but it does this on the basis of existing differences, which affect relative costs of production and access to markets.[46] Accumulation takes place through a hierarchy of modes of social relations of production linked within transnational production organizations. Some of these modes of social relations of production generate more surplus than others. Struggles take place over the proportions of the surplus to be captured by the central decision makers of the transnational production organization and by the political authorities of the different jurisdictions in which it functions. The crucial problem for transnational production organizations is continually to increase the surplus through higher productivity and to lower production costs.

Production costs are determined by (1) the cost of producer goods, (2) the cost of raw materials, (3) the cost of labor, (4) the cost of externalities such as environmental degradation insofar as the producing organization is required to bear them, and (5) the combinations in which (1), (2), (3), and (4) are put together.

Most research and development has taken place in the advanced capitalist countries and most of that in the United States. Very little of it has been located in the less developed countries.[47] A great deal of this research has been done by large corporations or by government agencies working on projects from which large corporations could benefit (e.g., nuclear and space research). Advance in productive technologies was concentrated in core-country headquarters of transnational production organizations. These organizations have been in a position to maintain a lead in the productivity of industrial processes.

Access to cheap raw materials, especially energy, but also other minerals, was a major initial goal of the postwar expansion of U.S. corporations and those of some other advanced capitalist countries.[48] There is little question but that raw materials exported from less developed countries as inputs to advanced-country industries were cheaper than similar raw materials extracted in the latter countries, though the exact extent of the cost difference was obscured by the fact that prices were controlled by advanced-country-based multinational corporations (MNCs). Nevertheless, from 1969 to 1974 all raw materials prices (including but not confined to the price of oil) rose, signifying a major readjustment in international accumulation.[49]

Cheaper labor was available either by employment of immigrants from poor countries or by relocating plants from rich to poor countries. Japanese firms, for cultural reasons, never encouraged immigration and preferred to locate subsidiaries or use subcontractors in South Korea, Taiwan, and other countries with cheaper labor, while countries of Western Europe resorted to immigration on a large scale and with corresponding social and political costs. U.S. industries have used both immigrant labor and foreign location as means of tapping cheaper labor. Often these methods have been used in sequence: French-Canadian labor was imported to man the textile plants of New England before these plants were relocated, first in the southern states, then abroad. The future expansion of European industries seems more likely to take place through relocation in less developed countries than by any recurrence of the massive immigration of cheap labor that took place in the 1960s and 1970s.

Somewhat similar to the search for cheaper labor has been the impact of environmental controls imposing cleanup or anti-pollution costs on industries. Such regulations proliferated in the rich countries from the 1970s as public awareness of environmental degradation became aroused. Poor countries offered sites that did not impose such costs.

Transnational production organizations can maximize cost advantages by combining these various factors in complex hierarchical systems. Inputs to the production process organized by dominant firm A can be provided by (1) foreign-located dependent firm B, which produces raw materials, or (2) foreign-located dependent firm C, which produces components by employing labor cheaper than is available to A in its home country and/or which pollutes the environment in ways not allowed in

A's country. Thus part of A's profits are derived from cheaper raw materials, the degradation of nature, and cheaper labor in the countries of B and C. If fact, A may not derive any profit from the workers it directly employs in its own country. These are highly skilled and well paid and enjoy considerable job security and benefits. They are necessary to maintain the sophisticated technology at the core of this transnational production organization and to do the nondirectly productive work of research and development, market research and promotion, and financial operations crucial to the planning of the transnational organization. Labor costs at the core of the industrial process have, in fact, been absorbed into the fixed capital costs of the organization. The difference between sales and costs comes rather from the dependent units in the production organization and thus ultimately from the differences in social relations of production prevailing among them.[50]

An illustration can be had from one of the most recent industries, microchip information technology. Microchip manufacturing began in 1971 and grew rapidly during the 1970s, peaking in 1974 and then declining as there was more competition and growing capacity, leading to a crisis of overproduction in 1981. Initially, computers were made by male electrical engineers in core installations; as the industry grew, chips made in Silicon Valley, California, were sent to Far East assembly plants to be placed in their carriers by semiskilled enterprise-labor-market women using microscopes. As industrial capacity became surplus, some of these women were sent back to the rural communities from which they had been recruited. The labor costs to the manufacturer of expanding and then contracting production were thus minimized.[51] The poor-country enterprise-labor market became the buffer for economic downturn.

The formal institutional, legal, or proprietary relationships involved in transnational production organizations may be of many different kinds. These include the internalizing of a dual labor process within firm A by the recruitment of an immigrant labor force alongside a core skilled labor force of national origin; outright ownership by A of foreign subsidiaries B or C; supply of A by foreign joint venture firms using capital subscribed in part by A and in part by nationals and states of countries in which they are situated that use technology supplied by $A$; subcontracting by $A$ to foreign firm $D$; leasing of patented technology by $A$ to foreign firm $D$; compensation agreements through which $A$ provides technology, and foreign firm $D$ or $E$ repays with part of its production of goods (used as components by $A$); and ad hoc commercial agreements worked out by $A$ with a variety of foreign firms on the basis of its superior information about the sourcing of required inputs throughout the world. Any or all of these arrangements constitute aspects of the internationalizing of production.

Preferences differ in the choice among these various techniques for putting together transnational production organizations. Internalizing of dual labor processes and outright ownership of subsidiaries was the preference of MNCs, especially in the first phase of expansion. Subcontracting was extensively used by Japanese corporations in their overseas movement. Joint ventures were urged on MNCs by the governments of industrializing Third World countries and some socialist countries as a means of enhancing local participation. Compensation agreements are associated with the relationships between capitalist-country-based MNCs and socialist-country enterprises. Electronic information processing has been applied by Japanese firms to put together deals for the acquisition of components and other inputs in a variety of countries.

Political pressures can influence within limits the distribution of power in transnational production organizations. The success of OPEC in capturing a larger share of petroleum rents is an outstanding case of a successful political coalition redistributing surplus. Neomercantilist states have successfully pressured MNCs to undertake more research and development locally, to do more processing of raw materials, and to manufacture more for export. Governments can intervene to contest administrative pricing by MNCs so as to maximize their fiscal take from corporate activities. The limits within which political influences can be effectively exerted on foreign capital are the points beyond which capital loses its incentive to invest. A less-developed-country location presents a balance of advantages and disadvantages to the decision-making centers of transnational production organizations. This balance is calculated in terms of access to raw materials, market opportunities, the preempting of competitors, political security, and so forth. The range of what is acceptable to foreign capital may be fairly wide. It may include changes in formal ownership; indeed, the transnational decision-making center may turn the nationalization of a peripheral subsidiary to advantage if it becomes a means of acquiring capital infusions from the peripheral country government and giving that government an interest in the profitability of the transnational production organization as a whole.[52] What is negotiable concerns the relative shares of the surplus. What is not negotiable concerns the goals and direction of the development process itself.[53] Actions by peripheral country governments that would disrupt the accumulation process, e.g., by default on debts, rather than accept new terms for rescheduling, or that would redirect production toward meeting local basic needs rather than maximize profits on the world market, invite either a severance of economic relations or the political riposte of destabilization.

International production grew through a prolonged boom in the world economy extending from the postwar investment in European recovery through the Korean and Indochina Wars. Conditions were propitious. Trade restrictions were progressively lowered and international trade expanded. Major currencies became convertible from 1958 and international capital flows increased spectacularly, encouraged, in the case of U.S. capital exports, by the prolonged overvaluation of the U.S. dollar, which facilitated the financing of U.S. corporate expansion throughout the world for twenty years after World War II. U.S. government investment in nuclear and space research (and European governments' support of projects like the Anglo-French Concorde) supplemented the accumulation of capital in private industry.

These boom conditions faltered by the late 1960s. During the 1970s, industrial capacity became surplus to demand, incentives to invest withered, and a competitive struggle for limited markets became overt. What new investment took place in internationalized production during the 1970s was mainly in raising productivity and lowering costs. It reflected the search for competitive advantage either through greater capital intensity and technology intensity of production or through tapping sources of cheaper labor or lower environmental costs. It was not directed toward expanding capacity, since capacity was already in surplus. In face of the worldwide problem of marketing, world industry and trade was kept going during the 1970s by an infusion of credit facilitated by the increase in U.S. dollar holdings outside the United States generated by cumulative U.S. payments deficits. These foreign dollar holdings became the basis of a Eurodollar financial market that escaped effective regulation by any national monetary authority and to which the decision centers of international production had preferred access. The result was a struggle for relative advantages among the most highly productive organizations in a context of worldwide inflation, rising unemployment, and surplus capacity.[54]

The problem of markets is inherent in the mode of capitalist development. Investment choices in this mode of development are determined by prospects of realizing a profit through sales. Demand is determined by the existing structure of incomes, which, being skewed inequitably, gives an edge in demand to things the rich or relatively rich are able and prepared to buy. In Third World countries, for instance, there is a local demand among the rich for consumer durables that may remain strong while effective demand for basic necessities of food, clothing, and shelter for the masses is weak. At some point, however, this elite market on the world scale may become saturated, and when this happens, the mode of development runs up against its limits. Up to this point, development proceeds by capital-deepening, through which new and more sophisticated products are introduced that appeal to the elite market.[55] During the 1970s, it seemed that the limits of the global elite market were being probed. Geographically, the elite market had been broadened from the rich countries to include the rich people of the poor countries; the domestic markets of Third World countries had become internationalized in the sense that the consumer products of the rich countries were now available there, too, through local production. The limits were also probed in respect of the scale of production organizations; in some industrial sectors, the scale of production of the most cost-efficient technologies had become greater than what could be absorbed by any single national market.[56]

If the limits had, indeed, been reached in a confrontation of supranational-scale production organizations with a nonexpanding level of demand determined by existing income distribution, then the alternatives appeared as: (1) a more intensive struggle for survival among the largest production organizations in which states would become involved as supporters of national champions; (2) a radical redistribution of income shifting the structure of effective demand to a mix of products different from those produced for the elite market, i.e., products responding more closely to basic needs; or (3) a political takeover of production organization to be run on a redistributive basis determined by states. Alternative (1) implies interimperial competition, and alternatives (2) and (3) imply social and political revolutions or an overturning of the political structures that have hitherto guaranteed the capitalist mode of development.

What has been the impact on labor of the internationalizing of production? What have been labor's responses?

It must be remembered that only a small fraction of world labor is directly involved in international production. The process indirectly affects, however, a much larger proportion of workers, and the behavior of these others, as well as of those directly employed by MNCs, in turn affects the process. Multinationals have been in the forefront of enterprise corporatism as regards their more skilled employees; they have also, especially in Third World countries, resorted increasingly to use of semiskilled, nonestablished workers, operating with a dual labor force on a world scale. Some international trade union organizations have tried to bargain collectively with MNCs by establishing affiliates in their branches in different countries and coordinating their actions against the employer. Some voices in the late 1960s proclaimed international collective bargaining as the wave of the future. Achievements have not matched the advance publicity, and international bargaining has suffered the same setbacks as national labor movements under the pressure of the world economic crisis of the 1970s and 1980s. To the extent that there were modest successes, these tended toward consolidating the positions of the most favored employees, in effect working as a kind of conflictual enterprise corporatism through which the upper echelons of workers became increasingly dependent for their welfare on MNC employers. Union action tended if anything to conform with the managerial thrust toward a dual labor force.[57]

Established workers in the advanced capitalist countries, through their trade unions, were generally successful in raising wages during the boom years of the 1950s and 1960s. These were passed on to the consumer in the form of higher administered prices but probably had some effect in squeezing profits and consequently provided management with the incentive to relocate production in cheap labor areas.[58] Established labor fought back at the national level by urging protectionist measures against the export of jobs. However, the rising unemployment levels of the 1970s and 1980s placed established labor on the defensive in all the core countries; unions reluctantly accepted concessions on labor costs in order to save jobs and acquiesced in management's almost exclusive powers over production rationalization and technological innovation. Thus, in a first stage, union power gave management an incentive to relocate, and in a second stage, union weakness gave management full control over the restructuring of production processes.

During economic recession and the restructuring of the production processes of international production, the burden of adjustment has been disproportionately borne by noninternationalized subordinate sectors. Households in the core countries have had to support unemployed male workers by drawing on savings and the aid of relatives and by the uncertain secondary-labor-market earnings of wives. In Third-World countries, the relative cheapness of employed labor is sustained not only by the existence of a massive reserve army of available labor but also by the relative cheapness of food and other necessities through local networks of farm and artisan production and marketing. Something analogous has occurred in the advanced capitalist countries with the burgeoning of "black" or underground economies in which goods and services are traded and bartered outside formal markets and legalized exchange.

The overall effect of the internationalizing of production has been to emphasize the disparities in the conditions of workers subject to different modes of social relations of production. It has enhanced the relative privilege of established workers in enterprise-corporatist relationship to the core services of international industry. It has weakened bipartite relations in the major heavy industries—automobiles, steel, shipbuilding, etc.—where workers have been hit by the "deindustrialization" of advanced capitalist countries and the shift of production to Third World locations. This same shift has favored the growth of state-corporatist relations in the Third World countries into which these industries have been moving. The secondary effects of the internationalizing process have likewise stimulated the expansion of enterprise-labor-market employment in Third World and in advanced capitalist countries in the national sectors symbiotically linked to international production, and they have encouraged the further expansion of the primitive labor market through urbanization in Third-World countries.

## THE INTERNATIONALIZING
## OF THE STATE

The internationalizing of the state is the global process whereby national policies and practices have been adjusted to the exigencies of the world economy of international production. Through this process the nation state becomes part of a larger and more complex political structure that is the counterpart to international production. The process results in different forms of state corresponding to the different positions of countries in the world economy. The reshaping of specific state structures in accordance with the overall international political structure is brought about by a combination of external pressures (external, that is, to particular countries though arising within the overall international political structure) and realignments of internal power relations among domestic social groups. Like the internationalizing of production, the tendency toward the internationalizing of the state is never complete, and the further it advances, the more it provokes countertendencies sustained by domestic social groups that have been disadvantaged or excluded in the new domestic realignments. These countertendencies could prove capable of reversing the internationalizing tendency, especially if the balance tips simultaneously in a number of key countries. There is nothing inevitable about the continuation of either the internationalizing of the state or the internationalizing of production.

The meaning given to the term *internationalizing of the state* can be expressed in three points: *First*, there is a process of interstate consensus formation regarding the needs or requirements of the world economy that takes place within a common ideological framework (i.e., common criteria of interpretation of economic events and common goals anchored in the idea of an open world economy). *Second*, participation in this consensus formation is hierarchically structured. *Third*, the internal structures of states are adjusted so that each can best transform the global consensus into national policy and practice, taking account of the specific kinds of obstacles likely to arise in countries occupying the different hierarchically arranged positions in the world economy. State structure here means both the machinery of government administration and enforcement (where power lies among the policy-elaborating and enforcement agencies of states) and the historic bloc on which the state rests (the alignment of dominant and acquiescent social groups).[59]

In considering stages in the internationalization of the state, it is useful to refer back to the distinction made above between the international economy and the world economy. In the international economy model, the state acts as a buffer between the external economic environment and the domestic economy. Its political accountability is *within*, its principal task being to defend the interests embodied in the domestic economy against disturbances from without, to give priority to domestic over external forces. Inward-directed accountability in a generally hostile external environment was expressed in the economic nationalisms of the Depression years of the 1930s. Countries turned inward to revive economic activity and employment, finding the eventual solution in rearmament and world war.

The Bretton Woods stage, conceived in the mid-1940s and put into practice ultimately in the late 1950s, placed the state in a halfway position mediating between international economy and world-economy structures. Bretton Woods was a compromise between accountability of governments (especially of debtor countries) to institutions of the world economy and accountability of governments to domestic opinion for their economic performance and for the maintenance of welfare. In order to be able to borrow or to renew debt abroad, governments would have to satisfy conditions laid down by the international institutions. The ability to borrow would make it possible for governments to soften the impact of external economic developments, e.g., the rise of rivals with a competitive advantage over domestic producers or falling prices of commodity exports, so as to allow time for internal adjustments and to maintain internal welfare commitments. The center of gravity shifted from national economies to the world economy, but states were recognized as having a responsibility to both. The prospect of open contradiction between the two was obscured in a confidence that time and resources would be adequate to effect a reconciliation. The compromise worked as long as the world economy was indeed expanding.

The International Monetary Fund was set up to provide time and money to countries with balance of payments deficits in order that they could make the kind of adjustments that would bring their economies back into payments equilibrium and avoid the sharp deflationary consequences of an automatic gold standard. The World Bank was to be a vehicle for longer term financial assistance. Economically weakened countries were to be given assistance by the world system itself, either directly through the system's institutions or by other states once their credit worthiness had been certified by the system's institutions. The institutions of the world economy incorporated mechanisms to supervise the application of the system's norms and to make financial assistance and other benefits of the system conditional upon reasonable evidence of intent to live up to the norms.

This machinery of surveillance was, in the case of the Western allies and, subsequently, of all industrialized capitalist countries, supplemented by elaborate machinery for the harmonization of national policies. The incentive for policy harmonization came with the promise of external resources, initially through the Marshall Plan. The practice of harmonization shifted the balance of accountability one step further in the world-economy direction. This practice began with the mutual criticism of reconstruction plans in Western European countries, which was the U.S. condition for Marshall funds. It evolved further with the annual review procedures instituted by NATO to oversee the sharing of defense burdens and defense support programs. It became an acquired habit of mutual consultation and mutual review of national policies from 1960 onward when the postwar reconstruction phase passed into a phase of world-economy expansion under the aegis of Bretton Woods.

The notion of international obligation moved beyond a few basic commitments, such as observance of the most-favored-nation principle or maintenance of an agreed exchange rate, to a general recognition that measures of national economic policy affect other countries and that such consequences should be taken into account before national policies are adopted. Conversely, other countries should be sufficiently understanding of one country's difficulties to acquiesce in short-term exceptions to general norms of behavior. Adjustments were thus perceived as responding to the needs of the system as a whole and not to the will of dominant countries. External pressures upon national policies were accordingly internationalized.

Of course, such an internationalized policy process presupposed a power structure, one in which central agencies of the U.S. government were in a dominant position. But it was not necessarily a power structure with lines of force running exclusively from the top down, nor was it one in which the units of interaction were whole nation-states. It was a power structure in which the components sought to maintain consensus through bargaining and one in which the bargaining units were bureaucratic fragments of states. The power behind the negotiation was tacitly taken into account by the parties.

Not only were pressures on state behavior within this power structure internationalized, they were also, through ideological osmosis, internalized in the thinking of participants. Susan Strange explains how British policy makers formulated policies in anticipation of the kind of external influence they had come to expect and how U.S. policy makers were more concerned with British policy's conforming to the conventional orthodoxy (so as not to set a bad example to others and to undermine the first line of defense for the dollar) than they were with getting their money back. She explains the internationalizing/internalizing policy process with great clarity:

During and immediately after negotiations for a large new international debt, a debtor-government's main and most difficult problem is to maintain its precarious balance between the two conflicting pressures with which it is certain to be assailed. The wording and form of its commitments in this period is less decisive than the balance-of-power relationship with the creditors. On the one hand, its domestic security is jeopardized if it seems to lay itself too wide open to charges of abdicating sovereignty and signing away the country's independence to foreign bankers and governments. It is obliged to shout in a deafening stage whisper: "Look, no strings!" to the gallery. At the same time it is obliged to reassure the stalls, in soothing tones compelling confidence, of its "correct economic behavior," according to the terms agreed for the loan. The only way in which such a conflict can be reconciled and such an absurd contradiction overlooked is by finding a middle path of policy which does not too badly upset either side and which does not seem too responsive to either source of pressure. By such means, the pantomime of multilateral surveillance can be played to everybody's satisfaction.

The one certain result, therefore, of adopting a debtor's posture is to give both national officials and their foreign or international opposite numbers a strong incentive to fudge the issues and to conceal and obscure any possible conflict between the national interests of the debtor-states and the national (or special international) interests of the creditors. This will be all the easier by reason of the sort of international freemasonry that has grown up over two or three decades between English-speaking economic officials; and by reason also of the international sympathies felt by professional economists for each other. The belief is therefore propagated by the experts on both sides of the creditor-debtor relationship that there is no feasible alternative to the policies adopted. Discussion becomes muted, if not altogether silenced: no one discusses the ultimate consequences of taking on the debt, and of the possible alternative courses of action open to debtors and creditors.[60]

The European Economic Community offers a case of intensive internationalization of a group of states—internationalization in the double sense in which these states become more closely bound up with each other, and as a group they become more responsive to world-economy pressures. The European

Monetary System (EMS) established in 1978, for example, was part of a "grand design" by Chancellor Helmut Schmidt and President Valery Giscard d'Estaing to create a European center of political-economic stability by linking the major European currencies together in common defense against the destabilizing effects of uncontrolled dollar proliferation. The EMS also opened the prospect of even closer monetary (and hence economic policy) unification among the EEC countries.

The growth in policy unification of the EEC countries in an overall sense has come about only to a limited degree through a transfer of powers to supranational agencies; to a greater extent it has been the result of interpenetration of national policy-making processes. Coordination mechanisms have been divided between the "hard" and the "soft"—hard coordination flowing from authoritative central decision making, and soft from the practice of mutual consultation. The soft type of coordination, which is basic to the development of European constitutional practice, takes place within the same kind of evolving ideological osmosis in regard to the norms of correct European behavior as was noted by Susan Strange in the sphere of debtor-creditor relations between Britain and the United States. European coordination is fairly hard in areas like trade policy, agriculture, and regional assistance; it is softer in respect of control of money supplies and credit regulation, industrial policies, and incomes policies. The mechanisms in place for soft coordination include monthly meetings of the EC finance ministers preceded by preparatory meetings of a coordination group and the preparation of an annual report every autumn that serves as a reference document for policy analogous to those of the U.S. Council of Economic Advisers. Further developments in the soft coordination area could be envisaged in the form of machinery of a European corporative kind to deal with industrial and incomes policies.[61]

Looked at as a whole, the international political structure that is in process of formation appears to be more evolved, more definitive, in some of its parts; less formed, more fluid, in others; and the connections between the parts are more stable in some cases and more tenuous in others. Any attempt to depict it must not be taken teleologically, as an advanced stage toward the inevitable completion of a latent structure. Rather it should be taken dialectically, as the description of tendencies that, as they become revealed, may arouse oppositions that could strive to confound and reverse them. With these reservations, the internationalizing state structure can be described in terms of three linked levels.

At the top level, consensus formation takes place among the major advanced capitalist countries. In this process, the central agencies of these states—prime ministerial and presidential offices, foreign offices, treasuries, central banks,—interact with each other, sometimes through formal institutions like the IMF, the World Bank, and the OECD with their own autonomous bureaucracies; sometimes through more ad hoc multilateral forums, including economic summit conferences; sometimes in a complex of bilateral relationships. U.S. agencies have a dominant but not necessarily determining role; they are determining only when they rally a broad measure of support on specific policy measures. The international institutions are particularly important in defining the ideological basis of consensus, the principles and goals within which policies are framed, and the norms of "correct" behavior. When, during the 1970s, the explicit norms of Bretton Woods (fixed exchange rates and most favored nation treatment, for instance) were either totally or partially abandoned, the practice of policy harmonization became correspondingly more important to the maintenance of consensus. The habit of policy harmonization had been institutionalized during the two preceding decades and was, if anything, reinforced in the absence of clear norms. Ideology had to substitute for legal obligation.

Within this top level, the European Communities are a particularly evolved instance of the internationalization process. The European process is a microcosm of the larger internationalizing process encompassing all the advanced capitalist countries. The EC contains, however, an implicit option: either to be a more effective transmission belt between the world economy and the European regional economy, promoting the internationalization of Europe, or to give a better defense of Europe, particularly in relation to the United States and Japan, than separate European countries could provide by themselves. If, up to the present, the EC has worked more in the first sense than in the second, the tendency could be reversed if the United States, disheartened by European and Japanese behavior, should move in a more protectionist or isolationist direction.

A second level comprises the links between the redistributive systems of socialist countries and the world economy. These expanded during the years of détente—roughly from the German *ostpolitik* beginning in 1966 to the Soviet military occupation of Afghanistan in 1979—taking the forms both of conventional trade and of industrial cooperation arrangements. The latter were agreements between Western-based or Japanese-based multinational firms and socialist country enterprises. They usually involved exchange of socialist-country production for Western technologies. The socialist state retained control of the linkage and could break it off if political conditions were so to dictate. Western governments, too, could cool the relationship as politics might require. The relationship had advantages for both sides but neither became inextricably enmeshed. Apart from the changing fortunes of direct economic relations between countries of East and West, there is a systemic effect neither side can escape. The principal form it takes is the arms race. This bears more heavily on the Soviet side since that country must devote a higher proportion of its national product to defense than the Western countries do just to retain arms parity.

At a third level, a stricter regime than that applying to advanced capitalist countries has been enforced on Third World countries. One element in the top-level consensus concerns the conditions for financing Third World debt. Consensus in this matter has generally been internationalized through the IMF and then applied case by case to Third-World countries. The top-level countries in effect jointly fix the parameters of the developmental options of late-industrializing countries. Third World elites do not participate with the same effective status as top-level elites in the formation of the consensus. The consensus does, however, gain ideological recruits and places ideologically conditioned agents in key positions within Third World countries. The networks through which international finance flows to these countries are staffed within these countries (e.g., in top positions in central banks and finance ministries) by people who have been socialized to the norms of the consensus and of its professional cadres. These people are often graduates of major advanced-capitalist-country universities and have often passed through the IMF Institute and similar bodies that bring Third World technical financial personnel into personal contact with the milieu of international finance. These are not the political decision makers of Third World countries but those who inform those decision makers about what their options are.

President Salvatore Allende of Chile underlined the impersonal and almost invisible nature of the relationship in his speech to the General Assembly of the United Nations on December 10, 1972:

> We find ourselves opposed by forces that operate in the shadows, without a flag, with powerful weapons that are placed in a wide range of influential positions.
>
> We are not the object of any trade ban. Nobody has said that he seeks a confrontation with our country. It would seem that our only enemies or opponents are the logical internal political ones. That is not the case. We are the victims of almost invisible actions, usually concealed with remarks and statements that pay lip service to respect for the sovereignty and dignity of our country. But we have first-hand knowledge of the great difference that there is between those statements and the specific actions we must endure.[62]

The Chilean coup and assassination of Allende less than a year following this speech was a salient but by no means unique instance of how recalcitrant Third World governments are ultimately removed by violence if they do not conform to minimum standards of correct world-economy behavior. More frequently, internal policy shifts are effected through changes in the composition of governments in these countries, together with realignments of the domestic forces backing regimes, giving them a more conservative basis.[63] The internationalization of the Third World state is externally determined and imposed, but it attracts internal allies and collaborators.

During the expansive years of the 1960s and their inflationary prolongation up to 1974, the contradictions between the welfare of vulnerable domestic groups and the requisites of international capital accumulation were usually obscured. In the advanced capitalist countries, the ideological osmosis between the agents of world-economy financial management and their domestic counterparts patched up policies that prevented open cleavage of interests. These policies oscillated between the restraint and stimulus of stop-go balance-of-payments management. Apart from an acute crisis like the Chilean coup of 1973, Third World nonconformity proved to be manageable, and some of these countries experienced economic miracles of growth.

The deep and prolonged recession in the world economy following 1974, however, brought the latent contradictions into the open. In the advanced capitalist countries, official ideologues opined that countries had become "ungovernable," by which they meant that the guarantees for vulnerable social groups built into social policy during the years of expansion would not cede before the demands of capital accumulation without touching off a serious internal struggle.[64] A return of Cold-War behavior between the United States and the Soviet Union ended détente and raised obstacles to the continuing expansion of financial, trade, and industrial cooperation between capitalist and socialist countries. Third World indebtedness reached proportions threatening the stability of the international financial system, raising the prospects of both more stringent and unpopular internationally imposed conditions for rescheduling debt and greater chances of debt repudiation with incalculable (but dangerous from the standpoint of world-economy management) political consequences. Neomercantilist protectionism loomed in advanced capitalist countries and so did radical revolution in the Third World.

As has been suggested above, the state structures appropriate to the internationalized process of economic policy harmonization contrasted with those of the welfare-nationalist state of the preceding period. National- and industry-level corporative structures tended to raise protectionist or restrictive obstacles to the adjustments required for the adaptation of national economies to the world economy. Corporatism at the national level was a response to the conditions of the interwar period; it became institutionally consolidated in Western Europe just as the world structure was changing into something for which national corporatism was ill suited.

As national economies became more integrated in the

world economy, it was the large and more technologically advanced enterprises, those participating in internationalizing of production, that best adapted to the new opportunities. A new axis of influence linked international policy networks with the key central agencies of government and with big business. This new informal corporative structure—a corporatism with international tendencies—overshadowed the older and more formalized national corporatism and reflected the dominance of the sector oriented to the world economy over the more nationally oriented sector of a country's economy.[65]

The shift from a national to an internationalizing corporatism involved a realignment of social forces underpinning state power. When consensus on world-economy requisites replaced consensus on national economy goals as the basis for policy formulation, some nation-based interest groups that had been included in corporatist coalitions became more marginal or were excluded. These found little sympathetic response in the central agencies of government but could exert influence at other points in the governmental process, notably in elected legislatures at national and provincial or local levels. Industries that were nation based and faced severe international competition, such as steel, shipbuilding, and textiles, were naturally protectionist and hostile to the internationalizing tendency. Medium and small businesses were also potential allies in the protectionist cause. Trade unions of established labor, which had won recognized status and material concessions within the postwar state structures of corporative Keynesianism, became threatened both by exclusion from the process of world-economy consensus formation and by the rise of enterprise corporatism. These social and economic forces were gradually pushed into opposition to the dominant internationalizing power bases of governments, but, weakened by the recessionary conjuncture of the world economy that prevailed in the 1970s, they lacked both the cohesion and the political clout sufficient to reverse the trend.

In the Third World, the internationalizing of the state produced a different kind of state structure. In the first flush of postcolonial independence in Asia and Africa, successor states were imitative of the pluralistic structures of core states. It was during this period that populist regimes thrived in Latin America,

as well as in some Asian and African countries, based on dispar-
ate coalitions in political cartels grouping landowners, urban
bureaucratic middle classes, and urban industrial workers. The
credit balances accumulated by some of these countries during
World War II allowed for a period of free spending during which
the appetites of politically significant domestic groups could be
appeased. During the 1960s and early 1970s, when the reserves
of Third World countries were depleted, these countries confronted separately the consolidated structures of the world economy. The world-economy consensus, operating through world-
economy institutions, exacted certain conditions from Third
World debtors in return for allowing them to continue to draw
on world-economy resources for their continuing development.
These conditions determined the path of development; i.e., development must be conducive to accumulation on the world scale
and complementary to the internationalizing of production.
These conditions also determined internal political structures
since they could be met only by regimes willing and able to use
force to carry through unpopular economic policies.

The Peruvian case is a paradigm for the internationalizing
of the state in periphery countries with a significant world-economy linkage. A nationalist military group took power in 1968
that began a program to nationalize major foreign investments
and to control future foreign investment, while at the same time
broadening its popular base of support by introducing land reforms aiming to mobilize peasant participation and measures for
worker participation in the management and profits of industrial
enterprises and by organizing squatters in the urban barriadas.
This regime was unprepared to extract from the national economy
an investment surplus sufficient to pursue its developmental
goals. At the same time, it encountered a credit barrier in U.S.
and world financial markets because of its nationalization policy.
In 1974 the military regime settled claims for compensation for
the nationalizations with the United States and thereby obtained
access to new foreign financing. Escalation of foreign borrowing
combined with less-than-anticipated export earnings brought
Peru into a severe exchange crisis by the beginning of 1976.
Meanwhile, in 1975, new government leadership of a more conservative bent replaced the initiators of the nationalist-mobilizing

experiment. Alfred Stepan relates the pressures arising in the exchange crisis to the change in the character of the regime thus:

> In April 1976 Peru had virtually exhausted its foreign reserves and initiated a major loan request. While other factors were also at work, it is impressive that in the thirty days before the vital loan was finally approved by a consortium of U.S. bankers, the [new] government (1) imposed a stabilization package involving a wage freeze, devaluation, and public sector budget cuts, a package that led one radical minister to apologize for the "capitalist cut" of the measures; (2) announced a state of emergency by which the unions' right to strike was cancelled; (3) changed the cabinet, in which the most prominent remaining military radicals . . . were removed, while the civilian head of social property resigned; (4) ended the ban on new oil contracts with foreign firms; (5) announced the first sale of a state company to the private sector; and (6) reached agreement in principle to pay compensation for the expropriation of Marcona Mining.[66]

Thus the foreign exchange crisis is typically the inescapable event that precipitates a restructuring of Third World state personnel, policies, and supportive coalitions in line with the requirements of international production. The internationalizing of the Third World state is more openly induced by external pressures than the internationalizing of the advanced capitalist state is and thus provokes more awareness and resentment. The IMF has become a known political enemy to nationalist and popular forces in Third World countries; it has never become known to the public to the same extent in advanced capitalist countries. In the latter countries, the internationalizing process appears to the public to be the result of ineluctable impersonal forces that can be separated from the symbolisms of domestic political debate.

## ONE MORE ANALYTICAL PROPOSITION

In this chapter I have argued that new state forms—the neoliberal and the neomercantilist developmentalist forms of state— emerged in the same historical process as produced a new hegemonic world-order structure, the Pax Americana. This historical process did not bring into existence any new modes of social relations of production nor did it change fundamentally the social structure of accumulation. A new hierarchical arrangement of modes of social relations of production was, however, structured by the new forms of state. Enterprise corporatism confirmed and stabilized the preferred status of employees at the core of world industrial processes. Tripartism was relegated from the top status it had achieved in the welfare-nationalist state to a secondary though still relatively preferred position in the neoliberal state. State corporatism grew with relatively privileged status in neomercantilist developmentalist states. There was a general expansion (encouraged intentionally or unintentionally by both forms of state) of modes of social relations of production in which workers are relatively unprotected—enterprise-labor-market and primitive-labor-market modes.

The hegemonic character of the Pax Americana showed a number of facets. The new world order was founded by a country in which social hegemony has been established (proposition six at the end of chapter 5) and in which that hegemony was sufficiently expansive to project itself onto the world scale. U.S. methods of production became the world model, exported and emulated abroad. Furthermore, the ideological and political power of global hegemony restricted the forms of state that were tolerated within this world order (proposition ten at the end of chapter 6). A combination of rewards and penalties—access to credit for compatible and political destabilization of incompatible national regimes—enforced conformity.

Hegemony was more secure at the center of the world system, less secure in its peripheries (proposition eight at the end of chapter 5). The weakness of hegemony in the peripheries took two forms. The neomercantilist developmentalist state was a form of caesarism that substituted for an absence of social hegemony where it governed. Elite members of peripheral societies participated in the global hegemony while ruling over nonhegemonic societies. But the Third World was also the site of some revolts against the global hegemony, which took the form of efforts to build up locally based counterhegemonies. While caesarism secured the passive acquiescence of some Third World societies in a global hegemony centered in the advanced capitalist countries, counterhegemonic movements in other Third World countries constituted open and active challenges to global hegemony. Corresponding to this differentiation in hegemonic intensity between core and periphery of the world system, class struggles were muted by corporatist structures in the core but more open and self-conscious in peripheral areas.

One further analytical proposition, to add to those advanced at the end of the previous two chapters, can be presented here. It is an elaboration of the already enunciated proposition that in a hegemonic order, economics is separated from politics (proposition seven, chapter 5). This final proposition (number eleven) is that international finance is the preeminent agency of conformity to world-hegemonic order and the principal regulator of the political and productive organization of a hegemonic world economy.

Finance is the fungible form of surplus accumulated from production. Its origin is in the production process and in production relations that allow for surplus accumulation. In its form as money capital, this derivative of production becomes autonomous in relation to production and able to shape the development of the production process and the future nature of production relations. When a business tries to borrow, the credit mechanism decides in effect whether or not that business will be able to acquire a certain technology to expand its profit-making capacity. The technology to be acquired implies a certain pattern of production relations. The financial mechanism will thereby strengthen or weaken that pattern, depending on whether credit is granted or withheld. When governments borrow, similar consequences follow: international credit is extended to the extent that the policies of states are deemed by the credit managers to be consistent with accumulation in the world economy. In addition, governments incur political obligation, through the financial mechanism, to adjust national economic policies so as to facilitate service on the debt, and this has further implications favoring certain kinds of production relations.

International finance, accordingly, is analogous to social-class formation, in that both are forces derived from production but that achieve an autonomy from production and can become a power over production relations. Finance is the economic form, social class the political form, taken by these forces derivative from production.

CHAPTER EIGHT

# THE WORLD ECONOMIC CRISIS: IMPACT ON STATE AND WORLD-ORDER STRUCTURES

Since the word "crisis" is so frequently abused for dramatic effect, it is well to be precise here about its meaning. Economists distinguish a crisis from a cyclical downturn: the economy must undergo some structural change in order to emerge from a crisis; in a cyclical downturn, the same structure contains the seeds of its own revival. Crisis signifies a fundamental disequilibrium; the cyclical downturn, a moment in the diachrony of equilibrium.

In a more political vein, Gramsci wrote of "organic crisis" and "crisis of hegemony." What he identified by these terms was a disarticulation between social groups and their putative political leaders, in sum a crisis of representation. In such a situation, old and new social forces coexisted, but the old ones had become detached from the political organizations that had formerly represented them, and the new ones had not produced organizations or "organic" intellectuals who could lead them effectively and bring them into coalescence with existing social forces to form a new hegemonic bloc. Two outcomes are possible in an organic crisis: either the constitution of a new hegemony or caesarism, i.e., the freezing of unresolved contradictions.

The risks in trying to comprehend the present are considerably greater if the present turns out to have been a phase of structural transformation. There are grounds for thinking that the years 1973–74 marked the beginning of such a historical turning point—the start of a period comparable in its long-range effects to the onset of the long depression of the late nineteenth century, which initiated a nonhegemonic sequel to the Pax Britannica, began the transformation of the liberal state into welfare-nationalist and other contemporary forms, and put into place a new social structure of accumulation led by mass-production industry.

Putative transformations in these three orders are currently the object of concern and debate. Has the Pax Americana come to an end and with it the hegemonic world order that gave a framework for world-economic expansion in the post-World War II decades? Do the phenomena of Thatcherism and Reaganism herald a new form of state radically different from the neoliberal corporative state, or are they but evidence of transitory convulsions in political structure that will lead to other novel forms? Has mass production or Fordism reached its limits as the preeminent form of industrial organization? Although each of these questions has attracted scholarly analysis, their interconnections have so far not received much attention. Part 3 of this work attempts to bring the concepts and analytical propositions discussed above to address these matters.

The starting point must be a consideration of the nature of the economic crisis that has affected the world economy since the mid-1970s. Inflation and indebtedness were the principal indicators of that crisis. The financial indicators were, however, manifestations of social and political conflict linking the three levels of our inquiry: production, state, and world order. They point directly to the disintegration of hegemony in world order, to a weakening of historic blocs, and an opening of hegemonic crises within states. These are, accordingly, the first objects of attention.

Somewhat less apparent than the changes taking place in the structures of states and world order are those transforming production processes, changes both in the international division of labor and in the social relations of production. These changes seem in part to arise out of the conflicts inherent in the power relations of the production processes themselves but are encouraged or thwarted both by state power and by the international configuration of power. Hence the prospects of a new social structure of accumulation (for the emergence of the previous structure, see chapter 6) are linked to the issues of structural change at state and world levels.

Finally, we are led to the human energies whose activity or passivity will make the future. These energies are both determined and free in their development. They are determined insofar as they are nurtured and shaped in certain directions by existing social practices. Thus, they constitute identifiable bundles of social forces—an emerging global class structure. They are free insofar as people conditioned in these ways have opportunities to seize or to forgo. This will take us as far as I aim to go: to try to delineate the human material, the social forces shaped by production, state, and world orders that are themselves the shapers of tomorrow's orders, and to discern the options open to these forces in their building of the future. Beyond that is the task of mobilizing action. It is implicit in my analytical effort but my book stops short where that task begins.

# Part 3

# Production Relations in the Making of the Future

Up to now we have been considering the interconnections of modes of production relations, forms of state, and world orders as complex historical structures in which elements of coherence and stability are matched against contradictions and conflicts. Out of these conflicts ultimately come structural transformations. The advantage of looking to the past is to be able to see some of these processes completed—completed, that is, by the initiation of a new phase of stabilization leading, after a time, to a further transformation. From a consideration of these completed phases a series of propositions have been advanced as guides to the analysis of historical-structural changes.

These considerations have brought us to a threshold of the world system during the 1970s. The purpose of acquiring knowledge about past processes is to be able to apply this knowledge to an understanding of the present in such a way as to gain more initiative in the making of the future. The present is in its nature incomplete. It has to be seen as movement, whereas the past can more clearly be grasped as structure. The structures of the recent past fix the circumstances in which the historical action of the present takes place. The actors have power to shape their future both in relation to their command over material resources and in relation to their understanding of the processes of change. This work aims to be a modest contribution to the latter.

It is postulated here that economic crisis is but one manifestation of a Gramscian organic crisis. In order to bring about structural change in the economy it is necessary to realize a realignment of social forces, either by consent (through hegemony) or by the more or less forcible stabilization of contradictory forces (through caesarism).

## THE CRISIS: INFLATION AND SOCIAL POWER

The economic symptoms of crisis during the 1970s are a familiar catalogue: high levels of inflation accompanied by mass unemployment, low growth, the emergence of substantial surplus capacity, and low rates of investment. To a generation conditioned by reaction to the Depression of the 1930s, unemployment had been the most politically sensitive indicator. Recessions during the postwar period, which brought about an increase in unemployment, had been countered by governments giving a moderately inflationary stimulus to the economy. A little inflation was a small price to pay for renewed growth and resorption of unemployment. During the 1970s, however, inflation became more serious and persistent. Inflation in the industrialized capitalist countries during the three years 1970–72 averaged 5.3 percent annually, in 1973 it was 8 percent, and from 1974 more than 10 percent annually.[1] During the midyears of this decade, a shift of perception came over policy makers in these countries: inflation rather than unemployment became the principal enemy.

The impact of economic crisis was not uniform in time or intensity. It was felt first in Western Europe in 1973–74 with the joint impact of a wage explosion, continuing from the events of May 1968 in France and thereafter encompassing all of industrial Europe, and the OPEC-initiated oil price rise. The United States was less vulnerable and managed to continue antipoverty and full employment policies at home while escalating its overseas expenditures, thanks to the U.S. privilege of printing the world's money. This free ride on an ever-declining dollar was interrupted in 1979 with a radical switch to tight money policies following the appointment of Paul Volker as Chairman of the Federal Reserve in the last year of the Carter administration, policies continued under the Reagan administration, which followed from 1981.[2]

The industrializing neomercantilist developmentalist states had a somewhat longer enjoyment of relatively unconstrained growth, thanks to their ability to borrow heavily from private transnational financial markets. This borrowing facility came to an abrupt end in the debt crisis of 1982. The same stringency also beset the economic and financial relations that had developed between the redistributive and the capitalist economies during the détente of the 1970s. This sequence of impacts signified, not a series of national crises, but the unfolding of a single world-economy crisis. This crisis manifested itself principally in the form of inflation of which ballooning debt was one aspect. If inflation was the indicator, it was not the explanation. The explanation lay in the conflict of social and political forces at the three levels of production, state, and world order.

The moderate creeping inflation of the advanced capitalist countries during the 1960s was a direct consequence of the corporative structure of the neoliberal state. Wage increases agreed between big corporate employers and trade unions were passed on to the public in price increases. Less powerful social groups were protected by the safety net of the welfare state. The state's expenses tended to rise both because of welfare-state transfer payments and because of the higher wages secured by increasing numbers of state employees through unionization of the state sector and the growth of welfare-state programs. Cost-push inflation was supplemented by state deficit financing. This took place within a broadly consensual political and ideological framework.[3] There was a national consensus in the major states on the goals of growth, productivity, high employment, and welfare. Labor by and large participated in this consensus; even in Italy and France, where communist movements represented a substantial majority of industrial workers, there was no open challenge to the neoliberal state. During this time, trade unions of established workers gained strength, and labor's political influence through social-democratic and analogous political parties won enactment of social legislation in many Western countries, putting in place comprehensive welfare and employment-sustaining state policies. Labor also in a number of countries secured protection against inflation in the form of wage indexation to the cost of living.

Signs that the limits of this consensus had been reached occurred in the explosion of social conflict that occurred in May 1968 in France and the *autunno caldo* of 1969 in Italy. These events were followed by an acceleration of wage increases in other advanced capitalist countries, including West Germany and Japan and the Scandinavian countries, where labor-management relations had been least conflictual. In all these countries, higher levels of inflation temporarily attenuated social conflict, postponing rather than avoiding it.[4]

In neomercantilist developmentalist states inflation has been the natural consequence of caesarism, i.e. the temporary stabilization of an unresolved confrontation of social forces none of which can subordinate the others without at the same time risking its own survival. Caesarism, in what we may call its benign phase, tends to accommodate this situation by acquiescing in the demands of all groups (though favoring some over others) and allowing the market to inflict the consequences in the impersonalized form of inflation. Caesarist regimes will lean toward one side or another in using inflation as a redistributive mechanism. Populism, in economic terms, was a policy of distributing incomes toward workers and other popular groups—a leftist inflation. The first Peron government of Argentina and the Allende government in Chile presided over inflations of this kind.[5] Other types of caesarist inflation favored some bourgeois sectors over others—import substitution manufacturers over agricultural exporters, for instance. Albert Hirschman recounts how in Argentina the industrial bourgeoisie would make common cause with the urban masses under populist leadership during recession in order to secure an expansionary policy and to hold down the price of meat, the principal export product and wage good, but would shift to ally with the cattle breeders in backing military intervention when workers in a tightening labor market were able to demand higher wages.[6] Military regimes have been just as inflationary as nonmilitary forms of caesarism in their propensity to offer incentives to many different industrial groups and to satisfy the demands of the military and other influential segments of the state bureaucracy. During the 1970s heavy international borrowing by authoritarian regimes became a substitute for the locally induced inflations of an earlier period. Indebtedness for countries, as well as for individuals, is grounded in inflationary expectations: money borrowed now can be used to generate future income flows that will enable the borrower to repay the principal in future depreciated currency. The newly industrializing countries of the 1970s expected to be able to service their growing debts from rising prices for their raw material exports and expanded export of their manufactures.

The United States was in a special position as founder and guarantor of the hegemonic world economy. Its role was critical in the internationalizing of what otherwise were a series of domestically induced inflations. The critical factor in the internationalizing of inflation was the U.S. payments deficit. This deficit grew apace during the 1960s as a direct consequence of U.S. military expenditures abroad, notably because of the escalation of war in Indochina, and the international expansion of U.S.-based multinational corporations. The deficit was thus directly related to the costs of U.S. hegemony. U.S. governments were unwilling, and in practice politically unable, to bear these costs domestically in the form of reduced expenditures at home. The administration of President Lyndon Johnson was committed to an antipoverty program, an offset to the unpopular war in Vietnam. The succeeding administrations of Presidents Richard Nixon and Jimmy Carter countered recessionary conditions by stimulating the economy toward full employment. This political inability to choose between foreign and domestic goals, between guns and butter, was acquiesced in by foreigners, who came to hold an increasing volume of U.S. treasury bills and dollar bank balances. The U.S. public debt became a world debt increasingly held by foreigners. This gave foreigners cause to admonish U.S. governments for irresponsible financial management, but it also made the holders of debt increasingly dependent on the system that generated it.

The international transmission of inflation took place through several mechanisms that dominated international financial networks during the 1970s.[7] One was the rising prices of raw materials, of which the fivefold increase in petroleum prices

brought about through the agency of the Organization of Petroleum Exporting Countries was the most dramatized instance. A
second was the growth of an unregulated transnational Eurodollar market, a financial market trading in foreign-held liquidities,
continually fed by the U.S. deficit and the dollar balances accumulated by the petroleum-exporting countries. This market became a source of credit for major corporations and governments
of newly industrializing countries. A third mechanism was the
system of flexible exchange rates, which the international financial system fell back upon from 1973 after abandoning successively the gold-parity and fixed-exchange-rate principles of the
Bretton Woods accord. This enabled the United States in particular to pursue full-employment policies at home while allowing
the dollar to deteriorate in value abroad throughout the decade.
The debasement of the dollar also advantaged U.S. exports and
offset to some extent the increased price of imported petroleum.
Through these transmission mechanisms even the surplus countries like West Germany and Japan imported inflation. This imported inflation stimulated a wage push in these countries too—
a phenomenon hitherto restrained there by cooperative labor-
management relations.

　　The wage push in the neoliberal states, caesarist inflation
in the neomercantilist developmentalist states, and the worldwide rise in raw-material prices can all be seen as the effects of
a diffusion of power. The wage push reflected the growing power
of labor; caesarist inflation, the absence of a consensus that would
enable conflicting social forces to act cooperatively; and rising
raw material prices, the slipping of power away from core managers of the world economy toward periphery forces. The factor
that tied these distinct origins of inflationary pressures together
into a generalized world inflationary process was the growth in
liquidities fed by the U.S. deficit. The United States was able to
run this deficit throughout the 1970s because of its political
dominance. Increasingly, however, political pressures were required to secure the acquiescence of foreigners to accept growing
amounts of decreasingly valuable dollars. In Susan Strange's
terms, the dollar was slipping from top-currency to negotiated-
currency status.[8] In the late 1960s, the U.S. negotiators used the
"financial deterrent" (the threat to sever the link between the

dollar and gold)[9] as a bargaining chip; in the 1970s, that weapon having been expended, they made acceptance of U.S. debt the quid pro quo for U.S. military commitments in Western Europe and the Far East, and they argued that general recovery would depend on recovery of the U.S. economy, which other major capitalist countries would have to help finance.

The dollar's contested status in the system thus also reflected a shift in power. Although the United States remained predominant, it faced a challenge to its policies from economically recovered Western Europe and Japan. Pressure on the U.S. government from the other advanced capitalist countries reached a peak in 1978, but the final blow that precipitated a radical change in U.S. monetary policy came, not from them, but from the periphery. The Ayatollah Khomeini triggered a sequence of events that led to Paul Volker's installation as chairman of the New York Federal Reserve and the beginning of restriction on the U.S. money supply.[10] Meanwhile, ideologues of the hegemonic order had sounded an alarm that the diffusion of power within states as within the international system had led to a problem of "ungovernability"[11]

## THE DISINTEGRATION
## OF THE NEOLIBERAL HISTORIC BLOC

A key indication that the world system confronted crisis rather than conjunctural adjustment came with a reevaluation of official thinking about the hierarchy of economic problems that took place at the midpoint of the 1970s. Inflation ceased to be regarded benignly as the inevitable but relatively innocuous consequence of a necessary stimulus to growth and began to be perceived by the dominant groups and state economic managers as the principal obstacle to economic revival and renewed growth. Inflation at the new higher rates now signified unpredictability of the future economic environment and became an inhibition to investment.

Behind the disincentive to invest was a long-term narrowing of profit margins beginning in the 1960s.[12] Part of this squeeze on profits was perceived by business as coming from the successive wage increases extracted by the entrenched power of labor in the neoliberal state. This may have contributed more to the psychology than to the reality of narrowing profitability during the earlier phases of the decline. Higher production costs from wage increases had been passed on to the consumer in higher prices. There had been very little change in the relative returns to labor and capital from production.

During the 1970s, however, the factor of international competition became a major constraint on pricing. Exports from Western Europe and Japan gained an advantage in international markets over those from the United States, where productivity in industry had risen more slowly.[13] U.S. exports regained a competitive edge on price for a few years in the mid-1970s thanks to the depreciation of the dollar, but U.S. industry faced a long-term challenge of competition that could be met only by investment in technological renovation. Surplus countries like West Germany and Japan with revalued currencies had to pare export costs so as to maintain the competitiveness of their products just as industry in a deficit country with a devalued currency, as the United States had become, attempted to increase the competitiveness of its products.

Capitalist management was caught in a profit squeeze between labor on the one side keeping wages high and foreign competitors on the other holding prices down. The tension between these opposing forces rose with the wage explosion that engulfed the capitalist world in the early 1970s when the bite of international competition was being acutely felt.

Behind this contradiction was another that affected the problem of productivity. The strength of worker organizations limited management's control in the production process just when management foresaw the need for radical restructuring of production. The imperatives of international competition seemed to require a more technology-intensive production process with fewer established workers and a more flexible use of semiskilled, nonestablished workers. Unions would be bound to resist these changes.

Another squeeze on capital in the neoliberal state, for some analysts the crucial factor in precipitating the crisis, has been a reduction of the share of capital in total output as a result of the transfers effected by state welfare programs.[14] An increased proportion of workers' (and also middle-class) incomes was now coming from various statutory entitlements financed through taxation. These programs were an integral part of the consensus on which the neoliberal state rested. They increased the proportion of GDP passing through the state budgets in all the advanced capitalist countries. Ultimately, they brought about a fiscal crisis. Unemployment automatically increased the social expenses of the state while at the same time it reduced state revenues. The costs of much-expanded state sectors continued to rise, since wages in the state sector were frequently indexed to inflation, a practice that had also spilled over from the state sector to large-scale private industry. Cumulative deficit budgeting not only contributed to inflation; it also raised interest rates as governments borrowed in domestic and international financial markets. The burden of service on public debts in turn became a growing claim on current state revenues. Middle-class tax revolts erupted in a number of countries. The social consensus was eroded as those who paid taxes were pitted against those who benefited from state revenues—private-sector against state-sector workers, middle classes against welfare recipients, small businessmen facing bankruptcy against "corporate welfare bums."[15]

The social contract that had been the unwritten constitution of the neoliberal state's historic bloc was broken in all the advanced capitalist countries in the years following 1974–75. These years were a threshold in class struggle. Governments allied with capital to bring about conditions that business people would consider favorable to a revival of investment, and they pushed labor into a defensive posture. Thenceforth tripartism ceased to be the preeminent mode of social relations of production. A new structure of production relations emerged that tended to polarize the working class into a relatively secure and protected minority, encompassed as a rule by enterprise corporatist relations, and a fragmented and relatively unprotected majority of nonestablished workers.

It has become a commonplace on both left and right of the political spectrum that the capitalist state has both to support capital in its drive to accumulate and to legitimate this accumulation in the minds of the public by moderating the negative effects of accumulation on welfare and employment. As growth stagnates, the contradiction between the two functions of accumulation and legitimation sharpens. The contradiction manifests itself internally in the advanced capitalist country in the form of a fiscal crisis, just as for the late-industrializing Third World country it manifests itself as an exchange crisis. As growth stagnates, the costs of social policies rise and the tax base on which to finance them diminishes. Budget deficits become inflationary, while capital argues that the tax burden inhibits investment. There is strong pressure from capital to cut back on legitimacy by reducing social expenditures of government and rolling back real wages, thereby denouncing the social-democratic compromise worked out among capital, labor, and governments during the postwar economic boom. Governments have to balance the fear of political unrest from rising unemployment and exhaustion of welfare reserves against the fear that business will refrain from leading a recovery that would both revive employment and enlarge the tax base. In this circumstance, governments in the advanced capitalist countries, whatever their political coloration, have leaned toward the interests of capital.[16]

During the years of postwar consensus it had become accepted wisdom that society would not tolerate high unemployment or any dismantling of the welfare state. If these things were to occur, it would, it was said, cost the state the loss of its legitimacy. The truth of this proposition has not been demonstrated uniformly. Indeed, it would more generally seem to be the case that the legitimacy of state welfare and of labor movements has been undermined in public opinion, not the legitimacy of the state. Large-scale unemployment has produced fear and concern for personal survival rather than collective protest. The unions are in strategic retreat, losing members, and unable, in general, to appeal to public opinion for support.

The disintegration of the neoliberal historic bloc was prepared by a collective effort of ideological revision undertaken through various unofficial agencies—the Trilateral Commission, the Bilderberg conferences, the Club of Rome, and other less prestigious forums—and then endorsed through more official consensus-making agencies like the OECD. These agencies of latterday neoliberalism prepared its demise. A new doctrine defined the task of states in relaunching capitalist development out of the depression. There was, in the words of a blue-ribbon OECD committee, a "narrow path to growth," bounded on one side by the need to encourage private investment by increasing profit margins, and bounded on the other by the need to avoid rekindling inflation.[17]

The methods advocated were strict control of national money supplies, strict restraint on government spending, and equally strict deterrence of increases in real wages. High and persisting levels of unemployment, it was recognized, would inevitably accompany this kind of adjustment. The new doctrine rejected positive government intervention in the economy while underlining the imperative nature of these negative measures of intervention. This seemed to rule out corporative-type solutions like negotiated wage and price policies and also the extension of public investment. It placed primary emphasis on restoring the confidence of business in government and in practice acknowledged that maintenance of welfare and employment commitments made in the course of the postwar development to politically important but economically subordinate groups would have to take second place. While applauding wage restraint and state budget cutbacks, business also demanded a strengthening of managerial authority over the organization of work, an authority that had been weakened by worker power on the shop floor, and the freedom to restructure production so as to be able to make greater use of technology-intensive processes and flexible employment of temporary and part-time nonestablished workers and support services.[18]

The goals of the government-business alliance could be achieved only through a weakening of trade union movements. Rising unemployment created the conditions for undermining organized labor's power by fragmenting and dividing the working class. This did not come about in quite the same manner as the classical effect of unemployment lessening labor's bargaining power in general vis-à-vis capital. From 1970 onward a new phenomenon appeared in the inflationary process. Unemployment ceased to have a restraining effect on wage increases. Thenceforth wages continued to rise at the same time as unemployment increased.[19] Those workers who retained jobs did as

well or better during phases of high unemployment as during
periods of employment expansion. The link between wages and
unemployment was broken. At the same time, those workers who
remained in the established category while unemployment was
spreading around them became more dependent on their employers. Objective conditions were propitious for enterprise corporatism among the dwindling proportion of relatively secure
and relatively well-off employees. They were not badly served
by the economic program of the government-business alliance.
They could perceive their interests as distinct from and possibly
opposed to those of the nonestablished and unemployed.

Another line of cleavage that could be exploited by the
government-business alliance separated state from private-sector
workers. In a number of advanced capitalist countries, the most
recent forward thrust of the trade union movements had been in
the organizing and securing of collective-bargaining rights of
state-sector workers. These now found themselves in the front
line of attack by the new program of budget cutbacks and wage
restraint. Where the private sector had set the pattern for wage
demands and trade-union organizational drives by state-sector
workers, governments now set the example of wage resistance
and employment rationalization for the private sector. The attack
on state-sector workers eroded both public sympathies for the
labor movement and working class solidarities. State-sector
strikes always appeared to hurt the public, and private-sector
established workers, like middle-class people, could identify
themselves as taxpayers interested in reducing government
spending.

Among the unemployed and nonestablished there were
also divergent interests. Downgraded former established workers
might cling to trade-union solidarity as a hope for revival of the
halcyon days of the neoliberal social consensus. Migrant target
workers, women seeking part-time employment, illegal workers
in the burgeoning underground economies, unemployed ghetto
youths all would have quite different orientations to work and,
distinct in their own ways, all be far less attracted to trade-union
solidarities.[20]

This fragmentation and growth of divisions within the
working class has not been uniform. In many Western European
countries, a long history of ideological education has maintained
a sense of solidarity. The force of this tradition is much weaker

in North America. (It remains stronger in Canada than in the United States.) In both Italy and France there have been instances where unions have maintained solidarity of action between migrant workers and local established workers, whereas in other instances these groups have been juxtaposed in opposition one to another. Fragmentation has, however, been the underlying trend that explains the weakness of labor in preventing the disintegration of the neoliberal social consensus and opposing the program put in its place by the government-business alliance.[21]

If the strains tending toward a disintegration of the neoliberal historic bloc have been visible since the mid-1970s, it would be premature to define the outlines of a new historic bloc likely to achieve a certain durability as the foundation for a new form of state. One can, however, prudently speak of a crisis of hegemony as having opened in some of the leading countries of the capitalist world. Its symptoms are an uncertainty of direction among the dominant groups and a fragmentation and absence of cohesion among the subordinate groups. Some of the dominant groups espouse a classical liberal view of national and world economy; others envisage a more state-interventionist national capitalism with some revival of corporatist methods of consensus building. The lack of cohesion among subordinate groups is evidenced by the incoherence of opposition politics. The crisis of hegemony is a crisis of representation: one historic bloc is dissolving, another has not taken its place. Such a condition is ripe for caesarism, not necessarily in its man-of-destiny (or, pace Thatcher, woman-of-destiny) form, but quite possibly a caesarism without caesar. Indeed, a parallel can be drawn between the inflations of the advanced capitalist countries during the late 1970s and the inflations of the neomercantilist developmentalist states. With the erosion of social contract, the former were slipping into the same condition of uncooperative competition among social forces locked in a political impasse that had characterized the latter.

## TENDENCIES IN THE TRANSFORMATION OF THE NEOLIBERAL STATE

Two principal directions of movement in political structures are visible in the erstwhile neoliberal states: one is exemplified by the confrontational tactics of Thatcherism in Britain and Reaganism in the United States toward removing internal obstacles to economic liberalism; the other by a more consensus-based adjustment process as in Japan, West Germany, and some of the smaller European countries. The crisis of hegemony is more apparent in the former, while the latter seems to suggest the possibility of an adaptation of neoliberal structures to the prospect of a more power-managed world political economy. In France, the structures of economic management present analogies to those of the latter, while the polarization of society and politics is more like the former. Meanwhile, minority left-wing groups in some of these countries (e.g., the CERES group in the French Socialist Party and the Labour Party advocates of the Alternative Economic Strategy in Britain) propose more self-reliant strategies to protect national economies from world-economy influences so as to be able to plan production of use values rather than rely on competition in the production of exchange values for the world market. These divergent tendencies draw strength from factors differentiating the different countries: position in the world economy, the structures of production and finance, entrenched ideologies, and political practices. Each of these tendencies toward an alternative form of state posits a changed structure of world order and presupposes a reconstructed pattern of production relations. Underlying these different prospects for a new order of production is the implication of a transformation of the social structure of accumulation.

The Thatcher-Reagan model can be treated teleologically as the anticipation of a hyperliberal form of state—in the sense that it seems to envisage a return to nineteenth-century economic liberalism and the rejection of the neoliberal attempt to adapt economic liberalism to the sociopolitical reactions that classical liberalism produced. The whole paraphernalia of Keynesian demand-support and redistributionist tools of policy are regarded with the deepest suspicion in the hyperliberal approach. Government spending to create employment, and transfer payments to targeted groups intended to sustain their purchasing power and thus indirectly to maintain employment, fall under this suspicion. So also do other kinds of government intervention to support industries in difficulty such as credits, bailouts, price supports, and subsidies—although in these respects principles are not consistently followed in the practice of the hyperliberal tendency. Government-imposed regulations to protect the public with respect to industrial activities (antipollution, safety and health controls, etc.) are also to be weakened or dismantled. The market is to determine how much protection the public really wants. (People will not, according to the reasoning of this tendency, buy unsafe products if they do not want them and will move away from polluted areas if they find them unpleasant. The economist's assumption of perfect information and freedom of decision is touchingly naive.)

The hyperliberal tendency in the state actively facilitates a restructuring, not only of the labor force, but also of the modes of social relations of production. It renounces tripartite corporatism. It also weakens bipartism by its attack on unions in the state sector and its support and encouragement to employers to resist union demands in the oligopolistic sector. Indirectly, the state encourages the consolidation of enterprise corporatist relations for the scientific-technical-managerial workers in the oligopolistic sector, a practice for which the state itself provides a model in its treatment of its own permanent cadres. Finally, state policies are geared to the expansion of the new enterprise-labor-market type of employment in short-term, low-skill, high-turnover jobs. The overall impact of the hyperliberal tendency on the social formation is thus toward a polarization of labor between a privileged minority enterprise-corporatist component and a large-scale, unstably employed enterprise-labor-market component, with a declining but aggravated and conflictual bipartite residue. Cohesion among enterprise-labor-market workers is obstructed by the fact that they are segmented along age, sex, and ethnic lines.

The political implications, as mentioned above, are a complete reversal of the coalition that sustained the neoliberal state. That state rested on its relationship with trade unions in the oligopolistic sector (the social contract), an expanding and increasingly unionized state sector, readiness to support major businesses in difficulty (from agricultural price supports to bailouts of industrial giants), and transfer payments and services for a range of disadvantaged groups. The neoliberal state played a hegemonic role by making capital accumulation on a world scale appear to be compatible with a wide range of interests of subordinate groups. It founded its legitimacy on consensual politics. The would-be hyperliberal state confronts all those groups and interests with which the neoliberal state came to terms. It does not shrink from open opposition to state-sector employees, welfare recipients, and trade unions.

The government-business alliance that presides over the transformation of the neoliberal into a would-be hyperliberal form of state generates an imposing list of disadvantaged and excluded groups. State-sector employees made great gains as regards their collective bargaining status and their wages during the years of expansion and have now become front-line targets for budgetary restraint. Welfare recipients and nonestablished workers, socially contiguous categories, are hit by reduced state expenditure and unemployment. Farmers and small businessmen are angry with banks and with governments as affordable finance becomes unavailable to them. Established workers in industries confronting severe problems in a changing international division of labor—textiles, automobiles, steel, shipbuilding, for example—face unemployment or reduced real wages. So long as the excluded groups lack strong organization and political cohesion, ideological mystification and an instinctive focus on personal survival rather than collective action suffice to maintain the momentum of the new policy orthodoxy. If at least a small majority of the population remains relatively satisfied, it can be politically mobilized as necessary to maintain these policies in place against the dissatisfaction of an even very large minority that is divided and incoherent.

This confrontational posture of the would-be hyperliberal state toward the various excluded groups requires a new basis in legitimacy. The answer has been sought in a nonhegemonic, populist appeal to the sanctity of traditional values. At the oratorical level, the new legitimacy stresses the work ethic, family, neighborhood, and patriotism.[22] At a subliminal level, the appeal is tinged with racism—against immigrants and minorities stereotyped inconsistently both as welfare bums and as threats to jobs. The ideological appeal is nominally classless, though in practice aimed at an amorphous blue-collar and petty-bourgeois constituency. The managerial elites and scientific-technical cadres of enterprise corporatism are by and large too sophisticated for this kind of appeal. They are more likely recruits for a state-capitalist alternative.

The appeal to traditional values is strengthened by the strong military stance of the hyperliberal state. The state justifies militarism as necessary to defend the capitalist world order. In economic terms, there is a "military Keynsianism" effect in stimulating the economy, but inflated arms budgets and military adventure abroad increase the state's budget deficit far beyond the cuts achieved in the welfare and social services.[23] Persistent and mounting state budget deficits expand the public debt, keep interest rates high, and act as a deterrent to productive investments. Military expenditures, moreover, being increasingly of a technology-intensive and capital-intensive kind, are less able than during earlier phases of military expansion (the Korean and Indochina wars) to expand employment.[24] The ideological benefits of military expansionism are probably greater for the would-be hyperliberal state than its economic benefits are.

The international consequences of militarism reveal the ambiguity of the hyperliberal model. The state disengages from civil society—it reverses the trend toward interpenetration and blurring of the edges between state and society that corporatism promoted—in order to force more radically the adjustment of national economies to the world economy. In this respect, it is the fullest, most uncompromising instance of a liberal state. But the militarism with which it is entwined is the harbinger of a reversion from the hegemonic capitalist world order, which called the neoliberal form of state into being in the first place. Militarism is a symptom of the regression of global hegemony on which the world economic order has rested. The more that military force has to be increased and the more it is actually employed, the less the world order rests on consent and the less it is hegemonic. Economic benefits appear to flow less from the operation of universal laws of the market that is the basic article of faith of liberalism and more from power positions backed by force.

While the hyperliberal model reasserts the separation of state and economy, the alternative state form for relaunching capitalist development promotes a fusion of state and economy. This state-capitalist path may take several forms differentiated by national positions within the world economy and by institutional structures and ideologies. The substance common to these differentiated forms lies in a recognition of the indispensable guiding role of the state in the development of the nation's productive forces and the advancement of their position in the world economy through a conscious industrial policy, and in an equal recognition that this can be achieved only through a negotiated understanding among the principal social forces of production arrived at through the mediation of the state in a corporative process. Such an understanding would have to produce agreement on the strategic goals of the economy and also on the sharing of burdens and benefits in the effort to reach those goals.

The state-capitalist approach is grounded in an acceptance of the world market as the ultimate determinant of development. No single national economy—not even the largest—can control the world market or determine its orientation. Furthermore, unlike the neoliberal approach, the state-capitalist approach does not posit any consensual regulation of the world market as regards multilateral trade and financial practices. States are assumed to intervene not only to enhance the competitiveness of their nations' industries but also to negotiate or dictate advantages for their nations' exporters. The world market is the state of nature from which state-capitalist theory deduces specific policy.

The broad lines of this policy consist of, in the first place, development of the leading sectors of national production so as to give them a competitive edge in world markets, and in the second place, protection of the principal social groups so that their welfare can be perceived as linked to the success of the national productive effort.

The first aspect of this policy—industrial competitiveness—is to be achieved by a combination of opening these industrial sectors to the stimulus of world competition, together with state subsidization and orientation of innovation. Critical to the capacity for innovation is the condition of the knowledge industry; the state will have a major responsibility of funding technological research and development. In its task of guiding productive development, the state will have to balance strategic security values against competitive efficiency. Competitive efficiency dictates specialization, but if specialization in comparative advantages were to neglect sectors essential to national security, e.g., automotive, aerospace, and computer sectors, the state would seek to retain a national position in these sectors despite higher costs. Obviously, the trade-offs between security and efficiency are more difficult for smaller economies than for a continental economy like that of the United States.

The second policy aspect—balancing the welfare of social groups—has to be linked to the pursuit of competitiveness. Protection of disadvantaged groups and sectors (industries or regions) would be envisaged as transitional assistance for their transfer to more profitable economic activities. Thus training, skill upgrading, and relocation assistance would have a preeminent place in social policy. The state would not indefinitely protect declining or inefficient industries but would provide incentives for the people concerned to become more efficient according to market criteria. The state would, however, intervene between the market pressures and the groups concerned so that the latter did not bear the full burden of adjustment. (By contrast, the hyperliberal model would evacuate the state from this cushioning and incentive-creating function, letting the market impose the full costs of adjustment upon the disadvantaged.)

Where internally generated savings were deemed to be essential to enhanced competitiveness, both investors and workers would have to be persuaded to accept an equitable sharing of sacrifice, in anticipation of a future equitable sharing of benefits. Thus incomes policy would become an indispensable counterpart to industrial policy. Similarly, the managerial initiative required to facilitate innovation and quick response to market changes might be balanced by forms of worker participation in the process of introducing technological changes. The effectiveness of such a state-capitalist approach would, accordingly, depend on the existence of corporative institutions and processes, not only at the level of enterprises and industries, but also of a more centralized kind capable of organizing interindustry, intersectoral and interregional shifts of resources for production and welfare.

The state-capitalist form involves a dualism between, on

the one hand, a competitively efficient world-market-oriented sector, and, on the other, a protected welfare sector. The success of the former must provide the resources for the latter; the sense of solidarity implicit in the latter would provide the drive and legitimacy for the former. State capitalism thus proposes a means of reconciling the accumulation and legitimation functions brought into conflict by the economic and fiscal crises of the 1970s and frozen in caesarist polarization by hyperliberal politics. In its most radical form, state capitalism beckons toward the prospect of an internal socialism sustained by capitalist success in world-market competition. This would be a socialism dependent on capitalist development, i.e., on success in the production of exchange values. But, so its proponents argue, it would be less vulnerable to external destabilization than attempts at socialist self-reliance were in economically weak countries (e.g., Allende's Chile and post-carnation-revolution Portugal). The more radical form of state-capitalist strategy thus presents itself as an alternative to defensive, quasi-autarkic prescriptions for the construction of socialism through reducing dependency on the world economy and emphasizing the production of use values for internal consumption.[25]

Different countries are more or less well equipped by their historical experience for the adoption of the state-capitalist developmental path with or without the socialist coloration. Those best equipped are the late-industrializing countries (from France and Japan in the late nineteenth century to Brazil and South Korea in the late twentieth), in which the state (or a centralized but autonomous financial system as in the German case) has played a major role in mobilizing capital for industrial development. Institutions and ideology in these countries have facilitated a close coordination of state and private capital in the pursuit of common goals. Those least well equipped are the erstwhile industrial leaders, Britain and the United States, countries in which hegemonic institutions and ideology kept the state by and large out of specific economic initiatives, confining its role to guaranteeing and enforcing market rules and to macroeconomic management of market conditions. The lagging effects of past hegemonic leadership may thus be a deterrent to the adoption of state-capitalist strategies. It can also, however, be asked whether strategies that were appropriate to catching up the hegemonic leaders (when the industrial model of the future was present before the late-developing rivals) will prove equally successful in the uncharted realms on the frontiers of technological development, where many countries find themselves today.

Recent U.S. literature comparing the policy structures of advanced capitalist states has pointed to factors both propitious and unpropitious to taking the state-capitalist route. Peter Katzenstein has contrasted states that have used policy instruments for specific industrial interventions (France and Japan) with those that have limited their action to macroeconomic instruments 'Britain and the United States),[26] and he has illustrated the varieties of experience of small European countries in combining offensive world-market export strategies with commitment to state welfare.[27] John Zysman has underlined the importance of very different financial structures in either facilitating (France and Japan) or inhibiting (Britain and the United States) state leadership in the orientation of investment and thus industrial development.[28] Like Katzenstein, he points to West Germany and the small European countries as instances of compromise among the principal social groups being negotiated in relative autonomy, though sanctioned by the state in a process characterized by another author, Philippe Schmitter, as "societal corporatism."[29]

These authors discuss the state as an ensemble of governmental instruments and goals of policy. I have stressed also the historic bloc as a constitutive component of the state. It was argued above that the world economic crisis of the 1970s dismantled the neoliberal historic blocs of the advanced capitalist countries. The hyperliberal project sustains itself with a political coalition of the relatively satisfied, excluding a significant but ideologically and politically fragmented part of the nation, and it mystifies this polarization with an appeal to patriotism. This constitutes a caesarist response: the temporary stabilization of a basically contradictory and conflictual situation.[30] The state-capitalist project must be read, by contrast, as an attempt to reconstitute social hegemony within the nation through corporatism. If the incentives to this endeavor may appear attractive, the obstacles are great and differ from country to country.

One condition for its success would seem to be the exis-

tence of a corps of persons around whom a coalition of social
forces could be constructed—those whom Gramsci would have
called the organic intellectuals. In France, the graduates of the
grandes écoles, in particular the Ecole nationale d'administration, provide such a corps, linking the upper echelons of state,
finance, and industry. In Japan, the graduates of the prestige
universities, in particular Tokyo University, give the same kind
of leadership. These groups are capable of defining a "national
interest" transcending particular economic interests of firms, industries, or regions, and they dispose both of instruments to
implement such policies and of influence to secure conformity
of diverse business interests with the overall objectives. In Britain
(as John Zysman has pointed out) the civil service has the necessary autonomy to evolve a "national" perspective but lacks the
instruments of policy and channels of influence to carry it out.[31]
The tradition of separation between state and economy is a major
obstacle to effective state leadership of economic development.
U.S. political practice and ideology has made government officials the creatures of interacting special interests, to the point
where the very concept of the state has been somewhat alien to
U.S. thought.[32] The principal objection to the idea of an industrial
policy in the United States is that the U.S. political process would
inevitably make of it a panoply of protectionism for the inefficient. (The reasoning is that those industries that hurt most will
be the most effective pressures on government, and since interests
are fragmented, each can see only its own success or failure and
will not have confidence in adjustment policies that require abandonment of existing positions.)[33]

     A second condition is the availability of a potential
coalition of social forces adequate both to carry through the project for enhancing the competitiveness of national production and
to agree on the burden and benefit sharing to be incurred in the
process. One most critical aspect of this condition is the ability
to convince the weaker, less productive sectors of industry of the
need for change. In Japan, development has hitherto taken place
through a dual economy: the leading high-productivity, technology-intensive sector based in the Japanese homeland has progressively stripped down and upgraded its labor force; the lower
productivity, more labor-intensive industries have multination-
alized themselves, making increasing use of cheap labor over-

seas.[34] A senior French official writing on industrial policy, Christian Stoffäes, has advocated a similar policy for France: high
wages in the leading sector to encourage technological upgrading
of industrial processes and "delocalization" (or movement
abroad to make use of cheaper foreign labor) for the more labor-
intensive processes.[35] In the United States, Reaganism has
achieved a political unification of U.S. business in support of the
Republican Party, but it is a unity based on a contradictory economic policy. Defense-related industries benefit from big military
budgets while Wall Street's confidence is shaken by uncontrolled
budget deficits. Main Street, i.e., businesses that are not internationally competitive and have had their profit margins squeezed
by union wages, remain ideologically in the Republican fold but
suffer from the high interest rates of Reagan-era monetary policy.
This contradictory coalition precludes any industrial policy, except insofar as the defense budget underpins a de facto but un-
avowed industrial policy.

   Another aspect of the coalition-building problem is the
availability of an *interlocuteur valable* on the side of labor. Only
in West Germany and the small European countries have broadly
representative labor movements acquired, since World War II,
experience as negotiating partners enjoying a certain equality of
status with business and government in deciding matters of national economic and social policy. This experience was, as noted
above, interrupted by the economic crisis that pushed labor in
all the advanced capitalist countries into a defensive position. In
both France and Japan, where industrial policies were successful,
labor was relatively weak. In France, the largest and most representative segment of the labor movement was politically excluded during the years of industrial modernization supported
by the Marshall Plan. In Japan, the labor force was institutionally
segmented into established and nonestablished, the trade unions
being confined to the former group and within it fragmented into
enterprise-corporatist organizations. In Britain, by contrast,
where the trade union movement was relatively strong, it was
unable (because of shop floor versus top leadership tensions) to
constitute a valid partner in industrial policies, and industry was
unwilling to countenance any union voice in investment
decisions.

   In principle, the corporative forms of organization required to negotiate the industrial and incomes policy bases for state-capitalist development would involve a revival of tripartism. The industrial-policy proposals for the United States drafted by Felix Rohatyn envisage a top-level industrial development board composed of members of cabinet, business, and labor, located in the Executive Office of the President, and disposing through a new Industrial Finance Administration of funds to support industries or firms whose competitiveness is critical to the national interest. "The Board's administrative authority would be limited, but the stature of its members and its access to the President would give it influence to marshal the resources of the executive branch in support of a coherent development strategy."[36] Such a mechanism seems to assume not only that labor representatives be accorded considerable influence in the determination of national economic priorities but also that these representatives will be able to arbitrate the differences among different unions and groups of workers that will inevitably arise in any readjustment of production structures. Both assumptions are most doubtful in the light of the weakening of the trade union movement by the economic crisis and the restructuring of production. The lack of centralized control over economic negotiations has differentiated the U.S. labor movement from those in Scandinavia and West Germany.

If tripartite corporatism appears an unlikely prospect in the United States, Christian Stoffäes perceived some risks for industrial policy in France of allowing tripartism free rein. The world-market-conquering offensive strategy he saw as France's salvation would require a strong state capable of defining and implementing specific policy choices while at the same time associating economic and occupational interests with the pursuit of national goals. He feared, however, that a more politically likely outcome would be a defensive protectionist policy dictated by the diverse interests with access to government.[37] In other words, the more "societal" (to borrow Philippe Schmitter's term) tripartite corporatism becomes, the less apt it is for the management of an effective world-market competitive strategy, but the more tripartite representation is subordinated to state-led corporatism, the more chance there is that competitive rather than protectionist policies will be consistently followed. This, at any rate, may be a valid proposition for countries with a relatively weak labor movement—and one has to bear in mind the general weakening of labor movements in the advanced capitalist countries since the mid-1970s.[38] It may well prove that the Japanese model of state-capitalist development, in which trade union participation takes place through an enterprise-corporatist relationship with big enterprises rather than through national-level union representation on tripartite bodies, is the more likely form for state-capitalist development in the 1980s.

The corporatist process underpinning state-capitalist development, which would include business and labor in the world-market-oriented sector and workers in the tertiary welfare-services sector, would at the same time exclude certain marginal groups. These groups have a frequently passive relationship to the welfare services and lack influence in the making of policy. They are disproportionately the young, women, immigrant or minority groups, and the unemployed. The restructuring of production tends to increase their numbers. Since these groups are fragmented and relatively powerless, their exclusion has generally passed unchallenged. It does, however, contain a latent threat to corporatist processes. Part of this threat is the risk of anomic explosions of violence, particularly on the part of the young male unemployed element. Such explosions often, however, strengthen by reaction the established authority.[39] The other part of the threat is the risk of political mobilization of the marginals, which would pit democratic legitimacy against corporatist economic efficiency. These dangers are foreshadowed in the writings of neoliberal scholars about the "ungovernability" problem of modern democracies.[40] The implication is that the corporatist processes required to make state-capitalist development succeed may have to be insulated from democratic pressures.[41] To the extent this becomes true, the prospects of internal socialism sustained by world-market state capitalism would be an illusion.

In short, the state-capitalist alternative has some potential for reconstructing internal hegemonies and overcoming the caesarist impasse that hyperliberalism tends to rigidify. The narrowing basis of corporatism (particularly as regards its labor component) on which state-capitalist development must rest does, however, contain a latent contradiction to democratic legitimacy.

Its historic bloc would be thin. The excluded groups available
for mobilization into a counterhegemony would be considerable,
though the fragmentation and powerlessness of these groups
would make the task formidable. In the medium term, state-
capitalist structures of some form seem a feasible alternative to
the hyperliberal impasse. The long-term viability of these forms
is a more open question.

## STRUCTURAL CHANGE
## IN THE WORLD POLITICAL ECONOMY

The propositions emerging from the study of preceding historical
periods suggest that changes in forms of state will be conditioned
by both the social structure of accumulation (including in particular the social relations of production) and the structure of world
order. At the present time, changes in both of these structures
can be perceived. Those affecting the social structure of accumulation, which may well be the most profound and of the
longest duration, will be discussed in the next chapter. Structural
changes in world order and their implications for the direction
of change in forms of state are considered here.

These can be summarized under three points: (1) a virtual
abandonment of the central regulatory functions of the world
economy entrusted under the Pax Americana to the institutions
of global hegemony, accompanied by a weakening of central
authority and increasing reliance by states and corporations on
their political-economic bargaining power; (2) little change in the
basic bipolarity of the military-strategic system, but a relative loss
of control by the superpowers outside their homelands and loss
of credibility in their leadership and of confidence in their sense
of priorities, particularly among U.S. allies; and (3) a heightening
of competitive pressures, beginning with the arms race and extending through world markets for raw materials, capital equipment, and manufactured goods, which tends to encourage an
emulative uniformity in the way problems are confronted and
solved rather than withdrawal into isolated spheres within which
distinctive solutions can be attempted.

The last point implies that the world is not moving toward

a system of self-contained economic-strategic blocs similar to the trend of the 1930s. It is, however, moving into an aggressively competitive trading pattern in which negotiating power, rather than the impersonal rules of liberal economic behavior, determines outcomes in a zero-sum game. The system has become more decentralized and power more diffused, a diffusion that is more pronounced in the economic than in the military-strategic realm. To this diffusion of power corresponds a loss of hegemony in the sense of a consensual norms-based system. The continuing military and economic predominance of the United States outside the Soviet sphere rests more openly on its strength and bargaining power. Hegemony has given place to dominance.

Does this greater diffusion of power mean that the world order is becoming more permissive in the sense that there is more freedom for the development of novel forms of state and of production relations? Not likely, because of the competitive pressures present in the world system. These are likely to act on all states outside the redistributive societies in such a way as to encourage the adoption of similar forms of state-capitalist development geared to an offensive strategy in world markets and sustained by corporatist organization of society and economy. Production in these societies will most likely be organized through a combination of enterprise-corporatist and enterprise-labor-market social relations, and tripartism will be invoked in some countries as a process for the formulation of industry policies and incomes policies under state leadership. Any countries driven by internal pressures to adopt a defensive-withdrawal strategy vis-à-vis the world economy would incur the risk of economic failure with a drastic drop in living standards.

The redistributive societies will also be constrained by the competitive pressures of the world order, though not to the same degree as other states. The developmental possibilities of the Soviet Union and China are limited above all by the arms race. To the increased defense budget of the United States corresponds a proportionately greater economic effort by the Soviet Union with a smaller margin remaining for social development. Nevertheless, both the Soviet Union and (to an even greater extent) China have entered phases of experimental change in social productive organization regarded by their leaders as essential to the maintenance and strengthening of their power within the world system. These social and economic experiments are guided by the internal criteria of the redistributive systems, even though some aspects (e.g., the greater use of market mechanisms and decentralization of management in economic development) may appear to reflect some practices of capitalist development. The links that redistributive societies establish with the capitalist world market are limited and controlled by them to serve the specific purposes of these societies. Their economies are not in the position of competing for world market shares as are the countries of capitalist development. Exports are important to these countries, but as surplus from their internally determined production requirements. These countries are constrained externally by the world military power competition and internally by the limits to their ability to mobilize population and resources for national goals. Furthermore, the diffusion of power outside the Soviet sphere and the decline of U.S. hegemonic leadership open more options for the Soviet Union and China. The arrangements concluded by the Soviet Union with Western European countries for the construction of a natural gas pipeline giving Western Europe access to Soviet energy are suggestive of a range of possible international economic arrangements the Soviet Union and China could make with different partners (or with each other) in a world economic order governed by negotiated contracts.[42]

The decline of centralized management characteristic of the world economy of Pax Americana can be traced through the 1970s. The top management of this world economy can more adequately be represented as a system than as an institution—a system only partly composed of state-like institutions. During the 1960s, the U.S. Department of the Treasury might have appeared to be the apex, its general policy criteria being internationalized through the medium of the IMF, World Bank, the General Arrangements to Borrow, the Bank for International Settlements, the OECD, and several other agencies. Through these institutions, linked by the overlapping personnel of their principal decision makers, there took place the process of policy osmosis among the leading personnel of advanced capitalist states and of policy projection into Third World countries that has been described in

Chapter 7. However, during the 1970s, private transnational banks assumed such an important role that the top management structure could no longer be convincingly represented exclusively in terms of state and interstate institutions. Of course, financial markets had always shaped the way the system worked. The World Bank had depended on the private banks to market its bonds, and in this way capital markets in New York and in Europe constituted a check on the kinds of policies that both the World Bank and its potential borrowers could in practice pursue. The capital markets in question cannot realistically be thought of as nonpolitical. They are not cast in the classical model of an infinity of buyers and sellers of money; rather they are composed of a limited number of oligopolists whose consensus can be ascertained by a few telephone calls and whose individual judgments are based on a balancing of financial risk-taking and prudence, of political pressures and personal prejudices.

When, during the 1970s, the chief expanding source of international credit was the lending operations of the transnational banks, the exact nature of the interrelationship between state and private structures at the apex of the world system became both more important and more mysterious. U.S. and German state policies encouraged the private banks to lend to the Soviet Union and Eastern European countries as part of the policy of détente. Simultaneously, industrializing Third World countries found borrowing from the private banks less politically distasteful than going to the IMF. Ultimately, it must have been accepted by all concerned that the advanced capitalist states through their central banks would have to back up the private banks in case of payments crisis or default in order to avoid an unacceptable shock to the international financial system. Indeed, the principle of ultimate state responsibility was multilateralized through a decision of the central bankers at the Bank for International Settlements in July 1974 that the central banks of the major capitalist countries would act to prevent the collapse of private banks within their jurisdictions.[43] The private banks were being encouraged to take on quasi-state-like functions in international lending and in return had some assurance that the central banks would, in crisis, bail them out. The mystery concerns how much latitude private bankers had and how much political restraint they operated under. It seems evident in retrospect that this was not a very tightly managed system.

When, in the early 1980s, a sequence of crises revealed the inability of some Eastern European and Third World countries to meet their debt obligations, proposals emerged to move the official institutions, particularly the IMF, back into a central role supervising international lending and at the same time to enhance the political character of the IMF, i.e., to reassert the state character of international finance. This is something desired not just by governments as a means of controlling their risks but also by the transnational banks as a means of limiting theirs.[44] However, a more central and perhaps essentially symbolic role for the international institutions in debt management and the multilateralizing of debt renewal conditions was not accompanied by any reform of the international monetary system such as would make possible enlarged centrally controlled credit and greater exchange stability.

The relative enlargement of the private, nonstate character of international financial management during the 1970s may be seen as an effect of weakening hegemony. Private international credit expanded for lack of any agreement on how the official intergovernmental structures in the system could be reformed. The impasse on reform was the consequence of stalemate between the United States and the European countries on the future role of the dollar. The United States had an effective veto on reform and was not prepared to forgo the advantages of the dollar's international status. The United States could run a continuing deficit so long as the dollar remained the principal currency for settling international accounts and the principal reserve currency.

The relatively greater dependence of Europe and Japan on imported oil denominated in dollars tied these countries ever more tightly to the dollar standard as OPEC, following 1973, raised the price of oil. It weakened these countries' chances of gaining U.S. acceptance of any reform displacing the dollar from its dominant position. As confidence in U.S. management waned, private transnational banks took on more of the actual management of the system. In the absence of agreement on management by official institutions, dollar hegemony shifted to the financial market, that is to say, to the very largely unmanaged dollar itself. Perceptions of impending crisis in the early 1980s revealed the risks in this hegemonic cop-out, but the political prospects of consensual reform of the system at the interstate level, though apparently more necessary to the system's survival, did not seem for all that more likely. Authority weakened at the apex of the international financial system. Crisis did not produce effective centralization. U.S. power was too great to be brought under any externally imposed discipline but no longer great enough to shape the rules of a consensual order.

In trade, the erosion of the GATT system and the growth of neomercantilist practices through the 1970s and into the 1980s have been abundantly described: the negotiation of special sectoral agreements like the multifiber one; the difficulty of dealing with nontariff barriers; state backing for corporate "national champions"; the growth of countertrade, compensation agreements, and other forms of barter.

Although for long perceived by Western commentators through the lenses of hegemonic liberalism as unfortunate departures from the rational course of policy—departures dictated by selfish interests—this complex of trade measures is now coming to be understood, at least by some analysts, in its own terms as a rationally coherent strategy under existing world-economy conditions. Susan Strange has proposed a "web-of-contracts model" as a more adequate substitute for the liberal model, pointing out that the neomercantilist reality does not imply less trade than was the case heretofore under liberal hegemonic rules.[45] Under the web-of-contracts practice, deals are negotiated by states with states, by states with corporations, and by corporations with corporations. The total volume of trade is limited much more by the capacity of the financial system to provide credit than by protectionist exclusions of products. In other words, the failure of the financial system—which in the 1970s provided too much credit and in the 1980s too little—is a more serious constraint than the shift in the mode of trade relations is.

If finance is the chief determinant of the level of economic activity, technology is the principal factor in competitive success or failure. Those states most concerned to capture and expand a share of the world market must invest heavily in technological research. The advanced countries on the frontiers of technology must become innovators in order to compete successfully. Third World countries pursuing rapid industrialization likewise seek to build up a domestic technological capability, in order not to remain forever dependent on outside knowledge; to this end they require foreign investors to do some research and development in the host country, in addition to acquiring up-to-date equipment from abroad.

Technology is a field in which the military and economic aspects of power overlap. Defense spending has been a major stimulus to technological advance, not only in defense production per se but also as a spillover from defense to civilian industrial applications. The European countries and Japan have succeeded in supplanting U.S. world leadership in some fields of engineering and electronics. President Reagan's Strategic Defense Initiative ("star wars") contains the potential for reasserting U.S. leadership in high technology backed by a huge state budget and conceived so as to attract industrial research in allied countries into a contributory relationship to the U.S. effort. All the more reason for France and her European associates to advance the Eureka proposal as a means of furthering European technological autonomy, not only in armaments, but, even more, in the area of industrial competitiveness.[46]

The diffusion of economic power and the internationally competitive nature of the world political economy put pressure on states to adopt an offensive strategy in world markets. Through such offensive strategies, states would lead and assist national industries to conquer market positions. At the same time, internal pressures come from interests disfavored by competition to adopt a defensive strategy of protection and partial withdrawal from world competition. The prospect that the defensive strategy would lead to a long-term decline in both power and plenty argues against it. But, as discussed above in connection with the transformation of the neoliberal state, to follow an offensive strategy requires both a competent corps of state personnel practiced in the use of adequate policy instruments and the negotiation of a social contract distributing the costs and benefits of industrial readjustment among the most influential socioeconomic groups. These conditions may prove to be beyond the capacities of some states.

The defensive strategy would close off certain external flows to and from the national economy, e.g., by the use of foreign exchange and trade controls. The offensive strategy, by contrast, would preserve the openness of the national economy in its leading sectors while it involved the state to a significant extent in their development. It is precisely this openness to competitive pressure with free international movement of capital that would tend toward a uniformity of economic structures and also of the culture underpinning economic activity. It would lead toward a number of competing national entities increasingly similar in their broad political, economic, social, and cultural outlines.

The international financial network, despite its manifest failings (lack of consensus on key currency reform, on recentralization of management, or on mechanisms for credit creation and distribution) remains the principal external constraint on national policies, acting as an incentive to openness and as a deterrent to the defensive strategy. The very hint of a threat by some government to control capital movements or foreign exchange can lead to an investment strike and a capital flight, precipitating thereby an exchange crisis that will require foreign borrowing and possibly devaluation of the national currency. Reluctance to follow a policy of openness makes foreign or domestic borrowing by the state difficult, as does a perception in the financial markets that the state is not managing its expenditures in relation to its revenues. The British Labour government was forced in 1976 to reduce state expenditures as a proportion of GNP by a combination of IMF pressures and the high cost of borrowing in the domestic finance market. The alternative to borrowing would have been to print more money and provoke a run on the pound.[47] The French Socialist government under President François Mitterand introduced during its first year a number of social measures, including a fifth week of paid holidays, retirement at sixty, reduction of working hours to thirty-nine a week, and improvement of conditions for part-time and temporary workers, and it also carried through nationalizations of banks and industrial groups. In its second year, however, the government had to face deficits in the social services and unemployment insurance, in public and private enterprises, and in the balance of payments of the country, which resulted in an alignment of state policies on those of the other advanced capitalist countries: priority to antiinflation measures, imposition of a wage freeze and abandonment of wage indexation, and cutbacks in government spending in general and in social expenditures in particular.[48]

A combination of internal pressures from domestic social forces and external constraints operating through financial markets and institutions of the world economy sets practical limits to the options of governments. If a government were determined not to heed the external forces, it would have to be prepared to rely exclusively on internal means of stimulating and coordinating the productive forces in its society. In the extreme case, this would mean mass mobilization, collective and egalitarian austerity, and the organization of production geared to use (or the basic needs of society) rather than exchange (or the possibility of profits on world markets). This would imply a shift, not toward the defensive-protectionist strategy, but toward the construction of a redistributive system.

The defensive strategy, in opposition to competitive openness, is advocated by conservative groups (of both capital and labor) who want to protect their existing positions, not to revolutionize society. It is less a strategy, in the sense of a coherent program, than a demand for concessions. But the mobilizing redistributive alternative is something else. There is no indication that public opinion in advanced capitalist countries is psychologically prepared for such an alternative. The ethic of personal choice that nourishes the hope of a personal salvation on earth, as well as in heaven, is too widespread to succumb to a collectivist solution except perhaps under conditions of social and economic catastrophe.[49]

In some Third World countries, the magnitude of foreign debt is so great and the domestic political and social pain of making the kinds of adjustments likely to be required so intense that the prospect of defaults cannot be ruled out.[50] Susan Strange's observation with respect to Britain, that rich creditors are much more concerned with appearances than with getting their money back, doubtless applies also to the Mexicos, Brazils, and Perus.[51] The international financial networks, to the extent they can maintain coherence, will doubtless make the maximum compromise to keep these countries within the system, and to tolerate the reality of default so long as the forms of financial obligation are respected. The political elites of these countries in turn will shudder before the political consequences of overt default, which would cut off foreign resources and require them to rely on the committed support of their own populations. These governments are more likely to gamble on the understanding of the world financial networks. Regimes that have held power by excluding popular groups cannot readily transform themselves into mobilizing regimes. At the same time, there are limits to the economic exactions they can be perceived to inflict upon their own populations for the satisfaction of foreign capital.

For the Third World country caught in this financial bind, the alternative to either authoritarian repression or the stalemate of a cartel state is a national-populist revolution of the kind that overthrew the Shah of Iran—an alliance of the excluded. Such alliances are difficult to build because of the fragmentation of potential opposition groups and the effectiveness of modern technologies of repression. Nevertheless, the Iranian revolution, as well as other movements like the liberation struggles in southern Africa and Central America, show it to be possible. The survival of such movements depends on the dispersion of power in the world system. The chances may be somewhat better in the Persian Gulf than in a small Caribbean island.

Are there prospects for a comparable alternative in the advanced capitalist countries? As a general proposition, the pressures for conformity are stronger at the center than at the periphery of a system. There would seem to be very little chance for a successful war of movement leading to the capture and retention of power by forces committed to radical social restructuring in any of the advanced capitalist countries. There is some possibility of a longer, slower growth of an alternative political culture in some countries that would give greater scope to collective action and place a greater value on collective goods. For this to come about, whole segments of societies would have to become attached, through active participation and developed loyalties, to social institutions engaged in collective activities. They would have to be prepared to defend these institutions in times of adversity. Although the basic strength of such a movement is necessarily derived from its roots in society, it is extremely unlikely that it could break through successfully to reorganize the polity in isolation in any single country. Success would be conditioned by the strength of similar movements in other countries, as well as by a diffusion of power at the world level such as would preclude a concerted external effort at suppression.

The condition for a restructuring of society and polity in this sense is to build a new historic bloc capable of sustaining a long war of position within capitalist society until it is strong enough to become an alternative basis of state power. This effort has to be grounded in the popular strata of any particular society, but at the same time it must be able to mobilize sufficient strength in the world system to protect its national bases. The adversity that has befallen the left during the economic crisis of the 1970s and 1980s may perhaps be turned to advantage if it were to provoke reflection on the conditions for such a long-term strategy.

# CHAPTER 9

# MUTATIONS IN THE SOCIAL STRUCTURE OF ACCUMULATION

In a fascist prison during the late 1920s and early 1930s Antonio Gramsci reflected upon the transformation of productive forces he called "Americanism and Fordism" and its significance for the development of capitalism in Europe. His thoughts probed the connections between technology and the power relations of production, between both of these and the moral order of society and role of the state, and the relevancy of all these factors to the process of accumulation. Gramsci's reflections raised a number of issues involved in the putting into place of the social structure of accumulation that came to govern world economic processes during the first half of the twentieth century. They are a useful starting point for considering whether this structure has, during the last decades of the century, entered a new phase of mutation.

## TECHNOLOGY AND SOCIETY

Fordism, in Gramsci's thinking,[1] did not bring into existence a basic change in the class relations of capitalism but was rather a rationalization and extension of these relations shorn of all extraneous and precapitalist baggage. Fordism, through its ability to mass produce consumer goods for people's needs, showed the progressive face of capitalism, its ability to develop the productive forces. This productive capacity was opposed, not by workers, but by the regressive and parasitical forces in existing society that lived off the fruits of capital but were not themselves productive: the traditional intellectuals, the rural bourgeoisie, and the multitudes who battened upon state office for their incomes. If Fordism had achieved its breakthrough in America, it was largely because these regressive forces were relatively powerless in America. This was also why American industry could at the same time achieve high levels of accumulation and afford high wages for its workers—the weight of the unproductive elements of society was relatively light. Subsequently, the lash of competition compelled European industries to emulate American methods, but in Europe the regressive forces were relatively more powerful, and the state mediated between the rationalization of production, on the one hand, and the regressive forces on the other.

The fascist corporative state was caught on the horns of this dilemma. There were some elements in fascism that envisaged the corporative state as the means of making a gradual transition toward the adoption of American methods throughout Italian industry. Gramsci was, however, skeptical that this tendency within fascism could triumph, because of fascism's dependence on the entrenched, dominant, plutocratic landlord and traditional intellectual elements of society. This made a breakthrough by the technical-managerial cadres of industry improbable. Fascism would remain a passive revolution, stabilizing through coercion an impasse in social development, verbally espousing certain aims of industrial concentration, but stopping short of the agrarian and industrial reform a thoroughgoing Fordism would imply.

There is a strong sense of historical dialectic in Gramsci's thoughts about Fordism. The condition for the successful installation of Fordism in industry was the breaking of worker power, achieved by a combination of coercion (the weakening and destruction of trade unions) and persuasion (high wages). The implications of Fordism, once established as a general model of production organization, were, on the one hand, economic planning for the economy as a whole, and on the other, a moral transformation creating new types of personalities both masculine and feminine. Gramsci's skepticism about the prospect that state capitalism, through fascist corporatism, would be able to achieve the planned economic environment for Fordism relates to the first of these implications. So does the adoption by the Soviet Union of Fordist principles of industrial organization as the production basis for a planned economy.

The second implication—the prospects of a new moral order convergent with mass production—was closer to Gramsci's continuing preoccupation with historical materialism, with the relationship of social being to social consciousness. Hitherto all major changes in modes of existence had been the result of coercion, i.e., the dominance of one social group over another. (He gave the example of the shift from nomadism to settled agriculture, accompanied by the imposition of serfdom.) What fascinated Gramsci about the installation of Fordism was the effort on the part of employers to reshape working-class morals that accompanied their use of coercion against working-class institutions.

Mass production, by its fragmentation of tasks and assembly-line organization, reduced work to a sequence of physical movements. It required a worker who would be disciplined and attentive. A dissolute and irregular life outside the factory would render a worker unfit for factory discipline. Strong puritanical social and moral controls over the worker's life as a whole would compensate for the inherent interest in and creative commitment to work characteristic of the artisanal methods that had been displaced by Fordism.

Perceptive capitalist employers like Henry Ford understood this problem of bringing about concordance between factory work and social existence. They approached it by trying to manipulate the social lives of workers whose collective power had been broken. Their initiatives at moral reform went on at the level of the worker and the factory: "Hegemony here," wrote Gramsci, "is born in the factory and requires for its exercise only a minute quantity of professional political and ideological intermediaries." It would, Gramsci foresaw, become a problem for the state; the capitalist state would take over and extend the ideological work of employers.[2]

The Russian Bolsheviks were aware of the same problem.

They approached it by imposing an external discipline upon the factory while attempting to spread among the working class as a whole a spirit of dedication to the goals of revolution. The "militarization of labor" associated with Trotsky's organization of war communism was revived in practice by Stalin in the First Five-Year Plan. Gramsci's acknowledgment of American capital's effectiveness in "the biggest collective effort to date to create . . . a new type of worker and of man"[3] can be read as a rebuke to wrong methods employed by the Soviet leadership in what Gramsci agreed was a right purpose.

The focus on the workers and the factory as the bases on which a new order would have to be built conformed with Gramsci's earlier experience with the workers' councils movement in Turin. Contrary to both Henry Ford and Stalin, he envisaged the new order emerging through the autonomous interaction of workers with their organic intellectuals in the revolutionary party—the modern prince—creating a worker-led counterhegemony.

Gramsci saw two contradictions arising with Fordism. One was the hypocrisy inherent in the growth of libertinism among the dominant classes, who would abandon in their own behavior the puritanical standards prescribed for the working class. (He might also have foreseen the growth of cynicism in countries of actually existing socialism as a reaction to the self-serving behavior of Party and bureaucratic cadres.) The other contradiction arose directly out of the transformation of work, which emptied work of creative or intellectual challenge and content, aiming to turn the worker into a "trained gorilla."[4] Contrary to Adam Smith[5] and subsequent writers on alienation, Gramsci did not see this as "the spiritual death of man"[6]—a progressive brutalization and mental deprivation of the working class. The workers who had no longer to think about the conceptual content of their work would have other things to absorb their mental capacities, including projects that could become quite threatening to the ruling classes. Fordism, for the working class, was but a stage—a liberation of the mind consequential upon a defeat in class struggle—in the historical development of an alternative society.

Gramsci's analysis of Fordism brings out several guiding principles for the examination of evidence regarding current change in the social structure of accumulation. One of these principles is that technology has specific implications for social organization, productive organization, the role of the state, and ideology. These implications are not, however, dictated in a singular one-way-only manner by technology. Different ideological and social forms may be devised as consistent with a given technology. Another principle is that technologies are spread through competition engendering the necessity of emulation. This is precisely where differences in social, productive, and ideological forms arise as different adaptations are made to the same diffused technology.

Two further points to those guiding principles examined by Gramsci can be added for our own consideration. One concerns the possibility of alternative technologies and the factors determining the choice of those technologies that become dominant, like Fordism. The other is that dominant technologies do not absorb the whole of production even in the era of their greatest dominance. They coexist with other previously developed technologies, each with its own different form of social relations of production, and accumulation takes place through the structured interconnections of the coexisting variety of dominant and subordinate modes of production relations. Gramsci did not consider these points. They are additional to but not inconsistent with those he did.

The question contained in the first of these points can be phrased as an alternative: Does technology develop on its own, from its own internal logic, thereby dictating what adjustments society must make to it? Or is technology itself a product of society and of society's power relations?

There is a strong bias in modern thought in favor of the autonomy of technological development. By adopting the idea of a "natural history" of technology, three phases in a progression have been perceived as taking place since the industrial revolution of the late eighteenth century:[7]

1. Manufacture based on skilled manual trades. The factory workshop consists of an assemblage of artisans or skilled tradesmen, each carrying out a relatively complex task in the

course of which he can control the quality of his work and the pace at which it is carried out.

2. Mass production with conveyor-belt technology (Fordism) in which tasks have been highly fragmented and are carried out by quickly trainable, semiskilled workers. The motions to be performed by each worker and the pace at which they are to be performed is determined by the technical system, not by the worker's judgment.

3. Automated or continuous process production in which work is reintegrated on the scale of the workshop or enterprise but is carried out by machines that are not directly controlled by the worker. The worker plays a supporting role as dial-watcher or maintenance mechanic.

These three "stages" have the form of abstract ideal types more than of fair representations of the historical development of production. The image of the workshop as an assemblage of skilled craftsmen is, for instance, hardly representative of early cotton textile mills, in which many women and children were employed.[8] Nevertheless, the sequence craftsmanship-Fordism-automation has a certain validity in simplifying the modern history of leading technologies.

Based on this, various theories have attempted to explain the social "consequences" of changes in production technology, for example, the kinds of worker organization evolved as a response to each phase. Thus the crafts-based phase evoked the response of unions composed of skilled tradesmen. These workers identified with their craft or profession and had a relatively high mobility among enterprises. Their unions controlled access to trades qualifications and defended their members' earning capacity by holding a strong position on the supply side of a labor market in which there was a scarcity of skilled labor. The workers of the mass-production phase responded differently, through industrial unionism. They had little or no control over the supply side of the labor market, being drawn from a large pool of unskilled migrants who could be trained in a few days to perform the work required of them. Their strength lay in their numbers and their potential political impact, and they consequently sought to influence the industrial system through the state, for example, by gaining protection against unemployment and other social benefits. Unlike the craft workers, they had no sense of deprivation at losing control over the work process. The arrival of the automation phase in the 1960s brought with it speculations concerning a third type of worker response. Observers noted the emergence of a new category of scientific and technical personnel with professional qualifications of a more general or polyvalent order than the craft-specific skills of old, i.e., mathematical, analytical, and communications skills. Such people were thought likely to identify with the enterprise and with the integrated production processes in which they worked. Speculation has centered on whether they would assert their functional autonomy and lead a movement demanding both more self-management by technicians' work groups at the enterprise level and more influence over future investment policy at the level of society as a whole, or whether they would become more dependent on the enterprises into which they were integrated and would identify more with management goals.[9]

These theses treat technology as a given and infer worker responses from the nature of the technical organization of production.[10] There is no suggestion contained in them that technological choices themselves may be determined by social power relations.[11] The alternative approach considers technology as a part of a strategy of social conflict inherent in the process of capital accumulation. Technology consists, after all, in the practical methods selected for the purpose of solving production problems. Thus defined, the questions that arise are: Problems for whom? Solutions toward what purpose? The answers are simple: For the accumulators and for the purpose of accumulation.[12] The basic and related thrusts of technological change from the nineteenth through the twentieth centuries have been (1) to gain greater control for management over the execution of work through labor discipline, and the consequential ability to minimize labor costs and increase the intensity of work; (2) to substitute capital for labor as labor costs increase; and (3) to separate the tasks of conception and direction of production from the tasks of execution in such a way as to strengthen management control and weaken worker autonomy in the work process.[13] The cumulative effect of these technological changes tilts the odds in social conflict in favor of management and against labor. In doing so, it has enabled management to continue the accumulation process on more favorable terms. The same technologies serve both capitalist and redistributive accumulation. Accumulation is the common factor, not capitalism, though capitalism pioneered the process and first put the technologies into practice.

Looked at in these terms, the three sequential ideal types of technology described above are phases in a continuous movement enhancing the accumulator's power over labor. In a first stage, capital brought the machinery of production under its control in factories. It did so because the existing method of "putting out" production of goods to artisans working in their own cottages had specific disadvantages for the mercantile entrepreneur: there was no control over the pace of work and no effective restraint on pilfering and embezzlement of raw materials and goods. The factory was created as a means of enforcing employer discipline, not because newly invented machinery required a factory form of organization of production. Factory-scale machinery followed the introduction of the factory and further facilitated reduction of labor costs, e.g., by enabling employers to hire women and children as machine tenders rather than pay craftsmen's wages. The factory and the technology that flowed from it were the result of the triumph of capitalists over dispersed laborers whose only power had lain in their control over their own work. The factory much diminished this control. As Marglin (1974) put it: "The steam mill didn't give us the capitalist; the capitalist gave us the steam mill."[14]

Even in the factory, however, the capitalist's control over work was not complete. The worker could still, individually or as part of a team, pace the use of machinery. This residue of worker control was the target of the innovations in production technology begun in the late nineteenth century that became widespread in large-scale industry during the interwar period through mass production, scientific management, Taylorism, etc.—the complex of changes signified by Fordism. These changes inaugurated a long process of deskilling labor by separating the manifold motions that the skilled worker coordinated in his own mind into simple, repetitive movements carried out separately by unskilled workers and coordinated through the engineering design prepared by management.[15] Automation and robotics are, in this sense, a further extension of Fordism. The movements at the core of the production process are carried out by machines coordinated by other machines, with some scientific and technical staff standing in a support and monitoring relationship to the process.

Characteristics of societies other than the power relations between capital and labor also played a role in the selection of technologies. Charles Sabel has drawn attention to the nature of markets, itself a consequence of social structures.[16] It was in the United States that a mass market for standardized machine-made goods became most firmly established. Social and geographical mobility and the relative weakness of particularistic cultural traditions and social distinctions facilitated the emergence of a homogenized taste that led Americans to buy the goods mass produced by machines. Social and cultural values supported the Fordist innovations. In Britain, the same propensities existed, though in a more restricted way. The large population uprooted from rural life and subjected to the experience of mass urbanization during the early nineteenth century became a mass market. The social stratification and particularisms that characterized the rest of British society, however, demanded more differentiated products. France provides a third type of social demand. The Revolution stabilized a large population of agricultural smallholders who provided for much of their own consumption, and the rest of French society, as in Britain, maintained a demand for customized or individually crafted products. As a result, a different mode of industrial production persisted and developed in centers like Birmingham and Sheffield in Britain and Lyons in France, a mode in which technological progress was consistent with small-scale production and product differentiation.

Given the existence of two alternative directions of technological development—large-series production of standardized goods for a mass market and small-series production of differentiated goods for segmented markets—the ultimate triumph of the mass-production mode is attributable to two factors. One was the cost advantage of mass production, which enabled it to cut competitively into specialized markets. Once a technological innovation cutting costs had been introduced by one capitalist, competition would oblige others to follow.[17] The other factor was the advantage of mass production for the supply of war materials. States thus saw the existence of national mass-production industries as a condition for war preparedness. Both factors can be assimilated to competition: competition for shares of consumer markets and interstate competition. Thus a mode of production that originated in the power struggle of capital with labor became generalized through the effect of competition. The most unlikely instance of this diffusionary effect was the adoption of Fordist production organization by Lenin and the Bolsheviks in Russia.

Motivations in this matter of technological change—how much is due to conscious strategies of class struggle and how much to diffusion through competition—are less important than consequences. The consequences point to the further principle mentioned above: that dominant technologies coexist with earlier technologies in complex hierarchical relationships. Different production methods are linked together in a system of complementarities and compatibilities. New technologies do not necessarily displace older ones; they form a relationship with them, dividing and allocating production between them.[18] Particular technologies express a power relationship between labor and the accumulators, and the compatible coexistence of different technologies expresses a power relationship between the groups engaged in each. Thus the description of the global pattern of technologies of production is a map of global power relations. This point is illustrated in the discussion of current tendencies in production organization that follows.

## THE CORE-PERIPHERY STRUCTURE
## OF PRODUCTION AND JOBS

In order to grasp whether and in what way the global accumulation process may be changing, it is necessary to ascertain the mutations taking place in the relationships among different technologies of production and the modes of social relations associated with them. These mutations can be observed only as tendencies that are still fluid. The patterns that ultimately emerge will be shaped both by social power relations and the technological solutions that are available. States will orient the choices made, thereby reinforcing certain social forces, and state actions will in turn be influenced by international competition, military and economic. It is unlikely that the total process of change in production and jobs will prove to be reducible to any single factor and futile to look for such a determining factor. It will be more to the point to consider the variety of factors underlying observable changes so as to try to estimate their relative weight in different situations and therefore the probabilities of alternative futures.

Chapter 7, in the discussion of the internationalizing of production, noted the development of a core-periphery structure of production on a world scale. The more capital-intensive phases of production and the innovation of more sophisticated technologies through research and development take place in the core. The more labor-intensive phases and standardized technologies shift to the periphery. The core concentrates increasingly on software while the periphery takes a growing share of hardware production. The hardware production of the periphery, however, usually remains technologically dependent on the softwares of the core.

This differentiation in production organization corresponds to differences in labor supply. Labor for the capital-intensive, technologically sophisticated phases of industry is high-cost labor, but because of the capital-intensity of the production process, labor costs are a lesser proportion of total production costs than they are with standardized labor-intensive technologies. Managements accordingly seek to retain in their service the core workers in whom they have made an investment in training and whose skills and dedication are necessary for the continuing flow of production by high-cost equipment. Managements also seek to find for the labor-intensive phases workers who are quickly trainable, readily disposable, docile, and cheap.

While it is relatively simple to describe these characteristics of core and periphery, it is more difficult to give the terms core and periphery generalizable concrete points of reference. The terms originated with a geographical connotation that they still retain. The core was first located in the leading industrial countries and the periphery in the economically less developed countries.[19] Yet it is quite possible to note shifts in industrial leadership within the geographical core (from the United States to Japan for certain aspects of electronics), as well as instances of conventional core-type industry in certain less-developed counties (e.g., steel in Brazil and South Korea). Similarly, within so-called core countries, there exists a core-periphery division within industries between the principal centers of innovation and development, on the one hand, and regional or provincial production units of a lower technological level, on the other. Geographical shifts of the core have also taken place within countries, the most recently celebrated being that from the northeast to the southwest of the United States. Although the functional characteristics of core and periphery remain analytically valid, their association with specific geographical positions must be considered to be a matter of perhaps transitory circumstance, not of immutable destiny.

Similarly, the association of core and periphery with sectors of industry, i.e., that large-scale corporate industry constitutes the core and small- to medium-scale industries the periphery, has been and remains questionable. The difficulties of the automobile industry illustrate those of large corporate multinational enterprises that have some of the features of periphery production: relatively labor-intensive and standardized technology. At the same time, some of the breakthroughs in innovative technology have been made by relatively small enterprises.

As regards labor supply, two strategies have been followed with opposite geographical consequences in the search for cheap and disposable labor. One lay in the design of plant, which would combine a reduced proportion of high-cost, high-skill labor with a higher proportion of low-skill, quickly trainable labor. The European automobile industry followed this route. Immigrants from the Mediterranean countries provided the cheap labor. There was, however, a limit to the tolerance of societies for immigrants and their ability to absorb and provide them with services. Xenophobic reaction ensued.[20] Another answer was to transfer plant into geographically peripheral zones either within the same country or abroad. Within countries this usually means shifting away from centers of strong trade-union organization to tap a new labor force of former farmhands, immigrants, and women workers lacking a tradition of trade-unionism. In movement abroad, countries that had extended primary education to a large part of the population and that have strong regimes ready and able to control or suppress unions have had the advantage. Taiwan, South Korea, and Singapore are preeminent examples. This movement provoked a response in the form of pressure for state policies to counteract "deindustrialization."[21]

Although the geographical and industrial-sector connotations of core and periphery have become increasingly confused, the analytical validity of the differentiation between core and periphery has been strengthened by the economic crisis since the mid-1970s. The basis for the distinction, however, needs to be redefined so as to avoid tying it too closely to these factors of geography and industrial sector.

The combination of heightened international competition for market shares in a nonexpanding world economy with the existence of surplus capacity in already installed technologies has oriented new investment toward cutting production costs. This takes two directions: the introduction of automation, robotics, and analogous methods of displacing labor by equipment, and the more systematic use of cheap labor. At the same time market demand has become more differentiated, particularly the effective demand of the elite markets that pull forward the process of innovation in capitalist development. Thus, in tandem with cost cutting, enterprises seek greater flexibility in adjusting production to this differentiated demand. The knell is sounding for the mass production of standardized articles made possible by Fordism. The consequences of this search for cost-cutting and diversification of output as the keys to competitiveness are to be found in the variety of divergent tendencies now observable in contemporary production processes.

A general pattern underlies these various tendencies. Employers under competitive pressure have been very sensitive to labor costs, fiscal burdens, and costs imposed by regulation (for example, antipollution controls). They have sought to stabilize their work forces at as low as possible a level consistent with continuous production. They have also sought to achieve with this work force the maximum versatility to meet changing market demands. As regards increases in demand, they have tried to meet this either by investing in more highly productive equipment or by using sources of labor that involve no long-term employment commitments and in some cases that facilitate evasion both of fiscal controls and administrative regulations.

Employers are now tending to envisage their work forces as composed of fixed and variable elements.[22] At the core of the enterprise is a group of full-time career employees engaged directly in the production process and in managerial, financial, and marketing work. This core group does not vary with fluctuations in the enterprise's level of activity. It has long-term security of employment. For this group, management emphasizes flexible utilization made possible by training, retraining, and redeployment within the enterprise. The skills of the members of the group become increasingly polyvalent but also increasingly specific to the enterprise. Their security and their knowledge bind them to it.

Next to this core group is a peripheral category of full-time employees who have few opportunities of career development and less job security. Many of these are semiskilled workers or else downgraded skilled workers who did not make it into the core group. Management tolerates or encourages a relatively high turnover among this group so as to facilitate adjustments to market-dictated changes in output. Most conflict is likely to arise from within this group, particularly on the part of downgraded workers who look to their trade unions for protection.

A further peripheral category consists of employees of the enterprise on contracts of a type that allow for adjustment of employment levels to demand changes. These include part-time and short-term contracts and also work-sharing arrangements.

Finally, employers make increasing use of outwork and externally contracted services. This includes contracting for certain operations within the plant, such as maintenance and cleaning services, and also contracting for work done outside the plant either by self-employed individuals or by subcontracting enterprises.

The more stable and permanent jobs are those with the best working conditions and prospects of advancement. Low-paid, dangerous, dirty, or polluting work and work for which

there is a more variable demand are relegated to the technologically peripheral category for subcontracting, etc.[23] An international extension of the subcontracting practice is a most likely
development, whereby Third World enterprises would contract
to undertake the most energy-consuming and most polluting
early stages of industrial processes, reserving the cleanest, most
sophisticated stages for the core installations in their home countries. Such a differentiation between categories of tasks and terms
of employment was pioneered in Japanese industry. Now all
major world industries, from their cores outward, are undergoing
a process of Japanization.

   Through such strategies, employers are able to shift the
burden of uncertainty from themselves and the core group to the
various peripheral groups. The cumulative consequences of these
strategies can be observed in a declining proportion of securely
employed, relatively highly paid, and enterprise-integrated workers, together with a growing proportion of less securely employed,
low-paid, peripheral workers segmented into several distinctive
groups having little cohesion with one another. The social relations of production of the core group are typically on enterprise-
corporatist lines. Those of the peripheral groups range from a
declining bipartism among the first category of peripheral workers, through a vastly expanded enterprise-labor-market mode encompassing both in-plant part-timers and temporary personnel
and workers in subcontracting enterprises, to a self-employed
sector of outworkers in effect dependent on enterprise contracts.

   These changes in the social relations of production in the
advanced capitalist countries are particularly marked since the
onset of the economic crisis in the mid-1970s. In the United
States, it has been observed that new jobs created have been
predominantly in the low-skill, low-pay category, and mainly in
services (of which temporary clerical work and fast-food restaurants are preeminent examples).[24] In West Germany, before the
crisis, labor market segmentation into isolated categories was not
significant; there was a general mobility flow from less to more
attractive jobs within enterprises, and where workers were displaced by technology, they were rapidly reemployed elsewhere.
Since the crisis, boundary lines have become visible separating
(1) a core labor force with secure employment, (2) a secondary

labor force of more precariously employed workers vulnerable to economic cycles and doing the less attractive work, and (3) a marginal category of the more or less permanently unemployed.[25] At the same time as these changes are increasing social vulnerability for a large section of the labor force and for those excluded from the labor force, the fiscal crisis of the state leads to a reduction of social services.

The trend toward a declining proportion of core jobs and an increasing proportion of peripheral jobs in the advanced capitalist countries, accelerated by the economic crisis, can be described as the peripheralization of the labor force. The structure of employment in these countries begins to take on some of the features hitherto associated with industrializing countries of the Third World. The trend has also been perceived as a regression to the heroic age of competitive capitalism in the nineteenth century.[26]

Peripheralization takes both legal and extralegal or illegal forms. The legal avenues include part-time and temporary employment and subcontracting. The extralegal forms, i.e., avoidance of legal regulations and nonobservance of legal norms, and the illegal forms, i.e., those involved in the activities of criminal organizations, together comprise what has been called the underground or submerged economy,[27] a counterpart in many ways to what in Third World countries has been described as the informal sector.

The underground economy covers a multitude of different forms of work and of social relations of production. Most underground activities are very poorly paid, a few are highly rewarded. There is work by undeclared workers: some work as outworkers in their homes, others in clandestine workshops often removable so as to avoid state inspectors. There is also undeclared work (and therefore untaxed income) by workers who hold legally declared jobs. Some of this takes the form of unreported overtime paid outside the official pay envelope. Often it takes the form of a worker having two jobs, one legally regulated and declared, the other undeclared and unregulated. Different kinds of people typically enter into these different kinds of illicit production relations. Women and children are commonly employed as outworkers. These groups are joined by illegal immigrants in clandestine workshop employment. Skilled male workers are more commonly practitioners of double employment. A further form of exchange in the underground economy is barter, for example, of services among higher income professionals. The only common features among these various forms of work in the underground economy are that no taxes are paid on the transactions, and legal norms and regulations are ignored.[28]

These various forms of underground production have been noted in the United States. Illegal work is prevalent in agriculture, hotels and restaurants, cleaning services, and the clothing industry. Most striking has been the revival of sweatshops in the garment industry in New York City, employing many illegal immigrants from the Caribbean. But the underground economy is implicated also in the shift of industry toward nonunionized sites in the Southwest and in the expansion of domestic outwork.[29] Among Western European countries, the phenomenon of the underground economy has been most pronounced in Italy and may have comparable dimensions also in Spain. In these countries, it is well represented in construction, clothing, shoes, gloves, hotels and restaurants, mechanical maintenance and electronics, agriculture, and domestic services but is present to some extent in virtually every branch of economic activity. In Naples alone, it is estimated that more than 100,000 persons are engaged in clandestine work, whole neighborhoods being organized for the production of gloves, shoes, and articles of clothing. In Prato, near Florence, a town noted for its booming small-scale textile manufacture, the vast majority of enterprises employ illegal workers. Double employment is particularly common among government employees in Italy. It has been estimated that about one third of the shoe production in one region of Spain is either in clandestine workshops or by undeclared outworkers, the latter about 70 percent women and 25 percent children.[30]

The underground economy is not separated from the regular economy. The two are closely interconnected. Factories that operate to a degree within the law also employ illegal workers; some may declare a few workers but employ in practice many more, others pay undeclared overtime to their declared workers. Clandestine factories subcontract to supply large-scale enterprises of the regular economy. Self-employed workers enter into undeclared contracts with legally recognized enterprises. Individuals, holding two jobs, divide their time between the regular and the underground economy. The underground economy is clearly an extension of the regular economy, symbiotically linked to it. The two make a functional whole.

The underground economy has attracted a good deal of attention since the early 1980s. The way in which the problem has been defined and the questions being asked indicate the source of this interest. The concern of the state is primarily fiscal. The underground economy is a counterpart to the fiscal crisis of the state. Underground production does nothing to increase state revenues, but it does benefit directly or indirectly from state expenditures.[31] Clandestine workers benefit from certain social services, e.g., health services and education for their children. Their employers benefit indirectly from the state's subsidization of some of the costs of reproducing their labor. With high unemployment, many unemployed in receipt of benefits have undeclared jobs. Civil servants, who benefit from job security, pension rights, etc., have second, undeclared incomes on which no taxes are paid. High-income professionals, like lawyers and accountants who exchange services with no invoices, avoid taxes on these services. The state is therefore interested in finding out how much revenue it is losing because of these practices. Accordingly, the underground economy is defined very largely in terms of tax evasion, irrespective of the very different kinds of activity, the very different categories of workers, and the very different forms of production relations covered by this definition.

Another concern of the state is with the maintenance of a satisfactory level of economic activity and of employment. This brings out the ambiguity of the state's position with reference to the underground economy, for despite the loss of revenue and the undermining of the state's regulatory authority, the underground economy is recognized as providing a considerable number of jobs and incomes. Indeed, the expansion of the underground economy since the onset of the economic crisis has been attributed in some measure to the fiscal pressures of the state on business. The good news for the state behind the bad news of revenue shortfall and loss of authority is that the existence of the underground economy means that GNP has been understated.

How much it has been understated becomes a matter of interest to the state. Since there are no hard figures because the very nature of the underground economy is that it falls outside collected statistical data, various methods have been devised for estimating its size. (In this respect, i.e., its nonappearance in official statistics, the underground economy is analogous to domestic production for family consumption.)

These estimates vary widely. The low estimates are those made by the OECD. They suggest an underground economy in the United States and other highly industrialized member countries (UK, West Germany, Japan) of about 4 percent of GNP, while in Italy and other Southern European countries, where it is generally assumed the underground economy is relatively large by the standards of advanced capitalist countries, it would be more than twice that level, i.e., in the range of 10 percent. The high estimates for the United States and Italy are in the 35 percent range, for West Germany more than 25 percent, for Sweden more than 15 percent, and for the United Kingdom about 10 percent. All estimates, high or low, agree that these figures for the early 1980s reflect a considerable growth in underground activity since the onset of the economic crisis in the mid-1970s.[32]

The definition of the underground economy is thus derived from certain concerns of the state, which are different from those of the present study. The category "underground economy" does not, as such, have much meaning for the social relations of production. Neither, for that matter, does the category "informal sector" as applied to Third World countries.[33] Both are blanket terms covering a range of different modes of social relations of production. The expansion of the informal economy and its relative importance in certain advanced capitalist countries do, however, underscore certain broader tendencies in the social relations of production. It is one aspect of the restructuring of production in advanced capitalism. This restructuring is accentuating what I have called the peripheralization of the labor force within a core-periphery structure of production. Peripheralization, for the workers concerned, involves both precarious employment and segmentation into distinct groups having little possibility of achieving collective action. Its concomitants are a weakening or dismantling of state services for these groups and an undermining of regulatory protection of working conditions, health and safety, i.e., a general disengagement of the state from the production process. The growth of the underground economy is a manifestation of these tendencies. In regard to the social relations of production, it takes the form of an expansion of enterprise-labor-market conditions and a revival of putting-out as a form of dependent self-employment. The terms *core* and *periphery* increasingly express position in the social relations of production rather than either geographical location or size and type of industry.

## FLEXIBILITY, DECENTRALIZATION AND THE BALANCE OF SOCIAL POWER

The keynotes in the restructuring of production in the advanced capitalist countries are flexibility and decentralization. The employer's incentive to experiment in these directions is the desire to cut costs and to be able to respond to a more variegated and shifting market demand. Some workers, too, are attracted by certain forms of flexible staffing arrangements and decentralized production.

Industry's reorganization of production methods has taken several forms. Some of these constitute a development and rationalization of Fordist production. Others move away from the Fordist pattern in the direction of smaller scale production units and more ad hoc coordination of autonomous units in complex production processes.

The model that most represents a further development of Fordism is one in which a small core of managers and planners monopolizes the conception and organization of work, and a largely unskilled contingent of easily replaceable workers executes work tasks. It is noteworthy that some of the clearest cases of this model are in service industries rather than in manufacturing. Department stores and fast-food restaurants are prime examples.

Department stores have a highly paid managerial core engaged in long-run planning, and a secondary-labor-market sales force of part-time and temporary workers.[34] Cost-cutting to meet competitive pressures has eliminated the salesperson who through long experience in the same department has learned enough about product qualities and differences to be able to advise customers. The sales function has been Taylorized.

The organization of the fast-food business is somewhat more complex. The management structure in form is an arrangement between a big business and a multitude of small businesses, each of which has purchased the franchise for exclusive marketing of the big-business product in its locality. The big-business franchiser thus shifts part of the profit-and-loss risk onto the small-business franchisee. The latter benefits from the brandname advertising of the franchiser but must use the prescribed methods, equipment, and materials provided by the franchiser. Since production is labor-intensive, the methods prescribed by the franchiser include the organization of the labor process. Production of the limited range of standardized food items offered by fast-food restaurants is structured by the machinery. Workers are unskilled and readily transferable from one phase of the process to another. The franchisee is bound by the operations manual of the franchiser and has no autonomy with regard to the organization and management of the labor process, and operations allow for no worker discretion. The whole process is programmed from corporate headquarters and regulated through inspection from headquarters. Employees consist of a majority of part-time teenagers paid at the lower student minimum wage, whose careers with the fast-food chain end at the age of eighteen or when they must legally be paid the full minimum wage, and a minority of full-time women workers paid at the full minimum wage. Labor turnover is fairly high and of little concern to management since workers are so easily replaceable. Because the only means of demonstrating opposition to management is to quit, the high turnover acts as a safety valve reinforcing management's authority.[35]

An alternative route that also combines core and peripheral work forces within the same large-scale production organization is the creation of a complex in which innovative research and development, together with the more capital-intensive production techniques, are concentrated in a central plant, and standardized, labor-intensive phases of production are carried out in peripheral factories. The latter may be part of the same firm, or alternatively consist of small businesses dependent on the central factory. The latter case is often the means whereby a central factory makes use of the underground economy. Obsolete textile equipment, for instance, is not abandoned or destroyed; it finds its way into the underground economy to produce with labor subjected to substandard wages and working conditions.[36]

Subcontracting and outwork also provide avenues of flexibility for big firms. Strong trade union power in core factories may lead management to seek cost reduction through subcontracting and outwork, together with a stabilization or reduction of core-factory personnel. Outwork and subcontracting are also used to provide specialized services. Some such services require high skills and are well remunerated. Some of the subcontractors of big enterprises are themselves organized on a national or even on an international scale, e.g., in the case of some business services and engineering agencies. These subcontractors are often retained when their big-enterprise clients shift the geographical location of some of their industrial activities. Local small enterprises come in at the bottom of the scale to pick up the subcontracting and temporary work not taken by the interregional subcontracting firms. These local subcontractors typically provide the worst conditions of employment, with minimal juridical protection for employees, who have ambiguous informal contracts of employment and may not be covered for safety and health risks. When such subcontracting employees work within plants alongside core workers, as is frequently the case, the result is a coexistence of highly protected, secure career-type jobs with a revival of archaic labor practices and unprotected forms of employment.[37]

A second direction of change in the labor process is toward making large-scale organizations more flexible so as to meet a more diversified product demand. This represents a revision of Fordism, retaining the Fordist scale of production while adjusting to the fact that the product-standardization for uniform demand in mass markets that made Fordism possible can no longer meet competition.[38] This type of adaptation has been most in evidence in the consumer-durable industries where Fordism made its breakthrough, for instance, in automobiles.

Product standardization was based on special-purpose

machinery planned as a production system to be operated by unskilled or semiskilled workers. This is a low-trust pattern of organization in which workers are technically controlled by the mechanical process and have a minimum of discretion or initiative in their work. If, however, a production organization is to be able to respond to changes in demand by shifting to different models or products, it will require general-purpose machines, i.e., whose functions can be quickly adjusted, and a more skilled and adaptable work force. This implies a high-trust pattern of organization that will rely to a considerable degree on the initiative and discretion of workers. The separation of conception from execution that was a basic principle of Fordism has to be reversed, and the unity of conception and execution once again enacted on the shop floor. Any such reorganization contains contradictions: management wants flexibility in production and cooperative initiative on the part of workers but does not want to lose control of the production process; workers may perceive greater shop floor responsibility in the production process as an opportunity to regain control and to assert a claim to self-management. In determining how these contradictions develop, much will depend on the culture and institutions of labor relations and the level of trust present in them.

The contribution that reorganizing production could make toward greater competitive efficiency (as distinct from better human relations) was underlined in a report on an international conference of persons from labor, management, government, and academia held in Toronto in 1981:

> An often overlooked dimension . . . is the pressure of competition and resulting needs for flexibility, that can best be handled through solutions that are efficient from a technical point of view and at the same time improve the quality of work. For example, machine-paced assembly lines are known to be defective because they generate stress, boredom, alienation, psychologically damaging social isolation, and a generally poor working environment. But it is less widely recognized that they are inadequate in the view of the urgent need in today's business environment for more flexibility and capacity to adapt to model variations and rapid shifts in product lines. A conventional assembly line cannot cope with this type of need, but small, self-regulating, multi-skilled groups can.[39]

"Humanization of work" and "quality of working life (QWL)" are code terms for this second direction of change in the labor process. In practice, employer initiatives have ranged from application of occupational psychology techniques to encourage more "positive" worker attitudes without making any significant changes in assembly-line methods, through job-enrichment and job-rotation practices to make work more interesting and workers more adaptable, to the restructuring of assembly lines into a series of autonomous work groups. Union reactions have ranged from resistance to manipulatory techniques that seek to have workers identify with management goals, through cooperation with management in productivity raising as quid pro quo for some participation in management, to aggressive union action to enhance workshop control on "humanization of work" grounds.[40] Where management had virtually won the battle for control of the labor process through Fordism, the adaptation of Fordism to diversified demand has once again brought workplace organization onto the agenda of social conflict.

An alternative to making large-scale production organizations more adaptable while retaining their size and scale of output is to break down large organizations into a series of small-batch producing units. This has been done by some steel producers, in a shift away from the large-scale integrated plants geared to maximum demand that were the ultimate in massive modernization investment in the 1970s and that contributed to worldwide surplus capacity in the industry in the 1980s. Specialty steels are produced in smaller batches, require a more skilled work force, and, on the part of management, more imaginative marketing to think of new applications of steel and to respond to new industrial opportunities. An example is the Ruhr steel manufacturer Thyssen, which began in the 1970s to produce a variety of specialty steels in order to counter the competition of new integrated steel mills in Japan and Third World steel production in Mexico, Brazil, and South Korea. The French steel firm Solmer, which built a new steel complex at Fos-sur-mer near Marseilles in the late 1970s with a view to supplying a growing heavy industry in the south of France and the adjacent Mediterranean region, converted the plant to specialty steels as the initial project threatened to add to surplus capacity during years of recession. Some Japanese and U.S. steel producers are following the same route, while the more conservative integrated steel producers seek refuge in protectionist pressure on the state.[41]

One stage further in decentralization of production beyond the specializing of subdivisions of a big corporation is production by small independent units. In manufacturing, technological developments have made sophisticated equipment efficient for use by small-scale producers. Numerically controlled machines, for instance, can be reprogrammed for different tasks.[42] Large scale no longer necessarily has economic advantage and may have the competitive disadvantage of rigidity, a rigidity derived both from heavy investment in a technology that must be amortized over a long time and from bureaucratic rules often reinforced by trade-union-protected workshop rules. The small enterprise can often economize on capital, plan for actual demand rather than the cyclical peak, and enjoy more flexible organizational structures and staffing practices.

In the steel industry, so-called minimills have taken an increasing share of the market while the big integrated producers have been suffering surplus capacity. Minimills are the dynamic component of an otherwise sick steel industry in the United States. They compete successfully with the big integrated producers by using quite different technology and materials. (They use electric-arc furnaces, which can efficiently produce much smaller quantities than the giant blast furnaces that set the minimum economic scale of production for integrated mills, and they use scrap, which is cheaper than iron ore.) In 1981, minimills had about 15 percent of total U.S. steel shipments, and it is projected that by 2000 they should be competitive in up to 40 percent of the U.S. market. Their technology and marketing methods are seen as the most likely means of revitalizing an industry badly hit by foreign competition, and the big integrated producers have been adopting some of their features, along with decentralizing toward more specialized production.[43]

The social relations of production in minimills make a complete break with those of the strongly unionized integrated steel industry. Minimills have located close to their markets, away from the old centers of steel production. They are generally nonunionized, pay lower wages than integrated mills (though incentive-wage schemes allow some workers to achieve the same or higher levels), and allow management greater flexibility in organizing work and in taking productivity-raising initiatives. Managements have also followed the Japanese practice of fostering a team-oriented corporate culture. The most publicized minimill, Nucor, has even introduced lifetime employment. The minimill has, in other words, embraced enterprise corporatism.[44]

Speculation has also centered on the idea that really small-scale (or cottage) industries could become the focus for an autonomous industrial development, breaking out from a dependency on big corporations. (Minimills in steel are small only by comparison with huge integrated plants.) The recent economic history of central Italy provides the paradigm for this model.[45] Analysts of this development have seen three stages to it. The first phase came about as an employer response to the peak of trade union power in the big factories of northern Italy in the late 1960s. Management began to reduce staff in the core plants by attrition and to shift production to small-scale subcontractors. Concurrently, some skilled workers from the core factories, restive under the wage solidarity policy of their unions, which had recently concentrated on upgrading the status of migrant workers from the south, sought to enhance their earning power by going into business as suppliers to their former employers. This also coincided with big industries' need to adapt production to the demand for more customized short-run output, which recourse to subcontracting facilitates. In this phase, the expansion of small industry took place under the umbrella of big industry. In a second phase, cottage industries discovered they could supply more than one client by equipping themselves with up-to-date machinery and by maximizing inventiveness to shift production to meet market demand. In a third phase, the more technologically advanced small producers discovered a capacity to innovate new techniques of production and new products for the national and even for world markets.

The expansion of sophisticated world-class cottage industries in the Emilia-Romagna region was sustained by the penetration of the region's economy into more backward regions of the country, e.g., the Marches and Apulia, to which Emilian businessmen could put out or subcontract labor-intensive work. The existence of this external labor force made it possible to maintain steady employment and relatively high incomes in the cottage-industry and artisan sector of Emilia-Romagna, by shifting the burden of economic fluctuations onto the region's newly acquired periphery, where the classic conditions of low pay, obsolete machinery, and employer freedom to dismiss redundant workers prevailed.

The social relations prevailing in these world-class cottage industries are conditioned by the specific Italian context. The income range is very considerable: skilled maintenance workers may earn twice as much as their counterparts in big industry, while the worst paid homeworkers are paid only about one third of the lowest factory wage. Jobs fall broadly into two categories: routine machine-tending work, which is not demanding of skill and offers no opportunities of upgrading; and versatile skilled work in setting up production processes and designing products, which is often based on skills once applied in big industry but offers scope for more initiative than big industry ever could.

Many of the founders of these cottage industries are strong union men and Communist Party supporters. (Some were purged in the antiunion campaigns waged by management of big industries during the 1960s.) Unions are present in the small-industry sector but allow for much more flexibility in staffing and organization of work than in the big factories. Furthermore, the regional and municipal governments of Emilia-Romagna, a strongly Communist region, have been helpful to cottage-industry development by promoting common services for small business and by mobilizing pressure on the central government to secure state investment in local infrastructure. (In this the local Communist-led authorities have to counteract the bias of the Christian-Democrat-led central authorities against disbursing public funds to Communist-controlled regions.) Communists and Socialists have been concerned not to leave the defense of small-business interests to the political right.

The experience of cottage-industry development in Emilia-Romagna suggests a reincarnation of the entrepreneurial spirit vaunted by Schumpeter in at least temporarily auspicious circumstances. There are longer term problems besetting such a development. One is how the small enterprise can reproduce itself. Typically, its leadership comes from outside, from the ranks of skilled workers in big industry, and it does not train and develop successors to these leaders as big bureaucratic managerial structures do systematically. Moreover, there is little or no chance that the relatively unskilled machine tenders employed in cottage industry could make the transition to leadership. Another problem is how the spirit of innovation can be kept alive when the easy course may seem to be to try to continue to supply existing demand rather than continually to search out new opportunities. Related to a happy solution to both of these problems is the maintenance of a favorable political and institutional environment for small industries such as exists in the Emilia-Romagna region. A good part of the secret of innovation lies in the maintenance of a collaborative relationship among technicians in many small firms so that they can share experiences in solving problems. Two analysts of the Italian cottage-industry development have compared the relations among innovative firms to the collegial relation among good doctors, good lawyers, or good university teachers: "each firm is jealous of its autonomy, overproud of its capacity, but fully conscious that its success and very survival is linked to the collective efforts of the community to which it belongs and whose prosperity it must defend."[46] Through cooperation small businesses can pool administrative, marketing, and purchasing services and can secure bank loans on better terms than they could individually. The culture and political context of the development is, moreover, conducive to cooperative development.

By looking back over the range of tendencies in the restructuring of industrial production in advanced capitalist countries, it can be seen that cumulatively they have been destructive of labor's autonomous collective social power. Nevertheless, it cannot be denied that some aspects of the restructuring are attractive to certain groups of workers, a fact that raises additional obstacles to the achievement of a common working-class strategy.

The context of mass unemployment generates pressures and some incentives for workers to adapt for their own survival. A male worker displaced from his job in one of the old strongly unionized industries—e.g., steel or automobiles—cannot easily make the transition to a job in the much-vaunted "high tech" sector. For one thing, the job will be in another part of the country, probably an area in which unions are weak; for another, it will pay only about one third of the unemployed worker's former wage. The underground economy, however, offers some incentives to supplement unemployment benefits or welfare payments. Ex-workers' wives and teen-age children are similarly attracted into secondary-labor-market part-time or temporary employment or outwork in order to sustain the family's existence. A close relationship has, indeed, been found between welfare and the underground economy. Welfare is insufficient for the family's survival. Clandestine employment makes this survival possible as a supplement to welfare. From the clandestine employer's standpoint, welfare is a wage subsidy.[47]

Another group of people, nurtured in the revolution in lifestyles of the 1960s, seek alternative ways of working—alternatives to the clock-punching, externally controlled work environment of Fordism.[48] These people are willing to trade income potential for leisure and for autonomy in determining the pace and timing and site of their own work. Their attitude toward work is partly instrumental: it gives them an income to live the way they want to. It is also partly qualitative: they want their work to be consistent with their primary values in life. Outwork of a dependent self-employed type with flexible schedules and a home environment fits these concerns for many young people. Part-time or short-term temporary work suits many women who want to adjust their earning capacities to their family responsibilities.

For other workers, oriented more toward maximizing income than personal autonomy, double employment is a solution. The basic "official" job gives the element of security, especially if it is in government service or of some equally guaranteed permanent status, and the second "irregular" job produces a perhaps higher but more uncertain income, rewarding, for example, skills that are underutilized in the official job. Still others, frustrated by limits to their wages and opportunity for initiative in large organizations, choose to trade relative security for the risk of independent-artisan or small-business status. This is the case for those skilled workers who have led the successful cottage industry development of central Italy. The successful ones have maximized both income and autonomy.

Finally, there is the impact of the economic crisis on the

family and more broadly on the production of use values by individuals and through informal social networks. Certainly, unemployment and the cutback of state social services have placed great strains on the family. Where the family structure is weak, it has frequently succumbed, leaving many people in an isolated, anomic condition. The challenge has also produced responses of resilience in which the informal, "natural" structures of society have attempted to compensate for the inadequacies of some of the formal structures of social protection and social opportunity first created and then starved by the state. Do-it-yourself around the household and in vehicle maintenance has been given a stimulus by unemployment. One can assume also an increase in reciprocal exchanges of services on a neighborhood and friendship basis. Informal friendship and extended family networks take on more functions of child care, care of the aged, minor medical services, education and skill development, organization of leisure, and so forth. Families have also taken on more market-oriented exchange-value production in the form of outwork alongside production for their own use. The strengthening of interfamily cooperation in respect of household needs not only cushions the impact of unemployment; it also facilitates the family's adjustment to the expansion of this form of dependent market activity.[49]

Restructuring of production in the advanced capitalist countries centers on industrial processes and has been accelerated by the economic crisis following the mid-1970s. From there it has extended throughout society with impact on all production structures, including the family. These changes in the advanced capitalist countries are likely to set new patterns of social power relations on the world scale through the effects of competition, emulation, and penetration. Changes are also taking place in the production processes of Third World and redistributive societies, some of which have been going on for a longer time.

In the Third World, transformations in agriculture have had particularly dramatic impact. Since the nineteenth century, a dualism has developed in agriculture between a sector oriented to world markets and another oriented to self-sufficiency and local supply. In the Sahel region of Africa, as in other Third World regions but with more devastating effect, the growth of export-crop agriculture linked in various ways to multinational agribusiness has appropriated much of the best land, leaving marginal land to subsistence production. The consequence is that these nonindustrialized countries have had to import food to supply their urban populations, and their rural populations have been recurrent victims of famine.[50] International economic and financial links have made it difficult for Third World countries to move back from a position of dependence on the earnings of export crops toward an agriculture geared more to local supply. When Mexico envisaged such a policy, including a splitting-up of large export-oriented holdings into farms for small-scale producers of crops for local consumption (the *sistema de alimentación mexicana* or SAM), it was disrupted by the debt crisis of the early 1980s, which put a premium, for example, on the growing of luxury strawberries by large-scale producers for sale in the U.S. market as one means of securing foreign exchange for debt service.

In Brazil, a three-stage development in agricultural production can be seen. Cheap food for urban consumers was in a first stage produced in *latifundia-minifundia* complexes as a surplus extracted from peasant communities. These communities, besides providing labor for the *latifundista*, existed on the margin of the exchange economy, providing for their own reproduction, including handicraft manufacture of the nonfood items they needed. The *latifundista* used surplus labor for relatively inefficient extensive cultivation of export crops. In a second stage, local handicrafts were very largely destroyed by the extension of the national market for manufactured goods. Food production for local consumption was increasingly taken over by small farmers renting land from *latifundistas* or by squatters on unoccupied lands. These small farmers sold their produce to middlemen who supplied the urban markets. In a third stage, export-crop production (meat, coffee, soya, sugar cane) has expanded and modernized, enclosing large areas and using machinery with minimal amounts of wage labor. (This has also happened in other Third World countries, e.g., in Iran under the Shah, as Third World agriculture becomes linked into a global food-processing industry.) Small farmers, and particularly squatters, are vulnerable to government-supported expansion of large-scale export agriculture. They are driven from the lands they till into the *favelas* and *alagados* surrounding the urban centers.[51] Urban crowding increases the primitive labor market, which, in turn, serves as a reserve army for the recruitment and disciplining of the enterprise labor market in both small and larger scale industries.

The redistributive economies, since the mid-1950s, have been preoccupied with the issue of decentralization of management and production. Developments in these countries have implications for the social relations of production.

Redistributive systems function according to a different logic from that of capitalist development, in which production is directed by anticipations of profit. Production of use values is in principle planned on a nationwide scale according to the political priorities of the leadership. All able-bodied members of society are available for work, and all share in some manner in the redistributed product. Accordingly, labor is a fixed, not a variable cost; therefore the productive effort of any individual is a net gain to the whole society, even if it is not sufficient to reproduce that individual's own labor power and in addition to create a surplus value. (This would be the condition of its employment in a capitalist economy.)

Planning in redistributive systems achieved considerable success in initiating rapid growth. Capital and labor could be fully employed and directed toward attaining the redistributors' goals for output. Redistributive planning also encountered serious problems, the reverse side of its success. The redistributors' preference for large-scale production units and for bureaucratic regulation led to inefficiencies. Labor shortages emerged as bottlenecks to production, often the result of labor hoarding, as enterprises wanted to retain underemployed workers so they would be available in peak periods. After the initial phase of revolutionary enthusiasm and despite campaigns of socialist emulation, workers began to withhold effort. The consequences were the frequently mentioned deficiencies of the planning system: output does not match demand, particularly for consumer items; goods are shoddy; and workers perform at a sometimes lackadaisical pace.[52]

Since the end of the Stalin era, during which military-type discipline was the model for factory and farm, the leaderships of the redistributive economies have been recurrently preoccupied with the reform of economic management so as to overcome the deficiencies of the system. Experiments in reform include decentralization of management decision-making authority to enterprises; simplification of plan procedures, for example through a reduction in the number of control figures; and a greater use of market mechanisms for the allocation of resources and final output.[53]

Contemporaneous with these reform efforts at the official level, a spontaneous compensation for the defects of the planning system took shape in what has been called the "second economy." This corresponds in some ways to the underground economies of capitalist countries but has to be understood within the different context of a redistributive system.

The second economy is part legal, part illegal. The legal part includes private plot cultivation by farm families and free marketing of their produce, some construction and maintenance of private homes, and some authorized artisan work. The illegal part includes diversion of state-enterprise equipment, materials, and labor for private purposes and trade in foreign goods, etc. More importantly it also includes the activity of enterprise managers who illicitly obtain materials they need in order to meet their plan target (not for their own personal gain but to meet the obligations of the enterprise) and who are thus tempted to dissimulate part of their enterprise's output in order to be able to make payment for such needed inputs not available through regular channels.[54] This amounts in practice to the spontaneous creation of an illegal market through which enterprises can make good the shortfalls in plan-directed inputs. The existence of this second economy has been functional to the planning system, despite its partial illegality, in helping both individuals and enterprises to meet their needs.

Outright repression of the second economy (or at least its illegal component) would be both impossible and dysfunctional to the system. There seem to be two alternative possibilities. One would be to keep things the way they are—illegal but nevertheless permeating the system, tolerated but with recurrent crackdowns on more notorious abuses. The other would be to legalize more of the second economy so as to integrate it with the planning system. By and large, the Soviet Union seems to have followed the first route, though that may change. Since some people generate substantial illicit incomes in second-economy activities and many managers are accustomed to operating partially within the second economy, there are undoubtedly entrenched resistances to change.[55] The second route has been followed in Eastern Europe and more recently in China.

The Chinese case concerns an economy with far less developed productive forces than exist in the Soviet Union and Eastern Europe. Its primary problems are: to put the whole labor force to work, to effect a gradual transfer of labor from agriculture to industry (and therefore to raise agricultural productivity so as to feed more industrial workers with fewer farmers), and to raise the productivity of industry through technological improvement. In confronting the employment problem, the Chinese leadership has reversed previous policies in order to encourage an increase of jobs outside the state sector. It is anticipated that future trends in employment will be low growth in the state sector and higher growth in the collective (especially small collectives) and self-employment sectors.

The transition from agricultural to industrial production is to be effected as much as possible through the development of rural industries, thereby avoiding large movements of population to the cities. Initially, rural industries were geared to local agriculture, processing of local crops, and production of tools and utensils, etc. used by local people. From the late 1970s, however, there has been greater official emphasis on interdependence and division of labor within China. A core-periphery structure has developed in which rural industries are closely linked as peripheral suppliers to urban-based core enterprises. This core-periphery structure also facilitates technological upgrading: urban enterprises displace their older machinery to a rural site, working it with locally available labor, making place for more up-to-date equipment in the core factory.

The social relations of production differ as between core and periphery factories. Core workers are state employees, established workers with considerable rights in their jobs (despite official urgings that there should be more flexibility in manning), but rural workers are nonestablished, technically "peasants" temporarily employed in rural industries. In addition, casual workers may be recruited from rural villages for specific types of fixed-duration work in urban factories. If enterprise managers have very little flexibility to dismiss established workers, they have much more scope for varying the size of staff to needs in the peripheral, nonestablished labor sector. These differences in workers' relative job security are probably more important than differences in money income, although nonwage benefits and subsidies also give advantage to the established urban over the nonestablished rural worker.[56]

In the more developed redistributive economies of Eastern Europe, opportunities for broadening the legality of the second economy raise prospects analogous to some of the developments in capitalist economies discussed above—as regards, for instance, the opportunities for decentralization and for applying sophisticated technology in small-scale production. Small co-operatives of professionals and technicians could contract services to state enterprises, for instance; the state could create a network of workshops to be leased for small-scale production.[57] This would be consistent with the existing practice of small-plot agricultural cultivation on state land, which has proven to be the most efficient way to grow certain more labor-intensive crops, and for which the inputs and outputs are included in state plans. Thus an expansion of self-employment, and of what could be called a plan-regulated small private-business sector, could evolve within an overall planned economy.

THE STATE
AND THE WORLD ECONOMY
IN THE RESTRUCTURING
OF PRODUCTION

The tendencies discussed above depict movements in a variety of directions, some seemingly negative, some more positive for the people involved in them. To focus on any single tendency creates the risk of bias and distortion in appraising the whole. Preoccupation with the fast-food chain may create an impression that the world is moving toward the ultimate in Taylorization of work, an impression that is controverted by evidence of movement away from Taylorism and Fordism in more technologically sophisticated spheres of production. Emphasis on the autonomy of new high-tech cottage industries on the Emilian model contrasts with the revival of more exploitative putting-out production in the Marches and Apulia. And so forth. Since all these tendencies are in a fluid state, they cannot give any firm picture of the new overall social structure of accumulation. Whatever form that structure ultimately takes will be determined by social choices to be made now and in the near future. Those social choices will, as suggested, be very largely shaped by the actions of states, which in turn will be influenced by the world context in which states exist. The most that can be done now is, first, to attempt to see whether the variety of tendencies observed fit coherently into a pattern, in which apparently opposite movements in different sectors and different geographical regions reflect contradictions within a complex structure; and, second, we can attempt to see what alternative directions of development may possibly emerge out of such a pattern.

The general features of the labor process are similar in both capitalist and redistributive development. The purposes to which accumulation is put and the mechanisms of deciding what is to be produced differ as between these two modes of development, but up to now the ways in which work has been organized and the technologies on which work organization is based are not very different. *Grosso modo*, this labor process as it is currently evolving can be analyzed in terms of four productive sectors: (1) a relatively small core of skilled polyvalent workers integrated with their enterprises on a quasi-permanent basis; (2) an increasingly large and segmented periphery consisting of people doing unskilled and sometimes unpleasant work whose employment is more precarious; (3) state workers in the social policy field providing services to the population in education, health, and welfare, etc.; and (4) production of use values outside the exchange economy, in the household or through informal networks, which contributes substantially to feeding, clothing, and housing those who produce in the exchange or redistributive economies, i.e., wage workers, and to raising a new generation of such workers.

In capitalist development, the core-periphery differentiation between the first two categories takes the form of a polarization in the social relations of production between enterprise corporatism for the core workers and enterprise-labor-market and dependent self-employment status for the periphery in the work force. (I am using core and periphery to designate social position, not geographical location, in the light of my earlier discussion.)

A seemingly positive aspect, from the standpoint of human emancipation, of the industrial restructuring that has been going on is the trend toward more decentralization and more autonomy for work groups and toward the reunification of conception and execution that had been severed by Fordism. Although these tendencies are apparent so far only among core workers and some small high-tech entrepreneurs and artisans, they do seem to herald the end of the Fordism that had been the industrial dynamic throughout most of the twentieth century.

Is, then, the fast-food chain the last gasp of Fordism, or is it the dawn of a new Fordist era? Fordism is, indeed, still alive and well but in new places and new occupations different from those that witnessed its early triumph where at present Fordism is in regression. Fordism has shifted to the periphery; it is developing there alongside a revival of more archaic production methods—sweatshops and putting-out. Fordism has colonized some of the service industries in advanced capitalist countries, e.g., fast foods, and also the production with standardized technology of consumer goods in Third World countries, destined both for domestic and world markets.[58] Gramsci's analysis with which this chapter began remains pertinent to the Third World today, where Fordism is being introduced as a passive revolution within the structures of state corporatism.

In the advanced capitalist countries, the fourth sector—state social services—has been cut back, major victim of the fiscal crisis of the state. These services are labor intensive, but their pay scales are influenced by the pattern of earnings of industrial core workers. The cost of state social services has in consequence risen sharply with inflation, but as these services expanded during the precrisis boom years, quality of output may have suffered from bureaucratic overexpansion. With the reduction in state social services following the economic crisis, more responsibility has fallen upon family and informal networks of use-value producers.

In the redistributive systems, analogous tendencies are present: a polarization of core and periphery jobs, a deterioration of state social services, and more reliance on informal relationships to get things done at both household and enterprise levels.

How these various tendencies develop will depend to a considerable extent on what states do or refrain from doing. If the present tendencies prevail, it is very largely because states have encouraged them. Some instances of state impact on the structuring of the labor process are the following:

- The most powerful states have invested heavily in research and development, e.g., nuclear and space research, mainly for military purposes, which has accelerated technological innovation in industry, including nonmilitary applications, and generally contributed to the development of a knowledge capability for certain kinds of technological innovation. Some Third World states have sought to bargain their way toward the acquisition of technological capability by requiring multinational corporations to locate some of their research and development within the host country as a condition of setting up operations there. The kinds of technology so encouraged are those propitious to world-economy competition (e.g., geared to elite demand rather than basic needs).[59]
- States have aided capital accumulation in specific industries by subsidies and tax write-offs. Where the aim has been international competitiveness, this has favored certain kinds of innovations in technology and labor process. Where it has been protectionist, the result is to stabilize existing production methods.
- States have encouraged the expansion of low-wage precarious employment through the management of unemployment benefit systems when they have required beneficiaries to accept less qualified work than they previously performed and when they exempt certain cate-

gories of enterprises from the application of labor and social security regulations.[60]

- Selective enforcement of work permit requirements has in practice encouraged clandestine employment of illegal immigrants and disciplined these workers to accept low wages and poor working conditions for fear of expulsion.
- Reduction in welfare benefits has also, as noted above, resulted in an increase in underground employment. (Public authorities have also, on occasion, contracted out services at substandard conditions.)[61]
- The role of a Third World state in the transformation of agriculture is illustrated by the Brazilian case mentioned in the previous section of this chapter: by extending a minimum wage to agriculture, the state encouraged large-scale export-crop producers to mechanize in order to save labor; by extending the national road network, it lowered transport costs and opened the interior market to manufactured goods, thereby helping to destroy local handicrafts that had made rural communities quasi-autarkic and encouraging farmers into more specialized production for urban markets; finally, the state put its political and repressive resources behind the enclosure of lands for large-scale crop production.
- Like the British state in the early nineteenth century, Third World states have encouraged urban industry through a cheap-food policy, helping employers minimize the cost of maintaining a labor force. By keeping the urban minimum wage low and by repressing or controlling trade-union activity, the state has protected the employer's margin between productivity and costs.

These points illustrate how the state has affected the restructuring of production. It is appropriate at this stage to ask how the possible transformations of state structures discussed in chapter 8 might translate into action (or inaction) shaping the future labor process.

In the hyperliberal model, the state is an ally of capital in a repressive restructuring of the labor process. The directly repressive effects on labor flow from the market. The state dismantles mechanisms hitherto built up to protect the labor force and ensures that the market can operate without obstruction. Hyperliberal ideologues, advocates of deregulation in all things, have glorified the underground economy as a struggle for market freedom against collectivist state interventionism.[62] The defense of traditional values by their populist-morality allies reveals a pressure toward relegating the recently expanded female wage-labor force to the home. The combination of market-imposed discipline and patriarchal family structure would be counted on to stabilize the periphery and household sectors of the economy with a minimal level of state social services. The hyperliberal state offers nothing to the industrial core other than the opportunity to exploit the periphery and the household in order to remain competitive in world markets.

The neomercantilist alternative, with its post-Keynesian industrial and incomes policies, does offer more to the core: aids to capital accumulation for technological upgrading, active political support in international competition, and negotiated corporatist consensus among core labor and industry. This state model also proposes to maintain the existing state social services so as to mitigate the social tensions inherent in the core-periphery polarization of work and the probability of long-term, ineradicable unemployment. The state, in this model, gambles that its success in international economic competition will be such as to make possible sufficient transfer payments through the social services to keep social discontent at a containable level. As noted in chapter 8, the historic bloc on which this model is based is thin and its institutions remote from the mass of the population. Its long-term survival depends on political demobilization and the fragmentation and isolation of dissent.

A speculative alternative that has claimed some attention in advanced capitalist countries envisages a "dual society." In this somewhat idyllic vision one small fraction of human activities would be engaged in highly sophisticated production of goods; another larger fraction would be devoted to labor-intensive services for people. Some people would be active exclusively in one or the other sector. Others would be able, by flexible time-sharing practices, to divide their efforts between the two sectors. The second or people-oriented sector would not consist primarily of expanded state services; it would rather emphasize networks of autonomous voluntary groups dedicated to the production of use values. The first sector would maximize efficiency; the second, conviviality.[63]

If this third model has not proven to be entirely convincing as an alternative direction of state-society relations, it may at least be credited with having posed both explicitly and implicitly a number of critical problems besetting the process of restructuring production and accumulation.

Critics of the dual-society model, who are at the same time critics of the hyperliberal state model, point out that both models imply the weakening of the social power of labor. The power of labor, they argue, has been the mainspring of social progress through this century; its weakening would lead to the dismantling of the welfare state that has been its principal achievement. They argue further that the benignly regarded people-oriented sector of the dualist model conceals a regression to nineteenth-century social conditions or an assimilation of advanced capitalist societies to contemporary Third World conditions.[64] The model says nothing about the negative aspects of the expansion of the enterprise labor market and dependent self-employment. Informal autonomous service groups have taken on more social responsibilities as a result of the same restructuring process that has created more sweatshops and outworkers. The hyperliberal model at least has the merit of frankness, whereas the dual-society model turns the stark reality of peripheralization into a mythical creative "informal sector." The dual-society vision is derived from those people who opted out of consumerism in the 1960s to search for alternative styles of life and work. It ignores the coercive force of peripheralization that has marginalized a much larger number of people against their own will.

Nevertheless, these critics of the dual-society model do not themselves have a convincing alternative to propose, one that would resolve the problems they can justly point to. Principal among these problems are structural changes in production that may make it possible for all the goods that society would need to be produced by 10 to 15 percent of the population. The Keynesian world in which infusions of monetary demand were from time to time required in order to ensure full employment of human resources becomes completely irrelevant in such a situation. A rethinking of the relationship of work, income, and society becomes necessary. The dual-society theorists have affirmed the need to separate work from income and instead to evaluate work in terms of its contribution to society.

The not-so-improbable assumption that no more than 15 percent of the population need be involved in goods production alone demonstrates the absurdity of linking individual incomes to the productivity of industry. There could be no principle of natural justice that would reward that small proportion of the population in relation to the high productivity of the equipment they use while others who do not work with high-productivity equipment are relatively deprived. In face of this absurdity, it becomes reasonable to regard work as a privilege, to be sought and performed for its own satisfactions. Those who do not work at producing goods with high-productivity equipment can work at producing needed services, or objects of some aesthetic merit, whose value to the people who benefit from them and to society as a whole is at least as great as that of the goods they consume. Dual-society theory has at least posed anew, if it has not resolved, the question of the social valuation of socially necessary work, as well as the problem of nonwork-related criteria and methods for the distribution of incomes.

Also posed is the question how to determine what is to be produced. The hyperliberal and neomercantilist models do not need to raise this question. Both begin with the proposition that the world market will decide what is to be produced. The issue they both confront is what the best method is for success in creating and responding to world-market demand. If, however, it turns out that 15 percent of the people are all it takes to produce the goods that are needed, it becomes rational to seek some criterion other than international competitiveness for determining the socially desirable composition of that production. The search for that criterion marks the dividing line between capitalist and redistributive development, between production impelled by exchange and production for use.

The dual-society theory also raises but does not resolve

the question of bureaucracy. It is sensitive to the criticisms that the social services have become self-expanding imperial entities, cultivating their own institutional interests and those of their staffs even more than the interests of their clients, and that they have become remote and alien to the people they are intended to serve. It proposes to remedy this by turning over most of the task of social service to less formal, autonomous groups. The virtue of bureaucracy, as Max Weber reminded us, lies in impartiality and the rule of law, the institutionalization of impersonal rational norms. It is fair to object that real-life bureaucracies do not match this ideal type, that they embody beneath the rational facade elements of clientelism, personal ambition, favoritism, and corruption. The corresponding ideal-typical defect of informal autonomous groups is particularism and discrimination, although they may also in practice evoke dedication and altruism on the part of those who work in them. The question that dual-society theory has not answered is how to retain the dedication while at the same time controlling against particularist abuses. How can the larger interest of society assert itself through a maze of small, autonomous groups?

The hyperliberal model rests ultimately on the patriarchal family. Women's work in the home reproduces a primarily male labor force. The male worker's top status at home compensates for his dependent status at the workplace. The wife's consumption habits and desires, assuming she behaves as the advertising industry would hope, keep the "patriarch" at work (and less inclined to strike) and keep the demand side of the economy active. This kind of family is functional to capitalist development. The patriarchal family may also have been functional to redistributive accumulation as it has so far been experienced, though redistributive societies have mobilized more women into the labor force and they have recognized an at least formal equality in the workplace, even as they did nothing to alter the sexual division of labor in the home. Alternative visions of society raise the question of a restructuring of family production, as well as of industrial production: a sharing of domestic tasks not based on sexual stereotypes; removal of the barriers between work for family consumption, social service, like education, care of the aged, and so forth; and production of some exchange values of a specialized kind by the application in the home of small-scale, high-tech productive equipment, craft skills, and tools, etc.

The principal objection to visions of an alternative society is the political one: these visions do not contain a clear strategy for changing existing society. Hitherto, the working class has been the political basis for the hope of change. The achievements of social policy through the twentieth century were based on the growth of worker power. Now, however, visionaries of an alternative society seem to have abandoned hope in the working class. It is too fragmented, they affirm, and those working-class elements that retain some power are too much bound up with the existing system. There is much truth in this. André Gorz founds his hopes on "a non-class of non-workers" (he uses "work" in the narrow sense of wage employment rather than in the broad sense of productive activity).[65] The members of this "non-class" would have to be defined more in terms of their subjective orientations than their objective position in production relations. They would comprise all those who feel alienated in existing society and who reject the idea of work (in the narrow sense) as personal fulfillment. Such a category, Gorz recognizes, has no positive principle of cohesion—only a common negation of established social order. The "non-class" cannot by any strategy take power (as a worker-based revolution might conceive of taking power). Taking power, moreover, would be inconsistent with its only common principle: negation. Rather, the goal asserted by Gorz is the erosion of power. The activities of the autonomous groups ideally comprising this "non-class" are not directed toward the state; they are directed toward social action. It would have to be out of the tension between such manifold social activity and the corporatist superstructures of state power that some transformation of the state-society relationship could be hoped for.

Whatever slim grounds for hope there might be for bringing about political change through these means, they are completely blocked by military confrontations in the new Cold War and the many active regional and civil wars. The very notion of a withering of state power has as precondition the absence of international threat and the enjoyment of internal security. For this reason, the peace movement is the necessary foundation for any alternative vision. Only a dismantling of the external and internal repressive capabilities of the state would permit such alternative societies to come into existence. The peace movement is logically the broadest basis for popular mobilization toward an alternative society. The war movement is the greatest threat to that alternative and the most powerful force in defense of the hyperliberal state, the neomercantilist state, and the redistributive regimes of "actually existing socialism."

The unlikelihood that the peace movement can succeed in disarming states in no way diminishes its utility as a means of broad popular mobilization. This unlikelihood does, however, make it reasonable to envisage strategies for change based on a more rigorous analysis of social forces than the concept of a "non-class." Strategies based on "non-classes" imply a leap into subjectivity that makes for ephemeral politics. The fact that the working class has become fragmented and that parts of it have been coopted into the established order is not sufficient ground for abandoning class analysis altogether. The inferences to be drawn from class analysis today may prove to be pessimistic with regard to the existence of a firm basis for change, but that pessimism would be a surer guide to building a coalition of forces— a prospective counterhegemony—than voluntarism resting solely on sentiments triggered by events. The "non-class" issues—peace, ecology, and feminism—are not to be set aside but given a firm and conscious basis in the social realities shaped through the production process. To the task of identifying these social forces and their directions of movement I turn now in the final chapter.

## CHAPTER TEN

# THE FORMATION OF CLASSES AND HISTORIC BLOCS

Class is to be understood as a real historical relationship and not as merely an analytical category in the mind of the analyst. Whether or not social classes exist is a matter for historical investigation. The social basis for the existence of classes comes from the way in which people are positioned in production processes, but if the production process creates the potentiality for classes, it does not *make* classes. Social practices shaped by events give people the common experience of class identity and of collective action. Some of these practices are oriented toward production, e.g., trade unionism, some toward the state, in the form of political parties or movements. The former have often tended toward an institutionalization of class relations within the established productive system. The latter have exhibited greater potential for transforming structures both of production and the state. Since the form of state has been found to be the determining influence on the development of modes of production relations, the orientation of classes toward the state, their channeling into political action, is a crucial historical question. However autonomous such political action may be, it is constrained by its social basis. People may be momentarily aroused by political enthusiasms, but in the longer run, political movements can do no more than their class basis allows.

Several factors affecting class arise out of the fact that distinct modes of social relations of production coexist within any society.

1. Not every dominant or subordinate group in each distinct mode of social relations of production necessarily forms a class; some may not attain the level of common identity and capacity for common action that constitutes class; they remain a latent or potential class.

2. Dominant or subordinate groups from two or more modes of social relations of production may combine to form a class, e.g., through the development of solidarity between established and nonestablished workers, or between small-scale entrepreneurs and corporate managers.

3. The different modes of production relations are hierarchically connected in dominant-subordinate relationships (peasant production providing cheap food for nonestablished workers in small-scale industries, who in turn produce cheap inputs for large-scale industries with established workers) that affect the class orientations of their component elements, e.g., through separating the interests of established and nonestablished workers.

4. The classes formed around the dominant mode of social relations of production have a predominant influence over the formation and orientation of classes derived from subordinate modes, including the opportunity to form a hegemonic relationship with these other classes.

The state creates and maintains the framework for the development of production by direct or indirect intervention in productive processes. It structures the hierarchical relationship among the coexisting modes of social relations of production. The way the state regulates production is conditioned by the class structure of support underpinning the state. Social revolutions, or radical shifts in class structures, can give a different orientation to the state's role in production.

Thus class is important as the factor mediating between production on the one hand and the state on the other. The building and disintegration of historic blocs is the process whereby class formation can transform both states and the organization of production.

The mediating role of class between production and the state is most clearly perceptible within particular societies or social formations. The same mediating role can also be examined at the global level. Here class formation and conflict mediates between the world economy of production and the interstate system. The classes that participate in this mediation have their origins in national societies, but form links across the boundaries separating national societies.

The study of emerging class structure is an exercise in social mapping at both national and global levels. The map will include the tendencies in class formation that are apparent in different kinds of national societies (e.g., advanced capitalist societies, industrializing Third World capitalist societies, the redistributive societies of "actually existing socialism," and societies with a still primitive level of productive forces). It will also show tendencies toward a globalizing of certain classes or transcendence of their origins in national social formations. The importance of attempting this kind of social mapping is to better understand the composition of existing historic blocs and the elements available for the formation of new historic blocs—and hence the potential for change in the form of state, in the interstate system, and in the future organization of production.

Outcomes in all three spheres are an open question. No independent and dependent variables are posited, no one-way causalities, e.g., from an "inevitably" emerging organization of production to consequentially "necessary" forms of state and interstate system. The future shape of production organization is just as open as the future form of state and just as constrained by the existing pattern of forces. The struggle goes on at the same time on all three terrains. The question to be addressed here is: what are the forces that are either present in combat or more passively available for mobilization into combat?

This approach, which regards class formation and the formation of historic blocs as the crucial factor in the transformation of global political and social order, has several advantages:

1. It avoids reducing states and the state system to the world economy, a tendency for which world systems theory has been criticized.[1]

2. It builds a picture of the world economy and the state

system from the bottom up by a mapping of production systems and historic blocs and thereby avoids reification of world systems.

3. It keeps historical dialectic at the center of concern, i.e., the confrontation of social forces and the strategies that can shape future structures of power (national and global) in one direction or another, and thus avoids attributing structural-functional homeostasis to world systems.[2]

This approach is grounded in the proposition that people do make their own history, though not in conditions of their own choosing. It aims to delineate what those conditions actually are and to identify feasible directions toward the building of historic blocs. For this reason, much of the discussion of global class structure below will appear indeterminate, opening questions instead of answering them conclusively. That is because the answers will be given only by future social practice.

Insofar as tendencies appear—tendencies that may, of course, be reversed by future practice—these give a picture that is the inverse of the one depicted by Marx and Engels in the mid-nineteenth century. In the Communist Manifesto, they saw capitalists aligned with their respective states while the vocation of the workers of the world was to unite. Recent developments in the late twentieth century suggest rather a movement toward the unification of capital on a world scale, while industrial workers and other subordinate classes have become fragmented and divided. Realistic strategies for social and political change should begin with the facts, however unpalatable.

## DOMINANT GROUPS

Consider first of all the dominant social groups. Their hierarchy can be plotted as (1) those who control the big corporations operating on a world scale, (2) those who control big nation-based enterprises and industrial groups, and (3) locally based petty capitalists. The middle category is a heterogeneous one that includes managements of private nation-scale corporations, public sector corporations in capitalist countries, and state enterprises in socialist countries.

The first group have attained a clearly distinctive class consciousness and, though they do not identify themselves as such, constitute what can be called the transnational managerial class. Being a member of a class does not mean submerging conflicts of interest with other class members—indeed, it is of the essence of a capitalist class that rivalries exist among capitalists. What it does mean is awareness of a common concern to maintain the system that enables the class to remain dominant. Various institutions have performed the function of articulating strategies in this common concern: the Trilateral Commission, the OECD, the IMF, and the World Bank all serve as foci for generating the policy consensus for the maintenance and defense of the system. "Interdependence" is the key symbol in an ideology linking economic rationality, social welfare, and political freedom or "modernization" (depending on whether the reference is to advanced capitalist or Third World countries) with a world economy open to corporate movements of goods, capital, and technology. Prestigious business schools and international management training programs socialize new entrants to the values, lifestyles, language (in the sense of shared concepts, usages, and symbols), and business practices of the class. The culture specific to the class is generically American and has been spread transnationally from a U.S. base, homogenizing the outlook and behavior of members of the globally dominant group in a way that distinguishes them from the differentiated cultures of national elite groups. It has, despite its pervasive Americanness, become nonetheless transnational. American executives try to repress native atavisms in order to embrace a style of interpersonal relations conducive to common action with Germans and Japanese—even with Frenchmen and Soviets. The participant Frenchmen, Germans, etc., have traveled a longer cultural journey into this homogeneity, seduced by its blandishments. Together, all of them enjoy a sense of superiority to the common run of mortals in their shared liberalism, efficiency, and enlightenment.

The transnational managerial class is not limited to persons actually employed among the managerial cadres of multinational corporations and their families. It encompasses public officials in the national and international agencies involved with economic management and a whole range of experts and specialists who in some way are connected with the maintenance of the world economy in which the multinationals thrive—from management consultants, to business educators, to organizational psychologists, to the electronics operators who assemble the information base for business decisions, and the lawyers who put together international business deals.

International financial management has become of growing importance as a component of this class. Finance is the principal mechanism for enforcing class dominance over the world economy within an order maintained by military strength. Finance binds countries into the world market and obliges governments, as a condition for renewing their international loans, to carry out the policies required for the transnational managerial class to flourish, policies that place the main burden of adjustments upon the more vulnerable social groups. Finance also contains the main endogenous threat to the world economy, from the excessive growth of indebtedness by both governments and big corporations, which has since 1982 revealed the world economy as a fragile structure liable to a financial collapse that could lead to a general movement toward neomercantilism.

The other two categories, associated respectively with national and local capital, are more diverse. Symbols are available to these groups—national symbols to national bourgeoisies and free-enterprise and populist symbols to petty capital. Whether or not these symbols are used to emphasize distinctive orientations is contingent upon the ways in which national groups react to world-economy developments and to the dominant position of the transnational managerial class.

National bourgeoisies took form historically in countries of early capitalist development. They evolved distinctive cultural traditions, as well as specific national economic power bases and different alliance relationships with precapitalist dominant classes (landowners, military nobility, and state bureaucrats) in the formation of national historic blocs. There was also, from the earliest phase of capitalist development, an international component—what Karl Polyani referred to as *haute finance*—which linked national capital into an international economic system. There was also a common understanding on the part of national capitalists of their mutual interest in supporting this system in the era of *les bourgeois conquérants*. National capital from the start had an internationalist dimension.

The world-economy expansion of the Pax Americana favored the internationalizing of production. Some national capital that formerly had rested on a national territorial base now became global in scope. It remained national in its reliance upon the political support of the home state but now came to operate in many countries. Elements of national capital were now won over to the neoliberal world order and absorbed into the transnational managerial class—they became its components within the nation, agents promoting the adjustment of national policies to the requisites of world-economy expansion. Some elements, however, often the least dynamic, remained apart from this movement, increasingly dependent upon state protectionist measures.

The economic crisis following 1974 brought out the conflict of interests between the nationally and internationally oriented capitalist interests. The policy debate between the adherents of a reconstructed neoliberal world order and the neomercantilists, and between hyperliberal and state-capitalist orientations in the form of state, reflects the stresses within contemporary capitalism. Does it signify a confrontation of the transnational managerial class by revived national bourgeoisies? Not necessarily. Neomercantilism with state-capitialist forms of management does not imply a retreat into autarkic spheres with quite separate class structures. Rather it implies an intensification of unregulated competition among national capitals, each implanted in a number of countries, for dominance in world markets. Each major nation's capital seeks to be everywhere that profits can be made, and all, by the very pressure of competition, are becoming more alike. The different national capitals engaged in this global competition are no more distinctive than firms competing in a national market—something that does not prevent competing capitalists from forming a common class. The transnational managerial class would, in a neomercantilist future, become somewhat more weighted than at present with state officials, and its common institutions would disappear or lose influence, but the social reality of a global class would not, for all that, necessarily come to an end.

There was little evidence of cleavage between international and national tendencies in U.S. capital during the expansive years of the 1950s and 1960s. The international orientation led the expansion, but there was room for all. Some linkages were established through subcontracting, and segmentation of labor markets minimized the competitive disadvantage of local capital. Cleavage between the two tendencies appeared more openly in the years of economic crisis following 1973, most notably in a variety of protectionist demands that contradicted the world-economy orientation of policy supported by the international sector.[3] The political impacts of each of the two tendencies is brought to bear at a different point in the U.S. political system. The international sector has privileged access to the executive branch and particularly to those agencies managing foreign economic policy, the State Department and Treasury. Protectionist interests are more effective through lobbies in the Congress and, along with local entrepreneurs, in the state legislatures. The result has been ambiguity in U.S. policy: continuing commitment affirmed by the executive to international commitments and ad hoc protectionist measures enacted by Congress.[4]

The ad hoc political influence of protectionist interests has been reinforced by the emergence of an ideological current that offers an alternative view of policy to that of liberal internationalism. Various strands entwine: concern for the "deindustrialization" of the United States resulting from the shift of manufacturing by multinationals into foreign (often Third World) locations; concern to avoid making the "British mistake" of the late nineteenth century by exporting capital and with it the technological capability to generate rival economic powers; advocacy of neomercantilist foreign economic policies geared to the protection and enhancement of U.S. economic power and more direct participation by the state in the mobilization of capital and direction of investment.[5]

Petty capitalists in the United States have, in post-1973 crisis conditions, become highly vulnerable to the reduced level of demand in the domestic market and to high interest rates, leading to lower profits and a high rate of bankruptcies. The grievances of small business have not, however, generated an autonomous class-fraction revolt. Small business has come increasingly under the dominance of large capital, particularly

through the "franchise" mechanism whereby the local businessman absorbs a major part of the risk for corporate giants, who
provide the technology, brand name, and market organization,
while the local businessman tries to draw his profits from the
cheaper labor available through labor market segmentation.

In other advanced capitalist countries, the balance between international and national fractions of capital has differed
historically. Britain is the exceptional case in which the internationally oriented financial interests of the City have traditionally dictated policy, allowing balance-of-payments considerations affecting the exchange rate of the pound to outweigh the
developmental concerns of industry.[6] In Germany, France, and
Japan, government and finance have been traditionally more
closely linked to the development of national industries. The
industrial recovery and expansion of the postwar years accentuated the differentiation between large-scale and small-scale
enterprises. The Japanese solution brought small-scale enterprises into a dependent subcontracting relationship within a national policy geared to export expansion by large-scale enterprises. The European countries sought markets to match the scale
of production of large units of capital both by export promotion
and by forming the European Common Market (EEC). While big
capital welcomed the EEC, local capitalists accustomed to stable
shares of local markets adapted less easily to the new conditions.[7]
Resistance to the rationalization and modernization promoted by
the coalition of big capital, states, and EEC provoked small business revolts.[8]

Through the 1960s, big capital in Europe became increasingly internationalized as U.S. capital flowed into the EEC to
produce behind the common tariff and to take advantage of the
higher rates of profit to be earned there.[9] Japan, always more
resistant toward intrusions of foreign capital, acceded in some
measure to U.S. pressures to permit certain forms of foreign
investment as a quid pro quo for Japanese full participation in
the rule-making and rule-supervising agencies of the world economy. Conflicts between international and national orientations
of capital become manifest at this point in the advanced capitalist
countries other than the United States. Jean-Jacques Servan-
Schreiber's book *The American Challenge* (1967) enlivened pub-

lic awareness of a struggle to resist consolidation of U.S. technological supremacy by strengthening an independent European capacity for industrial growth and innovation.[10]

The struggle was not, however, openly joined between two opposed segments, international and national, of capital within Europe. Alternative policy clusters emerged in national politics. The dominant ones (e.g., the regimes led by Valéry Giscard d'Estaing in France and Helmut Schmidt in West Germany) expressed continuing commitment to the neoliberal world-economic order with continuing enhancement of the competitiveness of big national capital in this sphere, combined with transitional protection and adjustment aid for the less competitive. Opposition clusters (e.g., the Gaullists in France) expressed the apprehensions of capital less able to adapt to world market conditions and of popular groups not benefiting from the growth of the more dynamic industrial sectors. Prolonged economic crisis following 1973 reduced the plausibility of the first and deepened the concerns of the second. Capital movements reversed, flowing now through Eurocurrency markets into the United States, while the depreciation of the dollar favored U.S. over European and Japanese exports on world markets and increased labor costs in Europe and Japan relative to the United States. The early advantages of European and Japanese capital in world market competition were now challenged by a revived U.S. industrial competitiveness—a competitiveness due more to the use of U.S. power to manipulate the world financial system than to real gains in industrial productivity. Capital in all the major countries became more than ever aware that world market success depended equally upon productive efficiency and political power.

In late-developing countries, from those of southern Europe to the industrializing countries of the Third World, national bourgeoisies never attained the same degree of hegemonic status as bourgeoisies in older capitalist countries. The state in most of these countries became a major agency for mobilizing and accumulating capital. The predominance of state officials in the accumulation process and in the control of the country's productive apparatus gives rise to an attempt to define the nature of the group that controls development. It is, of course, necessary to differentiate several distinct patterns of power relationship.

In some Third World countries, state structures coexist with evolved local propertied classes—landowners and nascent national bourgeoisies. The state, with its military-bureaucratic apparatus, has assumed the role of guiding national development and of managing the links between local and foreign capital.[11] In Brazil, the state has fostered the association of multinational capital with state corporations and some of the larger blocs of national private capital. The state has also used its international credit to raise and underwrite foreign loans for investment in state and private sectors. It has been the major force in capital accumulation. The Brazilian case may be exemplary but not unique.[12]

There is an element of rivalry in the relationship to foreign capital to the extent that state officials and national capitalists bargain with multinationals for a larger share of total accumulation. The notion of a comprador bourgeoisie, which suggests a role of subordinate agent to multinational capital, is totally inappropriate to this relationship. Nevertheless, the rivalry takes place within the framework of a common commitment to a pattern of development oriented to world markets. State-centered economic management is one of the manifold manifestations of world-economy capitalist development. (The alternative would be autocentric development, but to adopt such an alternative would imply a degree of mass mobilization too risky for the political survival of the dominant groups.)

In other less developed countries, an indigenous class structure based on property was less than fully evolved. In many African countries, it is difficult to speak of an indigenous land-owning or local capitalist class. Landowning, in the sense of capitalist farming, and local capitalist enterprise were the monopoly of foreigners. Even though state administrative structures were somewhat more sketchy and less thoroughly articulated with society than in some of the more developed postcolonial Third World countries, the state was relatively more powerful in relation to society. The civil and military cadres of the state and parastatal corporations became the dominant power and the exclusive link to outside capital and the interstate system with its potentials for aid and influence.

The personnel of this dominant group had a common

background. They were drawn from the educated petty bourgeoisie with some admixture of more traditional social authorities (although the children of the latter soon integrated with the former through education). This had led to a variety of efforts to identify the ruling group in the use of terms such as *bureaucratic bourgeoisie, managerial or organizational bourgeoisie,* and *state class.* They have been called a bourgeoisie by analogy because of the control they have over the productive apparatus through their control of the state but also, perhaps, because of an observed disposition of some of their elements to link up with foreign capital both as real compradors, e.g., in the role of local staff of multinational corporations, and as an autonomous group seeking external capital and allies for their own economic activities. The "state class" appelation, by dropping the "bourgeois" qualification, suggests an indeterminacy on the part of this group (it could move either toward integration with world capitalism or toward a more autocentric and socialist development). It also suggests that the group has attained a self-reproducing power status that can be opposed to subordinate classes in the society.[13]

The inherent ambiguity of the ruling group has been underlined by many observers. Amilcar Cabral, believing that in African conditions, only elements from the petty bourgeoisie could lead a successful revolution, proposed that the revolution would be able to maintain its integrity only if these petty-bourgeois elements were prepared to commit class suicide.[14]

Broadly, two courses of action are open to them. One is to maintain the revolutionary thrust toward autocentric development emphasizing basic needs and social equity—a course fraught with political risks. This is not inconsistent with selective links to the world economy through foreign investments and exports but must subordinate these links to national development goals. The other is to seek or accept foreign capital and produce for the world market as a means of servicing that capital. This is the soft option for a leadership tired of or threatened by continued popular mobilization. It is a course that may show evidence of economic growth, albeit with growing inequities and an external orientation to the economy. The state managers of a country possessing mineral resources in demand on world markets are especially liable to be attracted to the second course. Insofar as they derive rents from their control over access to minerals, they become in effect partners of the multinational capital that processes and markets their raw materials.[15]

Thus, if the state class does exist, it is an ambivalent structure that may move either in the direction of self-reliant development or in that of dependent integration into the world economy, with a natural inclination over time to the latter unless popular pressures can be recurrently rekindled to pressure the leadership to stay the revolutionary course.

A number of less developed countries are only of marginal interest to transnational capital. Their poor domestic markets offer little or no incentive for foreign investors to set up local production. Nor are export platforms a likely option so long as the industrializing Third World countries contain untapped reserves of more readily trainable and disciplined manpower. The financing of food and energy inputs poses problems of international credit. The greatest influence the state cadres of these countries have with those elements of the transnational managerial class they encounter lies in the threat of sociopolitical disorder inherent in their countries' lack of development and deteriorating economic and social conditions. Some hope to extract sufficient poor relief from the rich countries, averting the risks of popular mobilization. Others offer themselves frankly as repressive policemen in return for military and counterinsurgency assistance. Whether playing the benign or the malevolent role, these state cadres become accessories to the transnational managerial class thwarting the development of social forces in their countries.

Economic management in socialist countries is a special case. Industries in these countries operate under the tutelage of a political system centered in a Party whose leadership thinks in terms of totality, linking all significant activities in the society, including the management of industry, to overall goals. The concerns of different industrial sectors are reconciled within this total framework and managerial positions filled so as to conform with the general direction given by the central leadership. Potential exists for the emergence of a directing class in the Soviet system, but it is still difficult to speak of the emergence of class as a self-reproducing social category.[16] These directing groups adopt a perspective of national economic interest. (This does not, of course, mean that as individuals they are any less self-serving or corrupt than people in authority in other systems.)

They have entered into reciprocal relationships with particular elements of the transnational managerial class, e.g., through interindustry cooperation between some multinational corporations and some socialist enterprises. They have also joined in projects with the transnational managerial class, including the expansion of East-West trade, financing through the Eurocurrency markets, and participation (by a few of their countries) in the International Monetary Fund. Such reciprocal relations between dominant groups of state managements and the transnational managerial class remain subject to the veto of the former. They have not enmeshed the state managements irrevocably in the dynamics of a world economy led by the transnational managers.

## SUBORDINATE GROUPS

Looking downward from the dominant social groups, it is possible to spot tendencies in class formation among subordinate groups. In summary, these tendencies are: (1) the emergence of a new middle stratum of scientific, technical, and supervisory personnel comprised within enterprise-corporatist production relations and closely linked to the functions of industrial management; (2) an increasingly defensive posture of those established workers who remain within the scope of bipartite and tripartite production relations; (3) continuing expansion of nonestablished in relation to established jobs in advanced capitalist countries, accompanied by both a fragmentation of worker interests and a general spreading of instrumental values among all worker groups, both of which tendencies put in question the prospect of working-class solidarity; (4) the mobilization of new industrial labor forces in industrializing Third World countries, which will either be tamed in the protective embrace of state corporatism or become foci for revolutionary upheaval; and (5) the socially and politically destabilizing consequences of agricultural transformation in the Third World and of the increase in marginal populations and so-called informal-sector employment.

*The New Middle Stratum*

Technical, scientific, and supervisory personnel in the most technologically advanced sectors of industry have been hailed both as a "new middle class" and as a "new working class." The labels reflect different appraisals of the historical role this group is expected to perform. The "new middle class" designation describes a buffer layer within industry between those who control the accumulation process on top and the mass of the workers below—a status quo-protecting function.[17] The "new working class" designation expresses an anticipation that this group will become the cutting edge of change leading the rest of the working class toward self-managed socialism.[18]

The long-term trend toward industrial concentration has brought about a broadening and deepening of the management function. The individual entrepreneur assisted by several clerks whose managerial decision-making process went on within his own skull has been replaced by an ever more elaborated collective system of management, specialized into functions of finance, marketing, research and development, and production engineering, all coordinated at the top but collectively constituting an interdependent labor process of management. The new technical, scientific, and supervisory cadres constitute the lower layers of this managerial structure and its interface with those whose work is externally determined by this structure. Automation has created some new specializations based on theoretical knowledge of a polyvalent kind rather than on specific trades skills—on ability to think in systems terms and to interpret information and manipulate symbols. Often these skills become tied closely to particular enterprises and production processes. Those who develop such skills may thus develop at the same time an identity with and loyalty to the enterprise. The management structure as a whole depends on the continuity of action of the cadres. There are incentives on both sides to transform a contract for the purchase of labor power (determined by short-term market prospects) into a more integral form of employment relationship with the corporation, i.e., a salaried relationship with career development prospects and a pension at the end. What was once, in Marxian terms, thought of as variable capital becomes merged into constant capital. The form of social relations of production through which this is done is enterprise corporatism.[19]

Claus Offe has examined the ideological implications of the integration of such personnel. Achievement and merit are the principal legitimating criteria acknowledged in modern societies for differential rewards to individuals. The cooperative, interdependent nature of the work of "technostructures," however, makes it very difficult to measure objectively the contributions of individuals since the product is that of a team. In practice, selection and promotion to positions of higher status in the work process are based on criteria that have only a very approximate functional relevancy to the content of work but are good predictors of conformity to the social goals of management. Coupled with a tendency to recruit cadres, not from below, but from outside, this accentuates a social separation between cadres and workers. Offe concludes that the integration of employees through career prospects with the enterprise "means that large areas of motivation are now tied to the current status quo of power and income distribution."[20]

Integration does not, of course, eliminate conflict. Cadres have collective demands to press on top management. Their identification with the enterprise may well be matched by a sense of their own indispensability to the production process and capacity for technical self-determination. The conflicts in which they may be engaged, whether for a larger share of enterprise income or for more autonomy in decision making, remain issues within the enterprise family and have little or no bearing on generalized working-class action or political unionism. The "new working class" thesis recognizes that technical and scientific personnel tend to split away from class-based alignments and to engage in enterprise-oriented demands. It argues, however, that enterprise identification is not synonymous with an alignment to top management and that since cadres have the sense of being the authentic knowledge base for the production process, they are the group of workers most likely to envisage opportunities for self-management, in other words, for a regime in which management legitimated by property ownership can be replaced by management legitimated by technical competency.

The most doubtful part of the new working-class thesis, however, is that which envisages the cadres founding and leading a new kind of enterprise-based labor movement toward socialist self-management. There is little or no empirical basis for this proposition; scientific and technical personnel have not been at the forefront of strike action and labor agitation. Explosions have more characteristically broken out among the semiskilled.[21] It is true that scientific and technical personnel have usually gained more than proportionate influence in consultative schemes set up within enterprises, but these schemes are other instances of the social distancing of established workers in the larger scale, more integrated enterprises from the nonestablished and more precariously employed—another manifestation of enterprise corporatism.

What does remain plausible in the "new working class" thesis is the possibility that the cadres could be positively responsive to state action to nationalize industries. Any prospective change in the status of industry seems, indeed, more likely to come from state initiative as a result of a political change of regime than from any autonomous reform of the enterprise led by the cadres themselves. The financial dependency of enterprises on the banks, and of the banks ultimately on the state's capacity to mobilize capital, underlines this plausibility. Bankers may perceive a natural alliance with the technical cadres of industry since, in the last analysis, their work is more necessary to effective debt service than the formal owners are. This perception would, of course, be more vivid when a socialist government controls the banks. Possibly it is this that the French socialists, who have been foremost in advancing the "new working class" thesis have in mind.[22] One may, however, question how far such a change necessarily implies a transformation of social relations in production. It might well involve a consolidation of enterprise corporatism under state tutelage.

There is a lower stratum of personnel integrated within enterprises who can be categorized as "specialized workers." They have qualifications superior to those of the semiskilled though lacking the technological sophistication of the cadres. Their status depends on the role they play in supervising the flow of work by semiskilled operatives. Their power is thus identified with the technical organization of production specific to particular enterprises, and their main function is to ensure conformity with the norms of the enterprise on the part of subordinates.

Often such "specialized" jobs are to be found in older industries or older technologies that have adapted to the competitive impact of the technologically leading enterprises. The coexistence of old and new technologies is a further factor favoring a fragmentation of the interests of different groups of workers.[23] Some of the older industries that have traditionally been the preserve of skilled trades, e.g., printing, furniture manufacture, precision mechanics, have experienced a shift in the composition of their labor forces with a reduction in the proportion of skilled workers and an increase in the cheaper semiskilled. Where this has occurred, some of the skilled workers are often promoted into tasks involving preparation of work processes and supervision while some of the others are downgraded to less skilled work alongside a new lot of workers, often women or immigrants.[24] Under bouyant economic conditions such as prevailed in the 1960s, opportunities for individual promotion might outweigh resentment at the degradation of skills and impede any collective protest by erstwhile skilled workers. The restricted opportunities of the post-1973 crisis are more likely to engender a collective response. Such are the forces determining the borderlines of the enterprise corporatist consciousness.

### The Defensive Posture of Established Workers

Skilled manual labor has been the core of the trade union movement in the industrialized capitalist countries. Strong organizations of established workers gained recognition both as legitimate forces bargaining to determine the terms and conditions of employment in industry and also as a significant political force in influencing the development of social policies in the state through their association with mass-based, often social-democratic, political parties. Established labor became a key component of the coalition of political and social forces that constituted the social contract of the neoliberal state.

There were three variants of this general pattern. In the first, unions organized a relatively small proportion of the total nonagricultural labor force (not more than about 25 percent) and were effective in determining conditions of employment in large-scale enterprises of key industrial sectors but somewhat less effective in the realm of state policy. This was the case for the United States and Canada. In the second, unions were more strongly based in the labor force and were particularly influential in the determination of state policy through social-democratic parties, which held power through at least part of the postwar period. This was the case in Scandinavia, West Germany, and the Netherlands. In the third variant, unions were relatively weak in membership but became vehicles for occasional mass-based protests, which took on a class form (unions, in a sense, catching up with deeply rooted rank-and-file movements). These explosions secured a political response from a state controlled essentially by nonworking-class elements. This was the case in France and Italy, e.g., in the broadly based social movements of May 1968 in France and the "hot autumn" of Italy in 1969.

During the 1950s and 1960s, variations in strategies of social conflict and in the modes of resolution of conflicts can be explained very largely by these three variants. There was a steady level of strike activity in the United States and Canada (variant one); a decline of strikes to a negligible level in Denmark, the Netherlands, Norway, and Sweden (variant two); and some decline in Belgium, West Germany, and the United Kingdom (partial forms of variant two); and heavy concentrations of strike activity in France and Italy around moments of sociopolitical crisis (variant three).[25] These represented different ways in which established workers brought influence to bear on both industry and the state within the general framework of Keynesian-type economic management in an era of economic growth. Demand management maintained a welfare state with reasonably high levels of employment. Within the state, established workers' organizations were sought out as partners in national-level economic consultative bodies and economic planning commissions (with some exceptions, e.g., the French CGT and Italian CGIL, considered to fall outside the bounds of consensus because of their Communist Party connections). Workers were accorded some consultative status within industry, the most institutionally developed form being *mitbestimmung* in the German coal and steel industries. Established labor participated—albeit as a junior partner—in the power bloc that governed these countries during the postwar years. This accounts for the widespread acceptance of the ideology of "social partnership" in Western Europe and of "business unionism" in North America during these years.[26]

The years 1973-74 can in retrospect be seen as the threshold beyond which established workers were placed in a defensive posture and became alienated from the state. The rise of public expenditures to 50 percent or more of the national product, the prolonged decline and stagnation of economic activity, and the attendant exacerbation of the fiscal crisis of the state triggered a middle-class backlash against organized labor and against the welfare state. This change in the political environment was not necessarily accompanied by changes of regime. In the United Kingdom, Denis Healy's conduct of treasury policy in the Labour Party government of 1974-76 foreshadowed the more doctrinaire positions of the Conservative Thatcher government that followed, and in West Germany, the transition from the Willy Brandt to the Helmut Schmidt government marked a threshold presided over by the Social Democratic party. In Sweden, the country where the influence, even dominant influence, of labor over state and labor market policy had been most firmly entrenched, the Social Democrats, as the guarantors of this power structure, were ousted from office.

The background to this movement toward the exclusion of the established worker from political power has already been noted: the compression of the skilled-worker category in industry itself and a proportionate increase in the semiskilled. The compression of the skilled category eroded the power base of the bipartite and tripartite modes of social relations and the autonomous political influence of established workers. This compression in the traditional industries was offset to some extent by the progress of unionization among state-sector workers, which involved among other things the gaining of established status (i.e., more protected employment status) by groups of workers hitherto nonestablished, such as hospital and inside postal workers. State-sector workers, whose gains were mostly made in the 1960s, have also been placed on the defensive by the general pressure for budget cuts in all the advanced capitalist countries. Employers stiffened their resistance to union demands and reasserted their control over the organization of work so as to be able to decrease the proportion of skilled to semiskilled jobs.

Forced into opposition to the neoliberal state, the defensive posture of established worker organizations is expressed in a variety of ways. There has been a new emphasis in labor disputes on technological change—the natural attempt by skilled workers to reverse a vanishing control over the work process.[27] Unions have also tried to head off tendencies toward integration of worker interests with the enterprise (which would undermine the workers' collective autonomy of action) by reasserting the class basis of worker interests.[28] Realizing that the trends adversely affecting skilled employment cannot be resolved at the level of union-management relations, movements of established workers in some countries have been calling for a voice in investment policies with a view to promoting a kind of industrial reconversion that will not result in a large-scale displacement of skilled jobs.[29] This very demand, however, could become effective policy only if the the post-1973 trend toward alienation of established labor from the power blocs of advanced capitalist states were reversed. Whether at the enterprise level or the state level, established worker unions confront a problem of their own political weakness. Acquiescence in the political status quo, combined with industrial action, such as brought material results in the expansive 1950s and 1960s, is no longer adequate to their post-1973 situation.

Within established worker ranks, the post-1973 trends have enlivened suspicion and revolt against a union leadership perceived as too much accustomed to operating within the erstwhile system of power from which little or nothing now seems to be obtainable. One consequence has been to open opportunities for more radical leadership.[30] Radical tendencies within established labor that jostle conservative union leadership have shed the corporatism of earlier established worker movements: the radicals expect nothing from labor appointments to national consultative bodies, reject incomes policies (which in any case have not been much favored by the capitalist states since the crisis), and reject the cooptational implications of worker representation in enterprise-level bodies. Any forms of participation whether at enterprise or national levels would be envisaged by the radicals as opportunities for waging a power struggle for control of industry and industrial policy—for a definitely conflictual participation. Participation would become acceptable only to the extent that established worker organizations gained power.

Radical tendencies within established labor have, however, been an expression of frustration at labor's declining power. They represent little more than an exasperated awareness of the ideological cleavage that increasingly separates organized labor from capital and the state since the onset of the economic crisis. In their economic role, unions have found themselves in the degrading position of bargaining concessions to capital, trying to make their retreat as orderly as possible, trying to conserve their organized strength against the day when they might be able to use it more effectively. With some exceptions, union membership in the advanced capitalist countries has declined.[31] Labor's economic strength has eroded.

On the political level, the record has been scarcely more promising. Right-wing politics and ideologies have come to dominate in a number of the advanced capitalist countries. In France, the major exception, a Socialist Party government took power in 1981. During its first year of rule, social reform measures and nationalizations were put into effect. This was followed by a renewed policy of "rigor," the result of world-economy pressures, that brought this socialist experiment into conformity with the general pattern. Trade union strength has ebbed in France, too, underlining that the traditional basis of support for left-wing politics is no longer what it was.[32] Apart from eroding electoral support, the left has shown itself to be ideologically weakened. Various attempts have been made to build coalitions, but nowhere has a coherent policy alternative emerged to confront the actions of the state and capital, to counter deindustrialization and the expansion of the nonestablished workforce.

Some of the critical issues lie in the area of investments and incomes policies. Unions oppose incomes policies where workers are not an effective part of the power bloc that determines the whole of economic policy, including especially investments. Any gain with respect to union influence over investments might thus be met by a possible advance in the direction of incomes policy, ushering in a post-Keynesian type of national economic policy, the likely international implications of which are neo-mercantilist.[33] This would clearly imply a resurgence of labor's relative power and the reinsertion of established labor back into the historic bloc. However, unless and until this can be achieved, established labor may take the position that unions must rely on their own strength alone and remain suspicious toward the appeals and blandishments of states which have so obviously downgraded worker interests. Of course, what unions cannot achieve through economic strength they may try to achieve through political alliance. (This may be seen as the meaning of AFL-CIO support for the Mondale Democratic Party candidacy in the 1984 U.S. elections.) Labor politics have, however, been no more successful than union organization in most of the advanced capitalist countries since the mid-1970s.

## The Shifting Boundary Between Established and Nonestablished Workers

As noted in chapter 9, the transition from manufacture to Fordism during the late nineteenth and early twentieth century brought with it a new orientation of trade unions. As workers lost control over the work process, their organizations concentrated efforts on defending and improving their living standards through both industrial and political action. At the workplace, managerial authority became formally supreme; worker resistance was limited to informal restrictions of output. Models of personal behavior shifted from the work group to the street group[34] and from occupational solidarity to consumer conformity. In the late twentieth century, automation and high technology in the advanced capitalist countries accelerated these tendencies: there has been job enrichment for a relative few, job improverishment and a lowering of skills for others, and an introduction of still others to semiskilled work having no intrinsically satisfying content. At the same time, the communications media have spread consumerism, instrumental attitudes toward work, and acquiescence in the long-term stability of political systems.

The enlargement that has taken place in the sphere of semiskilled work has resulted in shifting and uncertain boundaries between established and nonestablished labor. Much of present-day social conflict concerns the definition of these boundaries. Three interacting sets of factors are involved in their demarcation. One is the technical organization of work and content of jobs, discussed in chapter 9. The second is the *weltanschauung* or form of consciousness of the workers concerned, their typical attitudes toward work and life.[35] The third is whether or not workers are organized in trade unions and the nature of their employment relationships.

One type of worker defined by the interaction of these three sets of factors is the "affluent worker" depicted in the studies by Goldthorpe and others at Luton in Bedfordshire, England.[36] These studies were done during a period of economic growth in a new industrial town among employees in three enterprises. They could be regarded as representative of male, British (i.e., nonimmigrant) workers in modern manufacturing. Being in a new town, these workers were relatively removed from close family and community influences such as might be assumed to be transmitters of traditional working-class culture. They were also in the younger age groups. The studies showed a high degree of attachment to consumer values as these arise in the nuclear family—what the authors characterize as "privatization"—and of instrumental attitudes toward work. Work, in other words, is valued only as a means for gaining the income required to satisfy consumer values. There was, however, little evidence of *embourgeoisement* in the sense of identification with the more traditional middle-class aspirations for independence and individual upward mobility. The worker was typically a union member who regarded the union instrumentally as the necessary collective means of defending and increasing income.

Objectively, the affluent worker has been presented as falling within the established worker category and as being typically a supporter of the status quo. This latter attribute most probably is to be explained by the favorable economic context and by an ideological milieu characterized by aspirations for a middle-class way of life shorn of the Protestant work ethic and manipulated by commercial advertising. Nevertheless, the possibility remains open, as the authors suggest, that a change in the economic environment could activate collective consciousness among affluent workers, most likely in a political form. Keener awareness of collective disadvantage in opportunities vis-à-vis other social groups or an economic downturn bringing deterioration of their relative incomes could spark such a change. In the absence of any such events, bipartite social relations of production among these workers are system maintaining rather than system transforming.

A second type of worker situated close to the established/ nonestablished boundary in the core industrial countries is in a full-time, low-status job. Many of these are relative newcomers, including people of rural background, ethnically differentiated imigrants, and women. They are employed in the large factories of the automobile industry, smaller regional plants of industries such as electronics, and in small or medium-sized local enterprises such as textiles or information processing. Some of the most explosive social conflicts of recent decades have broken out among this category. These generally focus on union recognition and the attempt to acquire established status. Often these efforts have foundered upon the hostility or indifference of already established workers, and this has made it easier for employers to resist nonestablished worker demands. Sometimes, however, a prolonged conflict sparks a movement of solidarity on the part of the established workers, and unions are formed or restructured to encompass and defend those attempting to gain established status.[37] Here the boundaries between established and nonestablished are most fluid and forms of consciousness range from social passivity and an instrumental view of the wage relationship, on the one hand, to active challenge to the structure of power and control in both management and unions, on the other.

It may well be that employment of full-time, semiskilled workers recruited from among groups suffering various forms of social disadvantage (minorities, immigrants, women) peaked during the precrisis years of the late 1960s and early 1970s and will not grow again. Thereby the established order in industry might spare itself the risk of generating an explosion. The functions performed by these workers can either be shifted to temporary jobs or reprogrammed into the sphere of the more integrated enterprise-corporatist work force through automation and robotization.

A third type encompasses those in a more precarious or

marginal employment relationship. These people are in temporary or part-time occasional jobs requiring a variety of skilled or
semiskilled qualifications. This includes people who welcome
short-term or temporary work as a means of maximizing their
free time and minimizing the sphere of their lives subject to work
discipline while providing them with a necessary, if minimal,
income. It also covers those who would prefer regular employment but have been unable to obtain it. The expansion of precarious employment was discussed in chapter 9.

According to the classical analyses of work and class formation, precarious employment would be unpropitious in the
extreme for the development of a class consciousness. Class consciousness was supposed to thrive on propinquity, whereas it is
the characteristic of temporary, part-time, and putting-out work
for workers to be associated only intermittently or not at all. The
work process isolates them rather than brings them together.
Furthermore, precarious employment of this kind expresses, for
many of the workers, a divorce between work and what is meaningful in their lives. Work becomes exclusively instrumental.
There is no satisfaction in it for its own sake, but only for what
earnings work can procure. Quite possible those participating in
occasional, temporary employment may devote some of their
energies to social and political action. Alternatively, they may
share passively in the manipulated desires of consumerism.
There is little or nothing in the work relationship itself that
predisposes to the one or to the other.

On the other hand, for some the precarious status does
involve a social and political consciousness, a rejection of the
authority structure of the established economic and political order, an option for an alternative. This is particularly the case for
some of the youth, who feel at the same time marginalized from
the established economic order and alienated from its values.
Perhaps, as is often alleged, this consciousness is more frequently
to be found among middle and upper-middle-class youth who
have reacted against an order to which their opportunities (in the
minds of their parents) were supposed to have been linked. Whatever their class origins, these elements of youth have given a form
of consciousness to a variety of informal, autonomous, use-value-
producing groups in a kind of parallel economy. This conscious-

ness is antipolitical rather than political and is directed more toward affirming a separate sphere of social action than putting pressure on the state for the extension of social policy.

These three types of social relationship to be found on the borderlines between established and nonestablished jobs embody contradictory tendencies, some supportive, some disruptive of existing industrial structures in the advanced capitalist countries. The affluent worker is objectively supportive during good economic times but could, in less favorable circumstances, become an opposition force. The newly recruited, still marginal, low-status worker may be kept in a relatively isolated and powerless position and be animated by a purely instrumental attitude toward work and an ambition to achieve personal upward mobility toward established status, but collective action can and has ignited these workers and has had a broader radicalizing effect on labor movements. The third type—precarious, temporary, and part-time employment—is equally ambiguous in its significance for class formation. Objectively, that is to say, in terms of the work relationship itself, it seems to favor the status quo of power relations in production or the increasing dominance of capital over labor. The instrumental attitude toward work it encourages, insofar as it provides a free run for consumerism, tends to perpetuate petty-bourgeois individualist ideology in enterprise-labor-market conditions of superexploitation. But subjectively, this particular realm of work can also harbor visions of an alternative society—visions sufficiently alive to trouble and even traumatize some members of the ruling class in Western Europe. Work in this sector of the economy can be a means of secession from established order, a secession that finds expression in non-work related movements like the peace, ecological, and feminist movements.

The apparent quiescence of labor in the advanced capitalist countries since 1974—quiescence relative to expectations that these societies would never again tolerate massive unemployment after the experience of the 1930s—is to be explained, not only by the coercive threat to employed workers made by high unemployment, but also by the politically and socially demobilizing effects of a growing enterprise corporatism at one extreme and of fragmented precarious employment at the other. Those sectors in which collective labor protest, in the classical analysis of labor and political action, would have been most expected have been steadily compressed. Traditional labor ideologies have been drained of their class substance. At the same time, new potential sources of protest have been created—frustration of the affluent worker's expectations, discrimination disadvantaging newly recruited immigrant and female work forces, the resentment of the craftsman downgraded to semiskilled status, the alienation of youth challenging the values of the dominant society. On the one hand are forces making for demobilization and social and political passivity—the condition for "governability" in the minds of the dominant groups. On the other, an opportunity appears for the formation of ideologies that could bridge the gaps between these fragmented sources of discontent. This opportunity for the construction of a counterhegemonic bloc has, however, not yet been very effectively seized.

## The Industrial Proletariat In The Third World

In Third World countries, work is at the heart of actual and potential social conflict. Three interrelated processes define the nature and occasions of such conflict: the formation of an industrial proletariat (most prominent and numerous in those Third World countries that were industrializing rapidly during the 1970s but occurring to a lesser degree in other Third World countries as well); expulsion of population from the rural areas as a consequence of the penetration of capitalist agriculture; and the growth of marginal urban populations and informal-sector activities in tandem with economic growth.

A natural history of class formation in peripheral capitalist development can be outlined. It will not fit every case precisely, but it does suggest a certain logic in the connections between sequential stages in patterns of economic growth, in state structures, and in modes of social relations of production.

The first links between a precapitalist formation and the capitalist world economy were established through trade. The precapitalist formation provided a market for some of the products of capitalist production and supplied some goods sought by capitalist traders (raw materials, slaves). These links were established through ports of trade regulated by the authorities of the precapitalist formation and initially tended to strengthen these local authorities insofar as they could remain in control of the trade.[38]

The expansive proclivity of capitalism and the superior force it mustered led to a second stage in which capitalist production implanted itself directly in the precapitalist formation. This was accomplished through the medium of imperialism, either by supplanting local powers with a colonial administration or by use of gunboats to compel acquiescence by local powers. The first capitalist undertakings might be raw-material extraction enterprises (mines, plantations) or facilities to penetrate further into domestic markets (ports, railways), or both. Whatever they were, they required wage labor and local cash demand. Local state administrations, whether colonial or formally independent, accordingly had to adopt measures to further a cash market economy and a supply of wage labor. Public borrowing and taxation produced these effects, supported by other instruments of public policy.

The social relations of production were transformed at two extremities. Production of agricultural products for markets, whether for regional urban food or long-distance commercial single crops, tended toward a consolidation of larger holdings using more capital (irrigation, fertilizers) in relation to labor and also to extensive engrossment of land by agribusiness. This left only the less productive lands for subsistence farming, and it transformed erstwhile peasants into agricultural wage laborers or sent them to the urban slums. At the other extreme, capitalist industry employed a relative few in jobs, which, alongside government services, seemed secure and well paid by comparison with what most of the urban population could hope to receive. Commercial agriculture and industrial and government wage earners provided much of the cash flow into the local economy. Between them was a heterogeneous group engaged in activities variously styled as traditional, informal, or marginal, comprising several modes of social relations of production. There were small workshops employing wage labor in the enterprise-labor-market mode; simple commodity production by artisans and providers of services (tailors, barbers) and small traders, all of the self-employment mode; and peddlers, domestic servants, and para-

sitical and illicit activities of all kinds, encompassed in the primitive-labor-market mode.[39]

The industrial work force and the modernized capitalist
form of the state grew up together, both a consequence of external
capitalist penetration of a precapitalist formation. The initial
forms of social relations of production in industry were sometimes enterprise labor market, i.e., completely unregulated, sometimes transplanted forms of enterprise corporatism, sometimes
forms of bipartism, often introduced under the tutelage of colonial administrations in imitation of metropolitan labor practices.
These initial forms represented the adaptation of practices in the
capitalist homelands to the opportunities and conditions of the
lands of capitalist implantation.

The state, which initially performed under metropolitan
surveillance the tasks requisite to create the conditions for local
capitalist production, became later an instrument that local elites
could use to gain greater control over the development process
and greater returns from it. The independent Third World state
confronted these social relations of production generated by metropolitan capital and sought to bring them within its sphere of
control. Two methods were adopted to achieve this. The more
short-lived method was populist mobilization of workers into
political support for a regime pursuing nationalist developmental
goals (see chapter 7). The more durable alternative method was
state corporatism: the imposition by the state of a single trade
union structure confined to the big undertakings of the industrial
sector. By substituting state corporatism for the initial enterprise
corporatism of some foreign investors, the state gained a bargaining counter vis-à-vis the foreign investor and made workers dependent on it rather than on the enterprise. State corporatism
also provided a framework for clientelism. Foreign investors
could buy tolerance and favors from the public authorities, and
local politicians could buy political support with jobs. Thus state
corporatism became the generalized mode of social relations of
production in the industrial sectors of Third World capitalism.

In those few Third World countries that have succeeded
in achieving extended periods of high economic growth, the state
depends on its control over official unions to ensure the supply
of trainable, docile, and cheap labor on which this growth is

based. To the extent that it can prevent the emergence of an alternative labor leadership and prevent prolonged disruptions of production, state corporatism underwrites the profitability of industry. It has not generally been able either to gain the allegiance of workers or to supress entirely the expression of worker interests and worker discontents. This is especially so where there has been some experience of autonomous worker organization. An official union is generally regarded by workers as an arm of the state or of industry, not as a worker organization.

Discontent typically breaks out in spontaneous wildcat strike movements, directed as much against the official union bureaucracy as against employers and the state—all part of the power structure from which workers are in practice excluded. One of the most important and unanswerable questions about future directions in the Third World concerns the consequences of such social explosions. Insofar as they can be quickly repressed, they will be little more than minor disturbances on the route to dependent development. To the extent that they gain in intensity and in duration, and the authorities falter or fail in repression, they could herald the possibility of alternative social and political structures. The Cordobazo in Argentina in the spring of 1969 was a warning that pent-up social pressures threatened an economically weakened regime.[40] The oil workers of Iran, in the insurrection that overthrew the Shah in February 1979, joined their discontent to the making of a revolution.[41] Is a less revolutionary transformation of state corporatism conceivable? Spain's experience with the growth of illegal workers' commissions alongside the official labor organizations during the late years of Francisco Franco's regime suggests a model—a model that might be reflected in the evolution of the workers' movement in Brazil, especially in the Sao Paulo region, during a phase of relaxation of military-political power in the early 1980s.[42]

Problems arise in the application of the class concept to Third World workers. A common thesis was that the full-time industrial wage earners in these countries form a labor aristocracy whose trade unions have made an economistic defense of their special interests.[43] Some facts support this thesis. Certain groups of workers in major undertakings, e.g., mines, ports, and railways, have become organized in effective unions.[44] Even where formal ideological affiliations were rhetorically expressed in class and revolutionary terms, as in the case of Chilean copper workers affiliated to the Chilean CGT in the pre-Allende period, actual practice was economistic. Moreover, the cleavage between established and nonestablished workers that grew up in the industrialized countries was reproduced in Third World countries. A striking instance of this occurred in Peru when a radical military junta in February 1969 expropriated the private sugar haciendas and transformed them into worker self-managed cooperatives. The new self-management committees, rather than expand membership of the cooperatives, preferred to hire nonmembers as wage labor and thus created two categories of workers, one privileged, the other not, leading to strikes and the threat of strikes by nonmembers.[45] The established/nonestablished cleavage has arisen outside the sphere of capitalist industry, as noted above in the case of China.

Whether this tendency has formed a stabilized, conservative upper class of workers is a much more questionable proposition. Several factors militate against the formation of a class-conscious upper proletariat. One is that although wage workers may be occupationally differentiated, in Third World urban centers they are often not socially differentiated from the amorphous category of the urban poor. Even those who as wage workers earn higher and steadier incomes live no differently from the others because social custom requires that they support larger numbers of extended-family members. Wage workers may also take on a second job, almost always in the so-called "informal sector," and members of the extended household will also be working in this sector. Thus occupationally based notions of class are muted.

A second factor is that instrumental motivations are generally common among low-status Third World urban residents, something they probably share with all workers most of the time, and this is combined with the rugged durability of the petty-bourgeois myth of upward social mobility. Work is the means of gaining the income indispensable to survival, and beyond survival, of nourishing the hope of amassing enough savings to become a petty trader or self-employed producer. Where mobility hopes seem frustrated and working conditions are oppressive, resentments are typically articulated in "we/they" terms of a populist character rather than in the development of class consciousness.[46]

The potentiality for a revolutionary role on the part of wage labor cannot, however, be discounted. As noted, state corporatism has been more successful in screening out alternative leadership than in positively attracting the loyalties of wage earners. A political void remains, though it is difficult to fill, given the obstacles to building opposition organizations, whether they be based on residence or on the workplace. Factors that enhance the possibility that an outbreak of industrial conflict could be transformed into a challenge to political and social authority include: (1) a prior history of autonomous worker organizations, (2) the existence of "occupational communities" generating a greater intensity of social interaction among particular groups of workers,[47] (3) the prevalence of a relatively high level of education among the workers concerned, and (4) the presence of radical intellectuals among workers who take advantage of crises in society to transform prevailing instrumental attitudes into class solidarities.

Of course, the first two of these factors could be conducive to economistic labor-aristocracy forms of consciousness, as well as to a revolutionary class-solidarity perspective. Furthermore, even an initial class-based revolutionary movement may be engulfed in a comprehensive populist consciousness, expressing itself more in nationalist or religious symbols such as those of Shiite Islam in Iran. Third World industrial development is generating conditions propitious for work-related social protest. Possibly the potential for revolt arising directly out of the social relations in the production process is greater in the Third World than in the advanced capitalist countries, and this despite the repressive instruments available to Third World states and the limited and fragile nature of worker class consciousness. Whether revolt, where it occurs, takes a class or a populist form remains moot and will depend on the ideological preparation of workers and the nature of the leadership.

## Peasants and Marginals

The third quarter of the twentieth century saw the global incidence of violence shift from the industrial heartlands to Third

World peasant societies.[48] Two world wars centered in Europe were followed by the success of a peasant-based revolution in China and by wars successfully prosecuted by peasant fighters against the arms and techniques of advanced industrial countries in Indochina, Algeria, and southern Africa. Peasants were slaughtered or repressed in Indonesia and fought continuing struggles in much of Central and South America.

This encouraged the notion that peasants—the wretched of the earth[49]—were the genuine revolutionary class. Nevertheless, by the last quarter of the century, new revolutionary perspectives in peasant societies appeared dim. In those countries where peasant-based revolutions had succeeded, established revolutionary regimes took the villages in hand; they reestablished compliance by peasants in the leadership of urban elites. The dynamic of revolution in the countryside was quelled. In the nonrevolutionary areas of Third World capitalist development, two tendencies became salient. One was rearguard action fought by peasants against the transformation of peasant agriculture into capitalist farming. Since the peasants were always the losers, the result was an increase in urban marginality as peasants were extruded from the land and flocked to the cities. The other tendency stemmed from a realization by the managers of the world economy that capitalist development would not absorb more than a fraction of the world's rural populations. It took the form of an attempt to stabilize the rural population left outside the effective scope of the capitalist economy through self-help schemes aiming toward self- sufficiency.[50]

The growth in marginality is the numerical consequence of (1) rising populations, (2) significant declines in the numbers of people supported on the land as capitalist agriculture displaces peasant cultivation, and (3) very small increases in industrial employment. These three factors explain why marginality grows with the level of economic growth and is highest (reaching about 30 percent of the labor force in some cases) in those peripheral countries that have achieved some degree of industrialization in both agriculture and manufacturing.

Objectively, the growth in marginality must be regarded as potentially destabilizing for the social and political order, since it implies a concentration of larger than necessary "reserve armies" of labor in conditions of extreme poverty proximate to the centers of economic, social, and political power. In practice, this threat is muted by the subjective conditions of marginality. The first generation of marginals have rarely evinced radical behavior, being similar in this respect to most immigrants. Their concerns are survival and adaptation. Their outlook is dependent and instrumental, conducive to clientelism rather than group solidarity and collective action.[51] Uprooted from traditional belief-systems, they have sometimes taken to messianic movements whose concepts of salvation tend to depoliticize. Attempts have been made to organize marginals from without, sometimes by state or church in structures consistent with the political order (e.g., in Peru by the military regime of the 1960s), sometimes by political parties or guerilla groups as a support for revolutionary change (the MIR in Chile and the Tupamaros in Uruguay, for instance). The threat of the latter becomes the overt justification for the apparatus of a repressive state. In all cases, the shanty-towns, *bidonvilles*, *favelas*, *barriadas*, etc., where marginals are concentrated, become foyers of crime, most of which victimizes the marginals themselves but some of which spills over to threaten the more privileged communities. This continuing danger, whose causes manifestly increase rather than decrease, generates the mentality of the garrison state among the settled population, further advancing the dynamic of repression. Thus the very existence of marginality, quite apart from any real revolutionary threat it may pose (and this has not usually been very credible), becomes a catalyst of the military-bureaucratic state, a systemic cause of human rights violations and institutionalized repression.

## IN SUMMARY

The foregoing suggests that class formation is not a given, determined historical process but a very fluid one—a dialectic of opportunities created by changes in the structure of production and of praxis evolved in response to those opportunities. It also suggests that powerful forces are at work, supported by the dominant classes, that obstruct class formation among emerging subordinate social groups—occupational fragmentation, exploitation of ethnic and religious identities and symbols, helplessness before the coercive repression of states and dominant groups (both official police and military repression and unofficial death squads), consumerism, and the petty-bourgeois aspiration to individual upward mobility.

The world economic crisis since 1973 has put these obstructive factors to the test. So far, in general, they have held. If, however, the crisis is long enough and deep enough, these obstructions are likely in some places to give way.

In the advanced capitalist countries, where labor historically achieved its greatest political and social gains, the past centers of labor's power—trade unions and social-democratic political parties—are almost everywhere on the defensive. Mutations in the production process are revealing new social bases of discontent, but so far the existing organizations of the official left have not been willing or able to encompass these in a coherent social and political movement. To do so is a challenge to the unions and especially to left-wing politics. The building of a new counterhegemonic historic bloc is a long-term task for organic intellectuals working in constant interaction with the groups whose dissent from the established order makes them candidates for inclusion—it is a task for Gramsci's "modern prince," the party as creator of a new state.

In Third World countries, the obstructions to class formation may well give way more easily because social and political structures are less solid, especially in those countries that have experienced the greatest economic growth in recent decades. The breakthrough of opposition forces could be triggered by a debt crisis accompanied by a failed attempt to enforce an austerity program whose main burden would fall upon the popular classes. The question here is whether class formation, and the organizational and ideological work it implies, will have kept pace with the socially destabilizing effects of rapid economic growth. Varieties of populism may provide a more likely form of revolutionary consciousness than class identity. Third World workers may not have acquired the degree of self-consciousness, organizational capacity and ideological maturity necessary to become the basis of a counterhegemonic bloc.

Wherever social revolt does break out, the capacity of the world system to maintain order comes into play. For any significant shift in the relations between classes to take place such as would allow for the formation of new historic blocs, it would probably be necessary that breaks in the present social structures occur in both advanced capitalist and Third World countries. Thus there could be support within the most powerful states for the struggle of repressed social groups in the Third World— support at least sufficient to prevent external intervention of a repressive kind.[52]

# CONCLUSIONS

Action is purposive. Social action can be broadly divided into that which tends to conserve the existing order and that which tends to change it. At the outset, I indicated my purpose was a critical one—to search for the most useful way of understanding the social and political world in order to change it. The model of change I adopted was to seek out the contradictions within the existing order, since it is from these contradictions that change could emerge. Implicit here is the assumption that even the most apparently stable order contains some areas of conflict and uncertainty.

Critical awareness of potentiality for change must be distinguished from utopian planning, i.e., the laying out of the design of a future society that is to be the end goal of change. Critical understanding focuses on the process of change rather than on its ends; it concentrates on the possibilities of launching a social movement rather than on what that movement might achieve. Utopian expectations may be an element in stimulating people to act, but such expectations are almost never realized in practice. The consequences of action aiming at change are unpredictable. Once a historical movement gets under way, it is shaped by the material possibilities of the society in which it arises and by resistance to its course as much as by the (invariably diverse) goals of its supporters.

An option for change rather than preservation of the status quo is dictated more by dissatisfaction with the prevailing order and hope for improvement than by any blueprint for an alternative society. It may arise from skepticism that prevailing political and economic mechanisms will satisfy human needs in a manner that is safe both for individuals and for the fabric of society as a whole. It will likely be driven by a sense of injustice and a hope for greater equity in the distribution of physical necessities and in the diffusion of social power. In the minds of those who opt for change, the solution will most likely be seen as lying not so much in the enactment of a specific policy program as in the building of new means of collective action informed by a new understanding of society and polity. These, rather than policy planning, become the primary objects of action.

The examination of conditions favoring the maintenance or transformation of existing social orders has, in this study, been posed in terms of the three levels of production, the state, and world order. No one of these levels determines what happens at the other levels in a one-way causal relationship. Changes come about through mutually sustaining developments at all three levels. Conditions found to be propitious for transformation include: (1) a weakening of global hegemony tending toward a more permissive world order in which it would be difficult for a dominant power or group of dominant powers to enforce conformity to its norms; (2) the existence of forms of state that are not merely different but that have different effects on the stability of world order (neoliberal and neomercantilist developmentalist states are different forms that both support the same kind of world order); and (3) the mobilization of social forces into new counterhegemonic historic blocs, particularly if this happens concurrently in several countries, including some of the more powerful countries, with links of mutual understanding and support crossing national boundaries. These three conditions add up to a diffusion of power.

Such conditions prevailed at the dawn of the liberal era in the early decades of the nineteenth century, permitting a new system of production—manufacturing under competitive capitalism—to become the material foundation for a new world order and new kinds of state. The long period of decomposition of the liberal world order in the late nineteenth century recreated such conditions, out of which ultimately emerged the basis for a new hegemonic era, the Pax Americana. Similar tendencies are observable at present. The question is whether they are sufficiently far advanced to allow for new experiments in social and political organization, or whether the existing order, even weakened, is still strong enough to eliminate the political threat of a consolidation of counterhegemonic tendencies. The answer to this question can be given only in political action. People in Nicaragua, Mozambique and Poland bear the cost of raising it.

The implication for theory of the approach taken in this study toward the transformation of social, political, and world orders is, in the first place, to forsake the actors-interactions paradigm that has been so influential in social science, in favor of one grounded in historical structures. The objective of the latter approach is to discern the structures that give a framework for action and that form the actors. Historical structures express the unity of the subjective and the objective. A nation, a class, a religion are not real physical objects, yet they give real form to the human situation. They are ideas shared in the subjectivity of innumerable individuals who are real physical beings. In being so shared, these ideas constitute the social world of these same individuals. They attain objectivity in the structures that circumscribe human action. These structures are as much a part of the material existence of people as the food they eat and the clothes they wear.

Structures are in one sense prior to individuals. They are already present in the world into which individuals are born. People learn to behave within the framework of social and political structures before they can learn to criticize or oppose or try to change them. But structures are not in any deeper sense prior to the human drama itself, as some structuralist theory would have us believe. Structures are not "givens" (data), they are "mades" (facts)—made by collective human action and transformable by collective human action. This historically changeable character of structures is what distinguishes the historical structures approach from *structuralism*. My approach has looked, not at individual actions and events, but at evidence of changes in the frameworks that set limits for thinking and acting.

I have found such frameworks or structures at the three levels of inquiry: modes of social relations of production, forms of state, and structures of world order. I have also found structures of structures linking together these three levels in systems that have had a certain stability for a certain duration. The point of my inquiry has, however, been less concerned with the synchronic conditions reinforcing stability than with the diachronic developments explaining structural transformations.

The chosen starting point has been the level of production. This was premised on the proposition that production is a universal human activity that conditions all other human activities. Production results not only in the supply of the physical requisites of life but also in the creation of the institutions and relationships through which life goes on and through which the accumulation of resources that sustain power and authority takes place. Production of physical goods plus the production of historical structures together constitute the material reproduction of society.

It would seem that Marx meant something like this when he wrote about the mode of production, though different authors in the Marxian tradition have interpreted his meaning in different ways. It is important to distinguish my usage from some of the ways in which this term *mode of production* has been used. One of these other ways has been to think of the mode of production as the discovery of the inner essence of capital, giving rise to notions like the "logic" of capital or the "laws of motion" of capital. My approach has rather been to infer structures from observable historical patterns of conduct. A coherence or logical unity is imputed to these structures, but that coherence is conceived as breaking down over time when new patterns of coherence come into existence. There are no privileged points in time at which an inner logic is revealed (such as the mid-nineteenth-century apogee of competitive capitalism). It is recurrently necessary to reconstruct explanatory hypotheses of structural transformation from the standpoint of each successive epoch. The method and approach of previous attempts to understand change may remain useful, although the conclusions drawn from them will almost certainly have to be revised. Inner essences remain forever elusive, but mental constructs of the ways prevailing structures condition action, and the openings they allow for change, can be of practical help in channeling collective action for structural transformation.

Another difficulty inherent in the usage "mode of production" lies in Marx's expectation that capitalism would bring about a unification and homogenization of production processes. In *Capital* Marx foresaw the transformation of scattered small-scale production into large-scale production. He went on: "These changes result in the destruction of all the antiquated and transitional forms in which the dominion of capital is still to some extent concealed, so that the rule of capital now becomes direct and conspicuous."[1] This demystification of capital's autocracy through the homogenization of work would, he thought, hasten the prospects for revolution.

In the short term, Marx's forecast was correct with regard to a progressive homogenization of production processes. The triumph of Fordism vindicated him on this point. (His forecast of the ripening of conditions for revolution was less accurate, since it underestimated the extent to which the transformation of the liberal state into the welfare-nationalist state could preempt revolutionary potential.) In the longer term, however, production processes have become once again very diverse. Fordism never encompassed more than a fraction of total production. There are today a great variety of modes of production, using that term in the simple direct meaning of how things are produced. Capital has shifted strategy away from concentration into ever larger homogenized units of production and toward a greater diversification of different modes of social relations of production linked together in complex production systems, sometimes global in extent. As a consequence, the term *mode of production* has with some authors lost its simple direct meaning and come to refer rather to the linking together or coordinating of these diverse social relations of production into a single complex process of accumulation. It is this ambiguity in meaning, shifting between how things are produced to how accumulation takes place, that empties the concept *mode of production* of much analytical usefulness.

This ambiguity can be dispelled, so I have argued, by distinguishing analytically among the social relations of production, the process of reproduction, and the process of accumulation. Focusing on the social relations of production reveals a number of distinctive structures. These structures originated in different epochs under different political auspices and have been associated in their origins with different accumulation processes.

Thus the enterprise-labor-market mode of social relations of production became the preeminent mode during the era of competitive capitalism, but this mode came into a world in which household production, subsistence production, slavery, peasant-lord production, and self-employment survived from an earlier epoch and became restructured in a subordinate manner into a capitalist accumulation process. Similarly, when central planning became the preeminent mode in a redistributive accumulation process installed by revolution, some other modes continued or subsequently revived in a subordinate relationship to it. There seems, indeed, to be little justification for attributing an indelibly or essentially capitalist quality even to the enterprise labor market or to bipartite relations despite their unquestionable historical association with the rise and development of capitalism. Enterprise-labor-market relations have been revived in subordination to central planning, and there is no reason to exclude even a possible compatibility of bipartism with central planning (the Polish *Solidarnosc* was a failed attempt to achieve this).

If the social relations of production are best distinguished analytically from reproduction and accumulation processes in order to be able to examine how different modes of social relations of production have become linked together in complex systems of production, it is otherwise with reproduction and accumulation processes. These seem to conform more closely one to the other.

I made a first distinction between simple reproduction (the reconstitution in the next production cycle of the same society as produced in the first) and expanded reproduction (the generating of a surplus that enables the society to grow and change through successive cycles of production). Only in expanded reproduction can one speak meaningfully of development, and accumulation is the means to development. Expanded reproduction, development, and accumulation designate different aspects of the same process.

I distinguish two basic modes of development: capitalist and redistributive modes. Both accumulate in order to grow. Both may organize production in similar ways in order to produce surplus for accumulation, but the mechanisms driving the accumulation process are different. Capitalist development is driven by opportunities for realizing profits in the market, and perceptions of these opportunities determine what is produced. In redistributive development what is produced is determined by decision of the redistributors, i.e., the political authorities. Subject to these distinctive mechanisms, there remains a range of choice in regard to the combinations of modes of social relations of production that are possible under either mode of development.

These combinations and the dominant and subordinate linkages among modes of social relations of production delineate the social structure of accumulation, i.e., the manner in which production in one mode subsidizes production in another or transfers surplus to that other (e.g., household production subsidizes both central planning in redistributive development and the dominant tripartite or enterprise-corporatist modes in capitalist development). If, hitherto, there has been a marked similarity in production methods under capitalist and redistributive development, this is to be attributed more to the effects of international competition (ultimately competition in military preparedness) between the two systems than to the inherent nature of either system.

Although production was the point of departure of this study, the crucial role, it turns out, is played by the state. States create the conditions in which particular modes of social relations achieve dominance over coexisting modes, and they structure either purposively or by inadvertence the dominant-subordinate linkages of the accumulation process. States thus determine the whole complex structure of production from which the state then extracts sufficient resources to continue to exercise its power. Of course, states do not do this in an isolated way. Each state is constrained by its position and its relative power in the world order, which places limits on its will and its ability to change production relations. A major point of emphasis in this study has been on the crucial importance of the state's relationship to production.

States undoubtedly act with a certain autonomy. Each state has evolved, through its own institutions and practices, certain consistent notions of interest and modes of conduct that can be termed its particular *raison d'état*. This autonomy is, however, conditioned by both internal and external constraints. State autonomy, in other words, is exercised within a structure created by the state's own history. The internal aspect of this structure lies in the historic bloc. The external aspect lies in the way the military and financial constraints of the world system limit the state's options and the extent to which its historic bloc is penetrated by class forces that transcend or are outside its own borders.

Class forces, and financial and military constraints, as argued above, all derive from production. They are different forms of power into which the accumulated results of the production process have been transformed. In being so transformed they have become divorced from the production process to become forces that can either maintain or change production relations. In defining the parameters of the state these forces mark both the dependence of the state on production and its dominance over the development of productive forces and production relations.

The world economic crisis following 1973 appears as a threshold marking a transition from one world order to another. It may prove to be comparable in importance to the crisis that began a century earlier and heralded the end of Pax Britannica. Even if it be premature to pronounce this historical verdict, it makes sense to think through the implications of tendencies now apparent on the premise that major structural changes are possible.

The crisis has been generated by the neoliberal order itself. This order, based for a long time quite successfully on a corporative social contract, on state-administered welfare, and on an internationalizing of production and internationalizing of the state regulated by international finance, created through these very practices the conditions of its undoing: stagflation, the fiscal crisis of the state, and the international debt crisis. The responses to the crisis by the dominant political and social forces have wittingly or unwittingly exacerbated internal and international polarizations. Internally, they have brought about a polarization between enterprise-corporatist protected workers, on the one hand, and a variety of much more socially vulnerable peripheralized workers, on the other. Internationally, strong pressures have been brought to bear on Third World countries to adopt

policies that would lay the burden of meeting their international
financial obligations on the popular classes. Initially, the consequence of the crisis has been to strengthen capital's power in
relation to labor and thereby provoke the disintegration of the
neoliberal historic bloc in the advanced capitalist countries. At
the same time, externally imposed fiscal discipline has choked
off some local developmental possibilities in the Third World.

In the longer run, the diversification of production relations results in the growth of a number of categories of producers
not included as full-fledged participants in existing forms of state.
These include nonestablished and self-employed workers who
have not been organized into trade unions or mobilized by political parties. In Third World countries new industrial workers and
growing numbers of urban marginals or informal sector producers
have not been included in industrial or political processes. There
is cynicism and alienation among workers in the countries of
"actually existing socialism." Within states of all kinds, there
exists a vast crisis of representation that would have to be resolved as a step toward the building of new historic blocs.

Beyond the crisis of representation there looms a crisis
concerning the nature of work and its place in society. This comes
about as a consequence of the development of the technical
capacity to produce abundance. Through all of history, the task
of physical reproduction—the making of what is necessary for
biological survival and for the nourishment of political power—
has absorbed the greater part of human effort. Now an era dawns
when most of this effort can be done by machines with relatively
little human effort. A vast reserve of potential human effort
thereby becomes available that could be devoted to social reproduction and development—the building and running of institutions and patterning of social relations. So long as physical reproduction has been the dominant task, social reproduction has
seemed to be constrained by blind necessity. Institutions installed
by different forms of compulsion, from the military coercion of
feudal lordship to the market coercion of capitalist property relations, took on the appearance of inevitability. People remained
for long stretches of time in a condition of passivity with regard
to the social order, so fully absorbed were they by the tasks of
physical survival. Where frustrations built up, these burst out in

revolutionary spasms, followed again by periods of social passivity. The concerns voiced recently by some ideologues of the established order that democracies were threatened by "ungovernability" was a signal that perhaps that passivity and abstentionism toward active involvement in political and social action, which these ideologues considered to be a condition for political stability, might be giving place to more active participation. If the reality is not obvious at present, the fear of it is.

A variety of practices exist that obstruct any such shift in the balance of human effort away from tasks of physical reproduction toward opportunities for social development. One is consumerism, which increases demands for unnecessary goods and promotes obsolescence and waste and thereby calls forth ever higher levels of physical production. Another is excessive individualism, whereby the duplication of private facilities is preferred to public or collective facilities. Yet another is the arms race, absorbing a substantial share of productive capacity and demanding ever more in response to a perceived mutual threat.

The prospect of such a shift in the balance of human effort, even vaguely perceived, appears as threatening to many. It is threatening, in the first place, to those benefiting most from the existing order—threatening to governmental and political practices, to the authority of employers, to established trade union leadership, to the deference shown by the public to the social policy bureaucracies, and so forth. It was on behalf of these interests that the cry of "ungovernability" was raised. It is threatening, also, to deeply entrenched notions of morality touching the work ethic and conventional sex roles. These have functionally reconciled people to a world preoccupied with physical reproduction and have given the social institutions of that world the aura of sanctity.

The existence of productive capacity that could satisfy the essential physical needs of the whole world's population contrasts with a situation in which that capacity is underutilized, and there is waste, inequity, and danger—threat of nuclear destruction, bloody conventional wars in the Third World, environmental damage, unemployment. Nowhere, perhaps, is the contrast more marked than between the capacity of agricultural science to produce abundant food with small numbers of workers and the soil erosion that brings recurrent famine to millions of marginalized subsistence cultivators.

The Cold War and the profit motive have been the two principal dynamics determining what and how much is produced and how it is distributed. Any shift in the balance of human effort away from physical and toward social reproduction would soon confront and challenge the implications of these two dynamics. The prospect of allowing people a greater scope for social participation and inventiveness is likely to increase pressures to tame both dynamics in the interests of a rational use of global resources and a more equitable distribution. Planning (which contains its own risks of inefficiencies, waste, and inequities) would have to be reconciled with variety in the needs and demands of different groups and with free expression in the creation of new social practices. A more participant society, one in which the balance of effort had swung from physical to social reproduction, could be the means of achieving that reconciliation.

Such a society will not come from wishing for it. It can be built only through a political movement capable of uniting sufficient of the segmented elements of existing societies into a counterhegemonic historic bloc. That task begins where part 3 of this book ended: with an awareness of the present social divisions generated in the production process, of the conditions of existence of these various groups and their modes of perceiving the world, and of their potential directions of movement.

# NOTES

## Preface

1. Several articles foreshadow earlier stages in the thinking that has gone into this volume, including Robert W. Cox (1971):139–64; Cox, Harrod, et al. (1972); Cox (1977c):113–37; and Cox (1973).

2. Some preliminary reflections on the levels of state and world order are to be found in Cox (1981):126–55; and Cox (1982): 37–58.

3. Gottfried Wilhelm Leibniz (1646–1716) named the irreducible simple unity or spiritual substance a monad. Monads, for Leibniz, had both individuality and development; each monad, differentiated from every other, had its own internal principle that guided its changes until all its possibilities were exhausted. Each monad also had a particular perspective on the world. For Leibniz, however, monads could not act upon one another; they were completely programmed from within at the moment of their creation, see Leibniz (1934). The monad concept is adopted here as a heuristic device, not as a metaphysical absolute. In particular, the notion that monads are not acted upon from outside is rejected. The sense in which the term applies here is one in which particular patterns of production relations are examined as distinctive forms of social life so as to discern their characteristic dynamics *as though* they developed according to a distinctive internal principle. This is merely, of course, a first step. Subsequently, these patterns must be examined in their interrelationships, i.e., explicitly recognizing mutual influences. On the contribution of Leibniz to the historicist concepts of individuality and development, see Meinecke (1972):15–30.

## Theme

1. This position was, for instance, taken by Kerr, et al. (1960) in a book that had a certain ideological impact in and beyond the United States in the early 1960s. A similar message was conveyed by Bell (1960).

2. Bahro (1978): esp. 183–202.

3. Gorz (1982): esp. 15.

4. Reinhard Bendix (1967) uses the terms "limited applicability concepts" and "contrast concepts" to designate such models of historical structures.

5. This is a standpoint of much French structuralism, from Claude Levy-Strauss to Louis Althusser, and also of the linguistics of Noam Chomsky. See Levy-Strauss (1966); Althusser and Balibar (1970):111–12; and Chomsky (1972).

6. This was the view of Giambattista Vico, who did not, of course, use the term *structure* but rather *cosa*, a rendition of the Latin *res*, which can be understood as "institution." Language and law were, for Vico, such institutions. See Thomas Goddard Bergin and Max Harold Fisch "Introduction" to their English translation of *The New Science of Giambattista Vico* (1970): li–lii. For Vico, "the nature of institutions is nothing but their coming into being *(nascimento)* at certain times and in certain guises" *(ibid,* para. 147, p. 22) and "the world of civil society has certainly been made by men, and . . . its principles are therefore to be found within the modifications of our own human mind" *(ibid.,* para. 331, pp. 52–53). I have elaborated the notion of historical structure in Cox (1981).

7. Before speaking of modes of development, it is well to consider the more nearly comprehensive notion of the mode of reproduction, i.e., the processes whereby societies are extended through time by giving birth to, raising, and educating a new generation and placing its members in their economic and social roles. Throughout much of human history, reproduction often seemed to have been a circular process, constantly repeated, through which the same structure of society was reproduced. Agrarian-based societies reproduced themselves in the forms either of small subsistence communities or of peasant villages part of whose product was extracted by a dominant political-religious class that took no part in material production but saw to the reproduction of the social-political order. Reproduction tended to be a circular, no-growth, nonaccumulative process.

Development implies a reproduction process with both accumulation and a consequential change of structures. (No positive valuation is necessarily intended in the use of the term *development,* e.g., as is conveyed by a term such as *progress.)* Development was initiated through the capitalist mode. In capitalism, the labor hired by the capitalist produces more than is required for its own reproduction. The surplus is taken by the capitalist who uses it, not for consumption and conspicuous display (like those extracted from precapitalist agrarian production), but for investment in expanding the capacity to produce in the next cycle, either by hiring more workers or by installing machinery that enables the same workers to produce more in the same time. Of course, the capitalist as a person may also indulge in excess consumption but to the extent that he does so he is not behaving as a capitalist.

The term *capitalism* is used here exclusively in this sense as a mode of development that breaks the cycle of continuous reproduction and introduces a purposive time dimension, an upward spiral of accumulation, investment, expanded reproduction, and so on. The term *capitalist* is not used in this study to apply to a single mode of *production.* Indeed, the capitalist mode of development has spawned several distinctive modes of social relations of production. To bracket these all together as a single capitalist mode of production confuses things that are significantly distinct. Moreover, the capitalist mode of development links modes of production that are distinctly noncapitalist into the capitalist process of accumulation.

The capitalist mode of development does not depend on individual capitalists or ultimately even on private property. It consists in (1) the appropriation of the difference between, on the one hand, the costs of maintaining and reproducing the labor force and productive equipment, and on the other, the returns from the marketing of what is produced; and (2) the use of this appropriated surplus to expand production in ways that will generate the largest additional surplus in the next production cycle as indicated by market demand. Who or what—e.g., individual capitalist or technostructure or state—actually appropriates or reinvests profits is fundamentally unimportant or nonessential to the mode of development, provided reinvestment is geared to profit-maximizing in a market context.

The redistributive mode of development also aims at expanded reproduction, but it departs from profit maximization as the criterion for investment in favor of a teleology that fixes goals for society and a production strategy for their incremental attainment independent of market or profitability. Welfare, in redistributive development, is a matter of political definition and conscious political choice, not something left to the market. Exponents of the capitalist mode of development maintain, of course, that welfare is in fact promoted through the market by an unconscious process, aggregating the whole mass of individual market decisions, that determines not only what people really want but how it can be most efficiently provided. Critics point out that capitalist development promotes social and interregional inequalities, that consumer choices are manipulated by advertising so that freedom of choice is an illusion, and that profit-maximizing growth, by taking little or no account of social costs, reduces welfare. Critics of redistributive development for their part argue that it fosters privilege, inequalities, and inefficiencies. It is no part of our intent here to argue the relative merits of these opposed perspectives. These arguments are examined in Lindblom (1977). The point to be made is that redistributive development substitutes consciously chosen social goals for the unconscious process of welfare promotion purported to lie in the market.

Just as capitalist development does not necessarily imply individual capitalists, so redistributive development does not necessarily imply a big state political bureaucracy. The Soviet central planning system did in fact create such a bureaucracy. Chinese central planning, which oscillated between antibureaucratic and bureaucratic phases, seems now also to be set in the direction of bureaucratization. Communal redistributionism can function with a good deal less bureaucratic superstructure and more scope for internal participation. Leftist critics of the bureaucratization of Soviet planning envisage nonbureaucratic methods for making the plan more responsive to social pressures and providing people with the necessary information and possibilities of intervention.

Historically redistributive development has not appeared as a successor emerging out of capitalist development. It arose in social formations that were very largely precapitalist, in which the capitalist mode of development had made only limited impact and was far from having transformed traditional reproduction (Russia and China). There it was not a successor to capitalism but an alternative mode of development.

8. Social class, as used in the present study, designates a real historical relationship and not merely an analytical category existing only in the analyst's mind. Class in this real historical sense is based on production, i.e., it is based on the fact that a certain group of people occupy a common position in production relations. But people who are members of a social class also know themselves to be members and they recognize others as members of their own or another social class. Class involves awareness of sharing common experiences of life and work, common perceptions of the cleavages in society (of being distinguished from and opposed to another class), and most likely of expressing this sense of community in collective action and shared aspirations. Whether or not classes have formed is a historical question that can be demonstrated only by historical evidence. I am adopting here *grosso modo* the standpoint of Thompson (1968).

Delicate problems arise in defining classes and relationships among classes. One extreme to be avoided is a priori deductive definition: this leads to the proposition that classes must exist because of the very juxtaposition of social groups in production, that a certain form of consciousness can be deduced from class position (other forms that may be found to prevail in practice being "false" consciousness), and that classes have historical roles attributed to them by a general theory of history. The other extreme to be avoided is an empiricism that aggregates the attitudes and opinions reported by a number of individuals who have been predetermined for survey purposes as members of the targeted social group; class consciousness is then assumed to be the aggregate of individual consciousnesses. Neither of these extremes gets at the historical phenomenon of class. To do this, it is necessary to relate the development of consciousness to real events and historical processes. A priori deductions concerning class lead to a dogmatism that may reconfirm the convictions of committed activists possessed of a sense of historical mission but are a poor guide to social and political practice. Empiricism reveals states of passive, manipulated consciousness that may well be transformed under pressure of events that channel individual responses into collective action. The sources of class identities and orientations are to be sought in events and changes of real social, economic, and political situations in which particular social groups are confronted by specific problems: either these events provoke a response through common action or they reveal an incapacity for action.

The social practices, i.e., the routinized means of collective action, of the social groups generated in the production process have taken forms oriented respectively to the spheres of production and of the state. In the sphere of production, these forms include trade unions and employer associations; in the sphere of the state, political parties. Trade unionism by itself has not usually become sufficiently free of the immediate context of production to be able to pose a challenge to the productive system. It has been immersed within that system and seeks its own advantage within it—seeks the maximum available to organized workers without threatening the system itself. Compared to trade unions, political parties of subaltern classes have had a greater capacity for autonomy with a potential for transforming production relations. Political parties are not the spontaneous emanations of social classes. Rather, where class-based political parties have come into existence, they have themselves been the means of arousing and channeling class consciousness. There is common ground between the Leninist and Gramscian views of party—and even between these and the oligarchy theory of Robert Michels based on trade union and social democratic politics or the elite theories of Gaetano Mosca and Vilfredo Pareto—in regard to the critical importance of organizational cadres. Gramsci's theory has, however, given a superior formulation to the relationship between cadres and class consistent with his broader understanding of the relationship between social being and social consciousness. The cadres cannot be merely manipulative; they are bound by the objective class experience within which they work. They can do no more than to give that experience consciousness of its own potential. Gramsci's views are to be found in Gramsci (1971) and in the full Italian edition (1975). Lenin's views on the roles of party and trade unions are expressed in *What Is To Be Done?* (1947). The elitist theories are in Michels (1959); Mosca (1939); and Pareto (1963). See also Hughes (1979): ch. 7; and Burnham (1943).

9. Since Gramsci's writings are fragmentary, unfinished, and unsystematic, they lend themselves to varying interpretations. They contain flashes of insight, many of which are not fully developed. What follows may be considered by some readers as developments of Gramsci's thought rather than propositions directly attributable to him in a literal sense. I am more concerned with following his inspiration than with textual exegesis. Generally speaking, there are two main tendencies in the interpretation of Gramsci. One comes out of the Marxist-Leninist

tradition and considers Gramsci primarily in relation to the issues of that current. An outstanding example is Buci-Glucksmann (1975), though unfortunately it is much influenced by the French structuralism of Althusser, which is wholly out of tune with the historicity of Gramsci's thought. The other tendency sees Gramsci more in relation to the Italian tradition from Machiavelli to Croce, including non-Italians like Georges Sorel, who was more appreciated in Italy than in his own country. Femia (1981) is a good example in the English language.

10. Gramsci's enlargement of the concept of the state includes the limited conventional idea of the state as the machinery of coercion or the monopoly of the legitimate use of physical force within a given territory, i.e., legal structure and machinery for law making, policy formulating, and enforcement through administration, police, and military. It also includes the machinery of organizing consent through education, opinion shaping, and ideology formation and propagation. This latter sphere of organizing consent covers many agencies usually thought of as nonstate or private—aspects of civil society such as political parties, the press, religion, and cultural manifestations. It does not include all such agencies but only such as tend to consolidate and stabilize a certain form of established power.

This enlargement makes the strength of the state much more comprehensively intelligible than the narrow coercive notion alone does, but it does not say anything specific about the content of the state, what it is in a concrete historical instance. This "what it is" is conveyed by the notion of the *blocco storico* or historic bloc (Gramsci, 1971: 366, 377, 418). The state, for Gramsci, cannot be separated as a technical instrument or agency, whether of coercion or of the organization of consent, from the social classes that sustain it. The historic bloc is the term applied to the particular configuration of social classes and ideology that gives content to a historical state. The term directs our attention to the analysis of the concrete nature of a particular state.

To conceive the content of the state—what it is—as the historic bloc focuses attention on certain problems in the history of a state, namely, what configuration of social forces lies at the origin of the formation of the historic bloc? What contradictions within the formed historic bloc are contained and minimized by its unifying ideology? Which social forces are the potential bases for a rival historic bloc? And is a political practice emerging that can give substance and cohesion to this alternative? These questions point both to the explanation of phases of relative stability in terms of the consolidation of a historic bloc and equally to explanation of phases in which the nature of a state is being transformed by the decomposition of an erstwhile established historic bloc and its displacement by a new one. The general concept of the state—machinery of coercion plus machinery for the organization of consent—is content empty. As soon as states are recognized as having content they become particularized and differentiated.

Historians have observed a stability and continuity of goals and methods of exercising power in particular states that is independent of the actual personnel holding positions of authority. This gives rise to the notion of national interest, or more accurately, of *raison d'état*, i.e., that for any particular state there is a discoverable logic of action necessary to maintain its power internally (with reference to its citizens or subjects) and externally (with reference to other states or other external forces). See especially Friedrich Meinecke (1957).

Closer historical inquiry will reveal that although there are indeed prolonged episodes of stability in *raison d'état* for particular states, there are also discontinuities, phases of upheaval in previously accepted goals and ways of doing things, following which a new *raison d'état* is inaugurated. Such discontinuities are not brought about merely by changes in the personnel of government; they involved more profound changes in the structure of societies. This leads to a deeper level in the concept of a state, namely, the complex of social class relations to which the raison d'état conforms, i.e., the historic bloc. This complex of social class relations, with its hierarchies of dominance and subordination and its cleavages and alliances, sets the practical limits for feasible goals and methods of exercising power. One can say that during periods of relative stability characterized by an identifiable raison d'état, this social substratum has been absorbed tacitly and unconsciously into the state. In these periods it is so much taken for granted in the framing and discussion of political action as to be virtually forgotten. Discontinuities occur when there are significant movements and shifts of social power relations among classes. During such periods, classes and ideologies and the political parties that shape and guide them form rival historic blocs contending over the very nature of the state. If one bloc displaces another, a new state is born and with it a new raison d'état.

Consequently, in the histories of particular states, one can look for disjunctions between successive forms of raison d'état as clues to a succession of forms of state. Then, with regard to each form, it becomes possible to reconstitute not only the persistent goals and methods of exercising power but also the particular social configuration to which they conform and the ideology through which the compatibility of social power and political authority is expressed.

Structural similarities between several states remove these forms from the particularity of national histories so that they become expressions of a common type. Thus forms of state become concepts of wider applicability, each positing certain conditions and a certain structure, and each containing certain internal contradictions likely to lead ultimately to its transformation into another form.

11. On hegemony as used here, see Gramsci (1971) passim and Cox (1983).

## Part 1. The Social Relations of Production

1. It is important to distinguish various Marxist usages of the term mode of production from the usage in this book of the term mode of social relations of production. I have deliberately avoided the use of the term mode of production because it has been given different meanings by different authors and so has lost whatever analytical value it may have had. An analytically scrupulous study of Marx by Cohen (1978) attributes three distinct meanings to Marx. The first equates mode of production with the technical or material way in which things are produced, or with what is sometimes called the labor process. Thus small-holder cultivation, the putting-out system, and the factory are different modes of production. By this reckoning, the Soviet truck assembly line would not differ in mode of production from the Detroit assembly line, or the Soviet state farm from the Midwestern wheat farm. The second of Marx's meanings is more complex, grouping together a number of social aspects of production. These include (1) the purpose of production, i.e., whether it is for use (direct consumption) or exchange (marketing), and, if for exchange, whether or not for the purpose of capital accumulation; (2) the form in which surplus labor is extracted from the worker, e.g., through feudal services or the realization of profit on the market; and (3) the mode of exploitation, i.e., the social mechanisms whereby workers are obliged to work. e.g., direct domination of serfdom versus the impersonalized compulsion to earn a wage felt by laborers who do not own means of production. The third of Marx's meanings, according to Cohen, was a combination of the first two or "the entire technical and social configuration" of production.

Cohen was concerned with economic structure, or the set of relationships or framework of power through which things are produced. A mode, he pointed out, is a way or a manner, not a set of relations. Whatever the merits of this distinction— and I am not sure that I would follow him here, since mode is also commonly used to mean the most frequent instance of a quality and thus as having the character of a type—Cohen obviously considered the term *mode of production* to be more ambiguous than clarifying, and he abandoned its use in his explication of Marx.

Cohen's rendition of Marx's combined usage is not very different from the way in which I have attempted to spell out in the present work the concept of a mode of social relations of production. However, the ambiguity of the term itself has been compounded by yet other usages current today, and this persuades me to avoid its use. One such common Marxian usage distinguishes epochs in a theory of history as modes of production, epochs that succeed one another as totalities linked by a dialectic between the development of productive forces and the relations of production. See Banaji (1977). In a similar manner, Wallerstein (1974a, b) uses "capitalist mode of production" to characterize a whole world system coming into being from the sixteenth century. Wallerstein conceives this system as linked by relations of exchange and accumulation, even though it comprises a variety of ways in which the things exchanged have been produced, e.g., by free labor, quasi-servile sharecroppers, and various forms of coerced labor. Louis Althusser (see Althusser and Balibar, 1970) made of the capitalist mode of production a Marxist equivalent of Talcott Parson's social system, a comprehensive structure of structures determined "in the last instance" by production but including, as "relatively autonomous" regions or levels or instances, state and ideology, etc. Still others have argued from Althusser's stress on "relative autonomy" the possibility of an "articulation" of distinct modes of production—though here, once again, the definition of mode of production becomes vaguer and more uncertain. See Foster-Carter (1978). In the present book modes of development and accumulation are distinguished from modes of social relations of production (see note 7 to the Theme).

## Chapter 1 The Dimensions of Production Relations

1. On intersubjective meanings, see Charles Taylor (1976) and Cox (1981).
2. Polanyi (1957):68–76.
3. The point is developed in chapter 9, below.
4. Landes (1969):54–62.
5. Braverman (1974):85–121.
6. Anderson (1974):371–87. In the wake of the Turkish conquest, peasant tenure was guaranteed and local ethnic nobility displaced. Concurrently, peasants in Eastern Europe were being subjected to stricter control and exactions. With the decline of Turkish power, by the eighteenth century, Turkish provincial landlords and the taxgatherers between them were taking two thirds of the peasant's output.
7. The contrast between community and association was made by Ferdinand Tönnies (1957) in the concepts *gemeinschaft* and *gesellschaft*. The formulation has been justly criticized for ideological bias. Tönnies looked back nostalgically to the warmth of *gemeinschaft*, confronted with the disintegration of social life in industrializing and urbanizing Europe. Subsequently, values in dominant social theory were reversed: modernization and rationalization of social relations became the goal and earlier forms of society were lumped together as "traditional," i.e., to be superseded. Eric Wolf (1982:10–13) has recently pointed out that such a dualist view of social process is nonhistorical in its singular disregard of the many differences among so-called "traditional" societies and in its unconscious acceptance of

an idealized U.S. society as the model of modernity. With these caveats concerning the ideological traps to be avoided, the contrasts between community and association, status and contract, remain useful tools of analysis.

8. Weber (1930), (1946):302–22.

9. Note Karl Polanyi's (1957):43–55 insistence that for most of humanity through most of its history, the economy, including all laboring activity, has been embedded in society. The exceptional case has been the self-regulating market of early capitalism which separated the economy from society or disembedded it.

10. There is a parallel here with Max Weber's (1946:245–64) charismatic type of authority that tends to become routinized into traditional or legal bureaucratic forms.

11. Points discussed here have been dealt with also in Cox (1977c).

12. Bendix (1963):8–10.

13. Hilton (1978):9–29. On the affinity of social rebels to heretical doctrines, see Engels (1956):part 2 and Cohn (1970). On the Anabaptists, who recuperated some of the peasant anger following the repression of 1525, see Clasen (1972). The Dolcinians of northern Italy provide the backdrop to Umberto Eco's novel *The Name of the Rose* (1983).

14. This loss of legitimacy in popular culture is well illustrated by von Grimmelschausen's picaresque novel of the Thirty Years' War *Adventures of a Simpleton* (n.d.).

15. Bahro (1978):176.

16. One significant reported case of strike action in the Soviet Union was at Novocherkassk in June 1962. It was triggered by a rise in food prices. See Boiter (1964):33–43. The Hungarian dissidents George Konrád and Ivan Szelényi (1979: 175) write: "It is hardly a coincidence that whenever a political upheaval culminates in a worker's rebellion . . . the first order of business for workers is to form their own, noncorporative organizations: workers' councils or soviets."

17. The United Nations has inherited from the League of Nations the task of investigating reports of the existence of slavery. This is done by the Working Group on Slavery, which reports to the Subcommission on Prevention of Discrimination and Protection of Minorities of the Human Rights Commission. In practice the definition of slavery has been broadened to include many situations in which people are not free to withdraw labor or in which conditions of superexploitation exist. See, e.g., Updating of the Report on Slavery, E/CN.4/Sub. 2/1982/20 and Add. 1. The conditions of superexploitation range from child labor, rampant in many countries, including European countries like Greece and Spain, as well as Brazil and other Third World countries; debt servitude, which continues to exist in India despite its outlawing; practices like the "sale" of sugar cane cutters by the Haitian authorites to the Dominican Republic—see Lemoine (1981); and traffic in women and children for the white-slave trade.

18. See Cox (1971) for the original definitions with which this process began.

19. The structural definitions included in this chapter are preliminary ones. The three volumes of this study that follow are devoted to an examination in depth, one after another, of these modes. The in-depth studies will, of course, give greater nuance and a fuller sense of developmental movement within each mode than is possible in this preliminary identification of its characteristics. The preliminary statement of the concept as structure is a necessary stage—a first approximation— in a research process in which the elaboration of the concept in the next three volumes is a further stage.

## Chapter 2. Simple Reproduction

1. On "embeddedness" of economy in society, see Polanyi et al (1971):67–83; Polanyi (1957):43–55, on "natural economy" in general; see also Polanyi (1966a) and Polanyi (1966b). The subsistence mode of social relations of production as described here is dealt with under different names by authors using somewhat different conceptualizations. Sahlins (1972:esp. 76–77) analyzes it as the "domestic mode of production," in which he includes production within extended families and also in lineage and village communities that allow for more extensive collaboration and division of labor than is possible within small-family producing units. Rey (1975) and Davidson (1978:54) both prefer the term *lineage mode of production* to designate communities in which most production is for local self-sufficiency, but there is also an accumulation of exploitable labor power in the hands of the heads of the communities. This term puts the emphasis on the political implications of lineage heads being able to manipulate this surplus labor power to become chiefs, pointing the way toward kingship, statehood, and the consolidation of a class-structured society. Catherine Coquery-Vidrovitch uses the term *African mode of production* in Gutkind and Waterman, eds. (1977):77–92. Wolf (1982:esp. 88–100) calls the same kind of structure the "kin-ordered mode of production." Friedmann (1980) prefers to set aside the concept mode of production as being analytically ambiguous and attempts to specify *forms* of production as concepts for the analysis of agrarian structures. The form of production is to be defined through a double specification of the unit of production and the social formation. She thus differentiates agricultural production using household labor according to the type of social formation in which it takes place, particularly in regard to whether there is limited factor mobility or active factor markets. The degree of commoditization becomes the critical variable for Friedmann, just as the degree of state formation and class formation is for Wolf. Friedmann's typology does not, however, include the subsistence form discussed here, though it does succeed in differentiating small-holder farming, sharecropping, combinations of these two, and hacienda or *latifundia* production. The problem pointed to by Friedmann, (the distinction between production unit and social formation) is discussed in a different sense by Banaji (1977) who takes the "historical laws of motion" as the basis for defining modes of production, making specific relations of production (and by implication what Friedmann calls *forms* of production) intelligible only in terms of a prior knowledge of these laws of motion. He concludes that "subsistence production . . . figures . . . as the specific *form of reproduction of labour-power* [italics in original] within a capitalist process of production." It becomes misleading, according to Banaji, to regard it as a specific, separate mode of production (e.g., a "domestic mode of production") in a system of modes of production dominated by capitalism" (p. 34). My reasons for rejecting this approach are discussed in footnote 1 to part 1 above.

2. Wolf (1982).

3. Sahlins (1972):37.

4. Wolf (1982:186–89) points out that economic power is not necessarily or even primarily the basis of authority in such communities. The *potlach* of the Northwest Pacific Coast Indians, for instance, validated chieftainship but did not create it.

5. Stavenhagen (1981):168–70.

6. Davidson (1978) categorizes this complementarily of subsistence cultivation with export enclave industries as the *colonial mode of production*. This is another instance to be added to those noted above (note 1 to chapter 2) of using

*mode of production* to apply to a complex of interconnected modes of social relations of production.

7. Wolf (1982):79–88, following Amin (1973) uses the term *tributary mode of production* to designate what we here call the peasant-lord mode of social relations of production. These authors put together both the Asiatic mode of production and the feudal mode of production in Marx's work as, for analytical purposes, constituting a single tributary mode in which surplus is extracted from peasant agricultural producers by a ruling class.

8. Anderson (1974):520–49; Wolf (1982):49–52, 55.

9. The importance of the clan as a link between members of the extracting class and the peasant communities supporting it has been stressed by Moore, (1967): 207–8, 469–70, 478. Noting that the revolutionary potential of peasant societies under the impact of "modernization" has varied considerably, he accounts for part of this variation by the following: ". . . an important contributing cause of peasant revolution has been the weakness of the institutional links binding peasant society to the upper classes, together with the exploitative character of this relationship" (p. 478). These links were stronger in the Japanese than in the Chinese case and much less strong in the Islamic context than in the Chinese.

10. See Anderson (1974):379–93; Wolf (1982): 367.

11. See Hilton, in Landsberger, ed. (1974); Hilton's introduction in Hilton, ed. (1978); Brenner (1976); and Brenner (1977). See also Wallerstein (1974a):25–27, 109–17, 139, 254–61, 293–94.

12. Anderson (1974):435–61.

13. Wallerstein (1974a):90–100.

14. Wolf, (1969).

15. Braudel, (1979):450–57. Braudel wrote "Le déracinement social, à une telle échelle, se pose comme le plus gros problème de ces sociétés anciennes" (p. 456).

16. Such movements flourished among the workers of the new and expanding textile industry of Flanders in the thirteenth century, uprooted from rural village life yet not protected by the urban guilds, and among shepherds, cowherds, and vagabonds in the same northern regions of rising population. Later, in the fifteenth and sixteenth centuries, when the cloth industry in Flanders was in decline and industrial and population growth passed to south Germany and the northern Netherlands, so did the incidence of popular millenarian expectations among the disoriented poor. See Cohn (1970):53–60, 107, 118–26, 282–84. The radical sectarianism of seventeenth-century England has been linked to the growing number and relative mobility of "masterless men" who by fate or by choice lived outside the conventional institutions of society—a condition accelerated by enclosures of land incidental to the introduction of capitalist development in agriculture. See Hill (1972):20, 39, 40–45, 85.

17. Piven and Cloward (1971).

18. Nelson (1979) considers four ways in which the members of what we have called the primitive labor market attempt to relate to and influence the established society: patron-client relationships, ethnic-based organizations, small special-interest organizations based on neighborhood or occupation, and mobilization by populist or Marxist political movements. She concludes that these people have not acted as a coherent class and do not destabilize the established order.

19. Pereira de Queiroz (1970):93–121.

20. In the United States, family production for direct consumption, if counted in GNP, would by rough estimates come close to one-fourth of total production. Lindblom (1977):108, citing Abdel-Hamid Sirageldin (1969).

21. Shorter (1975) uses a rather simple traditional/modern dichotomy to discuss the history of the family as a social institution from the eighteenth through the twentieth centuries. Something of the unease concerning the resiliency of the modern family in the advanced industrial world is caught in this historian's concluding sentences:

In the 1960s and 1970s the entire structure of the family has begun to shift. The nuclear family is crumbling—to be replaced, I think, by the free-floating couple, a marital dyad subject to dramatic fissions and fusions, and without orbiting satellites of pubertal children, close friends, or neighbours . . . just the relatives, hovering in the background, friendly smiles on their faces (p. 280).

## Chapter 3. Capitalist Development

1. Paul Sweezy, André Gunder Frank, and Immanuel Wallerstein put the stress on exchange relations. For Wallerstein, the capitalist world system exists already in the sixteenth century. Maurice Dobb, Robert Brenner, and Perry Anderson put the stress on production. For Anderson, absolutism was the final form of feudalism, even though it gave hospitality to mercantile accumulation of capital. The English historians Rodney Hilton and Christopher Hill agree. Maurice Dobb saw a long period of transition during which petty commodity production was preeminent. Much of the debate is summarized in Hilton (1978).

2. Wolf (1982):83–88.

3. Hilton, in Hilton (1978):25–27, 114–17, 150–53.

4. Hoffmann et al. (1956).

5. Anderson (1974):449–50.

6. Braudel (1979):tome 1, pp. 426–32.

7. Takahashi in Hilton (1978):79, 87–97. The parallel transformation from self-employment to the employment of hired labor for expanded reproduction in nineteenth-century United States is discussed in Gordon, Edwards, and Reich (1982):65–66.

8. Hilton (1978:22) writes: "In the 13th-century Flemish textile towns there was still confusion concerning the payment made to the textile craftsman by the merchant putter-out. It was not quite a wage, and yet it was not simply a payment for a job done by an independent craftsman."

9. Hobsbawm (1954):nos. 5 & 6, esp. no. 6, pp. 46, 51–52.

10. The importance of the national market is stressed by Braudel (1979):tome 3, pp. 235–330. Also Hobsbawm (1969):23–78; Williams (1980) passim.

11. Polanyi (1957):78–102. Polanyi saw the Speenhamland system, introduced in 1795, as a critical turning point. Speenhamland seemed initially to be a generous measure in the tradition of the Elizabethan poor law. It was designed to assure a minimum income linked to the price of bread irrespective of earnings. Its result was to subsidize low wages paid by employers and to put increasing numbers of people "on the rates," leading to widespread pauperization and demoralization while at the same time obstructing the formation of a working class by keeping the recipients in their counties. The triumphant middle classes through the Poor Law Reform of 1834 replaced this demoralizing protection with a harshly competitive labor market. Also see Hobsbawm (1969):104–5, 229; Thompson (1968):73.

12. Several studies in Landsberger, ed. (1974) illustrate these points, especially those by George D. Jackson (Eastern Europe), Yu. G. Alexandrov (Asia and North Africa), and Gerrit Huizer and Rodolfo Stavenhagen (Mexico and Bolivia). These studies underline the importance of peasant political pressures in bringing

about land reforms—a point also made by Rodney Hilton with reference to peasant resistance in the late middle ages. See Hilton, ed. (1978):22, and Hilton in Landsberger, ed. (1974). On the pattern of failure in land reforms, see Stavenhagen (1981): 27–28.

13. Engels (1969):106. Thompson (1968) recounts the undermining of skill differentiation with the repeal of apprenticeship laws, the increase of dependent "outworkers" and the factory employment of children, youth and women in such formerly skilled and independent occupations as weaving (pp. 259–346).

14. Schlesinger (1960):393–406.

15. Galbraith (1975).

16. de Grazia (1983).

17. On these tendencies, Carr (1945).

18. This is the basic thesis of Edward Shorter and Charles Tilly (1974).

19. Shorter and Tilly (1974); also Gordon et al. (1982):ch. 4.

20. On Bakunin and Marx, see Carr (1967):441–57. Lenin's views are in Lenin (1970); Fanon's in Fanon (1968). Gramsci's principal political concern was to breach the separation and to build an alliance of all workers and peasants under the leadership of the industrial workers.

21. Georges Sorel was the best known theoretician of revolutionary syndicalism. See especially his *Reflections on Violence* (1941). On the French activist and leader of revolutionary syndicalism Fernand Pelloutier, see Zeldin (1973):pt. 1, 10, pp. 246–50. Lichtheim (1961):223–33, deals with the syndicalist issue in ideological terms. Notwithstanding Sartre's disavowal of Georges Sorel in his introduction to Fanon (1968), the critical reader cannot but be struck by the similarity in the treatment of violence by Fanon and Sorel. In North America, syndicalism took form in the Knights of Labor during the late nineteenth century and in the Industrial Workers of the World in the early twentieth century. See Aronowitz (1973):62–106. The early CIO in the United States manifested some elements of syndicalism, notably in its practice of the sitdown strike. See Schlesinger (1960):393–406. On anarcho-syndicalism in Argentina in the 1920s, see International Labour Office (1930). Patrick de Laubier (1968) discusses syndicalism in the context of newly urbanized workers. His argument is examined critically by Shorter and Tilly (1974):272–73. They are concerned with organizational effectiveness and argue that established skilled workers have more resources to put into organization and are more effective than newly urbanized workers. This point is not in dispute here.

22. The "institutionalization of conflict" is a concept advanced by Dahrendorf (1958):64–66, 224–31. It implies the separation of industrial disputes from conflict over the social and political order and the adoption of a reformist, incrementalist strategy by unions. I have linked it here to Gramsci's concept of hegemony, in which a dominant class perceives the need to make concessions to subordinate classes that are not of such a kind as to weaken its dominance. Gramsci (1971):161.

23. The Derby-Disraeli ministry in 1867 sponsored the Reform Bill that extended the franchise to British householders, i.e., to the skilled worker and artisan classes. The Disraeli ministry in 1865 passed two acts giving a juridical status to trade unions and legalizing picketing, thereby grounding bipartite production relations in law. Disraeli's biographer Robert Blake (1966) discounts any basic philosophy of Tory democracy as the ground for Disraeli's action in these respects and sees them rather as successful attempts to take the political initiative from the Liberals: "The forces of property, commercial and industrial as well as landed, were by 1874 too deeply rooted in the Conservative Party to make it politically possible for the party to pursue the idea of an artistocratic anti-middle class alliance

with the working masses even if it had wished to do so" (p. 447). Blake also considered that

Disraeli, more than any other statesman of his day, had the imagination to adapt himself to this new situation [i.e., an enfranchised working class] and to discern, dimly and hesitantly perhaps, what the artisan class wanted from Parliament. Imperialism and social reform were policies which certainly appealed to them—or to a large section of them—and Disraeli seems to have sensed this in his curiously intuitive way, although even here it is important not to overstate the case (p. 553).

See also Hobsbawm (1969):125.

24. Ingham (1974) discusses some of the factors influencing employers to prefer negotiation at these different levels.

25. Schlesinger (1960) part 6. Franklin Roosevelt makes a striking parallel to Disraeli in this respect (see note 23). Schlesinger writes of him:

For Roosevelt, labour was not, like conservation or social welfare, a field in which he had primary experience or clear-cut views. He approached it quite without the preconceptions of his class—with, indeed, sympathy for the idea of organised labour as a make-weight to the power of organised business. But he sympathised with organised labour more out of a reaction against employer primitivism than as necessarily a hopeful new development in itself. . . . He saw himself as holding the balance between business and labour; and he viewed both sides with detachment. . . . Reared in the somewhat paternalistic traditions of pre-war progressivism and of the social work ethos, Roosevelt thought instinctively in terms of government's doing things for working people rather than of giving the unions power to win workers their own victories (pp. 387–88).

Senator Wagner took a more positive view of unions; he looked to collective bargaining to increase purchasing power that would keep the economy going, and he thought a strong labor movement would convince workers they could gain their own ends within capitalism so that unions would become "our chief bulwark against communism and other revolutionary movements" (p. 390). Skocpol (1980) concludes that the U.S. labor movement was too weak to have been a very effective pressure on the state in the early 1930s and that state initiatives, opposed by employer interests, to strengthen the labor movement and institutionalize collective bargaining were possible because the collapse of the international monetary and trading order had opened "political space" for the state, i.e., Roosevelt and Wagner, to act. This space was not, however, sufficient for the state to move further toward more thoroughgoing intervention of a Keynesian social-democratic kind (which would have implied a movement from bipartism to tripartism). The figures on the growth of the U.S. labor movement are cited by Skocpol from Derber and Young, eds. (1972):3, 134.

26. This proposition is confirmed by Shorter and Tilly (1974) with regard to France. They infer from their data on strikes through the nineteenth and twentieth centuries that "the government's main preoccupation in labor relations was the preservation of public order, rather than the strangulation of working-class political movements" (p. 39). Government intervention in strikes, mainly by state officials like labor inspectors and subprefects, would lean heavily on employers, as well as on workers, to limit the chances of public disturbances and force the parties to negotiate (pp. 39–41).

27. For example, Konrád and Szelényi (1979):220–52, esp. 232 writing of the countries of Eastern Europe:

. . . . economic reforms demand the creation of a political system in which arbitrary interpretation of the law is replaced by formal legal guarantees which will permit the legitimate expression of different interests, place the struggle of contending political forces in a legal and constitutional framework and make it visible to all, and guarantee public control over important decisions. The technocracy must accept the legitimate articulation of worker's interests even though they now conflict at times with its own interests and may do so systematically in the more remote future—up to and including worker self-management and the right to organize and defend their interests, even if such organizations may develop into rival power centers (p. 232).

   28. Bendix (1963):8–10.

   29. Galbraith (1968):71–82.

   30. Dore (1973):375–420 and Hanami (1979).

   31. Bendix (1963):41. On the effects of Taylorism and the ideological significance of industrial psychology, see also Braverman (1974):124–52. Mayo's work is described in Mayo (1945) and Homans (1951).

   32. Dore (1973) uses the term *welfare corporatism* to describe what is here called enterprise corporatism. In his comparison of British and Japanese industrial relations, the main point of which is to underline cultural differences that contradict the convergence theories inspired by technological and economic determinism, Dore nevertheless notes certain tendencies in Britain toward the Japanese model. (Convergence theories, by contrast, tend to forecast the disintegration of the Japanese pattern under the impact of markets.) See Dore (1973):338–71. He is, however, cautious about exaggerating these trends. One is sometimes tempted to see in the spread of enterprise corporatism the Japanization of industrial relations in Europe and North America. Enterprise corporatism has had its own dynamic in Europe and North America arising directly out of the processes of concentration of capital and segmentation of the labor force. Latterly, under the influence of Japan's economic success, there has also been some conscious imitating of Japanese practice, including naive transplants like compulsory morning exercises for workers and company songs—testimonials to the robustness of positivist thinking.

   33. Maier (1975).

   34. Schlesinger (1960):83–187.

   35. Memoirs by two of the senior officials involved who later played leading roles in the ILO are Sir Harold Butler's *Confident Morning* (1950) and Edward J. Phelan's *Yes and Albert Thomas* (1949). On the ideological role of the ILO regarding tripartism, see Cox (1977a).

   36. Maier (1975):513–15.

   37. Schlesinger (1960):83.

   38. Schlesinger (1960):83–187.

   39. A descriptive outline of these various tripartite organisms is given in Malles (1971). For a critical analysis of tripartite experiences, see Panitch (1984).

   40. Maier (1975):545–78.

## 4. Redistributive Development

   1. Carr (1952); Nove (1969):57–58, 63–72; Erlich (1967); Moshe Lewin (1974).

   2. Grossman (1977); Sauvy (1984):233–41.

   3. Stalin told Churchill that the ordeal of collectivization was even greater than that of World War II. Volin, in Black, ed. (1960):306.

   4. Bernstein (1967).

   5. Bendix (1963):8–10.

   6. Bendix (1963):181.

   7. Bendix (1963):206–7.

8. Meissner (1972):37, 40–44.

9. Schurmann (1966):263–84.

10. Teckenberg (1978).

11. Howe (1973a):95, 115, 153; and Howe, in Schram, ed. (1973b):234, 237, 253.

12. Shkaratan, in Yanowitch and Fisher, eds. (1973).

## Part 2. States, World Orders, and Production Relations

1. Ibn Khaldūn (1958).

## Chapter 5. The Coming of the Liberal Order

1. Burckhardt (1945) wrote of this period: ". . . a new fact appears in history—the State as the outcome of reflection and calculation, the State as a work of art" (p. 2). The Renaissance spirit, for Burckhardt, expressed "power in unity," e.g., Bramante's plan for the reconstruction of St. Peter's in Rome under Pope Julius II (p. 75). The succeeding baroque period, for Carl Friedrich (1952):39, expressed power as "movement, intensity, tension, force." On the importance of the revival of Roman law, see Anderson (1974):24–29.

2. Meinecke (1957) passim.

3. Mattingly (1973).

4. Albert Sorel (1922).

5. Roughly translated:

". . . all the powerful States are agreed not to allow any one of their number to raise itself above the others. Were any one to claim the lion's share, it would see its rivals form at once a league against it. There thus arises among the great States a kind of business association: each aims to conserve what it possesses, to take gains in proportion to its stake in the business, and to forbid any of the associates to dictate to the others. This is what is called the balance of power or the European equilibrium" (Sorel, 1922:33–34).

6. Clark (1947):98–114; Anderson (1974):29–33.

7. Clark (1947):30–61, on the developments in fiscal machinery. Braudel (1979: t.3, pp. 322–24) attributes British military successes during the eighteenth century to sound fiscal management. On the decline of Spain, see Vicens Vives, in Cipolla, ed. (1970):121–67.

8. The classic study on mercantilism is by Heckscher (1935). Heckscher's work has been criticized as both mistakenly perceiving a series of ad hoc measures as a coherent body of economic theory and as judging this purported theory by the canons of classical liberal economics. On these criticisms, see Coleman, ed. (1969). The royal charter of 1694 establishing the Bank of England was a critical act in putting the relationship between political power and merchant wealth on a businesslike basis. The Crown ceded control over the issuance of currency to a consortium of wealthy merchants in exchange for their funding of the royal debt. Thenceforth merchant and state interests had to be managed in common—an arrangement that prevailed unbroken until the economic crisis of the 1930s displaced control of the currency from the Bank of England to the Treasury. See Brian Johnson (1970).

9. Eli Heckscher, in reconsidering his work on mercantilism in the light of criticism that he gave insufficient attention to the differences among countries, contrasts the virtual absence of administrative controls in England in the late seventeenth century with the "vast administrative machinery" created by Colbert in France. Coleman (1969):23. Though vast, French old-regime bureaucracy was

ineffective by modern standards. Goubert (1966) depicts a situation in which government actions, though ambitious in their aim of economic promotion, penetrate only very marginally into society.

10. Marx linked the profits of trade, the import of gold and silver from the New World, and the transportation of African slaves to the Americas—all aspects of mercantilism—with the expropriation of the English peasantry, as elements in the primitive accumulation of capital necessary to launch the process of capitalist development. Keynes saw the virtue of mercantilism in its effect in encouraging foreign investment and, by reducing the interest rate, stimulating domestic investment. See Brown (1974):73–95. The classic study of the impact of the triangular trade with the West Indies on the development of British capitalism is Williams (1980). See also Hymer (1971).

11. Dehio (1963).

12. Skocpol (1979):56–60.

13. On the critical importance of the creation of a national market for the development of English capitalism, see Hobsbawm (1969):30–31, 41–51; and Braudel (1979 t.3,:pp. 235–53).

14. Becker (1932).

15. Meinecke (1957) epitomizes this contradiction in his treatment of Frederick the Great, who was an eminent practitioner of *raison d'état* in both its internal and external aspects—he rationalized state administration and founded his foreign policy in *realpolitik*—while at the same time he wrote a tract against Machiavelli and harbored universalist philosophers in his court. Immanuel Kant's essay "Eternal Peace" postulates that world peace is to be founded on the existence of states governed by the rule of law. Friedrich (1948) includes a translation of Kant's essay. List (1885:119–32) emphasized that the idea of perpetual peace was the foundation of all of Adam Smith's argument about the wealth of nations. Smith's model, which List called cosmopolitical, situates individual economic men in a fictitious universal commercial republic, whereas List himself reasoned in terms of a real world of national political economies. There is a concordance between the eighteenth-century ideas of universal peace and liberal economics that together expressed an emerging bourgeois concept of world order. Nannerl Keohane (1980) points to the link made between private vices and public virtues in the Augustinian revival led by Montaigne and the seventeenth-century Jansenists, and Hirschman (1977) traces the genealogy of the new vision of world order.

16. Albert Sorel (1922): vol. 1, p. 71.

17. Webster (1963): vol. 1, pp. 120–21, 127–28, 227–28, 492.

18. Briggs (1965a: 137, 182, 207, 210) points out that England was not spared internal dissensions during the war against France. Discontent arose, however, more as the product of changes in industrial structure than from sympathy with French revolutionary goals. Support for the war was widespread, if not unanimous. It was following the peace that discontent became more pronounced, since the fall in urban employment and rise in indirect taxation hit the workers most of all. The year 1819 was the most troubled one for working class distress, and it took a political form, repressed by the Tory regime in the Peterloo massacre and introduction of the Six Acts.

19. Talleyrand (1967): t.2, p. 159. The passage quoted may be rendered in English as:

The greatest need and most pressing concern of Europe was . . . to do away with the doctrines of usurpation, and to revive the principle of legitimacy, the only remedy for all the evils that have afflicted Europe and the only one capable of preventing their recurrence. . . . (I)t is above all a necessary element in the tranquility and happiness of peoples.

20. An Italian historian of imperial Rome, Gugliemo Ferrero (1941), sought to explain the upheavals leading to World War II as the consequence of disregarding the principle of legitimacy, the same principle that Talleyrand had perceived to be the only sure basis for internal and international order. Ferrero found in the doctrine of legitimacy, by analogy to the post-Napoleonic era, a conservative solution to the disruptions wrought by fascism and Nazism. There is a certain reminiscence of Machiavelli's metaphor of the centaur in Ferrero's statement: ". . . a legitimate government is a power that has lost its fear as far as possible because it has learned to depend as much as it can on active or passive consent and to reduce proportionately the use of force" (p. 41). The weakness of Ferrero's argument lies in treating legitimacy as a universal principle without regard to sociohistorical context. By contrast, Gramsci's concept of hegemony, also reminiscent of Machiavelli's centaur, makes the condition of acquiescence, stability, and tranquility dependent on the relationship between the principle on which a regime is founded and the historic bloc, i.e., makes legitimacy a historically contingent, not a universally valid, proposition.

21. See Webster (1963: vol. 1, p. 58) on Pitt's endorsement of the need to create a foundation of public law; and p. 498, on Castlereagh's view of the doctrine of legitimacy.

22. Nicholson (1947):17.

23. Webster (1963): vol. 1, p. 482.

24. Webster (1963): vol. l, p. 151.

25. Webster (1963): vol. 2, pp. 240, 406, 472.

26. Hinsley (1967):183–85.

27. Webster (1963): vol. 1, pp. 57–60, 493; vol. 2, p. 52.

28. Webster (1963: vol. 1, pp. 488–89) writes:

Castlereagh deliberately misled Parliament as to the part he had played in the Saxon and Neapolitan questions. . . . Similarly, his public policy towards the second restoration of the Bourbons was assumed in order to make his real policy possible. . . . The concealment, which was known to the other leaders of the Alliance, must have led them to believe that Castlereagh was prepared to deceive his own countrymen deliberately when he could not win support for his policy in any other way. . . . No wonder that the British people never understood the principles on which the reconstruction was based! He never fully took them into his confidence. Those who admire his honesty of purpose and diplomatic skill must regret this blot on his character which no casuistry can palliate.

29. Webster (1963): vol. 1, pp. 491–93; vol. 2, pp. 47–49, 407–9, 428. There was a good deal of British private enterprise involved in the independence movements in Latin America. Lord Cochrane's naval exploits on behalf of the South American rebels were highly popular in England, and large sums of money were raised for him in London. Castlereagh toyed with the idea of recognizing independent monarchies in South America. Canning ultimately recognized the new republics. Commercial recognition was necessary as a first step because Spain regarded British merchants trading with South America as pirates, and these merchants sought the protection of the Royal Navy.

30. Doubtless a bourgeois-run state would not have been able to grant subsidies rather than loans. This was the privilege of aristocrats dealing with finance. The one exception to the subsidy rule concerned Austria. The Austrians had apparently preferred a loan as being more consistent with Hapsburg dignity. The

repayment problem after the war became embroiled in Parliament, which demanded some return when the government would have preferred to cancel the debt. The Austrian government finally settled for some part of the sum due. Webster (1963): vol. 2, p. 401–2. The British practice in the Napoleonic wars compels comparison to the U.S. practice during World War I, which left a huge war debt and reparations problem to bedevil postwar international relations.

31. Halévy (1949b):36–40, 46–53. Ricardo and Parliamentary critics had objected to the government's expedient of renewing the debt by borrowing from the Sinking Fund: Ricardo wrote to a correspondent: "While Ministers have this fund virtually at their disposal, they will on the slightest occasion be disposed for war. To keep them peaceable you must keep them poor" (n., p. 40).

32. The perpetuation into the twentieth-century interwar period of this contradiction and of the myth that reconciles it is analyzed critically by Carr (1946).

33. Halévy (1949b):164. Nicholson (1947:266–78) is more inclined to stress the break between Castlereagh's and Canning's policies, whereas Halévy sees continuity. Nicholson's book has, at the end, the ring of Greek tragedy, in which Castlereagh's suicide coincides with the defeat of all his public goals, and particularly the end of the congress system. Hinsley (1967:222–25): points out that the basic goals of Castlereagh's policy were continued by Canning and Palmerston. Webster (1963: vol. 2, p. 504) also recognizes that, though the congress system came to an end, Castlereagh's fundamental idea continued in the Concert of Europe.

34. The prolonged political dominance of the aristocracies, not only in Britain but also in all European countries, up to the First World War is discussed in Mayer (1981.)

35. Hinsley (1967):220–21, 245.

36. A. J. P. Taylor (1957):xxxv, wrote: "Nationalism and mass-education, which had been expected to bring peace, were turned everywhere to the advantage of state-power. Where Germany led the way, Great Britain and France followed, though more slowly."

37. Hinsley (1967: 223) wrote: "It is not unreasonable to regard the Concert of Europe as being from one point of view the system which naturally replaced the aim of universal monarchy during the period of British predominance."

38. Adam Smith's views on the state are found mainly in books 4 and 5 of The Wealth of Nations. See also the Introduction by Andrew Skinner to the Pelican edition (1970):77–82. On the dismantling of guild and mercantilist restrictions, Landes (1969):145; Hobsbawm (1977):51.

39. Landes (1969):152, 199–200; Checkland (1964):329.

40. Polanyi (1957) discusses both the social implications of the Speenhamland system, evolved in the late eighteenth century to replace the Elizabethan poor law, in stablilizing the rural population and in stemming the flow into the industrial labor market and the effect of the 1834 poor law in effectively creating a general national market in labor. See also Thompson (1968):73, 244, 247–249; Hobsbawm and Rudé (1969):50–51.

Bendix (1963:21, 24, 61–62, 73–86, 115) shows the changes that took place in the prevailing attitudes toward poverty. Formerly regarded as a misfortune for which the community as a whole bore some responsibility, poverty now became a matter of personal responsibility that the "higher classes" could do nothing to alleviate (Malthus providing scientific justification for this view). Poverty was a self-inflicted deprivation that could be combated only by reforming the character of the poor under the strictest discipline. The optimistic counterpart to this was that the most industrious among the poor might themselves become capitalists. The importance of Methodism in convincing the poor themselves of this new doctrine was also emphasized by Elie Halévy, (1949a:424–25), the French historian. See also Thompson (1968:45–46), who sees an enhancement of working-class capacity for organization and growth in self-confidence as an unintended consequence of Methodism.

On poor law reform, see also Halévy (1950):119–29, 284–86. Halévy wrote: "The law appeared to regard poverty itself as a crime. The paupers were deprived of sufficient bedding, warmth, and nourishment. Indeed, it was the avowed object of the regulations to make the conditions of life in the workhouse harder than those of the worst-paid labourer in the district" (pp. 284–85). Hobsbawm and Rudé (1969:286) wrote concerning English labourers: "The New Poor Law of 1834 destroyed the last and most modest of their claims on society, namely the belief that it would not let poor men starve like dogs." Also Checkland (1964):329–30; Briggs (1965a):278–82.

41. Bendix (1964:82–83) discerns three policies concerning workingmen's associations followed by different European states during the liberal era: (1) a form of benign neglect (not Bendix's term), which consisted in allowing craft associations to continue to exist in accordance with the medieval concept of liberty as a privilege (Scandinavia and Switzerland); (2) the suppression of all associations filling the space between the state and the people (Prussian prohibition of workingmen's associations and French Loi Le Chapelier); and (3) a prohibition of combinations, i.e., affecting markets, while allowing association in other respects (Britain).

42. Halévy (1950):98; Halévy (1949b):46–53; Brian Johnson (1970):30–34; Checkland (1964):201; Briggs (1965a):339.

43. The Parliament that adopted the reform of 1832 also set about to centralize and strengthen state administration. Jeremy Bentham, who had converted from advocacy of "enlightened despotism" to support of democracy, retained a conviction in the need for a strong central power. His thinking inspired many of the administrative changes. Tories and traditionalists, Disraeli included, saw this as a tendency to impose a bureaucracy on the nation, aping Prussian and French models. See Halévy (1950):98–101.

44. Halévy (1949b:288) discounts the possibility that Peel's police reform of 1829 might have been intended to forestall a Jacobin-type rising. Suppression of crime was the only thought in his mind, Halévy considered. However, Behagg (1982:79–80) pointed out that working-class radicalism was repressed in Birmingham in 1839 by a detachment of London police drafted in by the middle-class mayor.

45. Halévy (1950):213–16; Behagg (1982):61.

46. Halévy (1951):20–22; Hobsbawm (1962):230–31.

47. Landes (1969):156–57. Habermas (1976:53–55) outlines functions of the capitalist state. The first two of his functions are (1) the state's tasks of constituting the mode of production and maintaining it through civil, property, and contract law and the establishment of the market and of providing certain basic prerequisites of production such as education, transportation, and communication; and (2) its aid to the accumulation process. Both are market-complementing actions. The other two functions he lists are market-replacing actions. The former correspond roughly to those of the liberal state. The latter arise in more recent transformations of the liberal state. Wolfe (1977) has attempted a typology of forms of capitalist state. His two initial forms are called the "accumulative state" and the "harmonious state." The former he regards as continuing from the absolutist (mercantilist?) period the state's role in encouraging capital accumulation; the latter expresses the ideological

conviction that the pursuit of particular business interests will be in the general interest. I do not find this distinction very useful or historically very convincing. The ideology of harmony did not await the late nineteenth century, as Wolfe seems to suggest; it was current in the eighteenth century and even earlier and influenced the new early-nineteenth-century legislation. Furthermore, there was an important break in the state's accumulation functions in the early nineteenth century with the dismantling of guild and mercantilist protections, the creation of a labor market, and the instituting of a regulated currency and banking and credit system. Ideology and accumulation were two aspects of the same historical structure, a structure that came into existence in Europe in the early nineteenth century and entered a crisis of transformation into a postliberal state in Europe during the last decades of the nineteenth century.

48. Adam Smith (1970) wrote that legislative proposals emanating from members of the mercantile classes:

ought always to be listened to with great precaution, and ought never to be adopted till after having been long and carefully examined, not only with the most scrupulous, but with the most suspicious attention. It comes from an order of men, whose interest is never exactly the same with that of the public, who have generally an interest to deceive and even to oppress the public, and who accordingly have, upon many occasions, both deceived and oppressed it (book 1, ch. 11, pp. 358–59).

49. Jones, in Epstein and Thompson, eds. (1982):18–21.

50. Briggs, in Briggs and Saville, eds. (1960):56.

51. Hobsbawm and Rudé (1969): passim and esp. 15–19, 24–36, 69, 76, 91, 195, 253, 262–63, 281, 283–84, 286–88, 297–98. "Swing" was the anonymous signature appended to threatening letters received by many landlords.

52. On Owenite trade unionism, Checkland (1964):347–49; Briggs (1965a):289–304; Halévy (1949b):281–82. On Chartism, G. S. Jones (1982); Briggs, ed. (1965c); Briggs (1965a):304–12.

53. Halévy (1950:63), commenting on the composition of the first Parliament elected following the reform of 1832, concluded: "the first Reformed Parliament, returned by a middle-class electorate, was like its predecessors a Parliament the overwhelming majority of whose members were country gentlemen and members of the aristocracy."

54. Jones (1982):48–49.

55. Briggs (1965b), in Briggs, ed. (1965c):296.

56. Halévy (1951):103–36; Briggs (1965a):312–23; Briggs (1965b):296–97; Briggs (1960):59–61.

57. Quoted in Briggs (1965b):298. Briggs (1965a) wrote that Chartism demonstrated "not the weakness of the working classes in the society of the 1840s but the strength of the middle classes" (as organized through the Anti-Corn Law League) (p. 312).

58. Briggs (1965b), commenting on the absence of revolution in England in 1848 and of counterrevolution in 1849, wrote: "The mid-Victorian years were years of social equipoise, and the militant class language withered on both sides of the class barrier. It became the fashion—particularly in 1851, the year of the Great Exhibition—to sing the praises of all classes." Jones (1982:50–51), who has argued that the appeal of Chartism depended on the perception that the state was being used by the propertied classes to oppress the poor, the workers, and those excluded from political power, observed:

Peel made no political concessions to Chartism, but his avowed aim was to remove the material sources of popular discontent and to avoid identifying the State with any particular fraction or economic interest of the propertied class. .... All this proved fatal to the conviction and self-certainty of the language of Chartism, especially in the period after 1842, when some real measure of prosperity returned to the economy.

59. Hobsbawm and Rudé (1969:47) pointed to a fundamental contradiction in English agrarian society:

Its rulers wanted it to be both capitalist and stable, traditionalist and hierarchical. In other words they wanted it to be governed by the universal free market of the liberal economist (which was inevitably a market for land and men as well as for goods), but only to the extent that suited nobles, squires and farmers; they advocated an economy which implied mutually antagonistic classes, but did not want it to disrupt a society of ordered ranks.

The hegemonic order stabilized and perpetuated that contradiction. As Anthony Brundage discovered, the effect of the new poor law of 1834 was to "strengthen the power of the country's traditional leaders over their localities," enabling the landed class, shaken by the Swing revolts, to restore labor discipline, lower the rates, and try to reestablish social cohesion by a flexible application of the new relief system. In practice, they made use, despite the new legislation, of outdoor relief as being less oppressive and also in some cases less costly than incarceration in the workhouse. Brundage (1978):90, 106, 144–45, 178–79, 182–84 (quote from p. 182).

60. Marx (1969):124.

61. Marx (1969):131.

62. Sellier, in Sturmthal and Scoville, eds. (1973); also Shorter and Tilly (1974): esp. 39–45.

63. On the U.S. economy in relation to government, Williamson, ed. (1951):100–4, 113, 359–63 (re land issue); 118–28, 282–84 (re government and capital formation); 228–31, 244–53, 297, 554–63 (re cheap versus sound money); 302–5, 535–39 (re the tariff).

64. *The Gilded Age*, a novel by Mark Twain (Samuel Clemens) and Charles Dudley Warner (1873), set in a context of speculation, graft, and corruption during the Grant administration years.

65. Beard and Beard (1940):esp. vol. 2, ch. 18, pp. 52–121.

66. Gordon, Edwards, and Reich (1982): ch. 3, pp. 48–99.

67. Landes (1969):201–10.

68. Morazé (1957).

69. Gallagher and Robinson (1953).

70. One of the earliest analyses of the impact of expanding capitalism on production relations in penetrated areas was in Luxemburg (1968; first published in 1913). A more recent attempt to theorize stages in the impact of capitalism on penetrated formations in the Marxist tradition is by Rey (1976). More recently still, the task of interpreting history in terms of the impact of capitalist development on precapitalist production relations has been carried forward by Wolf (1982): esp. ch. 10, pp. 296–309.

71. Luxemburg (1968):429–39; Wolf (1982):286–87.

72. Luxemburg (1968):371–77, 386–94; Wolf (1982):247–49, 252–61.

73. Wolf (1982):307.

74. Goldfrank (1975) gives an illustration of capitalist development in the periphery under the regime of Porfirio Diaz. The Mexican state, encouraged by the local bourgeoisie, sought foreign investment, expecting it would take the portfolio form. Foreign capital was forthcoming, but as direct investment along with U.S. policing of foreign indebtedness. The Mexican bourgeoisie was not strong enough

or independent enough to lead a national development and were willing to become accessories to foreign capital.

75. Polanyi (1957): esp. 130–77.
76. Cited in Checkland (1964):209–10.
77. Hobsbawm (1977):150–60.

## Chapter 6. The Era of Rival Imperialisms

1. Barraclough (1967):12.
2. A. J. P. Taylor (1957):255–56, 284, 346–47; Hinsley (1967):244–71.
3. Dehio (1963:230) explained the German gamble of the post-Bismarckian era as

a sad story of a consistent inability on the part of the Continentals [i.e., Dehio's concept of the continental power state] to appreciate fully the strange and hidden sources of strength among the insular nations. . . . The characteristic element in all the struggles for supremacy since the time of Philip II that I have discussed so far is a collision between a power dominating the old continent and the exponent, or exponents, of Western sea power. A secondary feature, appearing at the time of Napoleon I, is the collision between the dominant continental power and Russia.

See also pp. 232–42. Dehio's thesis, elegant in its economy of variables, takes the forms of state power—continental and insular—as given and does not attempt to probe their economic and social foundations. Types of state thereby tend to become idealized as modes of thought conditioned by history.

4. Landes (1969):269, 326–58; Hobsbawm (1969):127, 178–93.
5. Mayer (1981:277) argues that the landed interests were hard hit by the decline in agricultural prices brought about during the 1870s and 1880s from greatly expanded grain production for world markets in the Midwestern plains of North America, the Ukraine, and Argentina. This buttresses his case that it was the persistence of the old regime, not emergent capitalism, that lay behind the rise of protectionism and imperialism in the late nineteenth century, a thesis reflecting that earlier advanced by Joseph Schumpeter (1955:esp. 65, 67) in his essay on the sociology of imperialism. Schumpeter argued that "capitalism is by nature anti-imperialist" and that imperialism is "an atavism in the social structure" that "tends to disappear as a structural element because the structure that brought it to the fore goes into a decline, giving way, in the course of social development, to other structures that have no room for it and eliminate the power factors that supported it." The dubious quality of this thesis undercuts Mayer's principal argument, which lays the responsibility for aggressivity leading up to World War I entirely upon the old-regime aristocracies of Europe. It does not disallow the contribution of agricultural protectionism to that process.
6. In France, the state-initiated free trade policy of the Second Empire was reversed by a coalition of agriculturalists and manufacturers, first in a tariff law of 1881, and subsequently in the Méline tariff of 1892. Cobban (1965: vol. 3, pp. 42–43). In Germany, protectionism was an instrument of the state both to develop the economy and to consolidate a historic bloc. Bismarck secured the alliance of the most powerful group of industrialists through the protective tariff of 1879, while simultaneously, agrarian tariffs brought small farmers, hitherto liberals, into alignment with the Junker landowners who had been the mainstay of the government bloc. Barraclough (1947):426.
7. Bismarck's discussions with Lassalle are discussed in Carr (1950):72–87; the quote is from Carr (1945):19. Carr took the idea from Borkenau (1942).

8. Wehler (1972):77.

9. Barraclough (1947:433–34), citing Halévy in support, considered that a major factor in the decision of the Germany military to run the risk of war in 1914 was the perceived threat to them of the Social-Democratic success of 1912. In Britain, too, the coming of the war silenced a mounting revolt of both workers and suffragettes that threatened domestic peace and channeled both into a nationalist response. Note Wingfield-Stratford (1933:310): "if the war peril from Germany delayed much longer to materialize, it seemed quite on the cards that it might be forestalled by revolution. As the Edwardian passes into the Georgian age . . . class rises against class . . . faction against faction—it is a question whether international will not be anticipated by civil war." Note also Dangerfield (1961; first published 1935:388): with the outbreak of war, the suffragettes "turned patriot to a woman. . . . So in loyal fervor and jingoistic enterprise, ended the great Woman's Rebellion" (pp. 387–88); and ". . . even the proletarian movement, the Worker's Rebellion, which had carried its semi-revolutionary banner on to the very ramparts of Capital, now threw that banner aside, and hurled itself forward, in a new direction, against a more visible enemy, and beneath the Union Jack."

10. The classic analysis of long waves is by Nikolai Kondratieff, summarized in Kondratieff (1935). In his work, written in the 1920s, Kondratieff plotted two and a half long cycles. The upswing of the most recent cycle he dated from 1896 to 1914–1920. Ernest Mandel (1978) estimates the downswing of this long wave as lasting until the end of World War II. Kondratieff did not claim to explain the waves, only to plot them. He did hypothesize that they could be explained within the logic of capitalism and were not the product of exogenous forces. Different scholars have concurred in the probable existence of long waves while focusing on different explanatory factors. Joseph Schumpeter (1939) pointed to innovation (clusters of inventions) and availability of credit as factors conducive to launching a wave. Mandel (1978:108–46) considers the declining rate of profit to be the critical factor. Monetarists have stressed changes in the money supply, in particular the new gold mined in the Rand and the Klondike after 1896 (although Kondratieff thought that gold discoveries should be regarded as events triggered by the logic of the capitalist system and not as chance exogenous occurrences). Landes (1969:232–37) takes the balanced view that both innovation and expansion of the money supply were critical. Jay Forrester (1976:195–214) infers from his systems dynamic modeling that the explanation for long waves may be in the disjunction between capital goods and consumer-production sectors, the application of new technologies during an upswing leading to surplus capacity in the capital goods sector. He sees production planning rather than monetary policy as the appropriate approach toward initiating a new upswing. See also Forrester (1978) 145–48. For a summary analysis of long-wave theorizing, see also Research Working Group on Cyclical Rhythms and Secular Trends (1979) 483–500.

11. Gordon, in Hopkins and Wallerstein, eds. (1980). Gordon points to the weakness of earlier analyses of long waves, both Marxist and non-Marxist, which, he suggests, lies in the fact that they have dwelt upon the purely economic indicators of growth and crisis, ignoring the environment of social relations that conditions whether or not investors are confident in the prospects for accumulation. The composite of structures constituting this environment he calls the social structure of accumulation, hypothesizing it as a unified whole, instability in one element of which will tend to create instability in the whole. Gordon then explores the relationship between economic crises generated in capitalist development and social structures of accumulation. Crisis will, he suggests, undermine the stability of the

social structure of accumulation, so that the construction of a new social structure of accumulation will be necessary in order that investment take off again. Conversely, instability in the social structure of accumulation may contribute to economic crisis. Gordon then defines an economic crisis as "a period of economic instability in capitalist economies whose resolution depends upon the reconstruction of a social structure of accumulation" (p. 20). As elements in the social structure of accumulation, Gordon considers social class relations in the productive process, state investment in the economic infrastructures necessary for accumulation (transport, communications, etc.) and state investment in world-market control (imperialism, international monetary order, etc.). Gordon's thinking carries one step forward Trotsky's critique of the original Kondratieff thesis about long waves. Trotsky contested the affirmation that long waves could be explained within the logic of capital, asserting that they must occur as a result of the interaction of social and political forces with economic logic. Gordon provides the germ of a theory of how sociopolitical factors can be integrated with economic factors in an understanding of the unevenness of capitalist development. Implicit in such a theory, although not discussed by Gordon, is the problematic and unpredictable nature of sociopolitical changes. The "reconstruction of the social structure of accumulation" is a drama of social conflict that cannot be reduced to a sequence of objective economic data. The economic data define the stage on which the drama is played out, but they do not determine its outcome. On Trotsky's critique of Kondratieff, see Garvy (1943); Mandel (1978):126–29; and Day (1976).

12. Braverman (1974) deals with the United States; Georges Friedmann (1956), with France.

13. Edwards (1979):97–104 takes a narrow view of Taylorism, confining it to the application of systematic study of time and motion and production flow, which he sees as only a small part of the changes taking place in management practice. Braverman (1974) used it in a broad sense to name the whole movement toward fragmenting of work, which removed control of the work process from workers and placed it in the hands of management. Gramsci (1971):277–318 also used the term *Taylorism* in a broad sense, linking it with what he called Fordism and Americanism, which he perceived as a revolutionary development in productive methods that, in its impact on Europe, would have the potential both to eliminate the residues of feudalism and prepare workers for the next (proletarian) revolution. See also ch. 9.

14. Gordon, Edwards, and Reich (1982):112–64; Shorter and Tilly (1974):11–16, 180–84, 234–35. The restructuring of the labor process proceeded at a different pace in different countries, depending on the level of development of productive forces and the capacity for resistance of working classes. Halévy (1961) pointed to a contrast between the relative ease with which employers could introduce these innovations on the continent and in the United States and the resistance British employers encountered in the trade unions. On the continent, and especially in Germany, socialism as a political party movement was relatively strong, the trade unions as an industrial force relatively weak. In Britain, socialism was a negligible political force during the late nineteenth century, but the trade unions were relatively solidly entrenched among the established worker class in industry. Halévy wrote:

by the systematic restriction of the numbers employed in a particular branch of industry . . . they [the trade unions] either enforced an apprenticeship, extending over a large number of years, on all who wished to enter the trade, or fixed the proportion of children to adults that might be employed by any firm. Sometimes the men even reserved a definite proportion of the vacancies for their own children. The aim avowedly pursued by the vast majority of unions was the transformation of every industry and every trade into a species of guild closed to outside labour. ... The American or German employer was free to introduce into his factory the plant and process which made it possible to substitute unskilled for skilled labour. But the British employer was faced by the organized opposition of his men. In the engineering trade he could employ only skilled workmen, each of whom would serve only a single machine, whereas his German competitor could employ one unskilled workman to tend three machines at the same time (pp. 215–16).

Gramsci (1971) grasped the dialectical potential in Taylorism:

the brain of the worker, far from being mummified, reaches a state of complete freedom. The only thing that is completely mechanised is the physical gesture ... and not only does the worker think, but the fact that he gets no immediate satisfaction from his work and realises that they are trying to reduce him to a trained gorilla, can lead him to a train of thought that is far from conformist (pp. 309–10).

15. Gerschenkron (1962).

16. Carr (1946) underlined the hiatus, during the interwar period, between a residual hegemonic ideology of laissez-faire and the practice of states' adopting protectionism to defend their independence. See especially pp. 54–60.

17. Quoted in Bruce (1966):262.

18. The first use of the term *welfare state* has been attributed to William Temple, Archbishop of Canterbury, in 1941, as a contrast to the Nazi "power state." Schottland, ed. (1967).

19. Beveridge (1909).

20. Bruce (1966):163–69.

21. Keynes (1936).

22. Tinbergen (1964):esp. 8 and 70.

23. The dilemma for the social democrat of recognizing that welfare policies have involved economic nationalism is the theme of Gunnar Myrdal, (1967). Polanyi (1957:141) stressed the spontaneous, ad hoc character of the emergence of planning as a reaction to the social consequences of laissez faire: "While *laissez-faire* economy was the product of deliberate state action, subsequent restrictions on *laissez-faire* started in a spontaneous way. *Laissez-faire* was planned; planning was not."

24. Landes (1969):339–48; Hobsbawm (1969):172–94.

25. Shonfield (1965):177–82, 193–96. Lowi, in Lindberg et al., eds. (1975), defines the economic plan of a contemporary capitalist state as the state of permanent receivership: "a state whose government maintains a steadfast position that any institution large enough to be a significant factor in the community shall have its stability underwritten" (p. 117), a situation in which there is less socialization of production and distribution than socialization of risk (p. 118).

26. Cox, in Arthur M. Ross, ed. (1966).

27. On the role of British primary education as an agency of conformity, Landes (1969):341–42. Dunlop (1958) and Kerr et al. (1960) write approvingly of a perceived tendency toward decision making on the basis of technically defined options (from which "unrealistic" alternative conceptions of social order have been excluded), wherein the technical elites of the major interest groups (workers and employers) have more in common with each other in the understanding of problems than either have with their own rank and file. Wolfe (1977:298–321) writes critically of the depoliticizing tendency of late capitalism, which seems to require a passive, quiescent subject for its political system to work. Crozier et al. (1975) argue that high levels of participation are unpropitious for liberal democracy in advanced capitalism. The concept of government as a problem in technical engineering rather

than moral choice was illustrated by an incident in Canada. In January 1983, the Roman Catholic bishops issued a collective statement condemning a system that allowed high persisting rates of unemployment as being immoral and proposed policies for an alternative concept of society (Toronto Globe and Mail, January 1, 1983). The prime minister, echoed by leading newspaper opinion, could credibly reply that the bishops did not understand economics. (They presumably were technical specialists in theology. To each his own.) It will be evident by the dates of most of these references that the depoliticization of government became manifest from the late 1950s, the same period in which the "end of ideology" was proclaimed (Daniel Bell, 1960). This occurred, in other words, after the welfare-nationalist form of state had been transformed into a new form adjusted to the new hegemonic world order of the post-World War II period (see ch. 7 below). I believe the substitution of technical for moral choice in government to be functionally related to corporative-tripartite decision making. The depoliticizing effect of this was masked during the life-span of the welfare-nationalist state by the ideological importance of nationalism and its role in mobilizing cross-class unity behind nationalist economic policies. When the hegemonic order stilled nationalisms, the latent depolitization became manifest.

28. These percentages are based on tables in Feinstein (1972). This work gives figures for GNP at market prices (table 3, pp. T 10–11) and for combined public authorities' current expenditure on goods and services (table 14, pp. T 35–36). The exact percentages are 9.6 and 28.5 based on these figures. A different percentage for expenditures by all levels of government in relation to GNP is given in Russett et al. (1964): tables 15 and 23. This source sets the 1959 percentage for the United Kingdom at 45.3. Comparable percentages for other countries in 1959 given in the latter source are 52.9 percent for Sweden, 41.2 percent for the Netherlands, 38.8 percent for West Germany, and 27.9 percent for the United States. If defense expenditures are subtracted from these total government expenditure percentages, the hiatus between the United States and the others is magnified: 48.2 percent for Sweden, 38.6 percent for Britain, 37.2 percent for the Netherlands, 35 percent for West Germany, as against 18.3 percent for the United States.

29. Titmuss (1963), esp. ch. 1.

30. Therborn (1984):11–12.

31. Briggs (1965a):519. Universal manhood suffrage for elections to the lower house was instituted in Germany in 1871, reconfirmed in France in 1875. England, France, and Germany had all dispensed with property, tax, and educational qualifications by the turn of the century, but in all countries apportionment weighted representation in favor of rural over urban areas.

32. Halévy (1961):139–40, 303, has stressed the importance of "the Prussian model" of imperialism combined with social reform in the reshaping of British policy during this period. Other aspects of contemporary Germany were also objects of British admiration and emulation, especially the German educational system and the political philosophy of Hegel (pp. 140–63). Among the reformers, the Fabian Society looked to Joseph Chamberlain as the political leader most likely to bring German social reform to Britain (p. 142). On Chamberlain's social-policy initiatives, see Halévy (1961:231–43, 287, 312) and Bruce (1966):110, 122, 151. Halévy had a keen sense of the latent contradiction in Chamberlain's position (pp. 242–43). In Germany, a dominant old-regime military aristocracy arbitrated between the demands of an aroused proletariat and a dependent bourgeoisie, granting to bourgeois property the protection of the army but being quite willing to defend labor against the exactions of plebian capitalists. In Britain, the aristocracy, by dividing into two

parties, had managed to remain the governing class even as the dominance of industry over society was making the bourgeoisie a hegemonic ruling class. At the very time that Chamberlain was provoking a revival of the project of social reform in the Tory party, the financial and industrial bourgeoisie, threatened by the emerging specter of socialism, was moving into the Tory camp. Chamberlain's career heralded the transition of Toryism from aristocratic benevolence toward a progressive capitalism based on finance and large-scale industry, in which the prospects for social reform would always be subordinated to the requirements of capital accumulation.

33. Harcourt is cited in Bruce (1966):xv; the quote from the Fabians, in Bruce, p. 139; reference to the works of individual reformers in Bruce, pp. 10–11, 142–43.

34. Therborn (1984:16–17, 20–24) points out that the workers' organizations in Germany, Austria, and Denmark opposed state initiatives to introduce social insurance. Their attitude was based on ideological opposition to a paternalistic aristocratic state and affirmation of workers' rights. In late nineteenth-century Britain, trade union leaders thought of themselves as heirs of the liberal traditions of Cobden, Bright, and Gladstone. There was no significant labor participation in national politics before the end of the century other than as a modest representation within the Liberal Party. Halévy (1961):213–14.

35. Dangerfield (1961):235–49, 280–98.

36. Briggs (1965a):44–50. Halévy (1966:110) described the British wartime organization of production thus:

Raw materials and manpower were in short supply, but the needs of the military state were urgent. Now the chief consumer of the nation, the state set itself up as the final arbiter of production and distribution. To make its task easier, all the heads of firms in each industry were encouraged to combine; on the other hand, where their trade-union organizations were still incomplete, workers were urged to make them nearly universal. The state forced associations of employers and workers to become agents of its authority. It would consult them before acting. Once its decisions were taken, it was up to them to transmit its orders and to enjoin all employers and workers to carry them out (Text written in June 1919).

Regarding the New Deal see Chapter 3:67–8, 74–5, and note 25.

37. Barraclough (1947):436–40. Harold Butler, a senior civil servant in the British Ministry of Labour during the war, wrote in his memoirs of "the spectre of a great conspiracy, which would completely disrupt the production of munitions at the most dangerous moment of the war," which led the government to institute a nationwide inquiry under Mr. George Barnes, one of the Labour Party ministers. The inquiry calmed fear of an imminent worker revolt. The fear was not, however, definitely allayed; the government was perturbed again in the wake of the Russian army collapse, and George Barnes set off on a tour of the front line and bases in France to see if the spirit of mutiny had infected the troops. Once again, he concluded the fears exaggerated, although he found that British officers were much concerned that the future would be economically disastrous for victors and vanquished alike. Butler (1950):122–24.

38. Halévy (1966:105–57) gives an analysis of the significance of the Whitley councils written after the event in 1919.

39. Halévy (1966):167 refers to employer-initiated works councils in an essay on the problem of worker control written in March 1921.

40. Maier (1975):53–70. Although German tripartite corporatism as it emerged out of the débacle of World War I began as an employer initiative, this was by no means the origin of the corporatist idea in Germany. Therborn (1984:8–9) has

documented the corporatist theory underlying Bismarck's social reform initiatives of the early 1880s.

41. Maier (1975):138–41.

42. Halévy (1966):171–77, 189–94. Halévy, writing in 1922, described Lloyd George's proposals for the reorganization of the coal industry as "a mere smoke-screen behind which the government could beat a retreat and repudiate the proposals for nationalization" (p. 193). The anticipated nationalization of the railways was similarly averted. These failures of nationalization, Halévy wrote, "allow me to understand the silent and patient tactics by which the ruling classes in England under Lloyd George were able to defeat the working class agitation" (p. 197). Halévy went further to argue that the postwar weakening of the working class had been followed by a decline of the socialist idea in Britain, as the Labour Party abandoned nationalization in favor of the liberal pacifism of Cobdenite little England (p. 206).

43. Halévy's diagnosis of the contradictions between corporatism and so-cialist projects for nationalization and workers' control of industry was written in 1921:

In England—and I believe that it is still more true in Germany—some capitalists are wondering whether it would not be in the employers' interest to create a com-munity of interests in each industry between employers and workers in that industry by setting up a kind of corporative system. The employers would guarantee the workers what they are more concerned about than anything else—security. They would promise to establish a fund to insure them against the perils of unemploy-ment. They would offer them a system of profit-sharing. In return, once the workers were directly interested in the prosperity of the enterprise, the employers would ask their help in getting assistance from the state, protection against foreign com-petition, and higher prices by way of customs reform. . . . Now between these two conceptions—one working-class, the other emanating from the employers—the difference is obvious. One looks to the gradual expropriation of the employers and the elimination of profit. The other wants to interest the working class in the growth of capitalist profits . . ." (p. 79).

44. Gramsci (1971):238.

45. Regarding the ILO and corporatism, see ch. 3, note 35; also Cox, in Cox and Jacobson (1974). The United States, reluctant to join the ILO because of ideo-logical reasons, as well as because of the political isolationism that kept it out of the League of Nations, overcame these objections under the impact of the Great Depression, when corporatist initiatives (without the name) were taken by the Roosevelt administration during the first phase of the New Deal. The United States then took its place alongside the major European powers in affirming that the concept of tripartism was consistent with its state structures.

46. Following the British general strike of 1926, there was an attempt to negotiate a central arrangement between workers and managements through the Mond-Turner talks between a head of Imperial Chemical Industries (ICI) and a representative of the Trade Union Congress (TUC). The talks were inconclusive. British employers were weakly organized, and big corporations like ICI could op-erate on their own in labor matters without being able to rally the majority of employers. In the TUC, the left-wing opposition opposed the talks. See Ingham (1974):73–77; also Nigel Harris (1972):41–42.

47. Katzenstein, in Ruggie, ed. (1983):117–18.

48. Beer (1966):215–16.

49. Beer (1966):198–209. Skocpol (1980), in her analysis of the New Deal, stresses the limitations in the capabilities of the state and the constraints of political party organization impeding full development of social-democratic Keynesian plan-

ning. There are some analogies with the post-World War II British situation. U.S. trade-union strength grew during the 1930s with state backing—the organization of the mass-production industries by the CIO with the backing of the Wagner Act and National Labor Relations Board. But there was no possibility of central direction of the economy—government administrative reforms were blocked by rivalries among departments and between the executive and Congress. Powerful interests were divided, and when World War II came, the government leaned toward an understanding with business and muted the tendency toward social reform. The state, whatever its intentions, was limited by its own internal bureaucratic politics and by the pluralism of group interests.

50. Some of these postwar institutional frameworks are described in Malles (1971). See also Lambruch (1977):91–126; and Panitch (1984). On the Netherlands, Windmuller (1969):282–97.

51. Panitch (1981) sees corporatism limited by a revival of class solidarity. Corporatism, he argues, was a response of capital and the state to a growth in the power of labor in conditions of full employment and tight labor market. It represented a concession by labor (accepting less than its economic power could have extracted) to facilitate capital's continuing accumulation. This concession became an apparent weakness when renewed unemployment weakened labor's position. Panitch is discussing corporatism in the 1960s and 1970s, particularly in its incomes policy form, which, as I suggest below, is a residue of an obsolescent welfare-nationalist form of state.

52. Maier, in Hirsch and Goldthorpe (1978).

53. Offe (1972:487–88).

54. Titmuss (1959).

55. Harrod (1963:525–26) reported that Keynes himself, in the 1940s, speculated that the time might be ripe for Keynesianism at the world level. On the failure of postwar corporatist incomes policies, see Panitch (1976).

56. Maier (1975):339, 349, 427, 574, 578; Brian Johnson (1970):64–102; Landes (1969):414.

57. Maier (1975):562, 565, 567, 571; Landes (1969):404; Neumann (1944):337–40, 417, 419–28.

58. Neumann (1944) described how National Socialist cartel policy favored the big industrial combines (p. 264) and how the state contributed to investment in new technologies that were both instrumental to preparing Germany's war-readiness and profitable to private industrial combines (p. 280). National Socialism was not interested in nationalizing industry, but a section of the party acquired control over a segment of heavy industry (the Hermann Göring combine) as a means of access to the industrial bourgeoisie (pp. 298–302). Profit, Neumann concluded, remained the motive power of German industry under National Socialism. Neumann treats National Socialist pretensions to corporatism as a "myth" (pp. 228–32). In so doing he restricts the meaning of corporatism to an autonomous organization of industry and labor, whether of the kind realized in the practice of the Weimar Republic or envisaged in the theories of estates and in Catholic social doctrine. This restricts corporatism to what Schmitter calls "societal corporatism", excluding the "state corporatist" type instituted by fascism. See Schmitter, in Pike and Stritch, eds. (1974):103.

59. Landes (1969):414–17; Briggs, in Mowat, ed. (1968: vol. 12, ch. 3, pp. 70–75); Neumann (1944):222, 228.

60. Gramsci (1971):219–23, 228–29.

61. Gramsci (1971):59, 106–20, 289–94; Gramsci (1975): vol. 1 p. 504; vol.

2, p. 1220; vol. 3, p. 1781. The analyses of Maier on Italy and Neumann on Nazi Germany concord in this matter. Maier (1975:577–78) wrote:

Fascism did not suppress the causes of capitalist strife and class rivalry; it encouraged the centralization and coordination of that conflict such as was developing in other societies. There was a crucial difference: in Italy the outcome was predetermined . . . the Fascist regime remained in a reciprocal and symbiotic relationship with the old forces of order. Even as the state asserted new claims over the control of all policy, including economic decisions, it ceded to business leaders extensive control over industrial organization."

Concerning Nazi Germany, Neumann (1944:227) wrote: "the antagonisms of capitalism are [1944] operating in Germany on a higher and, therefore, a more dangerous level, even if these antagonisms are covered up by a bureaucratic apparatus and by the ideology of the people's community"; and "It was one of the functions of National Socialism to suppress and eliminate political and economic liberty by means of the new auxiliary guarantees of property, by the command, by the administrative act, thus forcing the whole economic activity of Germany into the network of industrial combinations run by the industrial magnates" (p. 261).

    62. Maier (1975):322.

    63. Maier (1975):46–50, 322–24, 428–29, 547, 557, 561, 572.

    64. Barraclough (1947):448–53; Neumann (1944): passim.

    65. Maier (1975):353.

    66. Barraclough (1947):441–43; Neumann (1944):11.

    67. Neumann and Maier agree that National Socialism did not change the Weimar corporative organization of business in any fundamental way. It did eliminate the autonomy of worker organization. See Maier (1975):592–94 and Neumann (1944):240, 471.

    68. Gramsci (1971):210–12.

    69. Gramsci (1971:220) cited Ramsay Macdonald's National Government in Britain after 1931 as caesarism without a caesar. He also saw the successive Italian governments from October 1922 up to January 1925, i.e., the coalitions formed by Mussolini, as "various gradations of caesarism."

    70. Regarding trasformismo see ch. 3, pp. 79–80 above.

    71. "Forze elementari," Ordine Nuovo, April 26, 1921. Cited in Alastair Davidson (1977):189–90.

    72. Reich (1975). Reich has expressed in Freudian terms a notion with a long genealogy in European thought. Giambattista Vico (1970), writing his New Science in eighteenth-century Naples, saw the return of barbarism as a recurrent possibility in human history.

    73. This point is cogently developed by Barrington Moore, Jr. (1967).

    74. Bendix (1963:119–91) recounts the transition of industrial labor from servile to nominally free status in Czarist Russia. The Czarist state was never content, as the liberal state was, to enact the conditions for the market and then let the market discipline the workers. The Czarist approach to the creation of an enterprise labor market can be regarded as protoliberalism within the structures of an old-regime bureaucracy. See also ch. 4.

    75. Skocpol (1979) stresses the factor of defeat in war as a determinant of the origins of revolutionary states.

    76. Konrád and Szelényi (1979: pp. 85–93, 127–30) advance the thesis that the Soviet pattern of redistributive state develops directly out of old-regime traditional redistribution without passing through capitalism.

    77. Carr (1952).

78. Schurmann (1974):228–36.

79. Cumings, "Introduction" in Cumings, ed. (1983).

80. Gramsci (1971):108–10, 229–39.

81. Schurmann (1966) gives the most explicit presentation of this thesis. Thomas Lowit (1979a,b) uses the term *polymorphous Party* to express the ramification of the Party through state and society.

82. The phrase "historic compromise" is used by Konrád and Szelényi (1979):187. It is obviously taken from the vocabulary of the Italian Communist Party, in which the term applies to a (proposed but not consummated in the Italian case) coalition between distinctive and quasi-permanent sociopolitical forces. Without using this term, Boris Meissner (1972:135–42) gives a somewhat similar analysis of an uneasy coalition between power elite and economic managers, and a more overt struggle between humanistic-intellectual and economic-bureaucratic segments of the intelligentsia, with the subaltern society very largely inert.

83. There is, of course, a continuing Marxist debate over the nature of the Soviet state. The official Soviet view is that since the October Revolution the state has gone through the phases of dictatorship of the proletariat, a socialist state, and a state of all the people. Trotsky's view that since the advent of Stalin's power the Soviet state has been a degenerate worker's state is maintained by contemporary Trotskyites (e.g., Ernest Mandel). Other Marxist critics of the Soviet Union characterize its form as state capitalism, i.e., the instrument of a state bourgeoisie (e.g., Charles Bettelheim or Tony Cliff) or else they see a "new class" that is not a bourgeoisie in control of the state (Milovan Djilas). These are all differing views about the class basis of the Soviet state. The conception of the Soviet state advanced here may appear to avoid the issue of the class basis. In fact, it asserts that the Soviet state stands outside class. It is the instrument of a Party that affirms its identity with the proletariat and gives industrial workers a relatively high status in the society but that commands the proletariat as effectively as it commands any other social group. Indeed, the Soviet state itself created the Soviet proletariat out of elements drawn from a peasant milieu, since the original proletariat that had participated in the October Revolution either disappeared in civil war and economic disorganization or was absorbed into the Party cadres. This form of state actively shapes and organizes a society in which preexisting class-based structures are eliminated and new social categories (workers, technicians, intelligentsia) are allowed to emerge, categories that have more in common with precapitalist status groups than with the social classes linked to the property relations of capitalism.

84. Przeworski (1981:30) refers to the worker revolt in Gdansk in the summer of 1980 that led to the organization of independent trade unions as "a sudden, massive rebirth of civil society."

85. Bahro (1978). On the Yugoslav case, see Benson, in Parkin, ed. (1974).

## Chapter 7. Pax Americana

1. These issues are discussed in Cox and Jacobson (forthcoming).

2. Among the many studies on the construction of the Bretton Woods system and the political significance of the postwar international monetary arrangements three stand out: Gardner (1969); Strange (1971); and in a more critical perspective than Gardner's, Block (1977).

3. Diebold (1959).

4. Cox (1977a); Maier (1977); on U.S. support for the European Movement,

Beloff (1963); on Jean Monnet's Action Committee for the United States of Europe, Haas (1958); Lindberg (1963); and Lindberg and Scheingold (1970).

5. Keynes was concerned with a situation in which wealth holders were unwilling to invest in productive assets because they had no confidence in the future, a lack of confidence that no reduction in interest rates would overcome. The only thing that would overcome their reluctance to invest would be an increase in effective demand, which he thought governments could bring about by public spending. Economic orthodoxy in the 1980s rejected Keynes' remedy, and President Reagan's advisers have taken the position that the way to promote investment is to make things more attractive for investors on the supply side, e.g., by tax cuts, deregulation, etc.

6. The argument that a U.S. payments deficit is good for everyone because it increases the liquidity on which international economic exchanges are based was expressed in Gardner (1960). A radical critique of the consequences of this policy is in Hudson (1968) and (1977). The evolution of U.S. policy is critically analyzed in Calleo (1982).

7. As instances, the Nicaragua of Anastasio Somoza, Bokassa's Central African "Empire," Idi Amin's Uganda, Bolivia under the international drug racketeer General Luis Garcia Meza, and the Duvalierist regime in Haiti.

8. In the literature exploring attempts to build socialist societies in poor peripheral countries under revolutionary leadership: Thomas (1974); Shivji (1976); Mittelman (1981); Ziegler (1983); and Saul, ed. (1984).

9. Up until the late 1960s hegemonic economic theory held that less developed countries would in the long run be caught up in the world-economy developmental process. Their development could be encouraged by measures calculated to facilitate the movement of private capital. The last major official international document to present this long-term optimism as a scenario was the report prepared by a commission chaired by former Canadian Prime Minister Lester B. Pearson for the World Bank (1969). Subsequently, forecasts have been less encouraging in respect to the prospects of a universal developmental process through the world economy. Sometime during the 1970s, a "Fourth World" was distinguished from the "Third World" to designate by implication the least developed countries now recognized to be marginal to the world economy. World Bank programs adjusted from the financing of projects deemed to be likely to result in growth through linkage to world markets in order to focus on projects designed to stem the buildup of sociopolitical pressures in areas marginal to the world economy through population limitation, self-help agricultural development, and encouragement of "informal-sector" employment expansion. Mittelman (1980) shows how the World Bank first opposed support for ujamma village development (a form of communal agriculture) while supporting private commercial farming and then switched to support of the ujamma villages in 1974–75 when it became concerned with the danger of social and political upheavals inherent in massive rural exodus and agrarian crisis.

10. John Gerard Ruggie has called this world-order structure "embedded liberalism," drawing his adjective from Polanyi's distinction between embedded and disembedded economic processes, i.e., whether or not economics is embedded in social relations. For Polanyi, the notion of a self-regulating market (classic liberalism) was a utopian construct in which the economy was conceived to be artificially disembedded from society. See Ruggie (1982). The threefold division of capitalist economies is from O'Connor (1973):13–18. Galbraith (1975) uses a twofold division into planning sector and competitive sector. See also Averitt (1968). O'Connor's monopoly sector would be included in Galbraith's planning sector.

Claus Offe considers the capitalist state to have two main functions: (1) allocation, which is determined by politics and carried out by bureaucratic methods, and (2) production. The latter function is required when private industry is incapable of providing certain of the inputs it requires because to do so would not be profitable. Offe argues that decisions about what the state is to produce are more complex than allocation decisions. Offe, in Lindberg, ed. (1975).

11. Calleo (1982):145–51; Blank (1977).

12. Maier (1978) passim; Calleo (1982):30–31, 40–43, 97–98.

13. Maier (1978):70.

14. Special issue of *International Organization* (1977):31(4) edited by Peter J. Katzenstein; Katzenstein (1983); and Zysman (1983).

15. Edelman, in Somers, ed. (1969), writes of the symbolic political consequences of institutionalized industrial relations. Business, labor and related government agencies:

are components of a single system whose functions are (1) to ensure and promote a continuing demand for production and a continuing flow of public contracts and (2) to arrange a mutual exchange of economic and political benefits. Once all the major dimensions of the transaction are brought into perspective, the assumption that union-management bargaining is a key forum for economic decision making is no longer tenable. It becomes at most a short-run and derivative influence upon economic trends and frequently a ritual, though it continues to make a significant organizational and political impact. . . . (T)hose directly involved in the bargaining and decision making can act only when they win support or neutrality from a large public of rank-and-file workers and political spectators. Any analysis that fails to take account of those aspects of the transaction that serve to win such acquiescence is bound to be superficial. The present analysis suggests that symbolic reassurances are partly what these large publics draw from the total transaction; reassurances that serve incidentally to tie them economically and psychologically to the political establishment and the status quo (p. 174).

16. On state sector unionization in Japan, Alice H. Cook et al. (1971).

17. Beveridge (1944):200.

18. Leo Panitch cites Jack Jones "the main union architect of the Social Contract" speaking in 1977 to a TUC conference:

I have yet to see . . . any firm evidence that the efforts of the sector working parties [i.e. the bodies charged under the NEDC with investment planning] . . . have produced any significant increase in investment or in employment, and that is the test. . . . In my view, an industrial strategy which relies only on the deliberations of sector working parties, on polite talks with industrialists and trade associations . . . is not a strategy at all, but an excuse for one. Cited in Panitch (1981):39.

19. The French CGT position was that the criterion proposed for an incomes policy, e.g., that wage increases should not exceed average increases in productivity, would only be acceptable "s'il s'agissait d'une société différente de la nôtre." La Documentation française (1964).

20. Reynaud (1968).

21. The breakdown of "concerted action" between unions and employers in Germany is analyzed in Markovits, Gibbs, and Allen (1980). Windmuller (1969) analyzes the strains affecting national wages policy in the Netherlands in the late 1960s.

22. See note 4 above.

23. OECD, Economic Surveys France, February 1977, p. 52. Direct controls were also used by the socialist Mauroy government in 1982. The arguments used were similar to those advanced for incomes policies in earlier social democratic

experiments: the Left must hang together to make it a success in order that the Left experiment in government can succeed. (In this vein, see an article by Maurice Duverger, "La gauche unie ou divisée?" addressed to the French Communist Party, in Le Monde, July 11–12, 1982.)

    24. OECD, Economic Surveys, Sweden, June 1981.

    25. Katzenstein (1983).

    26. Friedberg (1974):94–108; and Friedberg avec la collaboration de D. Desjeux (1976); also Zysman (1983):99–169.

    27. The transformation of French planning consequential upon France's entry into the EEC are discussed in Stephen S. Cohen (1977). Michael Crozier, who has appeared as the sociologist of Giscardien liberalism, wrote two articles for Le Monde entitled "Reflexions sur le VIIIe Plan" (August 8 and 9, 1980) in which he argued that the purpose of the Plan should be to assist the French economy to adapt to international competition:

C'est de l'analyse de l'évolution du monde qu'il faut partir et non pas de l'examen de la situation française. Notre competivité différentielle est notre guide. Pour obtenir le plein emploi, nous ne devons plus chercher à employer toutes nos capacités actuelles telles qu'elles sont, mais à les placer sur tous le créneaux où elles peuvent être compétitives.

Stoffaës (1978) also argued that the aim of industrial policy should be to make French industry more aggressively competitive on the world market, although he perceives that this can be achieved only by a more interventionist, neomercantilist state.

    28. Zysman (1983):168–69.

    29. French planners speak of an "80-20 ratio"; i.e., effective planning requires that close to 80 percent of production in a sector come from about 20 percent of the firms. See Shonfield (1965):138. Winkler (1976: t. 17, no. 1, pp. 120–21) also makes the point that corporatism is facilitated by concentration of capital since government can influence the whole economy by controlling a few big corporations.

    30. The development of enterprise corporatism among established workers in the leading sectors of industry emerges from the debate about the "new working class" in France. This is discussed in part 3 below.

    31. Girvan (1976) has used the term rentier state.

    32. Classic dependency is expounded by Frank (1969). The notion of dependent development was put forward by Cardoso and Faletto (1969) and has been elaborated in Evans, (1979).

    33. Frieden (1981). For the Third-World countries, borrowing from private transnational banks was more expensive, but it avoided the politically unpalatable conditions attached to borrowing from the IMF. The total external public debt of ninety-six developing countries rose from $U.S. 75.1 billion in 1970 to $U.S. 272 billion in 1977, the most significant change being in liabilities to private commercial banks whose net share of external borrowing of non-oil-producing, less developed countries rose from 6 percent in 1968 to 42.9 percent in 1977. Crough (1979):190.

    34. Regarding cooperatives, Fals Borda (1970) presents the case that such organizations in the Latin American experience have been dependent on states serving the interests of foreign capital. Korovkin (1985) has perceived a complex variety of possibilities among agricultural cooperatives in Peru, ranging from dependency on the state to autonomy in the market, although the role of the state has remained generally preponderant.

    35. The Peruvian military regime under General Velasco, 1968–1975, attempted to mobilize peasants and urban marginals into state-sponsored organiza-

tions. Following the Mexican and the Algerian revolutions, more conservative governments in those countries effected a demobilization of the rural populations through corporative organizations. State corporatism has also been used to exclude, domesticate, or replace preexisting class-based trade unions. Alfred Stepan (1978:74–81) has suggested a distinction between inclusionary and exclusionary corporatisms, the former partially mobilizing and the latter partially demobilizing.

36. Touraine and Pécaud, in Touraine (1976):207–9, 219–26; also Stepan (1978):160–81.

37. Dore (1973) analyzes the Japanese pattern of labor relations. This is a case of the enterprise corporatist mode as presented in this book. Dore subsequently examined the relevancy of the Japanese experience for present-day cases of late development (Mexico, Sri Lanka, and Senegal) and concluded that though there were similarities in the material organization of production—especially the dualism of the labor force and its implications for management—the two factors that stand out as different from the Japanese case are the proportionately greater role of the state and the importance of an international diffusion of ideas about labor relations. See Dore (1974).

38. Among political parties representative of populist leadership in cartel-type states have been the Partido revolucionario institucional (PRI) of Mexico and the Congress Party of India. Both institutionalized a stalemate among social groups based in different modes of social relations of production, none of which had been able to establish hegemony. President Getulio Vargas of Brazil in the 1930s institutionalized a corporative form of state, and President Sukarno of Indonesia attempted in the 1950s and 1960s to lead a cartel of indigenous social and political forces that included both the Communist Party and Islamic nationalist military officers.

39. See especially Evans (1979).

40. See ch. 6, notes 60 and 69.

41. Schmitter, in Chalmers, ed. (1972), adopting the Juan Linz typology of states, likened the corporatist-authoritarian type to the Bonapartist state analyzed by Marx in The Eighteenth Brumaire in which the executive power makes itself increasingly independent. Schmitter wrote: "external dependence contributes to the sort of nationally stalemated, nonhegemonic class and interest structure which Karl Marx postulated as the distinctive basis for Bonapartism . . ." (p. 101). Evans (1979):42 rejects the Bonapartist-technocratic version as regards Brazil and says that the state is, in fact, based on the national bourgeoisie, although this assertion is not so clearly borne out in his analysis (in which Brazilian national capital appears to have been dependent on the state for the opportunity of keeping a place alongside multinational capital, definitely the junior partner in a "triple alliance" of state, multinational, and local elite capital, which excludes smaller local capital). On the concept of "revolution from above," see Trimberger (1972). Gramsci perceived that passive revolution encouraged an idealistic view of the state. The technical and political practices of a genuinely hegemonic social group can most readily be seen to be related to that group's social existence and struggle for hegemony. Practices borrowed from abroad by nonhegemonic leadership appear as the result of intellectual choice. Gramsci (1974):116–17.

42. Stavenhagen (1981):106–47.

43. Many factors combined to bring about the debt crisis, varying from country to country. Those states that do not produce their own petroleum requirements or that import food had to face increases in their foreign deficits on these accounts. Those that had invested heavily in consumer goods manufacturing increased their

need to import foreign capital goods and intermediate goods. Those that counted on higher rents from exports of raw materials saw their expectations disappointed as world raw-material prices declined while their import bills for state-backed development projects exceeded forecasts. Whatever the particular combination of contributing factors, typically the neomercantilist developmentalist state found itself caught in the debt trap. The term *debt trap* is from Payer (1974).

44. Elsenhans (1983).

45. Stepan (1978) examined the case of sugar workers' cooperatives formed by the military government in Peru. Members of the cooperatives had an interest in limiting the number of full members to whom shares in the benefits of the cooperative would be paid. Rather than take on more members, they employed temporary laborers (who were not cooperative members) at lower rates of pay. This led to conflict between member and nonmember workers.

46. Michalet (1976:206–7) discusses what he calls the dialectic of homogenization-differentiation. The characteristics of the two models are examined in this book and also in Madeuf and Michalet (1978). Differences in labor costs among national economies become a basis for unequal exchange through the terms of trade in the international economy to the extent that commodities embodying more labor produced in poor countries are exchanged for commodities embodying less labor produced in the rich countries. The unequal exchange concept, for whatever it is worth as an analytical tool, applies only to commodities exchange. Emmanuel (1972); also Brown (1974:71–72, 278–79), who points out that the terms of trade are only a small part of the dependent relationship of satellite to metropolis.

47. Griffin (1974) cites figures to suggest that in 1970, 70 percent of research and development was done in the United States and only 2 percent in less developed countries.

48. U.S. President's Materials Policy Commission (1952). See also Krasner (1978):50–53, 93–133, 188–216; and Joyce and Gabriel Kolko (1972):620–30.

49. Biasco (1979):99–100.

50. Palloix, in Radice, ed. (1975a):63–88, esp. 73–83. Also Attali (1975):35–42. Surplus may be extracted without any organizational linkage between firms through royalties for patented technology. Vaitsos, in Radice, ed. (1975:198), writes:

If the licenser retains control of the volume, markets, prices and quality of goods sold, the sources, prices and quality of its intermediate and capital goods, the hiring of key personnel, the type of technology used, etc., then the only basic decision left to the licensee is whether or not to enter into an agreement to purchase technology. Technology, through the present process of commercialization, becomes thus a mechanism for control of the recipient firms. Such control supersedes, complements or substitutes that which results from ownership of the capital of a firm.

Vaitsos estimates that in 1969 royalties from Chile amounted to more than three times profits remitted by foreign subsidiaries (p. 206).

51. Duncan (1982).

52. Girvan (1976:36–50, 84, 141–43, 149, 152–56) argues that localization and nationalization of mineral extraction activities in Third-World countries constitutes the present new phase of their incorporation into world structures of dependency, not a break with dependency. The "buro-political managers" (state bureaucracy plus politicians) have through nationalization or localization succeeded in raising the revenues of the periphery state from its extractive industries. With these revenues, they undertake employment creation, support of the private sector, and maintenance of public order. From the perspective of the multinationals concerned, nationalization has been a source of new capital, has not weakened their

managerial control, and has committed the periphery state more nearly fully to the success of the international industry on which much of its revenues depend. In such circumstances, the moderate response of both multinationals and U.S. governments may be understood, not as resignation to fate, but as the working out of new mechanisms to preserve the essential features of the world-economy structure while accommodating to political groups in Third-World countries whose support is needed in order to maintain their part of the structure. See also Krasner (1978).

53. Evans (1979):74, 165, 194, 261, 288–90.

54. Strange (1979). On the decline of profits and investments from the mid-1960s, Arnoult (1978). On the origins of the Eurodollar market, Hirsch, (1967):236–42, and McKinnon (1979). Also Crough (1979):esp.73–92, 186–90. Paul Sweezy and the *Monthly Review* group have stressed the credit expansion phenomenon as an indicator of economic crisis in capitalism, e.g., Sweezy (1981), also the articles collected in Magdoff and Sweezy (1977).

55. Hymer, in Bhagwati, ed. (1972). Evans (1979):30–31 refers to the internationalization of the internal market of a peripheral country. Vernon (1966) propounds his product life-cycle theory to explain industrialization based on consumer-durable type products.

56. For example, no national economy (even the U.S. economy) was big enough to absorb the level of production reached by the computer industry by the 1980s. See Duncan (1982):93. On the question of scales of production with modern technology and less-developed-country markets, see Merhav (1969).

57. Cox (1976). Charles Levinson, one-time secretary-general of the International Chemical and General Workers, Geneva, was a leading publicist for multinational collective bargaining. See Levinson (1972). Levinson's claims are contested in a series of articles by Northrup and Rowan (1974).

58. Ozawa (1979:esp. 7, 80–81, 201, 203) points out that multinational expansion of Japanese industry was of particular concern to the low-productivity, labor-intensive sector of Japanese industry, which was hard hit by tight labor markets in the latter half of the 1960s. The availability of cheap labor in South Korea, Hong Kong, and Singapore was a boon to this sector, enabling it to survive competitively.

59. As background to the use here of the term *internationalizing of the state*, there is an extensive literature touching on the impact of external influences on nation-states. Beloff (1961) was perhaps the first to attempt to analyze systematically the mechanisms whereby participation in international organizations altered the internal policy-making practices of states. Cox and Jacobson (1974) represented the political systems of international organization as including segments of states. Keohane and Nye (1974) pointed to the processes whereby coalitions are formed among segments of the apparatuses of different states and the ways in which international institutions facilitate such coalitions. These various works, while they point to the existence of mechanisms for policy coordination among states and for penetration of external influences within states, do not discuss the implications of these mechanisms for the structure of power within states. It is this structural aspect I wish to designate by the term *internationalizing of the state*. Christian Palloix (1975b:82) refers to "l'internationalisation de l'appareil de l'Etat national, de certains lieux de cet appareil d'Etat . . .", by which he designates those segments of national states that serve as policy supports for the internationalization of production. He thus raises the question of structural changes in the state, though he does not develop the point. The various works on neo-Marxist structural views of the state seem generally to have neglected the international dimension of the state, e.g.,

Miliband (1969), Poulantzas (1968), Habermas (1976), Offe (1975), Anderson (1974). Keohane and Nye (1977), subsequent to the work mentioned above, linked the transgovernmental mechanism to the concept of "interdependence." I find this concept tends to obscure the power relationships involved in structural changes in both state and world order and prefer not to use it for that reason. Gourevitch (1978) does retain the concept of interdependence while insisting that it be linked with power struggles among social forces within states. A recent fashion has been to introduce the word "regime" to designate "principles, norms, rules, and decision-making procedures around which actor expectations converge in a given issue-area," as in the special issue of *International Organization* (Spring), 36(2), 1982, edited by Stephen D. Krasner. The objection I see to the method followed in this particular literature (though not, of course, to some contributions to it) is that the method tries to find general propositions about political behavior abstracted from historical process. I find myself in agreement with the criticisms of Susan Strange included in that special issue ("Cave! hic dragones: a critique of regime analysis," pp. 479–96). Closer to the notion advanced here is that suggested by Laurence Harris, in Miliband and Saville, eds. (1980):

I think it [the state] should be conceived as a hierarchical structure of state institutions, only one set of which are those encompassed by the idea of the nation state. At one level in the hierarchy we have to place international state institutions such as the IMF, the organs of the EEC, the Bank for International Settlements, and NATO. At a different level, we have to place the institutions of 'the local state' of towns and regions. With such a hierarchical concept of the state it is possible to analyze the relations between the actions of agents in its different parts, the manner in which organized class forces in one part affect the others, and how market forces affect each part of the structure (p. 260).

This definition is, however, limited to the government apparatus aspect of the state and ignores the historic-bloc aspect. My emphasis is more on the process of internationalization or formation of the hierarchical structure than on the structure depicted as a finished thing.

60. Strange (1971):291–92.

61. Emerson, in Abraham and Abeele, eds. (1981); Abraham and Lemineur-Toumson, in Abraham and Abeele, eds. (1981). François-Xavier Ortoli, the vice-president of the European Communities' executive, has stressed the need for closer coordination of internal monetary policies, including money supply, exchange rate, and interest rate policies, in Abraham and Abeele, eds. (1981):18.

62. Speech reproduced in Radice (1975):237.

63. Turkey, Peru, Portugal, and Jamaica underwent such internal changes during the late 1970s.

Turkey was confronted with a balance of payments crisis in 1976–77. An IMF team left Ankara in December 1977 without coming to an agreement on loan conditions with the Demirel government, which was unwilling to accept some terms of the IMF's stabilization package. A new government was subsequently formed by Mr. Ecevit, which did come to an agreement with the IMF and signed a letter of intent in March 1978.

In Peru, relations with the IMF were involved in the changeover from the government of General Juan Velasco Alvarado to that of General Morales Bermudez in 1976. Gen. Morales Bermudez tried to play the human rights card in Washington to get a better deal, telling President Jimmy Carter that the IMF deflationary stabilization program would inevitably lead to a cycle of social agitation and repression that would oblige Peruvian governments to violate human rights. His argument appears to have carried little weight in Washington. (Thierry Maliniak in Le Monde, November 15, 1977.) By the end of 1982, the Peruvian army and police were engaged in repression of an insurgency that had occupied much of the province of Ayacucho (Le Monde, January 3, 1983) while the government's austerity program was being monitored by quarterly visits from the IMF. Continuation of the IMF-dictated austerity program led, in March 1983, to a general strike. The government in reprisal imprisoned the trade union leaders. In June 1983, a government crisis forced the resignation of the minister of labor who had criticized the IMF-dictated policies for making the poorest bear the social costs of economic stabilization and for undermining local producers in favor of imports (Le Monde, July 1, 1983).

In Portugal, the first (minority socialist) government of Mario Soares was defeated by a confidence vote in Parliament in December 1977 when other political parties refused to support an austerity economic program worked out with an IMF consortium of which the Federal Republic of Germany was the key member. The crisis was resolved by the installation of a new Soares government with centrist party representation and a technocrat (Victor Constancio) in charge of a superministry of the economy (New York Times, December 9, 1977; Le Monde, January 29, 1978).

Foreign commercial banks cut off their credit to Jamaica in March 1976, citing inflation and wage increases as causes for alarm concerning the Jamaican economy. This left the IMF as the only possible source of foreign credit. The Michael Manley government had adopted economic nationalism and a social policy program that IMF sources regarded as responsible for persistent deficits and inflation. The government was considered in Washington to be "left-wing." Lengthy interrupted negotiations, punctuated by stop-go government measures, came to an end in December 1979 with the government's refusal to accept IMF conditions, which included an incomes policy designed to reduce real wages, devaluation, and cuts in government spending (which would have involved firing 11,000 employees at a time when unemployment was more than 25 percent). Manley appealed from the IMF officials to the executive board of the Fund, which preferred not to respond, awaiting the results of elections that Manley had had to advance for lack of funds. The Manley government's tractations with the Fund had resulted in austerity, falling real wages, and rising unemployment without meeting the Fund's conditions. The new government of Edward P. G. Seaga, which was formed after Manley lost the elections, quickly met with a delegation of U.S. business leaders and came to an agreement with the IMF. Loans once again flowed to Jamaica. See Paul Fabra in Le Monde, July 15, 1980; Phillips, in Holly Sklar, ed. (1980); and Girvan and Bernal (1982), and Arthur Lewin (1982).

As for Zaire, following the Shaba incursions of 1977-78, a conference of creditors laid down the condition that officials of the IMF be placed within the key ministries of the state to oversee the fulfilment of the conditions for debt renewal (New York Times, May 24, 1978, IV, 13:3; June 14, 1978, I:4; June 15, 1978, II:1). This is reminiscent of the arrangements put in place by the western European creditors of the Ottoman Empire and Egypt in the late nineteenth century whereby western agents administered the customs services of those states in order to ensure debt service. See Feis (1930):332–41, 384–97.

64. The argument of those who have written about "ungovernability" is couched in more general terms, i.e., the decline of deference, a growing intensity of political participation, the greater difficulty of states to serve capital accumulation needs. They consider a broad measure of public apathy necessary to make liberal democratic government workable. See Crozier et al (1975).

65. Industrial policy poses some interesting issues as between the old and the new corporatisms. See Diebold, (1980); and Pinder et al (1979). If planning evokes the specter of economic nationalism, industrial policy, as the Trilateral Commission study points out, can be looked upon with favor in a world-economy perspective as a necessary aspect of policy harmonization:

We have argued that industrial policies are needed to deal with structural problems in modern economies. Thus, international action should not aim to dismantle these policies. The pressure should, rather, be towards positive and adaptive industrial policies, whether on the part of single countries or groups of countries combined. Far from being protectionist, industrial policy can help them to remove a cause of protectionism, by making the process of adjustment less painful (p. 50).

66. Stepan (1978):287.

## Part 3.  Production Relations in the Making of the Future

## Chapter 8.  The World Economic Crisis: Impact on State and World-Order Structures

1. Biasco (1979):11. Biasco, an Italian economist, explores the social basis for world-economy inflation in the work cited. Although political analysis of inflation is sparse in Anglo-American literature, there are notable exceptions. Maier (1975) discusses the social coalitions and conflicts underlying inflation and stabilization in post-World War I Western Europe. Maier advanced his thinking on this subject further in Hirsch and Goldthorpe, eds. (1978). See also Hirschman (1981:177-207); and Maier and Lindberg, eds. (1984).

2. Calleo (1982):145–47, 152.

3. Maier's (1978:59–61) type of "creeping inflation." On the growth of industrial conflict from 1968, Adam and Reynaud, (1978). On its relationship to inflation, Biasco (1979):19–22, 102–19; and Jackson et al (1972).

4. Biasco (1979):19–21, 101.

5. Hirschman (1981) quotes the advice given by President Juan Peron of Argentina to his fellow populist dictator President Carlos Ibáñes of Chile in 1953:

My dear friend: Give to the people, especially to the workers, all that is possible. When it seems to you that already you are giving them too much, give them more. You will see the results. Everyone will try to scare you with the specter of an economic collapse. But all of this is a lie. There is nothing more elastic than the economy which everyone fears so much because no one understands it (p. 102).

6. Hirschman (1981):192–93.

7. Biasco (1979):37–9, 86–99, 113, 159–60; Block (1977):163–64, 206–10; Calleo (1982):136–38.

8. Strange (1971):1–21.

9. Block (1977):195.

10. Calleo (1982):152.

11. Crozier et al. (1975).

12. Bowles and Gintis (1982). Note here esp. pp. 54 & 86. Also Biasco (1979):101–23.

13. Calleo (1982):129.

14. This is a point on which some radical economists appear to agree with the analysis of conservatives. It is especially stressed by Bowles and Gintis (1982):69–78, who, though refraining from attributing to regulatory and redistri-

butive programs the sole or primary cause of the slowdown in the capitalist growth process, maintain that they have made an important contribution to that slowdown.

15. The phrase "corporate welfare bums" was used by David Lewis, former leader of the New Democratic Party of Canada, to castigate government readiness to provide relief for big corporations in financial trouble.

16. It is remarkable, in the light of scholarly stress on the "legitimacy" function of the welfare state, how little opposition there has been to this tendency to sacrifice employment in the fight against inflation and how little of that has been clearly grounded in alternative ideology. An exception was the 1982 year-end statement of the Canadian Conference of Roman Catholic Bishops, which asserted that the high unemployment rates resulting from government antiinflation policy reflected "a basic moral disorder" in society and indicated the need for a "basic shift in values" (Toronto Globe and Mail, January 1, 1983).

17. McCracken Report (1977).

18. Bowles (1982:49) calls this "the shift from an accumulation process constrained primarily by conditions of aggregate demand (or the realization of surplus value) to an accumulation process constrained primarily by conditions of exploitation."

19. Biasco (1979):104; Bowles (1982):64.

20. Sabel (1982):esp.78–126.

21. Italy is one country in which a policy of working-class solidarity has been effectively pursued by the left notably during the autunno caldo of 1969. The difficulties for the left presented by the fiscal background to political issues and by the segmentation of the work force were, however, apparent in the discomfiture of the PCI following the referendum held on June 9 and 10, 1985, on wage indexation, which the PCI initiated. The referendum proposed to reverse the Italian government's policy of ending wage indexation as part of an antiinflation program. It rallied less than 46 percent of the voters in favor, while the majority supported the government. The issue had the effect of dividing established employees (in government and big industry), who would have benefited from indexed wages, from the growing numbers of nonestablished and self-employed, who would not. Thus some otherwise loyal communist voters split with the Party on this issue, while neofascists of the MSI, who have many adherents among state employees, supported the referendum proposal. The event confirms that even in this most ideologically evolved and articulate political party, analysis of the implications of the economic crisis and the development of appropriate strategies are still far from adequate.

22. This rhetoric recalls the travail, famille, patrie slogan of the Pétainist French state. It tends to confirm the thesis that there is a contradiction between the undisciplined individualism and hedonistic values that capitalist society tends to produce and the ascetic individualism and other disciplined traditional or precapitalist values required to sustain the kind of state that can perpetuate capitalism. Habermas (1976):75–92. This thesis implies that fascism in some form is the ultimate recourse for the maintenance of capitalist development.

23. Ginsberg and Shefter (1984) argue that "supply-side" economics was more a political program than an economic theory; i.e., it was a rationale for overcoming the contradiction between cutting taxes and increasing defense spending, measures addressed to different segments of the political coalition Reagan's candidacy put together.

24. Magri (1982).

25. Stoffäes (1978) contrasts the quasi-autarkic approach to constructing socialism of the French Communist Party (PCF) and the CERES group of the Socialist

Party, in which France would have to isolate itself from European and world-economy influences, with the technocratic approach of the Michel Rocard faction in the Socialist Party, which advocates an offensive strategy of adjustment to the world economy (pp. 7–12). Stoffäes concludes: "On ne peut faire de bon socialisme à l'intérieur qu'en restant libéral vis-à-vis de l'extérieur: c'est là le sens du véritable *compromis historique* qui s'offre à la France" (p. 345). The British counterpart to the PCF-CERES position would be *The Alternative Economic Strategy. A Labour Movement Response to the Economic Crisis*, produced by the Conference of Socialist Economists London Coordinating Group (London: Blackrose Press, 1980).

    26. Katzenstein, ed. (1977).

    27. Katzenstein (1983), and Katzenstein (1984).

    28. Zysman (1983:306), like Katzenstein, inquires into the internal determinants of differences in national economic policies. Where Katzenstein looks for generalizable structural characteristics, e.g., strong/weak states, centralized/decentralized social processes, and the composition of dominant coalitions, Zysman pays more attention to economic organization and practices, especially the relationships among government, finance, and industry. Zysman argues that these institutional arrangements determine distinctive developmental types and that variations in the power of social groups account only for differences of outcomes *within* these types.

    29. Schmitter (1974).

    30. Ginsberg and Shefter (1984) point to the disintegration of the New Deal coalition with the progressive alienation from the Democratic Party of (1) the internationally oriented, technologically advanced, and capital-intensive sectors of business that Franklin Roosevelt had cultivated; (2) the defense-sector industries that had profited from the Korean and Vietnam War booms; and (3) manual workers who perceived the McGovern candidacy as geared to a shaky alliance between blacks and the "New Politics" segment of the upper middle class. The Reaganite coalition or "Reconstituted Right" politically reunified U.S. business, including the defense industry; social and religious conservatives; Southern whites; Northern blue-collar workers; and large segments of the suburban middle class. These authors conclude:

Each of Reagan's themes—tax cuts, social service reductions, expanded military spending, relaxation of business regulations, and so on—was designed to establish links between Reagan and a major national political force. The chief problem faced by the Reaganites was that these theses, however plausible individually, were mutually contradictory. The most important of these contradictions was the obvious discrepancy between Reagan's promise of substantial tax relief for the middle class and Reagan's pledge to drastically increase defense spending. (p. 39).

What these authors here describe is, in Gramscian terms, an unresolved crisis of representation, given a transitory stability through caesarism.

    31. Zysman (1983):182–84, 201–6, 212–16.

    32. Witness the self-conscious efforts of a neomercantilist like Stephen Krasner (1978:5–90) to rehabilitate a "statist" perspective in U.S. political science. The very term has a foreign ring in the U.S. cultural context.

    33. A *New York Times* editorial commenting on the industrial-policy proposals put forward in January 1984 by a study group co-chaired by Lane Kirkland of the AFL-CIO, Felix Rohatyn, an investment banker, and Irving Shapiro, formerly of DuPont de Nemours, was entitled: "Industrial policy = industrial politics" (January 23, 1984). It concluded: "Conventional political pressures could all too easily bring damaging remedies that favor one industry or region over another, or invoke protectionist measures, at enormous cost to consumers and competition."

This judgment confirms Krasner's view that the United States has a "weak state," i.e., one not sufficiently able to subordinate particular interests to a transcendent "national interest."

34. Ozawa (1979).

35. Stoffäes (1978):105–6, 265–68.

36. Rohatyn et al. (1984). Rohatyn has been one of the foremost advocates of the state-capitalist approach in the United States (see also Rohatyn, 1981). His is one voice in a broad band of economic opinion that Robert Walters (1985) has analyzed as a "structural-strategic" orientation that has arisen in challenge to the conventional liberal orientation.

37. Stoffäes (1978):224, 338.

38. The French Socialist government under President François Mitterand has found itself in the somewhat paradoxical position of trying to encourage a shift in French industrial relations practice from state regulation toward union-management negotiation at a time when the trade unions have been declining in strength. In part, this weakening stems from a relative decline in the manual work force common to all advanced capitalist countries; in part, it is also due to a relative drop in affiliations to those trade unions with a political orientation (CGT and CFDT) compared with those for which bread-and-butter issues are paramount. The more politicized unions have also become critical of and taken their distance from government policy. These tendencies raise questions about the future strength of labor in the French polity and the future orientation of bipartite and tripartite production relations. They may open the way for an increase in enterprise-corporatist patterns insofar as the politicized unions continue to lose strength. Jean-Daniel Reynaud (1984:54) has observed a widening gap between trade-union activists (militants) and the rank and file:

Cette distance n'a rien en soi d'anormal: le prolétariat a toujours eu une avantgarde. Encore faut-il qu'il se reconnaisse en elle, que l'écart soit moteur et mobilisateur. On peut se demander si aujourd'hui l'écart entre un appareil resté très fidèle à des traditions ouvrières et doctrinales et une base de plus en plus bousculée par les transformations des structures professionnelles et des cultures n'est pas un fossé.

Gérard Adam (1983) developed this viewpoint, which has, as might be expected, been much criticized by the various trade-union organizations. His thesis concords with our proposition that there exists a widespread crisis of representation in the advanced capitalist countries, including their working classes, and that this crisis is related to changes in the relationships among producer groups and the lack of adaptation of the organization, strategies, and ideologies of political parties and labor movements to these changes.

39. As, for instance, in British football "hooliganism," rampant for more than a decade and culminating in the massacre at the Heysel stadium in Brussels on May 29, 1985, which left 38 dead and 450 injured. The origins of the violence have been widely linked to the marginalization of some three million unemployed, predominantly youth, in Britain. The reaction has strengthened the call for more stringent police and security controls. Indeed, the disaster was in large measure attributed to the ineffectiveness of Belgian police measures compared with those practiced by their British counterparts.

40. Crozier et al (1975). The question is also posed by Stoffäes (1978:340): "Est-ce à dire que pour réussir le déploiement et mener une politique industrielle efficace, il faut sortir de la démocratie?" Stoffäes places his hopes (not entirely convincingly) in the efficacy of state leadership to persuade and assist people to

make the difficult changes in their lives that industrial redeployment would require.

41. The fiscal crisis of New York City in 1975 and its sequel could be a paradigm for the emergence and contradictions of the state-capitalist approach. It is not without significance that Felix Rohatyn, a principal architect of the settlement reached in the NYC fiscal crisis, is one of the major advocates of state capitalism in the United States. The crisis has been analyzed in political terms by Martin Shefter (1977):98–127. The background to the crisis lay in the emergence of three new political groups during the 1960s: the reform movement, the black civil-rights movement, and the movement to unionize city employees. In 1965, the reformers abandoned their allies in the municipal labor movement to back John Lindsay for mayor. To gain political support in an attack on the municipal bureaucracy and unions, this combination allied with the black civil-rights movement, an alliance that contained the promise of an expansion of municipal services to this client group. Lindsay found he could not govern the city without the support of the municipal unions, and to win their support he conceded their demands in the 1969–70 negotiations. Since the city could neither raise through taxes nor obtain through the budget of New York State sufficient revenues to pay for the enhanced expenditures resulting from these concessions to both blacks and unions, it had recourse to borrowing from the banks. By the mid-1970s, several factors combined to precipitate financial crisis: inflation raised the costs of municipal services, recession limited revenues, and there was an explosion in the costs of retirement benefits granted to city employees in the previous decade. In face of the evident inability of the city to service its expanded debt, banks and New York State officials were caught between unwillingness to concede more in taxes or loans and realization that city bankruptcy would have disastrous repercussions for themselves, as well as the city. The city was, in effect, placed in a kind of trusteeship. The state, at the urging of the banks, created an Emergency Financial Control Board empowered to freeze the wages of city employees, approve all city contracts, and supervise city finances. Members of the banking community were placed in positions of control over the city budget and administration. Retrenchment was directed at programs with black clienteles and at labor costs. The former were cut most easily, since the blacks, abandoned by the middle-class reformers who had mobilized them into the politics of the city, lacked effective organization to retain independent political clout. Municipal unions were a more difficult target because better organized; nevertheless, they were vulnerable to their corporatist involvement with the city—to prejudice the city's access to borrowing in the financial market, e.g., by forcing wage concessions, would undermine the source of their own salaries; and furthermore, the unions had been pressured to invest a substantial part of their pension funds in new city bonds, which would be rendered worthless by bankruptcy. The lessons of this episode are that (1) corporatism can provide a way out of a fiscal crisis provoked by the demands of new political groups; (2) this solution requires a restriction of decision power to elements acceptable to the financial market and the political demobilization or exclusion of elements likely to challenge that restriction; and (3) it is vulnerable to a political remobilization of the excluded elements.

42. Miller (1983).

43. Crough (1979):199; and U.S. Congress (1976).

44. Paul Volker, chairman of the U.S. Federal Reserve, has proposed that the IMF be both strengthened (by giving it a central position in the management of the world monetary system) and politicized (by giving it a permanent council of ministers): "The object here, quite frankly, is to bring a little more international political clout to the IMF and in turn to have international concerns reflected intimately and

directly in the councils of national governments." Volker, in Boarman and Tuerch, eds. (1976):18.

45. Strange (1985). Also Stoffäes (1978).

46. McGeehan (1985).

47. Laurence Harris, in Miliband and Saville, eds. (1980); citation from pp. 257–58.

48. Alain Vernholes, "1982: Les aléas du changement," Le Monde, December 31, 1982, and January 1, 1983.

49. Block, in Miliband and Saville, eds. (1980), examines the possibility that state intervention might pass a "tipping point" beyond which opposition on the part of capital would be ineffective. He thinks this is conceivable only in the case of a right-wing authoritarianism installed with the support of capital, e.g., the Nazi regime. Skocpol's (1980) analysis of the New Deal portrays a situation in which the limits set by capital block any radical action by the state to mobilize and release new productive forces.

50. President-elect Alan Garcia of Peru, in the summer of 1985, announced a program combining state encouragement of production of local basic needs rather than exports and a limit of debt service to 10 percent of export earnings. This program was the antithesis of IMF antiinflation recommendations for Peru, which were considered by the new government to have socially explosive implications. A more difficult case for the international financial networks because of its much larger debt is that of Argentina, where the elected civilian government of President Raul Alfonsin, which ended a long period of military rule, confronted, in the summer of 1985, an inflation rate of 1300 percent, noncooperation of the Peronist trade unions in an austerity program attempting to restabilize the currency, and inability to service the foreign debts. Fidel Castro, speaking to an international meeting in Havana in August 1985, called once again upon Latin American governments for a collective moratorium on foreign debt service.

51. Strange (1971):295.


## Chapter 9. Mutations in the Social Structure of Accumulation

1. Gramsci (1971):277–318.

2. There is an anticipation of the Reaganite alliance with the "moral majority" in this passage of Gramsci's prison notebooks (1971:304):

The attempts made by Ford, with the aid of a body of inspectors, to intervene in the private lives of his employees and to control how they spent their wages and how they lived is an indication of these tendencies. Though these tendencies are still only "private" or only latent, they could become, at a certain point, state ideology, inserting themselves into traditional puritanism and presenting themselves as a renaissance of the pioneer morality and as the "true" America, etc.

3. Gramsci (1971):302.

4. This is a reference to Frederick Winslow Taylor (1911:40), who wrote that "it would be possible to train an intelligent gorilla so as to become a more efficient pig-iron handler than any man could be."

5. Balancing his praise of the division of labor as the basis for expanding markets, raising production and increasing wealth, Adam Smith also wrote:

In the progress of the division of labor, the employment of the far greater part of those who live by labor, that is, of the great body of the people, come to be confined to a few very simple operations, frequently to one or two. But the understandings of the greater part of men are necessarily formed by their ordinary em-

ployments. The man whose whole life is spent in performing a few simple operations, of which the effects too are, perhaps, always the same, or very nearly the
same, has no occasion to exert his understanding, or to exercise his invention in
finding out expedients for removing difficulties which never occur. He naturally
loses, therefore, the habit of such exertion and generally becomes as stupid and
ignorant as it is possible for a human creature to become . . .

It is otherwise in the barbarous societies, as they are commonly called, of
hunters, of shepherds, and even of husbandmen in that rude state of husbandry
which precedes the improvement of manufactures, and the extension of foreign
commerce. In such societies the varied occupations of every man oblige every man
to exert his capacity, and to invent expedients for removing difficulties which are
continually occurring. Invention is kept alive, and the mind is not suffered to fall
into that drowsy stupidity, which, in a civilized society, seems to benumb the
understanding of almost all the inferior ranks of people.

From *The Wealth of Nations*, book 5, section 1, f, 50. See Smith (1976) vol. 2, pp.
781–783.

6. Gramsci (1971):309.

7. The threefold typology was proposed by Touraine (1955). It has been taken
over by a number of others, including Mallet (1963) and Shorter and Tilly (1974).

8. Thompson (1968):338–46; Landes (1969):60–63.

9. The first thesis was that of Mallet, (1963); the second is expressed in
Blauner (1964). In a third variant, Naville (1963) argues that automation, far from
integrating workers more closely with their enterprises, leads to a new form of
alienation as work is rendered more stressful and boring. This could, he speculated,
lead workers to attempt to regain control at a higher level (both in the enterprise
and in the coordination of the industrial system as a whole), which would undermine the legitimacy of the capitalist system.

10. Technological determinism has had an important place in theories of
industrial relations. One vein of theory, for instance, explains labor movements in
terms of the condition of labor markets, as in the work of Perlman (1928) and of
Sturmthal, in Arthur M. Ross, ed. (1966):165–81. Sturmthal's thesis is that an
abundance of labor leads to a labor movement focusing on political action, while a
scarcity of labor inclines unions toward collective bargaining, job control, and
economistic practices. The abundance or scarcity of labor derives at least in part
from the technology of industry, i.e., technologies that employ relatively unskilled
labor drawn from a homogeneous and abundant pool versus technologies that
require scarce skilled labor, whose supply can be regulated by craft associations.
This approach explains something about the nature of labor movements but nothing
about changes in technology or labor markets. Another theoretical approach treats
employer power as the determining factor in industrial relations and sees this as
shaped by what can very broadly be called the technological context, as in Ingham
(1974). Ingham compares Swedish and British industrial relations. Briefly, his
argument is that employer action in industrial relations is a consequence of three
main factors; (1) the degree of concentration of capital; (2) the extent of technological
complexity, i.e., coexisting varieties of technology; and (3) the degree of specialization or, conversely, of differentiation in production. Swedish industry is relatively more concentrated, less complex (mainly continuous process production),
and more specialized in export markets. This enables Swedish employers to achieve
greater unity and coherence in their industrial relations practices. British employers, by contrast, are divided along all three dimensions. Like the previously mentioned theories of labor movements, this theory explains something about the behavior of the parties to industrial relations but nothing about the technologies that
are assumed to determine this behavior.

11. Touraine does not espouse a simple technological determinism. Between technological changes and worker responses, he argues, the sociologist must insert the whole social life of the workers (attitudes, group patterns, communications, social relations). Nevertheless, the problem is stated in terms of technology's being the independent variable (see Touraine et al. (1965). S. Barkin, who sponsored this study for the OECD, makes clear in the preface that the purpose of the inquiry was to examine how to minimize worker resistance to technological change, e.g., through active labor market policies and possibly through forms of worker participation (p. 7). A special issue of *Sociolgie du travail* (no. 1, 1979) entitled "L'enjeu de la rationalisation du travail," by contrast, contains articles that put technology itself into the framework of investigation, seeing technological change, not as an independent variable or exogenous force, but as part of a strategy of social conflict.

12. On the question "for whom?", Griffin (1974) shows how research and development is concentrated in the rich countries and preponderantly in the United States. The problems that technology is to solve are defined by capital in the rich countries. Various exhortations toward redirecting research into the specific problems of poor countries have been voiced through the United Nations and conferences organized under its auspices to foster scientific and technological work in favor of less developed countries. Very little in practice seems to have come of this. More effective have been political pressures by some of the more powerful Third-World governments on multinational corporations to decentralize some of their research into their countries, e.g., Evans (1979):276–77. This achievement has resulted in the concerned countries' gaining a greater share of the research and development by multinationals; it has not resulted in a redefinition of development problems in a noncapitalist framework for which technological solutions are to be sought. A significant gap in technological development (indicative of the social power relations directing such development) is the neglect of innovations appropriate to collectively self-managed work. Most self-management thinking focuses on the institutions and procedures of worker participation and control rather than on the work process itself and the possibilities for autonomy and feedback within it.

13. The third point in particular is the central theme of Braverman (1974).

14. Marglin (1974:55). Landes (1969:60–61, 77 116–17), though he put most emphasis on the demand side in his explanation of the origins of the factory mode also recognized the incentive of employer control.

15. There is good evidence that Taylorism, in its origins, was a conscious effort by management both to gain greater control over labor and to make use of a cheaper kind of labor. Apart from Braverman (1974) passim, see also Bendix (1963):269–77.

16. Sabel (1982):39–45.

17. Mickler (1979) studied medium-sized enterprises in Germany in sectors that have been the traditional preserve of skilled professional workers (printing, precision mechanics, furniture making, construction, etc.). He concluded that the deskilling that took place in these industries derived from competition requiring rationalization of work in order to raise productivity, not from conscious management policies favoring deskilling as a means of gaining control over work. (He did, however, note some cases of systematic displacement of skilled workers by low-wage women workers.)

18. Other schematic histories of the labor process have used somewhat different categories from the technology-centered craft-Fordist-automated trilogy referred to here. Richard Edwards (1979) proposes a scheme conceived in terms of methods of worker control: simple control (i.e., face-to-face supervision), technical

control (i.e., control of the worker by the mechanically organized production process itself, e.g., the assembly line), and bureaucratic control (i.e., control embedded in the social organization of the enterprise according to its "rule of law"). These methods of control intersect with a labor force divided into three sectors: secondary (casual nonunion workers), subordinate primary (more stably employed and generally unionized manual workers), and independent primary (professional-technical, career-oriented employees). The resulting segmentation makes coherent collective action by workers very difficult. Gordon, Edwards, and Reich (1982) have added a theory of history to explain the development of this pattern. Basing themselves very largely on U.S. economic history, and focusing on the nature of the work force, they see three stages: (1) a stage of proletarianization during which small commodity production declines and most workers become dependent employees, (2) a stage of homogenization or leveling of status by deskilling and mass production, and (3) a stage of segmentation or the conscious arrangement by employers of separate treatment for different categories of workers, organized through personnel management in big corporations, and the existence of a dual economy of big core enterprises and small and medium peripheral enterprises. Lever-Tracy (1984) has criticized this cluster of theories, demonstrating that (1) there is little in common among some of the groups that are placed in the same categories, e.g., women, blacks, and immigrants in the secondary labor market; (2) there is no necessary and consistent fit between the categories of workers (white men versus women, migrants, etc.), jobs (primary versus secondary), and enterprises (core versus periphery); and (3) there does not appear to be any single causal mechanism to which the patterned historical changes and the existing differentiation is reducible. These points are well taken; they call in question the adequacy of the explanatory theories put forward, although they do not invalidate the observed differentiations that the theories were intended to explain. The present book approaches the same set of observations in a different way. My basic analytical category—modes of social relations of production—posits reciprocal relations among social forces of a dialectical kind, not fixed one-way power relations like systems of worker control. The historical stages observed do not assume a sequence of types (simple control, technical control, bureaucratic control; or proletarianization, homogenization, segmentation) but rather more a cumulative and shifting relationship among modes of social relations of production. The main problems to which this approach draws attention are (1) to understand the interrelationships among coexisting and connected modes of social relations of production and through that the accumulation process and (2) to discern the developmental possibilities arising out of the tensions and contradictions within and among these coexisting modes.

19. The case of Philips-Eindhoven illustrates the dilemma of a core industry headquartered in a country (the Netherlands) that is neither at the heart of the geographical core nor on the periphery. Philips reduced its Netherlands work force significantly from 1970 on, while employment in its plants increased both in peripheral countries (Singapore, Taiwan, South Korea) and in the United States (also in United Kingdom, France, and the Federal Republic of Germany). In the peripheral countries, production of standardized equipment for world mass markets went ahead under various arrangements, e.g., either directly in Philips plants or under arrangements with local firms for Philips distributors. The growth in the United States (and other core countries) was to be explained by the importance of the state as buyer of sophisticated electronic equipment for military and civilian purposes and the necessity of being located in the country to have access to this market. See Teulings (1980).

20. Castles and Kosack (1973).
21. Bluestone and Harrison (1982).
22. *Industrial Relations Review and Report* August 7, 1984. Also Caire (1982). Piore, in Berger and Piore (1980), has posited uncertainty as the principle of distinction between core and periphery of industry and between primary and secondary labor markets. The core is staffed in a permanent way to meet basic demand; the periphery, employing secondary workers, is staffed in a variable way to allow for fluctuations in demand above the basic level. The periphery of industry and the secondary-labor-market workers thus bear the burden of economic uncertainty. Lever-Tracy (1984:70–74) criticizes Piore on the grounds that secondary workers have been so integrated into industrial processes that their work is necessary to the maintenance of production, and consequently, the uncertainty factor cannot account for a good deal of the labor force segmentation that exists. It is, of course, quite possible to retain uncertainty as one of the factors conducive to segmentation without necessarily reducing all segmentation to that single causal principle.

23. Parodi (1978) covers employment strategies in steel, aeronautics, electronics, and agroalimentary industries in the Provence-Alpes-Côte d'Azur region of France in which the subcontracting practice is widespread. The distinction made here between skilled workers and semiskilled, on the one hand, and between permanent and subcontracted employees, on the other, corresponds to the general distinction between primary and secondary labor markets in the work of Doeringer and Piore (1971), who write:

Disadvantaged workers, the theory [of the dual labor market] asserts, are confined to the secondary market by residence, inadequate skills, poor work histories, and discrimination. Although the interconnections between primary and secondary labor markets are seen as either weak or non-existent, primary employers, through devices like subcontracting and temporary employment, can convert primary employment into secondary employment (p. 166).

Unions also contribute to the segmentation when they confine organizational efforts to certain sectors of work, leaving the more costly and difficult to organize outside their purview, e.g., the residential housing sector, which is typically nonunion in the United States (p. 174).

24. Rothschild, (1981), citing, inter alia, U.S. Labor Department, *Employment and Earnings*, March 1974, March 1980, and August 1980; and OECD, *Labour Force Statistics, 1967–1978* (Paris: 1980). Also Rein (1985):22–23.
25. Sengenberger, in Wilkinson, ed. (1981):243–58, esp. 248–51.
26. Wilkinson (1981) speaks of "the trend towards the casualization of the labour force in the metropolitan countries" as one of the broad conclusions emerging from a symposium on labor market segmentation in advanced capitalist countries (p. ix). Franco Chiarello, (1983:217), who uses the concept of "informal economy," which is generally held to cover household and friendship-network production, as well as the underground economy, e.g., Gershuny (1979), sees a systematic process of "informalization" (*un sistematico processo di "informalizzazione) taking place in the advanced capitalist economies. French authors, e.g., Caire (1982), have referred to "*précarisation*" from their contrasting of "precarious," e.g., short-term or temporary jobs, with secure, contractually protected jobs. My use of "peripheralization" includes these other usages. On the parallels with Third-World industrializing countries and nineteenth-century competitive capitalism, Amselle (1980).
27. De Grazia (1980, 1983); Redivo (1983); Tanzi, ed. (1982); Sauvy (1984); and Chiarello (1983). The involvement of organized crime is both as direct "em-

ployer" or "putter-out," as in prostitution and drug trafficking, and as provider of "services" for the extralegal elements of the economy, as in the channeling of illegal workers and protection of clandestine workshops. The Mafia, for instance, assures a supply of child labor to Milan factories; see Amselle (1980). On the size and ramifications of the organized crime "industry" in the United States, estimated to be second only to the first-place oil industry and ahead of the automobile industry in annual revenues, see James Cook (1980).

28. Salamone (1982). I recall an instance of well-paid double employment discovered some years ago to have been current among translators employed by the United Nations and specialized agencies in Geneva. Each organization had a complement of full-time translators on its permanent staff and in addition a budget for free-lance translations to cope with overload. The translators' freemasonry had worked out a system whereby translations for each organization were systematically put out to translators in the employ of other organizations so that translators were getting double pay for their time (official salary plus free-lance pay for work done often on office time). Of course, once discovered, a stop was put to this.

29. Ross and Trachte (1983); also Leichter, "The Return of the Sweatshop," part 2 of an investigation by State Senator F. S. Leichter, February 1981, mimeo., cited in Chiarello (1983):221; also De Grazia (1983):20.

30. De Grazia (1983):24–25; *Tribune de Genève,* June 13, 1983, re Spain. Also Marc Semo in *Le Monde,* March 14, 1981; and Veronique Maurus, "L'Espagne à mi-chemin de la CEE", III. *Le Monde,* June 24, 1982.

31. Emerson (1981):134.

32. Blades (1982); Tanzi (1982); De Grazia (1983); Philipp (1984). A survey article in *Business Week,* April 5, 1982, pp. 64–70, citing a variety of sources, comes to an estimate for the underground economy in the United States of about 14 percent of the officially measured GNP, with a rate of increase during the 1970s of two-and-a-half times that of GNP. Estimates for other countries were: Italy, 25 percent; West Germany, 10 percent; France, 10 to 15 percent; and Japan, 15 percent.

33. Jeffrey Harrod (1980) has criticized the concept of "informal sector" in Third-World countries in a similar perspective.

34. Bluestone and Stevenson, in Wilkinson (1981):23–46.

35. I am indebted to Ester Reiter for being able to consult her unpublished paper (1984?), "Life in a fast food factory," on which this paragraph is based.

36. Sabel (1982:49–56) summarizes recent German research on this kind of core-periphery organization in Bavaria. Mallet (1963:98, 111, 140), in a study of Machines Bull staffing strategy, showed a differentiation between an upgraded and relatively privileged work force paid by the month in the Paris operations and a new labor force of *ouvriers spécialisés* recruited from rural areas for provincial operations.

37. Rubery and Wilkinson, in Wilkinson (1981):115–32. Studies of Solmer's new steel complex at Fos near Marseilles showed that much of the subcontracting was to the same national-scale enterprises that had formerly served Solmer plants in Lorraine and the north of France. See Parodi (1978); note 23 above; and Broda et al. (1978).

38. Sabel (1982):194–219.

39. Jenkins (1981:15).

40. General Motors has focused on social-psychological aspects, leaving Taylorized assembly-line technology much as it was; the United Auto Workers have cooperated in programs at GM and Chrysler; Volvo inaugurated perhaps the most famous QWL experiment at its Kalmar plant in Sweden, replacing the conventional

machine-paced assembly line by a series of production "islands" based on the work of multiskilled, self-regulating groups. The Volvo experiment has been criticized as a kind of "democratization" of the work process imposed by management in an authoritarian manner. Jenkins (1981):27. German and Italian trade unions have given considerable attention to work organization issues in their bargaining, perceiving this terrain as propitious for enhancement of worker control and perhaps as an avenue for change of the capitalist system. Regarding West Germany, see Markovits and Allen (1979b). Pressure by Italian unions was instrumental in displacing assembly-line production at Fiat by a system based on "islands." Italian unions' concern with work organization questions was linked to their efforts to make investment policy a matter for collective bargaining. Amyot (1981). French unions have been generally suspicious and uncooperative regarding employer-initiated work reorganization schemes. Gallie (1978:311–12) studied comparatively the experience in British and French plants of the same company, both engaged in oil refining using highly automated, continuous-process technology. In both plants there had been a move toward greater team control by the process operators. In the French plant, unions were relatively weak in the plant, and union attitudes were derived from headquarters; workers sensed a great distance between themselves and management, and management asserted tighter control in supervision of detail. It was a low-trust situation. In the British plant, the union was stronger in the workplace and more defensive of workshop autonomy; and workers had less of a sense of distance from management. It was by comparison a high-trust situation. Gallie concludes that the need to negotiate technological change in the British situation of balanced power could result in inefficiencies, but the more authoritarian French managerial practice had high social costs. He speculates whether a more participative system might lead to more ready consent on the part of the work force to radical changes (the British practice giving the workers a de facto veto but little initiative). One might further question whether such a participative system would be possible short of more fundamental changes in the capitalist mode of development and accumulation.

41. Barnett and Schorsch (1983); Sabel (1982):204–5; Broda et al. (1978).

42. Redivo (1983):35; Sabel (1982):65.

43. Barnett and Schorsch (1983):83–103.

44. Barnett and Schorsch (1983):93.

45. Brusco (1982); Brusco and Sabel, in Wilkinson, ed. (1981); Sabel (1982):220–31.

46. Brusco and Sabel (1981):108 or Sabel (1982):255.

47. Chiarello (1983):233; Levitan et al. (1972). The underwriting of substandard wages by welfare is analogous to the operation of the Speenhamland system as analyzed by Polanyi (1957:77–85), with the difference that now the law is ignorant of the relationship. Polanyi attributed the pauperization of English country people to Speenhamland.

48. De Grazia (1983):60. In the summer of 1980, Le Monde (June 24, 25, 26, and 27) published a series of articles by Danielle Rouard under the general title "Travailler autrement" concerning various experiments in alternative forms of work in Berlin, Birmingham, Italy, and France.

49. Chiarello (1983) passim; Redivo (1983):37–42.

50. Barraclough (1975).

51. Brandao Lopes (1977). Charles Vanhecke, in Le Monde, July 27, 1982, described the situation in the Maranhao region in the northeast of Brazil:

Il y a dix ans, le Maranhao, c'était la terre promise: à l'entrée de l'Amazonie, une région immensément verte et immensément vide ouverte aux paysans qui fuyaient les sécheresses du Ceara, du Piaui, de Pernambouc voisins. Aujourd'hui, c'est l'un des haut lieux du "western" brésilien: un endroit où la terre peut se disputer à coups de feu entre les *posseiros* et les *pistoleiros*, c'est-à-dire entre les petits agriculteurs sans titre de propriété et les hommes de main des grands fermiers. . . .

Les grands éleveurs ont installé partout leurs barbelés. Les capitaux "industriels" venus du Sud ont envahi l'ouest et le nord du pays en quête de surfaces où le prix de vente du boeuf compenserait celui de l'hectare. L'Etat du Maranhao, grand comme les six dixièmes de la France, a été transformé en enclos d'où disparaissent peu à peu les cultures qui permettaient à la population de s'alimenter.

Pour payer l'industrialisation forcenée de ces quinzes dernières années, les militaires au pouvoir à Brasilia sacrifient les cultures vivrières aux grands produits d'exportation (soja, sucre, café). Ils ne peuvent y parvenir qu'en concentrant au maximum la propriété agricole. Ils ont donc décidé que le Far-West brésilien serait capitaliste ou ne serait pas . . .

52. Nove (1980); Dobb, in Abramsky, ed. (1974).

53. Braudel (1979:3:545–48) concludes his study by underlining the distinction with which he began (1:8) between the market and capitalism. The market is no more an exclusive feature of capitalism than it is inconsistent with socialism.

54. Simes (1975) quotes a report from the *Literaturnaya Gazeta* on the conviction of two collective farm chairmen for buying from thieves badly needed pipes for a cowshed and boxes to pack apples in. One of these chairmen subsequently asked: Which is the greater crime—to pay thousands of rubles to thieves, or to lose a harvest?

55. Grossman (1977):25–40.

56. Cox (1985).

57. Gábor (1979).

58. Fröbel et al. (1980).

59. Evans (1979):184–91.

60. Doeringer and Piore (1971:175–77) make the point that in the United States, enterprises that are exempt from the Wagner and Taft-Hartley Acts and from National Labor Relations Board decisions are all part of the secondary labor market. Furthermore, unemployment compensation, social security, and minimum wage legislation all exempt parts of the secondary labor market from coverage. In addition: "The public assistance system as at present structured . . . encourages people to work on the fringes of the labor market in jobs where earnings are not reported to official authorities." Markovits and Allen (1979a:10–11) point out how unemployment compensation in the Federal Republic of Germany is administered so as to encourage unemployed workers to take jobs below their level of qualifications.

61. In Sao Paulo, women street cleaners, who receive half of the minimum wage, work for enterprises that contract with the municipality for their services. Charles Vanhecke, in *Le Monde*, 28 juillet 1982, "Le tiers-monde brésilien. II. La civilisation du bidonville."

62. Milton Friedman has argued that the clandestine economy, by enabling individuals to get around state restrictions on personal initiative, was an important bulwark against state interference in the economy. Michel Crozier, a French sociologist who has become an ideologue for the liberal right in France, took the same position: clandestine work was an outlet for the spirit of initiative and a nursery for future enterprises. . . . "C'est peut-être un peu immoral, mais tant pis." De Grazia (1983:89), citing an article by M. Roy, "Le travail noir," *Le Point*, nov. 12, 1979, which reported these interviews.

63. Gershuny (1979):3–15; Heinze and Olk (1982). Both Gershuny, writing in Britain, and Heinze and Olk, writing in West Germany, reject both what I have called the hyperliberal model (what would come about for Gershuny if things are allowed to continue the way they are) and the alternative of "technocratic statism" (which Heinze and Olk seem to see as closer to German experience). They both advocate that the state amend regulations so as to legalize and facilitate the informal economy, taking over a range of social welfare functions (as well as providing a range of nonstandardized craft articles). Martin Rein (1985:28), in the United States, envisages the possibility that an anticipated reduction in the proportion of the work force required for goods production opens the possibility of a compensating expansion of the social services but without, so far as I know, taking a position on bureaucratic versus informal provision of these services.

64. Amselle (1980), Caire (1982), De Grazia (1983):90–91. The debate over the dualist model has been particularly articulate in France. A study prepared for the French Commissariat du Plan by a group under the leadership of Mme. Françoise Giroud (1980) envisaged economic futures in which either there would be an economic dualism segregating highly productive jobs integrated into world-economy processes from less productive, less well paid, more precarious employment, or there could be a dualism in each person's own working time between conventional (high-productivity) and "autonomous" (low-productivity) work. Both forms of dualism were rejected by Edmond Maire, secretary-general of the CFDT, a socialist-leaning trade-union organization favoring workers' self-management, who perceived the dualist vision as an ideological capitulation to the demands of big industry. Edmond Maire (1980) reasserted the importance of the principle of worker solidarity to fight against the institutionalization of dualism.

65. Gorz (1982). Heinze and Olk (1982) also recognize that support for their alternative society requires the political support of a social movement the basis for which is not nearly so homogeneous as the working class. The Green Party may be seen as the germ of such a politicized social movement in West Germany.

## Chapter 10. The Formation of Classes and Historic Blocs

1. Skocpol (1977).
2. Brenner (1977).
3. For instance, the Burke-Hartke bill in the U.S. Congress, the pressures from domestic producers that led to "voluntary" restrictions on textiles and other imports into the United States, and pressures on foreign automobile manufacturers to open plants in the United States in order to avoid import restrictions.
4. Krasner (1977) regards support for a liberal economic world order as the goal of the state—a state that is an autonomous actor not connected with an internationalist tendency in U.S. capital—and protectionist measures in Congress as the impact on the state of private interests. He sees the peak of consensus behind the liberal order occurring about 1960 and declining subsequently. He does recognize that corporations and banks, on the verge of foreign expansion in the 1960s, had a stake in the liberal international order. Krasner favors a policy of "controlled closure" that "would require dealing with domestic groups such as banks and corporations that are heavily involved in foreign activity" but thinks the "weakness" of the U.S. political system, i.e., its sensitivity to pressures of various domestic interests, will most likely result in U.S. policy's becoming "less coherent and the world economy more unstable." O'Connor (1973:64–96) considered that monopoly

capital has evolved a "class" position expressed through the executive branch as policies of national interest, while small-scale capital expresses "special interests" through lobbies in Congress, state legislatures, and local government. O'Connor does not distinguish national and international tendencies in monopoly capital.

5. On "deindustrialization" and the advocacy of a bigger role for the state in mobilizing capital, Rohaytn (1981). Also Rohaytn's article in the financial section of the New York Times Dec. 1, 1974. The U.S. Marxist analysts Harry Magdoff and Paul M. Sweezy (1977:63–75) also envisage the likelihood of a trend toward state capitalism on the lines advocated by Rohaytn. On the avoidance of the "British mistake" and the rationale for neomercantilism, Gilpin (1975) and Krasner (1978). On the contradiction between capital and community interests in the "deindustrialization" issue, Bluestone and Harrison (1982).

6. Strange (1971); also Blank (1977).

7. Dewhurst et al. (1961).

8. The best known case, which has become an archetype of small business populism, was the Poujade movement in France. Hoffmann et al. (1956).

9. Poulantzas (1974) argued that in the current phase of imperialism, U.S. monopoly capital does not dominate other advanced industrial countries by way of an external relationship but establishes its domination within them (in forms that extend to state apparatuses and ideologies). Hence the concept of "internal bourgeoisie" distinct from "national bourgeoisie," to designate what I have called the international tendency of capital in advanced capitalist countries other than the United States. This concept discounts the possibility of autonomous imperialisms.

10. Servan-Schreiber (1967). Reactions to U.S. corporate expansion began to be expressed about the same time in Canada. Cf. Canada. Task Force on the Structure of Canadian Industry, known as the Watkins Report, after Mel Watkins, University of Toronto political economist who led the task force appointed by former finance minister Walter Gordon on behalf of the Canadian government. Also Levitt (1970).

11. Alavi (1972).

12. Evans (1979) and Cardoso and Faletto (1969).

13. Saul (1974). The term managerial bourgeoisie is used by Richard L. Sklar (1979). The "state class" concept is from Hartmut Elsenhans.

14. Cabral (1979):119–37.

15. Girvan (1976).

16. The point made here is dealt with briefly in Goldthorpe, (1964). See also Giddens (1975):223–54.

17. Braverman (1974):403–9 estimates this group at more than 15 percent but less than 20 percent of total U.S. employment. Mills (1956) raised the questions of a bifurcation between old and new middle classes in U.S. society and the political ambivalence of the new. A U.S. marxist study edited by Dale L. Johnson (1982) argues both the proletarianization of the new middle class and its possible propensity for right-wing reaction.

18. Mallet (1963). There is a review of the debate in France over the historical role of this social category by Ross (1978) in which the author points out that whereas in most advanced capitalist countries sociologists have regarded the new middle stratum as tendentially conservative supporters of evolved capitalism, in France this group has been heralded as harbingers of a new social order.

19. Attali (1975) distinguishes enterprises into two categories: a dominant system of large integrated enterprises that have a global strategy and a dominated system of smaller enterprises that are more subject to their environment. The dom-

inant system, he argues, draws profits from its domination over its suppliers and clients more than from its own labor force; the dominated system finds the essential part of its profits internally, i.e., from exploitation of its own labor force. This distinction leads to relatively good conditions for the employees of the dominant system and relatively greater exploitation of the employees of the dominated system (esp. pp. 37–44). Attali's distinction between dominant and dominated systems is doubtless derived from François Perroux's (1973) concept of economy as a composite of market exchange and power relations. Doeringer and Piore (1971:34) note the incentives to management to stabilize employment of scientific and technical cadres in order to maintain its investment in the recruitment, screening, and training of an elite work force. Also Touraine et al. (1965):51.

    20. Offe (1976). Concerning the debate about automation and worker integration, see ch. 9, note 9.

    21. Adam and Reynaud (1978):245–52.

    22. Attali (1975) envisages a decentralized self-management system for the future, but he does not revive the argument, in Mallet (1963), that this will come about through an enterprise-oriented labor movement led by the new working class. Mallet argued that advanced technologies, e.g., producer goods in electronics, would develop most effectively under state capitalism where a technocratic direction of industry would share power with banking groups linked to the state (pp. 197–203). Bihr and Heinrich (1980:79–81, 105, 176) picture the Attali program as an alliance of bureaucratic-technical petty bourgeoisie with workers for the purpose of salvaging a reformed capitalism from the economic crisis.

    23. Dubois (1978).

    24. Mickler (1979) noted reductions in the proportion of skilled workers in German industries between 1950 and 1974: from 95 to 63 percent in composition (printing), from 70 to 10–20 percent in furniture assembly, from 50 to 23–29 percent in prefabricated construction, and from 80 to 20–30 percent in precision mechanics. These are all industries in which enterprises are typically of medium size. Mickler attributes these changes to competition, which stimulated rationalization and efforts to raise productivity. Neither supply and demand for skills in the labor market nor conscious management policies favoring deskilling were, he thought, significant factors. Sabel (1982:89–99) discusses the world views of craftsmen in decline and workers with plant-specific technical skills.

    25. Hibbs, Jr. (1978).

    26. On labor representation in national economic management, Shonfield (1969). On the implications of mitbestimmung, Cox (1977b). See also Panitch (1984).

    27. Issues in West German labor relations from about 1978 centered on the demand for the thirty-five-hour week, humanization of work and control of technological change, all raised by rank-and-file pressures. Markovits and Allen (1979b). See also chapter 9.

    28. Union suspicion of enterprise corporatism was discussed in Touraine et al. (1965). It has, if anything, grown during the ensuing twenty years.

    29. Italian metalworkers and chemical workers have been among the most explicit in linking the issue of reduction in the work force to a demand for a voice in investment decisions and industrial reconversion policies. See Trentin (1962); Momigliano (1962); and Amyot (1981).

    30. The challenge to union leadership preceded the coming of the economic crisis. Already in the 1960s a shift of power toward the shop floor had been noted. Reynaud (1968).

    31. Trade unionism in the United States and Canada, which historically has

many structural similarities, has, since the mid-1960s, diverged dramatically in respect of the proportion of the labor force that belongs to unions. At that time, just less than 30 percent of the nonagricultural paid workers in both countries belonged to unions. By 1980, however, that proportion had climbed to 39 percent in Canada and dropped to 23 percent in the United States. During the 1970s, structural differences became more accentuated. Whereas formerly most Canadian trade unionists had belonged to "international" unions, i.e., with headquarters in the United States, since 1975, Canadian-based unions have the majority of membership. The Canadian branch of a major union, the UAW, severed its connections with the U.S. headquarters to become an exclusively Canadian union. Organization of the state sector has also moved ahead more rapidly in Canada. Meltz (1983). It is indicative of the relative strengths and weaknesses of organized labor in the two countries that under the impact of the economic crisis, U.S. labor leaders have been more disposed to the negotiation of a social contract, i.e., revived tripartism, than their Canadian counterparts have, despite the greater historical experience with tripartism in Canada. U.S. businessmen have, however, been almost unanimously opposed to tripartism, an opposition only somewhat less manifest among Canadian businessmen. Maital and Meltz (1984).

  32. Reynaud (1984).

  33. For an outline of post-Keynesian policies, Eichner, ed. (1978).

  34. Doeringer and Piore (1971:175–77) observe that the street group determines behavior for the secondary labor market, and the work group, for the primary labor market. Rejection and abuse from the (white) work group may force the black worker back to the street group. A broader distinction is workplace vs. residence as the critical factor in identity.

  35. Discussed in Sabel (1982), esp. ch. 3.

  36. Goldthorpe et al. (1969).

  37. The strike at the French automobile manufacturer Talbot in June-July 1982 is a case where the *Confederation Général du Travail* (CGT) successfully acted to improve the status of the largely immigrant semiskilled (O.S.) work force. A mediator's report on the dispute recommended adoption of a Japanese practice giving to semiskilled workers a training equivalent to a French *baccalauréat* and thereby allowing the introduction of more advanced techniques. *Le Monde*, July 3, 1982. On the ambivalent attitude of male workers toward semiskilled female workers, see Rowbotham (1973):94.

  38. These initial contacts were associated with what Marx called the primitive accumulation of capital. Williams (1980) illustrates this phase. The port of trade concept is developed in Polanyi et al. (1971), in essays by Robert B. Revere, Anne C. Chapman and Rosemary Arnold. Rey (1976) advances a three-stages theory of the impact of external capitalism on a precapitalist formation: (1) initial contact strengthens precapitalist authorities, (2) capitalist production takes root and becomes articulated to precapitalist modes of production, and (3) capitalism reduces and absorbs all precapitalist elements (this stage having been reached only in the United States, according to Rey). In the Marxist classics, note the treatment of this problem in Rosa Luxemburg (1968). Lattimore (1960) gives a short account of a case in which imperialism did not lead to formal colonization. A recent addition to this literature is Wolf (1982).

  39. International development literature began to discuss the "informal sector" in the early 1970s. See, e.g., International Labour Office (1972). For a critique of this concept from the standpoint of production relations, Harrod (1980). Other scholarly treatments include Portes and Walton (1981) (esp. ch. 3), and Sandbrook, (1982).

40. Massari (1975); Jelin (1976). The *Cordobazo* was a strike movement that occurred in the northern Argentine city of Codoba in 1969. Since the 1950s, the city had become a center of the automobile industry, which had attracted a new, young, and relatively well-educated work force employed by multinational corporations. Some radical intellectuals were within this work force. Though the movement was ultimately repressed, it was sustained long enough to shock the political system and weaken the government, which changed ultimately as a result of it. It demonstrated the possibility of protest against trade union bureaucracies, employers, and government when a relatively well-educated work force, angered by frustration, links with a radical ideology. Stepan (1978:102) notes that the relative weakness in repression manifested by the Argentine state during the *Cordobazo* adversely affected its ability to attract international finance. Conversely, the relative severity of Brazilian coercion favored foreign capital inflows.

41. Azad (1980). Continuing strikes by the oil workers played a major part in the ultimate paralysis of the Shah's regime. Other industrial workers also took part in the movement, which set up workers' councils. This proletarian success was, however, short-lived, and the councils were soon dismantled by the Islamic revolutionaries, who destroyed oil workers' unity by pitting religious against non-religious workers. Azad attributes this defeat of class consciousness in a populist revolutionary wave to the youthfulness of the Iranian working class, a group very largely of peasant origin, and to the absence of independent working-class organization. The contradiction between a class orientation and a religious-populist orientation is endemic in Third World revolutionary movements. For a full examination of an earlier case—that of the Indonesian Communist party before 1926—see McVey (1965).

42. On liberalization in Brazil in 1979–80, a series of articles by Marcel Niedergang in *Le Monde*, December 9, 10, 11, and 12, 1980. The article of December 12 deals with the emergence of opposition unions analogous to the illicit workers' commissions in Spain during the last years of the regime of General Francisco Franco.

43. The most notable proponent of this thesis was Fanon (1968). For a critical discussion of the thesis, see Sandbrook (1977). Turner (1966) argues that organized workers in less developed countries have captured a disproportionate share of national income, and this has reduced the possibilities of employment creation. Organized workers have thus, he argues, entrenched their own privileged position at the expense of peasants and marginals.

44. Bates (1971).

45. Stepan (1978):195–229.

46. Sandbrook (1977).

47. The concept of "occupational communities" is taken from Kerr and Siegel, in Kornhauser et al., eds. (1954). Also Sandbrook and Arn (1977:57), in which "occupational communities" are defined as places "where, owing to a concentration of similarly-employed workers, their insulation from moderating outside influences, and their peculiar schedules occasioned by shift-work, work-mates interact both on and off the job to create and reinforce common images of the world."

48. Wolf (1969).

49. Fanon (1968).

50. See, for example, World Bank (1975). Also Feder (1976).

51. Nelson (1969 and 1979). Stepan (1978:158–89) points out that the urban squatters in Peru have not been notably radical or populist, but rather instrumental and clientelistic, and were relatively easily organized during the Velasco regime by state and church initiatives into structures articulating them with the state in a

vertical manner and thereby avoiding horizontal mass-based or class-based organization. Touraine (1976:142–56) associates a dependent or heteronomous pattern of behavior with the urban milieu of the marginals, whereas he sees the workplace as more conducive to autonomous behavior.

52. In a discussion on development and conflict among young people from various parts of the world brought together on the occasion of International Youth Year, in a conference on Issues for the Next Generation organized by graduate students of York University (Toronto, August 1985), the point emerged that the counterpart in the Third World to the peace movement in the advanced industrial countries was the armed liberation struggle. "Peace," in other words, did not mean pacifism. In order that liberation could succeed in the Third World, it was necessary to neutralize militarism in the dominant powers.

## Conclusions
1. Marx (1957):1:544.

# BIBLIOGRAPHY

Abdel-Hamid Sirageldin, Ismail. 1969. *Non-Market Components of National Income*. Ann Arbor: University of Michigan Institute for Social Research.

Abraham, Jean-Paul and C. Lemineur-Toumson. 1981. "Les choix monétaires européens, 1950–1980," pp. 69–83. In Abraham and Abeele, eds. 1981.

Abraham, Jean-Paul and Michel Van den Abeele, eds. 1981 *Système monétaire européen et réforme monétaire mondiale. European Monetary System and International Monetary Reform*. Brussels: Editions de l'université de Bruxelles.

Abramsky, C, ed. 1974. *Essays in Honour of E. H. Carr*. London: Macmillan.

Adam, Gérard. 1983. *Le pouvoir syndical*. Paris: Dunod.

Adam, Gérard and Jean-Daniel Reynaud. 1978. *Conflits du travail et changement social*. Paris: Presses universitaires de France.

Alavi, Hamza. 1972. "The State in Post-colonial Societies—Pakistan and Bangladesh." *New Left Review* (July-August), 74:59–81.

Althusser, Louis and Etienne Balibar. 1970. *Reading Capital*. Translated by Ben Brewster. London: New Left Books.

Amin, Samir. 1973. *Le développement inégal*. Paris: Les éditions de minuit.

Amselle, Jean-Loup. 1980. "Economie souterraine, économie sans mystère." *Le Monde diplomatique* (decembre).

Amyot, G. Grant. 1981. The Italian Unions: Radical Reformism or Imperfect Corporatism?" Paper presented at the fourth conference of the European Politics Group of the Canadian Political Science Association, Ottawa (December).

Anderson, Perry. 1974. *Lineages of the Absolutist State*. London: New Left Books.

Argyle, Michael et al. 1967. *Social Theory and Economic Change*. London: Tavistock.

Arnoult, Eric. 1978. "Hiérarchies et articulations internationales des économies." *Economie appliquée. Archives de l'I.S.M.E.A.* 31(3-4):529–45.

Aronowitz, Stanley. 1973. "Trade Unionism and Worker Control," pp. 62–106. In Hunnius et al. eds 1973.

Attali, Jacques. 1975. *La parole et l'outil*. Paris: Presses universitaires de France.

Averitt, Robert T. 1968. *The Dual Economy. Dynamics of American Industrial Structure*. New York: Norton.

Avery, William P. and David P. Rapkin, eds. 1982. *America in a Changing World Political Economy*. New York: Longman.

Azad, Shanrzad. 1980. "Workers' and Peasants' Councils in Iran" *Monthly Review* 32(5):14–29.

Bahro, Rudolph. 1978. *The Alternative in Eastern Europe*. Translated by David Fernbach. London: New Left Books.

Ball, George. 1967. "Cosmocorp: The Importance of Being Stateless." *Columbia Journal of World Business* 2 (November-December):25–30.

Banaji, Jairus. 1977. "Modes of Production in a Materialist Conception of History." *Capital and Class* (Autumn), 3:1–44.

Barnett, Donald F. and Louis Schorsch. 1983. *Steel: Upheaval in a Basic Industry*. Cambridge, Mass.: Ballinger.

Barraclough, Geoffrey. 1947. *The Origins of Modern Germany*. Oxford: Blackwell.

——1967. *An Introduction to Contemporary History*. Harmondsworth, Middlesex: Penguin.

——1975. "The Great World Crisis." *The New York Review of Books* (January 23).

Bates, Robert H. 1971. *Unions, Parties and Political Development: A Study of Mineworkers in Zambia*. New Haven, Conn.: Yale University Press.

Beard, Charles A. and Mary R. Beard. 1940. *The Rise of American Civilization*, revised and enlarged edition. New York: Macmillan.

Becker, Carl. 1932. *The Heavenly City of the Eighteenth-Century Philosophers*. New Haven, Conn.: Yale University Press.

Beer, Samuel H. 1966. *British Politics in the Collectivist Age*. New York: Knopf.

Behagg, Clive. 1982. "An Alliance with the Middle Class: The Birmingham Political Union and Early Chartism," pp. 59–86. In Epstein and Thompson, eds. 1982.

Bell, Daniel. 1960. *The End of Ideology*. New York: Free Press.

Beloff, Max. 1961. *New Dimensions in Foreign Policy*. London: Allen and Unwin.

——1963. *The United States and the Unity of Europe*. London: Faber and Faber.

Bendix, Reinhard. 1963. *Work and Authority in Industry. Ideologies of Management in the Course of Industrialization*. New York: Harper and Row. Originally published by Wiley in 1956.

——1964. *Nation-Building and Citizenship: Studies of Our Changing Social Order*. Berkeley: University of California Press.

——1967. "The Comparative Analysis of Historical Change," pp. 67–86. In Argyle 1967.

Benson, Leslie. 1974. "Market Socialism and Class Structure: Manual Workers and Managerial Power in the Yugoslav Enterprise," pp. 257–273. In Parkin, ed. 1974.

Berger, Suzanne and Michael Piore. 1980. *Dualism and Discontinuity in Industrial Societies*. Cambridge, England: Cambridge University Press.

Bernstein, Thomas. 1967. "Leadership and Mass Mobilization in the Soviet and Chinese Collectivization Campaigns of 1929–30 and 1955–56: A Comparison." *China Quarterly* (July-September), no. 31:1–47.

Beveridge, William Henry. 1909. *Unemployment. A Problem of Industry.* London: Longmans Green.

——1944. *Full Employment in a Free Society.* London: George Allen and Unwin.

Bhagwati, Jagdish N., ed. 1972. *Economics and World Order. From the 1970s to the 1980s.* London: Macmillan.

Biasco, Salvatore. 1979. *L'inflazione nei paese capitalistici industrializzati. Il ruolo della loro interdipendenza, 1968–1978.* Milano: Feltrinelli.

Bihr, Alain and Jean-Marie Heinrich. 1980. *La néo-social-démocratie ou le capitalisme autogéré.* Paris: Sycomore.

Black, Cyril E., ed. 1960. *The Transformation of Russian Society.* Cambridge, Mass.: Harvard University Press.

Blades, Derek. 1982. *The Hidden Economy and the National Accounts.* Paris: Organization for Economic Cooperation and Development (June).

Blake, Robert. 1966. *Disraeli.* London: Eyre and Spottiswoode.

Blank, Stephen. 1977. "Britain: The Politics of Foreign Economic Policy, the Domestic Economy, and the Problem of Pluralistic Stagnation." *International Organization* 31(4):673–721.

Blauner, Robert. 1964. *Alienation and Freedom.* Chicago: University of Chicago Press.

Block, Fred L. 1977. *The Origins of International Economic Disorder. A Study of United States International Monetary Policy from World War II to the Present.* Berkeley, Calif.: University of California Press.

——1980. "Beyond Relative Autonomy: State Managers as Historical Subjects," pp. 227–42. In Miliband and Saville. 1980.

Bluestone, Barry and Bennett Harrison. 1982. *The Deindustrialization of America. Plant Closings, Community Abandonment, and the Dismantling of Basic Industry.* New York: Basic Books.

Bluestone, Barry and Mary Huff Stevenson. 1981. "Industrial Transformation and the Evolution of Dual Labour Markets: The Case of Retail Trade in the United States," pp. 23–46. In Wilkinson. 1981.

Boarman, Patrick M. and David G. Tuerch, eds. 1976. *World Monetary Disorder. National Policies vs. International Imperatives.* New York: Praeger.

Boiter, Albert. 1964. "When the Kettle Boils Over . . ." *Problems of Communism* 13(1):33–43.

Borkenau, Franz. 1942. *Socialism, National or International.* London: George Routledge and Sons.

Bowles, Samuel. 1982. "The Post-Keynesian Capital-Labor Stalemate." *Socialist Review* (September October), 12(5):45–72.

Bowles, Samuel and Herbert Gintis. 1982. "The Crisis of Liberal Democratic Capitalism: The Case of the United States." *Politics and Society* 11(1):51–93.

Brandão Lopes, Juarez Rubens. 1977. "Développement capitaliste et structure agraire au Brésil." *Sociologie du travail* 1(77):59–71.

Braudel, Fernand. 1979. *Civilisation matérielle, économie et capitalisme, XVe-XVIIIe siècle.* t. 1 *Les structures du quotidien: le possible et l'impossible.* t. 2 *Les jeux de l'échange.* t. 3 *Le temps du monde.* Paris, Armand Colin.

Braverman, Harry. 1974. *Labor and Monopoly Capital. The Degradation of Work in the Twentieth Century.* New York: Monthly Review.

Brenner, Robert. 1976. "Agrarian Class Structure and Economic Development in Pre-industrial Europe." *Past and Present* (February):30–75.

———1977. "The Origins of Capitalist Development: A Critique of Neo-Smithian Marxism." *New Left Review* (July-August), vol. 104:25–92.

Briggs, Asa. 1960. "The Language of 'Class' in Early Nineteenth Century England." pp. 43–73. In Briggs and Saville, eds. 1960.

———1965a. *The Making of Modern England, 1783–1867. The Age of Improvement.* New York: Harper.

———1965b. "National Bearings." pp. 288–303. In Briggs 1965c.

———ed. 1965c. *Chartist Studies.* London: Macmillan.

———1968. The World Economy: Interdependence and Planning." pp. 37–86. In C. L. Mowat, ed. *The New Cambridge Modern History,* vol. 12, ch. 3. Cambridge, England: Cambridge University Press.

Briggs, Asa and John Saville, eds. 1960. *Essays in Labour History.* London: Macmillan.

Broda, Jacques, Serge Demailly, and Chantal Labruyère. 1978. "Crise de la sidérurgie et recomposition du procès de travail." *Sociologie du travail* 4(78):423–47.

Brown, Michael Barrett. 1974. *The Economics of Imperialism.* Harmondsworth, Middlesex: Penguin.

Bruce, Maurice. 1966. *The Coming of the Welfare State.* New York: Schocken.

Brundage, Anthony. 1978. *The Making of the New Poor Law. The Politics of Inquiry, Enactment and Implementation, 1832–39.* London: Hutchinson.

Brusco, Sebastiano. 1982. "The Emilian Model: Productive Decentralisation and Social Integration." *Cambridge Journal of Economics:* 6:167–84.

Brusco, Sebastiano and Charles Sabel. 1981. "Artisan Production and Economic Growth," pp. 99–113. In Wilkinson, ed. 1981.

Buci-Glucksmann, Christine. 1975. *Gramsci et l'état. Pour une théorie matérialiste de la philosophie.* Paris: Fayard.

Burckhardt, Jacob. 1945. *The Civilization of the Renaissance in Italy.* New York: Oxford University Press.

Burnham, James. 1943. *The Machiavellians: Defenders of Freedom.* Chicago: Regnery.

Butler, Harold. 1950. *Confident Morning.* London: Faber and Faber.

Byers, R. B. and R. W. Reford, eds. 1979. *Canada Challenged.* Toronto: Canadian Institute of International Affairs.

Cabral, Amilcar. 1979. *Unity and Struggle. The Speeches and Writings of Amilcar Cabral.* New York: Monthly Review.

Caire, Guy. 1982. "Précarisation des emplois et régulation du marché du travail." *Sociologie du travail,* no. 2, pp. 135–47.

Calleo, David P. 1982. *The Imperious Economy: U.S. Policy at Home and Abroad, 1960–1980.* Cambridge, Mass.: Harvard University Press.

Canada. Task Force on the Structure of Canadian Industry. 1968. *Foreign Ownership and the Structure of Canadian Industry* (The Watkins Report). Ottawa: Queen's Printer.

Cardoso, F. H. and E. Faletto. 1969. *Dependencia y Desarrollo en America Latina*. Mexico: Siglo Veintiuno.

Carr, Edward H. 1945. *Nationalism and After*. London: Macmillan.

——1946. *The Twenty Years' Crisis, 1919–1939*. London: Macmillan.

——1950. *Studies in Revolution*. London: Macmillan.

——1952. *The Bolshevik Revolution, 1917–1923*. London: Macmillan.

——1967. *Michael Bakunin*. New York: Vintage Books. Originally published by Macmillan in 1937.

Castles, Stephen and Godula Kosack. 1973. *Immigrant Workers and Class Structure in Western Europe*. London: Oxford University Press, for the Institute of Race Relations.

Chalmers, Douglas A., ed. 1972. *Changing Latin America. New Interpretations of Its Politics and Society*. New York: The Academy of Political Science, Columbia University. Proceedings. vol. 30, no. 4.

Checkland, S. G. 1964. *The Rise of Industrial Society in England, 1815–1885*. New York: St. Martin's Press.

Chiarello, Franco. 1983. "Economia informale, famiglia e reticoli sociali." *Rassegna italiana di sociologia* (aprile-giugno), 24(2):211–52.

Chomsky, Noam. 1972. *Problems of Knowledge and Freedom*. Bungay, Suffolk: Fontana.

Cipolla, Carlo, ed. 1970. *The Economic Decline of Empires*. London: Methuen.

Clark, G. N. 1960. *The Seventeenth Century*, ed. 2. Oxford: Oxford University Press.

Clarkson, Stephen. 1982. *Canada and the Reagan Challenge*. Toronto: James Lorimer, for the Canadian Institute for Economic Policy.

Clasen, Claus-Peter. 1972. *Anabaptism. A Social History, 1525–1618. Switzerland, Austria, Moravia, South and Central Germany*. Ithaca, N. Y., and London: Cornell University Press.

Clemens, Samuel (Mark Twain). 1873. *The Gilded Age*. London: George Routledge.

Cobban, Alfred. 1965. *A History of Modern France*, vol. 3: *France of the Republics, 1871–1962*. Harmondsworth, Middlesex: Penguin.

Cohen, G. A. 1978. *Karl Marx's Theory of History. A Defence*. Oxford: Clarendon Press.

Cohen, Stephen S. 1977. *Modern Capitalist Planning: The French Model*. Berkeley: University of California Press.

Cohn, Norman. 1970. *The Pursuit of the Millennium. Revolutionary Millenarians and Mystical Anarchists of the Middle Ages*. London: Paladin.

Coleman, D. C., ed. 1969. *Revisions in Mercantilism*. London: Methuen.

Collingwood, R. G. 1946. *The Idea of History*. Oxford: Clarendon Press.

Connerton, Paul, ed. 1976. *Critical Sociology*. Harmondsworth, Middlesex: Penguin.

Cook, Alice H. et al. 1971. *Public Employee Labor Relations in Japan: Three Aspects*. Comparative Studies in Public Employment, Labor Relations

Series. Ann Arbor: University of Michigan, Wayne State, Institute of Labor and Industrial Relations.

Cook, James. 1980. "The Invisible Enterprise." *Forbes* (September 29), pp. 60–71.

Cox, Robert W. 1966. "Trade Unions, Employers and the Formation of National Economic Policy," pp. 229–51. In Arthur M. Ross, ed. 1966.

——1971. "Approaches to a Futurology of Industrial Relations." International Institute for Labour Studies. *Bulletin*, no. 8, (Geneva), pp. 139–64.

——1973. "World Systems of Labor and Production." Paper presented to the Congress of the International Political Science Association, Montreal (August) (xeroxed).

——1974. "ILO: Limited Monarchy," pp. 102–38. In Cox and Jacobson. 1974.

——1976. "Labor and the Multinationals." *Foreign Affairs* 54 (2):344–65.

——1977a. "Labor and Hegemony." *International Organization* 31(3):385–424.

——1977b. "La participation: considérations sur la signification des expériences européennes," pp. 37–51. In Département des relations industrielles, Université Laval. *Participation et négotiation collective*. Québec: Les presses de l'université Laval.

——1977c. "Pour une étude prospective des relations de production." *Sociologie du travail* 2 (77):113–37.

——1979a. "Employment, labor and future political structures." pp. 262–292. In Byers and Reford. 1979.

——1979b. "Ideologies and the New International Economic Order: Reflections on Some Recent Literature." *International Organization* 33 (2):257–302.

——1981. "Social Forces, States and World Orders: Beyond International Relations Theory." *Millennium. Journal of International Studies* 10(2):126–55; republished with a postscript in R. O. Keohane, ed. 1986.

——1982. "Production and Hegemony: Toward a Political Economy of World Order," pp. 37–58. In Jacobson and Sidjanski. 1982.

——1983. "Gramsci, Hegemony and International Relations: An Essay in Method." *Millennium. Journal of International Studies* 12(2):162–75.

——1985. "China: A Redistributive System in the World Political Economy." Paper presented at the World Congress of the International Political Science Association, Paris (July).

Cox, Robert W., Jeffrey Harrod, et al. 1972. *Future Industrial Relations. An Interim Report*. Geneva: International Institute for Labour Studies.

Cox, Robert W. and Harold K. Jacobson. 1974. *The Anatomy of Influence. Decision Making in International Organization*. New Haven, Conn.: Yale University Press.

——Forthcoming. *Crisis in Hegemony. The United States and World Order.* .

Crough, G. J. (with a contribution from Victoria Chick). 1979. *Transnational Banking and the World Economy*. Sydney, Australia: University of Sydney, Transnational Corporations Project.

Crozier, Michel, Samuel P. Huntington, and Joji Watanuki. 1975. *The Crisis of Democracy. Report on the Governability of Democracies to the Trilateral Commission.* New York: New York University Press.

Cumings, Bruce, ed. 1983. *China from Mao to Deng. The Politics and Economics of Socialist Development.* Armonk, N.Y.: M. E. Sharpe.

Dahrendorf, Ralf. 1959. *Class and Class Conflict in Industrial Society.* Stanford, Calif.: Stanford University Press. Original German edition 1957.

Dangerfield, George. 1961. *The Strange Death of Liberal England.* New York: Capricorn. First published in 1935.

Davidson, Alastair. 1977. *Antonio Gramsci: Towards an Intellectual Biography.* London: Merlin Press.

Davidson, Basil. 1978. *Africa in Modern History.* London: Allen Lane.

Day, Richard B. 1976. "The Theory of the Long Cycle: Kondratiev, Trotsky, Mandel." *New Left Review* 99:67–82.

De Grazia, Raffaele. 1980. "Clandestine Employment: A Problem of Our Times." *International Labour Review* (September-October), 119(5):549–563.

——1983. *Le travail clandestin. Situation dans les pays industrialisés à économie de marché.* Genève: Bureau international du travail.

Dehio, Ludwig. 1963. *The Precarious Balance. The Politics of Power in Europe, 1494–1945.* Translated by Charles Fullman from *Gleichgewicht oder Hegemonie.* London: Chatto and Windus.

de Laubier, Patrick. 1968. "Esquisse d'une théorie du syndicalisme." *Sociologie du travail* 10:362–92.

Derber, Milton and Edwin Young, eds. 1972. *Labor and the New Deal.* New York: Da Capo Press.

Dewhurst, J. Frederick, John O. Coppock, P. Lamartine Yeats, et al. 1961. *Europe's Needs and Resources. Trends and Prospects in Eighteen Countries.* New York: Twentieth Century Fund.

Diebold, William Jr. 1959. *The Schuman Plan; a Study in Economic Cooperation, 1950–1959.* New York: Praeger.

——1980. *Industrial Policy as an International Issue.* New York: McGraw-Hill, for the Council on Foreign Relations.

di Tella, Torquato. 1965. "Populism and Reform in Latin America." pp. 47–74. In Veliz, ed. 1965.

Djilas, Milovan. 1957. *The New Class. An Analysis of the Communist System.* New York: Praeger.

Dobb, Maurice. 1974. "Some Historical Reflections on Planning and the Market," pp. 324–38. In Abramsky, ed. 1974.

La Documentation française. Recueils et monographies. No. 47. 1964. *Rapport sur la politique des revenus établi à la suite de la Conférence des revenus, 1964.*

Doeringer, Peter B. and Michael J. Piore. 1971. *Internal Labor Markets and Manpower Analysis.* Lexington, Mass.: Heath.

Dore, Ronald P. 1973. *British Factory, Japanese Factory. The Origins of National Diversity in Industrial Relations.* Berkeley: University of California Press.

——1974. "Late Development . . . or Something Else? Industrial Relations in

Britain, Japan, Mexico, Sri Lanka, Senegal." Brighton: Institute of Development Studies, University of Sussex, no. 61 (August).

Dubois, Pierre. 1978. "Techniques et division des travailleurs." *Sociologie du travail*, no. 2, pp. 174–91.

Duncan, Mike. 1982. "The Information Technology Industry in 1981." *Capital and Class* (Summer), 17:79–87.

Dunlop, John T. 1958. *Industrial Relations Systems*. New York: Holt.

Eco, Umberto. 1983. *The Name of the Rose*. New York: Harcourt Brace.

Edelman, Murray. 1969. "The Conservative Political Consequences of Labor Conflict," pp. 163–76. In Somers, ed. 1969.

Edwards, Richard. 1979. *Contested Terrain. The Transformation of Work in the Twentieth Century*. New York: Basic Books.

Eichner, Alfred S., ed. 1978. *A Guide to Post-Keynesian Economics*. White Plains, N.Y.: Sharpe.

Elsenhans, Hartmut. 1983. "Rising Mass Incomes as a Condition of Capitalist Growth: Implications for Today's World Economy." *International Organization* 37(1):1–39.

Emerson, Michael. 1981. "European Dimensions in the Problems of Adjustment," pp. 107–15. In Abraham and Abeele, eds. 1981.

Emmanuel, A. 1972. *Unequal Exchange*. London: New Left Books.

Engels, Frederick. 1956. *The Peasants' War in Germany*. London: Laurence and Wishart. Originally published in 1850.

——1969. *The Condition of the Working Class in England in 1844*. London: Panther Books.

——1972. *The Origin of the Family, Private Property and the State*. New York: International Publishers.

Epstein, James and Dorothy Thompson, eds. 1982. *The Chartist Experience: Studies in Working-Class Radicalism and Culture, 1830–60*. London: Macmillan.

Erlich, Alexander. 1967. *The Soviet Industrialization Debate, 1924–1928*. Cambridge, Mass.: Harvard University Press.

Evans, Peter. 1979. *Dependent Development. The Alliance of Multinational, State and Local Capital in Brazil*. Princeton, N. J.: Princeton University Press.

Fals Borda, Orlando. 1970. "Formation and Deformation of Cooperative Policy in Latin America." International Institute for Labour Studies, *Bulletin*, no. 7. Geneva:122–152.

Fanon, Frantz. 1968. *The Wretched of the Earth*. New York: Grove Press.

Feder, Ernest. 1976. "The New World Bank Programme for the Self-Liquidation of the Third-World Peasantry." *Journal of Peasant Studies* 3(3):343–54.

Feinstein, C. H. 1972. *National Income, Expenditure and Output of the United Kingdom, 1855–1965*. Cambridge, England: Cambridge University Press.

Feis, Herbert. 1930. *Europe the World's Banker, 1870–1914*. New Haven, Conn.: Yale University Press, for the Council on Foreign Relations.

Femia, Joseph. 1981. *Gramsci's Political Thought: Hegemony, Consciousness and the Revolutionary Process*. Oxford: Oxford University Press.

Ferrero, Gugliemo. 1941. *The Reconstruction of Europe. Talleyrand and the Congress of Vienna, 1814–1815.* New York: Putnam.

——1942. *The Principles of Power.* New York: Putnam.

Forrester, Jay W. 1976. "Business Structure, Economic Cycles and National Policy." *Futures* (June):195–214.

——1978. "We're Headed for Another Depression." *Fortune* (January 16), pp. 145–48.

Foster, John. 1977. *Class Struggle and the Industrial Revolution. Early Industrial Capitalism in Three English Towns.* London: Methuen.

Foster-Carter, Aidan 1978. "The Modes of Production Controversy." *New Left Review* (January-February), 107:47–77.

Frank, André Gunder. 1969. *Capitalism and Underdevelopment in Latin America. Historical Studies of Chile and Brazil.* New York: Monthly Review.

Friedberg, Erhard. 1974. "L'internationalisation de l'économie et modalités d'intervention de l'état: la 'politique industrielle.'" pp. 94–108. *Planification et Société.* Grenoble: Presses universitaires de Grenoble.

——1976. *L'état et l'industrie en France.* Rapport d'enquête, avec la collaboration de D. Desjeux. Paris: Centre national de la recherche scientifique, Centre de sociologie des organisations.

Frieden, Jeff. 1981. "Third World Indebted Industrialization: International Finance and State Capitalism in Mexico, Brazil, Algeria, and South Korea." *International Organization* 35(3):407–32.

Friedmann, Georges. 1956. *Le travail en miettes.* Paris: Gallimard.

Friedmann, Harriet. 1980. "Household Production and the National Economy: Concepts for the Analysis of Agrarian Formations." *Journal of Peasant Studies* (January), 7(2):158–84.

Friedrich, Carl J. 1948. *Inevitable Peace.* Cambridge, Mass.: Harvard University Press.

——1952. *The Age of the Baroque, 1610–1660.* New York: Harper.

Fröbel, Folker, Jürgen Heinrichs, Otto Kreye. 1980. *The New International Division of Labour. Structural Unemployment in Industrialized Countries and Industrialization in Developing Countries.* Translated by Pete Burgess. Cambridge, England: Cambridge University Press.

Gábor, I. R. 1979. "The Second (Secondary) Economy." *Acta Oeconomica* 22:291–311.

Galbraith, J. K. 1968. *The New Industrial State.* New York: Signet Books.

——1975. *Economics and the Public Purpose.* New York: Signet Books.

Gallagher, John and Ronald Robinson. 1953. "The Imperialism of Free Trade." *Economic History Review,* second series, 6(1):1–15.

Gallie, Duncan. 1978. *In Search of the New Working Class. Automation and Social Integration Within the Capitalist Enterprise.* Cambridge, England: Cambridge University Press.

Gardner, Richard N. 1960. "Strategy for the Dollar." *Foreign Affairs* (April), 38(3):433–45.

——1969. *Sterling-Dollar Diplomacy. The Origins and the Prospects of Our International Economic Order.* New York: McGraw-Hill. Original edition 1956.

Garvy, George. 1943. "Kondratieff's Theory of Long Cycles." *The Review of Economic Statistics* (November), 25(4):203–20.

Gershenkron, Alexander. 1962. *Economic Backwardness in Historical Perspective.* Cambridge, Mass.: Harvard University Press.

Gershuny, J. I. 1979. "The Informal Economy. Its Role in Post-industrial Society." *Futures* (February):3–15.

Giddens, Anthony. 1975. *The Class Structure of the Advanced Societies.* New York: Harper. First published 1973.

Gilpin, Robert. 1975. *U.S. Power and the Multinational Corporation: The Political Economy of Foreign Direct Investment.* New York: Basic Books.

Ginsberg, Benjamin and Martin Shefter. 1984. "The International Political Economy, Domestic Alignments and the 1984 Election" Paper presented at the 1984 meeting of the American Political Science Association, Washington, D. C. August 29-September 2).

Giroud, Françoise. 1980. *Réflexions sur l'avenir du travail.* Paris: Commissariat du Plan, la Documentation Francaise.

Girvan, Norman. 1976. *Corporate Imperialism: Conflict and Expropriation. Transnational Corporations and Economic Nationalism in the Third World.* White Plains, N. Y.: Sharpe.

Girvan, Norman and Richard Bernal. 1982. "The IMF and Jamaica." *Monthly Review* (February), 33(9):34–48.

Goldfrank, Walter. 1975. "World System, State Structure, and the Onset of the Mexican Revolution." *Politics and Society* 5(4):417–39.

Goldthorpe, John H. 1964. "Social Stratification in Industrial Society," pp. 109–17. In *The Development of Industrial Societies,* Sociological Review Monograph, no. 8, Keele, 1964. Papers read at the Nottingham Conference of the British Sociological Association (April 1964).

Goldthorpe, John H., David Lockwood, Frank Bechhoffer, and Jennifer Platt. 1969. *The Affluent Worker.* Vol. 1, *Industrial Attitudes and Behaviour.* Vol. 2, *Political Attitudes and Behaviour.* Vol. 3, *In the Class Structure.* Cambridge, England: Cambridge University Press.

Gordon, David M. 1980. "Stages of Accumulation and Long Economic Cycles," pp. 9–45. In Hopkins and Wallerstein, eds. 1980.

Gordon, David M., Richard Edwards, and Michael Reich. 1982. *Segmented Work, Divided Workers. The Historical Transformation of Labor in the United States.* Cambridge, England: Cambridge University Press.

Gorz, André. 1982. *Farewell to the Working Class. An Essay on Post-Industrial Socialism.* Translated by Michael Sonenscher. London: Pluto Press.

Goubert, Pierre. 1966. *Louis XIV et vingt millions de français.* Paris: Fayard.

Gourevitch, Peter. 1978. "The Second Image Reversed." *International Organization* 32(4):881–911.

Gramsci, Antonio. 1971. *Selections from the Prison Notebooks.* Edited by Quintin Hoare and Geoffrey Nowell Smith. New York: International Publishers.

——1975. *Quaderni del carcere.* Torino: Einaudi.

Griffin, Keith. 1974. "The International Transmission of Inequality." *World Development* 2(3):3–15.

Grossman, Gregory. 1977. "The 'Second' Economy of the USSR." *Problems of Communism* (September-October):25–40.

Günter, Hans. 1972. *Future Industrial Relations: The Federal Republic of Germany and Austria.* Research Project on Future Industrial Relations, International Institute for Labour Studies, Doc. no. 3, Geneva.

Gutkind, Peter C. W. and Peter Waterman, eds. 1977. *African Social Studies. A Radical Reader.* London: Heinemann.

Haas, Ernst B. 1958. *The Uniting of Europe. Political, Social and Economical Forces, 1950–57.* London: Stevens.

Habermas, Jurgen. 1976. *Legitimation Crisis.* London: Heinemann.

Halévy, Elie. 1949a. *A History of the English People in the Nineteenth Century.* Vol. 1, *England in 1815.* 1949b. Vol. 2. *The Liberal Awakening, 1815–1830.* 1950. Vol. 3. *The Triumph of Reform, 1830–1841.* 1951. Vol. 4. *Victorian Years, 1841–1895.* 1961. Vol. 5. *Imperialism and the Rise of Labour, 1895–1905.* London: Benn.

——1966. *The Era of Tyrannies.* Translated by R. W. Webb. New York: New York University Press.

Hanami, Tadashi. 1979. *Labor Relations in Japan Today.* Tokyo: Kodansha International.

Harris, Laurence. 1980. "The State and the Economy: Some Theoretical Problems," pp. 243–62. In Miliband and Saville. 1980.

Harris, Nigel, 1972. *Competition and the Corporate Society. British Conservatives, the State and Industry, 1945–1964.* London: Methuen.

Harrod, Jeffrey. 1972. *Trade Union Foreign Policy. The Case of British and American Unions in Jamaica.* New York: Doubleday.

——1980. "Informal Sector and Urban Masses: A Social Relations of Production Approach." The Hague: Institute of Social Studies, mimeographed.

Harrod, R. F. 1963. *The Life of John Maynard Keynes.* London: Macmillan.

Heckscher, Eli. 1935. *Mercantilism.* London: George Allen and Unwin. Translated from the original Swedish, published in 1931.

Heinze, R. G. and T. Olk. 1982. "The Development of the Informal Economy. A Strategy for Resolving the Crisis of the Welfare State." *Futures* (June):189–204.

Hibbs, Douglas A., Jr. 1978. "On the Political Economy of Long Run Trends in Strike Activity." *British Journal of Political Science,* no. 8, pp. 153–75.

Hill, Christopher. 1972. *The World Turned Upside Down. Radical Ideas During the English Revolution.* Harmondsworth: Penguin.

Hilton, Rodney H. 1974. "Peasant Society, Peasant Movements and Feudalism in Medieval Europe," pp. 67–94. In Landsberger, ed. 1974.

——ed. 1978. *The Transition from Feudalism to Capitalism.* London: New Left Books Verso.

Hinsley, F. H. 1967. *Power and the Pursuit of Peace. Theory and Practice in the History of Relations Between States*. Cambridge, England: Cambridge University Press.

Hirsch, Fred. 1967. *Money International*. Harmondsworth, Middlesex: Penguin.

Hirsch, Fred and John H. Goldthorpe, eds. 1978. *The Political Economy of Inflation*. Oxford: Martin Robertson.

Hirschman, Albert. 1977. *The Passions and the Interests: Political Arguments for Capitalism Before Its Triumph*. Princeton, N.J.: Princeton University Press.

——ed. 1981. *Essays in Trespassing. Economics to Politics and Beyond*. Cambridge, England: Cambridge University Press.

Hobsbawm, E. J. 1954. "The General Crisis of the European Economy in the Seventeenth Century." *Past and Present*, nos. 5:33–49, 6:44–63.

——1962. *The Age of Revolution, 1789–1848*. New York: Mentor.

——1969. *Industry and Empire*. Harmondsworth, Middlesex: Penguin.

——1977. *The Age of Capital, 1848–1875*. London: Sphere.

Hobsbawm, E. J. and George Rudé. 1969. *Captain Swing*. London: Lawrence and Wishart.

Hoffmann, Stanley, Michel Des Accords, Serge Hurtig, Jean du Rostu, et Jean-Michel Royer. 1956. *Le mouvement Poujade*. Paris: Armand Colin.

Homans, G. C. 1951. *The Human Group*. London: Routledge and Kegan Paul.

Hopkins, Terence K. and Immanuel Wallerstein, eds. 1980. *Processes of the World System*. Beverly Hills, Calif.: Sage.

Howe, Christopher. 1973a. *Wage Patterns and Wage Policy in Modern China, 1919–1972*. Cambridge, England: Cambridge University Press.

——1973b. "Labour Organization and Incentives in Industry, Before and After the Cultural Revolution," pp. 233–56. In Schram, ed. 1973.

Hudson, Michael. 1968. *Superimperialism. The Economic Strategy of American Empire*. New York: Rinehart and Winston.

——1977. *Global Fracture. The New International Economic Order*. New York: Harper and Row.

Hughes, H. Stuart. 1979. *Consciousness and Society. The Reorientation of European Social Thought, 1890–1930*. Brighton: Harvester Press. First published in 1958.

Hunnius, Gerritt, G. David Garson, and John Case, eds. 1973. *Workers' Control. A Reader on Labor and Social Change*. New York: Vintage Books.

Hymer, Stephen. 1971. "Robinson Crusoe and the Secret of Primitive Accumulation." *Monthly Review* (September), 23(4):11–36.

——1972. "The Multinational Corporation and the Law of Uneven Development," pp. 113–40. In Bhagwati, ed. 1972.

Ibn Khaldûn, Abd-ar-Rahmân. 1967. *The Muqaddimah*. Translated from the Arabic by F. Rosenthal. Princeton, N.J.: Princeton University Press. Original text fourteenth century.

*Industrial Relations Review and Report*. 1984. "Flexible Employment Strategies" (August 7) 325:13–16; based on John Anderson, "Manning for

Uncertainty—Some Emerging UK Work Patterns." Institute of Manpower Studies, University of Sussex.

Ingham, Geoffrey K. 1974. *Strikes and Industrial Conflict. Britain and Scandinavia.* London: Macmillan.

International Bank for Reconstruction and Development. 1975. *Rural Development: Sector Policy Paper* (February). Washington, D.C.

International Labour Office. 1930. *Freedom of Association,* vol. 5. Geneva: ILO, Studies and Reports, series A [Industrial Relations], no. 32.

——1972. *Employment, Incomes and Equality: A Strategy for Increasing Productive Employment in Kenya.* Geneva.

Jackson, D., H. A. Turner, and F. Wilkinson. 1972. *Do Trade Unions Cause Inflation?* Cambridge, England: Cambridge University Press.

Jacobson, Harold K. and Dusan Sidjanski, eds. 1982. *The Emerging International Economic Order. Dynamic Processes, Constraints and Opportunities.* Beverly Hills, Calif.: Sage, for the International Political Science Association.

Jelin, Elizabeth. 1976. "Spontanéité et organisation dans le mouvement ouvrier: le cas de l'Argentine, du Brésil et du Mexique." *Sociologie du travail* 18(2):139–68.

Jenkins, David. 1981. *QWL—Current Trends and Directions.* Issues in the Quality of Working Life. Occasional paper, no. 3. Toronto: Ontario Ministry of Labour.

Johnson, Brian. 1970. *The Politics of Money.* London: John Murray.

Johnson, Dale L., ed. 1982. *Class and Social Development. A Theory of the Middle Class.* Beverly Hills, Calif.: Sage.

Jones, Gareth Stedman. 1982. "The Language of Chartism," pp. 1–58. In Epstein and Thompson. 1982.

Katzenstein, Peter J. 1983. "The Small European States in the International Economy: Economic Dependence and Corporatist Politics," pp. 91–130. In Ruggie 1983.

——1984. *Corporatism and Change: Switzerland, Austria and the Politics of Industry.* Ithaca, N.Y.: Cornell University Press.

——ed. 1977. "Between Power and Plenty: Foreign Economic Policies of Advanced Industrial States." Special issue of *International Organization* 31(4).

Keohane, Nannerl. 1980. *Philosophy and the State in France. The Renaissance to the Enlightenment.* Princeton, N.J.: Princeton University Press.

Keohane, Robert O. 1978. "Neo-orthodox Economics, Inflation and the State: Political Implications of the McCracken Report," *World Politics* (October):108–128.

——1982. "Hegemonic Leadership and U.S. Foreign Economic Policy in the "Long Decade" of the 1950s," pp. 49–76. In Avery and Rapkin. 1982.

——ed. 1986. *Neorealism and Its Critics.* New York: Columbia University Press.

Keohane, Robert O. and J. S. Nye. 1974. "Transgovernmental Relations and International Organizations." *World Politics* (October), vol. 27:39–62.

——and——1977. *Power and Interdependence*. Boston: Little, Brown.

Kerr, Clark, John T. Dunlop, F. H. Harbison, and C. A. Myers. 1960. *Industrialism and Industrial Man*. Cambridge, Mass.: Harvard University Press.

Kerr, Clark, and Abraham Siegel. 1954. "The International Propensity To Strike," pp. 189–212. In Kornhauser et al., eds. 1954.

Keynes, John Maynard. 1936. *The General Theory of Employment, Interest and Money*. London: Macmillan.

Kolko, Joyce and Gabriel Kolko. 1972. *The Limits of Power. The World and United States Foreign Policy, 1945–1954*. New York: Harper and Row.

Kondratieff, Nikolai. 1935. "The Long Waves in Economic Life." *The Review of Economic Statistics* (November), 17(6):105–15.

Konrád, George and Ivan Szelényi. 1979. *The Intellectuals on the Road to Class Power. A Sociological Study of the Role of the Intelligentsia in Socialism*. Brighton, England: Harvester.

Kornhauser, A. et al., eds. 1954. *Industrial Conflict*. New York: McGraw-Hill.

Korovkin, Tanya. 1985. "The Politics of Agricultural Cooperativism: Peru, 1969–83," Ph. D. dissertation for York University, Toronto, Canada.

Krasner, Stephen D. 1977. "U.S. Commercial and Monetary Policy: Unravelling the Paradox of External Strength and Internal Weakness." *International Organization* 31(4):635–72.

——1978. *Defending the National Interest. Raw Materials Investments in U.S. Foreign Policy*. Princeton, N.J.: Princeton University Press.

Lambruch, G. 1977. "Liberal Corporatism and Party Government." *Comparative Political Studies* 10(1):91–126.

Landes, David S. 1969. *The Unbound Prometheus. Technological Change and Industrial Development in Western Europe from 1750 to the Present*. Cambridge, England: Cambridge University Press.

Landsberger, Henry, ed. 1974. *Rural Protest: Peasant Movements and Social Change*. London: Macmillan.

Lattimore, Owen. 1960. "The Industrial Impact on China, 1800–1950." *First International Conference of Economic History, Stockholm, August 1960.*, pp. 103–13. Paris and The Hague: Mouton.

Leibniz, G. W. 1934. "The Monadology." In *The Philosophical Writings of Leibniz*. Selected and translated by Mary Morris. London: Dent. Originally published in 1714.

Lemoine, Maurice. 1981. *Sucre amer: esclaves aujourd'hui dans les Caraïbes*. Paris: Encre.

Lenin, V. I. 1947. *What Is To Be Done?* Moscow: Progress Publishers. Originally published in 1902.

——1970. *Imperialism. The Highest Stage of Capitalism*. Peking: Foreign Languages Press. Originally published 1917.

Lever-Tracy, Constance. 1984. "The Paradigm of Dualism: Decay or Regeneration?" *Politics and Society* 13(1):59–89.

Levinson, Charles. 1972. *International Trade Unionism*. London: Allen and Unwin.

Levitan, S. A., M. Rein, and D. Marwick. 1972. *Work and Welfare Go Together*. Baltimore: Johns Hopkins Press.

Levitt, Kari. 1970. *Silent Surrender; the Multinational Corporation in Canada.* Toronto: Macmillan.

Lévy-Strauss, Claude. 1966. *The Savage Mind.* Chicago: University of Chicago Press.

Lewin, Arthur. 1982. "The Fall of Michael Manley." *Monthly Review* (February), 33(9):49–60.

Lewin, Moshe. 1974. *Political Undercurrents in Soviet Economic Debates. From Bukharin to the Modern Reformers.* Princeton, N.J.: Princeton University Press.

Lichtheim, George. 1961. *Marxism. An Historical and Critical Study.* New York: Praeger.

Lindberg, Leon. 1963. *The Dynamics of European Economic Integration.* Stanford, Calif.: Stanford University Press.

Lindberg, Leon et al. eds. 1975. *Stress and Contradictions in Modern Capitalism. Public Policy and the Theory of the State.* Lexington, Mass.: Heath.

Lindberg, Leon and Stuart Scheingold. 1970. *Europe's Would-be Polity. Patterns of Change in the European Community.* Englewood Cliffs, N.J.: Prentice-Hall.

Lindblom, Charles E. 1977. *Politics and Markets. The World's Political-Economic Systems.* New York: Basic Books.

List, Friedrich. 1885. *The National System of Political Economy.* Translated by Sampson S. Lloyd. London: Longmans Green. First published in German, 1841.

Lowi, Theodore J. 1975. "Towards a Politics of Economics: The State of Permanent Receivership," pp. 115–24. In Lindberg et al., eds. 1975.

Lowit, Thomas. 1979a. "Le Parti polymorphe en Europe de l'Est." *Revue française de science politique* (August-September), 29(4–5):812–45.

——1979b. "Y a-t-il des États en Europe de l'Est?" *Revue française de sociologie* 20:431–66.

Luxemburg, Rosa. 1968. *The Accumulation of Capital.* New York: Monthly Review. First published in 1913.

McCracken Report. 1977. See *Towards Full Employment and Price Stability.* 1977.

McGeehan, Robert. 1985. "European Defense Cooperation: A Political Perspective." *The World Today* (June).

McKinnon, Ronald I. 1979. *Money in International Exchange. The Convertible Currency System.* New York: Oxford University Press.

McVey, Ruth T. 1965. *The Rise of Indonesian Communism.* Ithaca, N.Y.: Cornell University Press.

Madeuf, Bernadette and Charles-Albert Michalet. 1978. "A New Approach to International Economics." *International Social Science Journal* 30(2):253–83.

Magdoff, Harry and Paul M. Sweezy. 1977. *The End of Prosperity. The American Economy in the 1970s.* New York: Monthly Review.

Magri, Lucio. 1982. "The Peace Movement and European Socialism." *New Left Review* (January-February), 131:1–19.

Maier, Charles S. 1975. *Recasting Bourgeois Europe. Stabilization in France,*

*Germany and Italy in the Decade After World War I.* Princeton, N.J.:
    Princeton University Press.
——1977. "The Politics of Productivity: Foundations of American Interna-
    tional Economic Policy After World War II." *International Organization*
    31(4):607:634.
——1978. "The Politics of Inflation in the Twentieth Century," pp. 37–72.
    In Hirsch and Goldthorpe, eds. 1978.
Maier, Charles S. and Leon Lindberg, eds. 1984. *The Politics and Sociology
    of Global Inflation.* Washington, D.C.: Brookings.
Maire, Edmond. 1980. "Le mouvement ouvrier face aux idéologies de la
    crise." *Le Monde* (August 21–22).
Maital, Shlomo and Noah M. Meltz. 1984. "Labour and Management Atti-
    tudes Toward a New Social Contract: A Comparison of Canada and the
    United States." Toronto: University of Toronto, Centre for Industrial
    Relations.
Malles, Paul. 1971. *Economic Consultative Bodies: Their Origins and Institu-
    tional Characteristics.* Ottawa: Information Canada for the Economic
    Council of Canada.
Mallet, Serge. 1963. *La nouvelle classe ouvrière.* Paris: Seuil.
Mandel, Ernest. 1978. *Late Capitalism.* London: Verso.
Marglin, Stephen A. 1974. "What Do Bosses Do? The Origins and Functions
    of Hierarchy in Capitalist Production." *Review of Radical Political Econ-
    omy* (Summer), 6(2):33–60.
Markovits, Andrei S. and Christopher S. Allen. 1979a. "The West German
    Trade Unions' Role in Democratization and Participation: Social Part-
    nership or Class Conflict." Paper presented at the 11th World Congress
    of the International Political Science Association, Moscow, August 1979.
——1979b. "The Human Experience of Labor in a Changing Market Econ-
    omy: The Ambivalence of the West German Trade Unions." Paper pre-
    sented to the 11th World Congress of the International Political Science
    Association, Moscow, August 1979.
——Kenneth Gibbs, and Christopher S. Allen (1980) "Class Power and In-
    dustrial Conflict in Advanced Capitalism: The Interaction of Business,
    Labor and the State in the Post WWII West German Steel Industry."
    Paper presented to the 1980 annual meeting of the American Political
    Science Association, Washington, D.C., August 1980.
Marx, Karl. 1957. *Capital,* vol. 1. Translated from the fourth German edition
    by Eden and Cedar Paul. London: Dent. Originally published in 1867.
——1969. *The Eighteenth Brumaire of Louis Bonaparte.* New York: Interna-
    tional Publishers. Originally published 1852.
Massari, R. 1975. "Le 'Cordobazo.'" *Sociologie du travail* 17(4):403–19.
Mattingly, Garrett. 1973 *Renaissance Diplomacy.* Harmondsworth, Middle-
    sex: Penguin.
Mayer, Arno J. 1981. *The Persistence of the Old Regime. Europe to the Great
    War.* New York: Pantheon.
Mayo, Elton. 1945. *Human Problems of an Industrial Civilization.* Boston:
    Harvard University, Graduate School of Business Administration.

Meinecke, Friedrich. 1957. *Machiavellism. The Doctrine of Raison d'Etat and Its Place in Modern History.* London: Routledge and Kegan Paul. Translated from *Die Idee der Staatsräson*, published in 1924.

——1972. *Historism. The Rise of a New Historical Outlook.* Translated by J. E. Anderson. London: Routledge and Kegan Paul.

Meissner, Boris. 1972. *Social Change in the Soviet Union. Russia's Path Toward an Industrial Society.* Translated by Donald P. Kommers. London and South Bend, Ind.: Notre Dame University Press.

Meltz, Noah M. 1983. "Labour Movements in Canada and the United States: Are They Really That Different?" Toronto: University of Toronto, Centre for Industrial Relations.

Merhav, Meir. 1969. *Technological Dependence, Monopoly and Growth.* London: Pergamon.

Michalet, Charles-Albert. 1976. *Le capitalisme mondiale.* Paris: Presses universitaires de France.

Michels, Robert. 1959. *Political Parties. A Sociological Study of the Oligarchical Tendencies of Modern Democracy.* Translated by Eden and Cedar Paul. New York: Dover. Original German edition published in 1911.

Mickler, Ottfried. 1979. "Rationalisation et déqualification du travail. Le cas de l'industrie allemande." *Sociologie du travail* (Jan.-Mars), 1(79):33–43.

Miliband, Ralph. 1969. *The State in Capitalist Society.* New York: Basic Books.

Miliband, Ralph and John Saville, eds. *The Socialist Register,* London: Merlin Press, various years.

Miller, Linda B. 1983. "Energy and Alliance Politics: Lessons of a Decade." *The World Today* (December).

Mills, C. Wright. 1956. *White Collar. The American Middle Classes.* New York: Oxford University Press.

Mittelman, James H. 1980. "International Monetary Institutions and Policies of Socialism and Self-Reliance: Are They Compatible? The Tanzanian Experience." *Social Research* 47(1):141–65.

——1981. *Underdevelopment and the Transition to Socialism. Mozambique and Tanzania.* New York: Academic Press.

Momigliano, F. 1962. *Lavoratori e sindicati di frente alle trasformazzioni del processo produttivo.* Milano: Feltrinelli.

Moore, Barrington Jr. 1967. *The Social Origins of Dictatorship and Democracy. Lord and Peasant in the Making of the Modern World.* London: Allen Lane, The Penguin Press.

Morazé, Charles. 1957. *Les bourgeois conquérants.* Paris: Armand Colin.

Mosca, Gaetano. 1939. *The Ruling Class (Elementi di Scienza Politica).* Translated by Hannah D. Kahn. New York: McGraw Hill. Original Italian edition published in 1896.

Myrdal, Gunnar. 1967. *Beyond the Welfare State. Economic Planning and Its International Implications.* New York: Bantam Books. Originally published in 1960.

Naville, Pierre. 1963. *Vers l'automatisme sociale? Problèmes du travail et de l'automation.* Paris: Gallimard.

Nelson, Joan M. 1969. *Migrants, Urban Poverty and Instability in Developing Nations*. Cambridge, Mass.: Harvard University, Center for International Affairs, Occasional Papers in International Affairs, no. 22.

——1979. *Access to Power. Politics and the Urban Poor in Developing Nations*. Princeton, N.J.: Princeton University Press.

Neumann, Franz. 1944. *Behemoth. The Structure and Practice of National Socialism*. New York: Oxford University Press.

Nicholson, Harold. 1947. *The Congress of Vienna. A Study in Allied Unity, 1812–1822*. Berne: Phoenix.

Northrup, H. R. and R. L. Rowan. 1974. "Multinational Collective Bargaining Activity: The Factual Record in Chemicals, Glass and Rubber Tires." *Columbia Journal of World Business* 9(1):112–24, (2):49–63.

Nove, Alec. 1969. *An Economic History of the USSR*. Harmondsworth: Penguin.

——1980. "The Soviet Economy: Problems and Prospects." *New Left Review* (January-February), 119:3–19.

O'Connor, James. 1973. *The Fiscal Crisis of the State*. New York: St. Martin's Press.

Offe, Claus. 1972. "Advanced Capitalism and the Welfare State." *Politics and Society* (Summer), 2:479–88.

——1975. "The Theory of the Capitalist State and the Problem of Policy Formation, pp. 125–45. In Lindberg, ed. (1975).

——1976. *Industry and Inequality. The Achievement Principle in Work and Social Status*. London: Edward Arnold. Originally published in German as *Leistingsprinzip und industrielle Arbeit* (1970), by Europaische Verlaganstalt.

Ortoli, François-Xavier. 1981. "Système monétaire européen: perspectives d'avenir." pp. 17–22. In Abraham and Abeele. 1981.

Owen, Roger and Bob Sutcliffe, eds. 1972. *Studies in the Theory of Imperialism*. London: Longman.

Ozawa, Terutomo. 1979. *Multinationalism, Japanese Style. The Political Economy of Outward Dependency*. Princeton, N.J.: Princeton University Press.

Palloix, Christian. 1973. *Les firmes multinationales et le procès d'internationalisation*. Paris: Maspero.

——1975a. "The Internationalization of Capital and the Circuit of Social Capital," pp. 63–88. ed. In Radice, 1975. Translation of an extract from Palloix. 1973.

——1975b. *L'internationalisation du capital. Eléments critiques*. Paris: Maspero

Panitch, Leo. 1976. *Social Democracy and Industrial Militancy: The Labour Party, the Trade Unions and Incomes Policy, 1945–1974*. Cambridge, England: Cambridge University Press.

——1981. "Trade Unions and the Capitalist State, or The Limits of Corporatism." *New Left Review* (January-February), 125:21–43.

——1984. "The Tripartite Experience." Brief prepared for the Royal Commission on the Economic Union and Development Prospects for Canada, July (xeroxed).

Pareto, Vilfredo. 1963. *The Mind and Society: A Treatise on General Sociology.*
Translated by Andrew Bongiorno and Arthur Livingston. New York:
Dutton. Original Italian edition published in 1916.

Parkin, Frank, ed. 1974. *The Social Analysis of Class Structure.* London:
Tavistock.

Parodi, Maurice. 1978. "La segmentation du marché du travail." *Projet*
123:298–311.

Patnaik, Prabhat. 1972. "Imperialism and the Growth of Indian Capitalism,"
pp. 210–29. In Owen and Sutcliffe. 1972.

Payer, Cheryl. 1974. *The Debt Trap. The International Monetary Fund and the
Third World.* New York: Monthly Review.

Pearson, Lester B. 1969. *Partners in Development: Report of the Commission
on International Development.* New York: Praeger.

Pereira de Queiroz, Maria Isaura. 1970. "Brazilian Messianic Movements: A
Help or a Hindrance to Participation?" International Institute for Labour
Studies, *Bulletin,* no. 7 (June). Geneva. pp. 93–121.

Perlman, Selig. 1928. *A Theory of the Labor Movement.* New York: Macmillan.

Perroux, François. 1973. *Pouvoir et économie.* Paris: Bordas.

Phelan, Edward J. 1949. *Yes and Albert Thomas.* London: Crescent Press.

Philipp, Beat C. 1984. "Hidden Economies in the Industrialized Countries."
*Economic and Financial Prospects.* Basle: Swiss Bank Corporation,
(April–May), no. 2.

Phillips, James. 1980. "Renovation of the International Economic Order:
Trilateralism, the IMF and Jamaica," pp. 468–91. In Sklar, Holly. 1980.

Pike, Frederick P. and Thomas Stritch, eds. 1974. *The New Corporatism:
Social-Political Structures in the Iberian World.* South Bend, Ind. London:
University of Notre Dame Press.

Pinder, John, Takashi Hosomi, and William Diebold. 1979. *Industrial Policy
and the International Economy.* New York: Trilateral Commission.

Piore, Michael J. 1980. "The Technological Foundations of Dualism and
Discontinuity." pp. 13–81. In Berger and Piore. 1980.

Piven, Frances Fox and Richard A. Cloward. 1971. *Regulating the Poor. The
Functions of Public Welfare.* New York: Vintage.

Pizzorno, Alessandro. 1978. "Entre l'action de classe et le corporatisme. A
propos de la représentation des travailleurs dans les pays capitalistes
avancés." *Sociologie du travail,* no. 2:129–152.

Polanyi, Karl. 1957. *The Great Transformation. The Political and Economic
Origins of Our Time.* Boston: Beacon Press.

——1966a. *Dahomey and the Slave Trade.* Seattle: University of Washington
Press.

——1966b. *Primitive, Archaic and Modern Economics: Essays of Karl Polanyi.*
George Dalton, ed. Garden City, N.Y.: Garden City Press.

——et al., eds. 1971. *Trade and Market in the Early Empires. Economies in
History and Theory.* Chicago: Henry Regnery. First published 1957.

Portes, Alejandro and John Walton. 1981. *Labor, Class and the International
System.* New York: Academic Press.

Poulantzas, Nicos. 1968. *Pouvoir politique et classes sociales.* Paris: Maspero.

——1973. *Political Power and Social Classes*. London: New Left Books. Translation of previous entry.

——1974. "Internationalization of Capitalist Relations and the Nation-State." *Economy and Society* 3(2):146–79.

Przeworski, Adam. 1981. "Democratic Socialism in Poland?" *Studies in Political Economy* (Spring), no. 5:29–53.

Radice, Hugo, ed. 1975. *International Firms and Modern Imperialism*. Harmondsworth, Middlesex: Penguin.

Redivo, Giampaolo. 1983. "Sistemi produttivi sommersi e mercati del lavoro: una analisi della letteratura." *Economia e lavoro*, (luglio-sett.), no. 3:31–52.

Reich, Wilhelm. 1975. *The Mass Psychology of Fascism*. Harmondsworth, Middlesex: Penguin.

Rein, Martin. 1985. "Social Policy and Labor Markets: The Employment Role of Social Provision." Paper presented at the World Congress of the International Political Science Association. Paris (July).

Research Working Group on Cyclical Rhythms and Secular Trends. 1979. "Cyclical Rhythms and Secular Trends of the Capitalist World Economy: Some Premises, Hypotheses and Questions." *Review* (Spring), 2(4):483–500.

Rey, Pierre-Philippe. 1975. "The Lineage Mode of Production." *Critical Anthropology*, no. 3, pp. 27–70.

——1976. *Les alliances de classes*. Paris: Maspero.

Reynaud, Jean-Daniel. 1968. "The Future of Industrial Relations in Western Europe: Approaches and Perspectives." International Institute for Labour Studies, *Bulletin*, no. 4. Geneva. IILS. pp. 86–115.

——1984. "France: la rigeur des temps." Mimeo for the Conservatoire national des arts et métiers, Laboratoire de sociologie du travail, Paris.

Rohaytn, Felix. 1981. "Reconstructing America." *The New York Review of Books* (February 5).

Rohaytn, Felix et al. 1984. *Restoring American Competitiveness: Proposals for an Industry Policy*. Washington, D.C.: Center for National Policy.

Ross, Arthur M., ed. 1966. *Industrial Relations and Economic Development*. London: Macmillan, for the International Institute for Labour Studies.

Ross, George. 1978. "Marxism and the New Middle Classes: French Critiques." *Theory and Society* 5(2):163–190.

Ross, Robert and Kent Trachte. 1983. "Global Cities and Global Classes: The Peripheralization of Labor in New York City." *Review* 6(3):393–431.

Rothschild, Emma. 1981. "Reagan and the Real America." *The New York Review of Books* (February 5).

Rowbotham, Sheila. 1973. *Woman's Consciousness, Man's World*. Harmondsworth, Middlesex: Penguin.

Rubery, Jill and Frank Wilkinson. 1981. "Outwork and Segmented Labour Markets," pp. 115–32. In Wilkinson. 1981.

Ruggie, John Gerard. 1982. "International Regimes, Transactions and Change: Embedded Liberalism in the Postwar Economic Order." *International Organization* (Spring), 36(2):379–416.

——ed. 1983. *The Antinomies of Interdependence. National Welfare and the International Division of Labor.* New York: Columbia University Press.

Russett, Bruce M., et al. 1964. *World Handbook of Political and Social Indicators.* New Haven, Conn.: Yale University Press.

Sabel, Charles F. 1982. *Work and Politics. The Division of Labor in Industry.* Cambridge, England: Cambridge University Press.

Sahlins, Marshall. 1972. *Stone Age Economics.* Chicago and New York: Aldine-Atherton.

Salamone, Nino. 1982. "Elementi per un'analisi del lavoro irregolare." *Economia e lavoro* (July-September), 16(3):87–106.

Sandbrook, Richard. 1977. "The Political Potential of African Urban Workers." *Canadian Journal of African Studies* 9(3):411–33.

——1982. *The Politics of Basic Needs.* Toronto: University of Toronto Press.

Sandbrook, Richard and Jack Arn. 1977. *The Labouring Poor and Urban Class Formation: The Case of Greater Accra.* Montreal: McGill University Centre for Developing Area Studies, Occasional Monograph Series, no. 12.

Saul, John S. 1974. "The State in Post-colonial Societies: Tanzania," pp. 349–72. In Miliband and Saville. 1974.

——ed. 1984. *A Difficult Road: The Transition to Socialism in Mozambique.* New York: Monthly Review Press.

Sauvy, Alfred. 1984. *Le travail noir et l'économie de demain.* Paris: Calmann-Levy.

Schlesinger, Arthur M., Jr. 1960. *The Coming of the New Deal.* London: Heinemann.

Schmitter, Philippe. 1972. "Paths of Political Development in Latin America." pp. 83–105. In Chalmers. 1972.

——1974. "Still the Century of Corporatism?" pp. 85–131. In Pike and Stritch. 1974.

Schottland, Charles I., ed. 1967. *The Welfare State. Selected Essays.* New York: Harper and Row.

Schram, Stuart R., ed. 1973. *Authority, Participation and Cultural Change in China.* Cambridge, England: Cambridge University Press.

Schumpeter, Joseph. 1939. *Business Cycles.* New York: McGraw Hill.

——1955. *Imperialism and Social Classes.* New York: Meridian.

Schurmann, Franz. 1966. *Ideology and Organization in Communist China,* ed. 2. Berkeley and Los Angeles: University of California Press.

——1974. *The Logic of Power.* New York: Pantheon.

Sellier, François. 1973. "The French Workers' Movement and Political Unionism," pp. 79–100. In Sturmthal and Scoville. 1973.

Sengenberger, Werner. 1981. "Labour Market Segmentation and the Business Cycle," pp. 243–58. In Wilkinson. 1981.

Servan-Schreiber, Jean-Jacques. 1967. *Le défi americain.* Paris: Denoel.

Shefter, Martin. 1977. "New York City's Fiscal Crisis: The Politics of Inflation and Retrenchment". *The Public Interest* (Summer). pp. 98–127.

Shivji, Issa G. 1976. *Class Struggles in Tanzania.* New York: Monthly Review Press.

Shkaratan, O. I. 1973. "Social Groups in the Working Class of a Developed Socialist Society," pp. 63–105. In Yankowitch and Fisher. 1973.

Shonfield, Andrew. 1965. *Modern Capitalism. The Changing Balance of Public and Private Power.* London: Oxford University Press.

Shorter, Edward. 1975. *The Making of the Modern Family.* New York: Basic Books.

Shorter, Edward and Charles Tilly. 1974. *Strikes in France, 1830–1968.* Cambridge, England: Cambridge University Press.

Simes, Dimitri. 1975. "The Soviet Parallel Market." *Survey* (Summer), 21:42–52.

Sklar, Holly, ed. 1980. *Trilateralism. The Trilateral Commission and Elite Planning for World Management.* Montreal: Black Rose Books.

Sklar, Richard L. 1979. "The Nature of Class Domination in Africa." *The Journal of Modern African Studies* 17(4):531–52.

Skocpol, Theda. 1977. "Wallerstein's World Capitalist System: A Theoretical and Historical Critique." *American Journal of Sociology* 83(5):1075–90.

——1979. *States and Social Revolutions. A Comparative Analysis of France, Russia and China.* Cambridge, England: Cambridge University Press.

——1980. "Political Response to Capitalist Crisis: Neo-Marxist Theories of the State and the Case of the New Deal." *Politics and Society* 10(2):155–201.

Smith, Adam. 1970. *The Wealth of Nations.* Books 1 to 3. Harmondsworth: Penguin. Originally published in 1776.

——1976. *An Inquiry into the Nature and Causes of the Wealth of Nations.* General editors R. H. Campbell and A. S. Skinner. 2 vols. Oxford: Clarendon Press.

Somers, Gerald, ed. 1969. *Essays in Industrial Relations Theory.* Ames, Iowa: Iowa State University Press.

Sorel, Albert. 1922. *L'Europe et la révolution française.* Paris: Plon.

Sorel, Georges. 1941. *Reflections on Violence.* Translated by T. E. Hulme. New York: Peter Smith. Original French edition published in 1906.

Stavenhagen, Rodolfo. 1981. *Between Underdevelopment and Revolution. A Latin American Perspective.* New Delhi: Abhinav Publications.

Stepan, Alfred. 1978. *State and Society. Peru in Comparative Perspective.* Princeton, N.J.: Princeton University Press.

Stoffaës, Christian. 1978. *La grande menace industrielle.* Paris: Calmann-Levy.

Strange, Susan. 1971. *Sterling and British Policy. A Political Study of an International Currency in Decline.* London: Oxford University Press.

——1979. "The Management of Surplus Capacity: Or How Does Theory Stand up to Protectionism 1970s Style?" *International Organization* 33(3):303–34.

——1985. "Protectionism and World Politics." *International Organization* (Spring), 39(2):233–60.

Sturmthal, Adolf. 1966. "Economic Development and the Labor Movement," pp. 165–81. In Arthur M. Ross, ed. 1966.

Sturmthal, Adolf and James G. Scoville, eds. 1973. *The International Labor Movement in Transition.* Chicago: University of Illinois Press.

Sweezy, Paul M. 1981. "Economic Crisis in the United States." *Monthly Review* (December), 33(7).:1–10.

Talleyrand, Charles-Maurice de. 1967. *Mémoires*. Paris: Jean de Bonnot, 2 vols.

Tanzi, Vito, ed. 1982. *The Underground Economy in the United States and Abroad*. Lexington, Mass.: Heath.

Taylor, A. J. P. 1957. *The Struggle for Mastery in Europe, 1848–1918*. Oxford: Clarendon Press.

Taylor, Charles. 1976. "Hermeneutics and Politics," pp. 153–93. In Connerton. 1976.

Taylor, Frederick Winslow. 1911. *The Principles of Scientific Management*. New York: Harper.

Teckenberg, Wolfgang. 1978. "Labour Turnover and Job Satisfaction: Indicators of Industrial Conflict in the USSR?" *Soviet Studies* (April), 30(2):193–211.

Teulings, Arnold W. 1980. "Internationalisation du capital et double déplacement de l'emploi." *Sociologie du travail* 4(80):369–89.

Therborn, Göran. 1984. "Classes and States. Welfare State Developments, 1881–1981." *Studies in Political Economy* (Summer), 14:7–42.

Thomas, Clive Y. 1974. *Dependence and Transformation. The Economics of the Transition to Socialism*. New York: Monthly Review Press.

Thompson, E. P. 1968. *The Making of the English Working Class*. Harmondsworth, Middlesex: Penguin.

Tinbergen, Jan. 1964. *Central Planning*. New Haven, Conn.: Yale University Press.

Titmuss, Richard M. 1959. *The Irresponsible Society*. London: Fabian Society, tract series no. 323.

——1963. *Essays on The Welfare State*, ed. 2. London: Unwin University Books.

Tönnies, Ferdinand. 1957. *Community and Society*. Translated from the German *Gemeinschaft und Gesellschaft* by Charles Loomis, ed. East Lansing: Michigan State University Press. Originally published in 1887.

Touraine, Alain. 1955. *L'évolution du travail aux usines Renault*. Paris: CNRS.

——1976. *Les sociétés dépendantes. Essais sur l'Amérique latine*. Paris: Duculot.

Touraine, Alain and Daniel Pécaud. 1976. "Conscience ouvrière et développement économique en Amérique latine," pp. 200–31. In Touraine. 1976.

Touraine, Alain, Claude Durand, Daniel Pecaud, and Alfred Willener. 1965. *Les travailleurs et les changements techniques. Une vue d'ensemble des recherches*. Paris: Organization for Economic Cooperation and Development.

*Towards Full Employment and Price Stability*. 1977. Paris: Organization for Economic Cooperation and Development. The McCracken Report.

Trentin, B. 1962. "Les syndicats italiens et le progrès technique." *Sociologie du travail* 4(2):105–22.

Trimberger, Ellen. 1972. "A Theory of Elite Revolutions." *Studies in Comparative International Development* 7(3):191–207.

Turner, H. A. 1966. *Wage Trends, Wage Policies and Collective Bargaining: The Problems of Underdeveloped Countries.* Cambridge, England: Cambridge University Press.

U.S. Congress. House Committee on Banking, Currency and Housing. 1976. *Financial Institutions of the Nation's Economy.* Washington, D.C.: GPO.

U.S. President's Materials Policy Commission. 1952. William S. Paley, Chairman. *Resources for Freedom.* Washington, D.C.: GPO.

Vaitsos, Constantine. 1975. "The Process of Commercialization of Technology in the Andean Pact," pp. 183–214. In Radice, 1975.

Vanhecke, Charles. 1982. "Le tiers-monde brésilien. II. La civilisation du bidonville," *Le Monde,* July 28.

Veliz, Claudio, ed. 1965. *Obstacles to Change in Latin America.* London: Royal Institute of International Affairs.

Vernholes, Alain. 1982. "1982: les aléas du changement." *Le Monde,* December 31, 1982, and January 1, 1983.

Vernon, Raymond. 1966. "International Investment and International Trade in the Product Cycle." *Quarterly Journal of Economics* 80:190–207.

Vicens Vives, Jaime. 1970. "The Decline of Spain in the Seventeenth Century," pp. 121–67. In Cipolla. 1970.

Vico, Giambattista. 1970. *The New Science of Giambattista Vico.* Abridged translation of the third edition (1744) by Thomas G. Bergin and Max H. Fisch. Ithaca, N.Y.: Cornell University Press.

Volin, Lazar. 1960. "The Russian Peasant. From Emancipation to Kolkhoz," pp. 292–311. In Black. 1960.

Volker, Paul A. 1976. "The United States and International Monetary Reform." pp. 13–20. In Boarman and Tuerch. 1976.

von Grimmelschausen, H. J. C. (n.d.) *Adventures of a Simpleton.* Translated by Walter Wallich. Original title *Simplicius Simplicissimus.* New York: Ungar.

Wallerstein, Immanuel. 1974a. *The Modern World-System. Capitalist Agriculture and the Origins of the European World-Economy in the Sixteenth Century.* New York: Academic Press.

——1974b. "The Rise and Future Demise of the World Capitalist System: Concepts for Comparative Analysis." *Comparative Studies in Society and History* 16(4):378–415.

Walters, Robert S. 1985. "America's Adaptation to a Changing International Economy: Structural Challenges Confronting Liberal Economic Traditions." Paper presented at the World Congress of the International Political Science Association, Paris (July).

Weber, Max. 1930. *The Protestant Ethic and the Spirit of Capitalism.* London: George Allen and Unwin.

——1946. *From Max Weber: Essays in Sociology.* H. H. Gerth and C. Wright Mills, eds. New York: Oxford University Press.

Webster, Sir Charles. 1963. *The Foreign Policy of Castlereagh.* London: G. Bell and Sons, 2 vols.

Wehler, Hans-Ulrich. 1972. "Industrial Growth and Early German Imperialism," pp. 71–92. In Owen and Sutcliffe (1972).

Wiarda, Howard J. 1978. "Corporative Origins of the Iberian and Latin American Labor Relations Systems." *Studies in Comparative International Development* (Spring), vol. 13:3–37.

——1980. "From Corporatism to Neo-syndicalism. The State, Organized Labor, and the Industrial Relations Systems of Southern Europe." Paper presented to the annual meeting of the American Political Science Association, Washington, D.C. (August).

Wilkinson, Frank, ed. 1981. *The Dynamics of Labor Market Segmentation.* New York: Academic Press.

Williams, Eric. 1980. *Capitalism and Slavery.* New York: Putnam.

Williamson, Harold F., ed. 1951. *The Growth of the American Economy,* ed. 2. Englewood Cliffs, N.J: Prentice-Hall.

Windmuller, John P. 1969. *Labor Relations in the Netherlands.* Ithaca, N.Y.: Cornell University Press.

Wingfield-Stratford, Esme. 1933. *The Victorian Aftermath.* London: Routledge.

Winkler, J. T. 1976. "Corporatism." *Archives européenes de sociologie* 17(1):100–136.

Wittfogel, Karl. 1957. *Oriental Despotism.* New Haven, Conn.: Yale University Press.

Wolf, Eric. 1969. *Peasant Wars of the Twentieth Century.* New York: Harper and Row.

——1982. *Europe and the People Without History.* Berkeley, Calif.: University of California Press.

Wolfe, Alan. 1977. *The Limits of Legitimacy. Political Contradictions of Contemporary Capitalism.* New York: Free Press.

World Bank. See International Bank for Reconstruction and Development.

Yanowitch, Murray and Wesley A. Fisher, eds. 1973. *Social Stratification and Mobility in the USSR.* White Plains, N.Y.: International Arts and Sciences Press.

Zeldin, Theodore. 1973. *France, 1848–1945,* vol. 1. *Ambition, Love and Politics.* Oxford: Oxford University Press.

Ziegler, Jean. 1983. *Contre l'ordre du monde. Les rebelles. Mouvements armés de libération nationale du tiers monde.* Paris: Seuil.

Zysman, John. 1983. *Governments, Markets and Growth. Financial Systems and the Politics of Industrial Change.* Ithaca, N.Y., and London: Cornell University Press.

# INDEX